The Treasury and economic policy
1964–1985

By the same author

Economic Images   Longman, 1983

The Treasury and economic policy 1964–1985

Peter Browning

Longman
London and New York

Longman Group Limited
Longman House, Burnt Mill, Harlow
Essex CM20 2JE, England
Associated companies throughout the world

Published in the United State of America
by Longman Inc., New York

First published 1986

British Library Cataloguing in Publication Data

Browning, Peter, 1920–
    The Treasury and economic policy, 1964–1985.
    1. Great Britain——Treasury——History——20th
    century 2. Great Britain——Economic policy——
    1945–
    330.941'0856   HC256.6
    ISBN 0-582-29672-2

Library of Congress Cataloging in Publication Data

Browning, Peter, 1920–
    The Treasury and economic policy, 1964–1985.

    Bibliography: p.
    Includes index.
    1. Great Britain--Economic policy--1945–
2. Great Britain--Economic conditions--1945–
3. Great Btirain. Treasury. I. Title.
HC256.6.B766   1986   338.941   85-24039
ISBN 0-582-29672-2

Set in 10/12pt AM Compedit Souvenir
Produced by Longman Singapore Publishers (Pte) Ltd.
Printed in Singapore.

Contents

Contents

In an old house there is always listening,
and more is heard than is spoken.
And what is spoken remains in the room,
waiting for the future to hear it.
And whatever happens began in the past,
and presses hard on the future.

T. S. Eliot   Chorus from *The Family Reunion*

Preface

> I have myself seen these sad events,
> and played no small part in them.
>
> Virgil

Alas, it is not entirely true: the part I played was small. But from where I was standing, stage left, carrying my spear, I had an excellent view of the performance; I knew when the actors fluffed their lines and when the scenery was about to fall down. I could watch the audience; and I understood the plot.

This is the story of an extraordinary twenty years in the history of the British economy and of the Treasury. I shall let the story speak for itself and not anticipate it here. The impatient reader – and the reviewer with 500 words to write – may, if he chooses, turn to the final chapter.

The book is in two parts. Part One is a narrative of economic events from 1964 to 1985 as seen, for the most part, from inside the Treasury. Part Two deals with specific themes. Chapters 10, 11 and 12, on public expenditure, sterling, and monetary policy, bring together topics that run through the narrative, with a little theory added. There is, inevitably, some repetition, but I have tried to keep this to a minimum. Some readers may find it helpful to read these later chapters first to provide background to the narrative. Similarly, readers unfamiliar with the work and organization of the Treasury may care to take Chapter 9 first. Chapter 13, on the secondary banking crisis, has been placed in Part Two as it is in a sense a digression from the main story; but the reader is free to read this chapter in its chronological place, at the end of 1973.

The period of the Labour Government from 1964 to 1970 is an important part of the story. But as it is a period that has been well documented, in ministerial memoirs and, notably, in Samuel Brittan's (1971) *Steering the Economy*, I have treated it relatively briefly. Readers familiar with the story of those years may choose to skim or skip the early chapters.

Purists may feel that in some parts of the book over-much attention is paid to Press reaction and Press opinion. History, they may feel, should be about what actually happened, not what people thought about it or what they thought ought to happen. I am unrepentant. The Press influences opinion, and opinion matters, at two levels: first, in a democracy any policy must be understood by, and have the broad support of, the people; secondly, and of more direct relevance to the story told here, Press opinion influences market opinion, and increasingly policy makers have come to realize that the markets cannot be ignored. Markets can make happen what they think ought to happen, or, second guessing, what they think the market thinks ought to happen.

A word about statistics. For perfectly respectable reasons – new information, new concepts, a wider coverage, re-basing – most (not all) statistical series are constantly being revised. This applies particularly to statistics of the balance of payments. In the narrative I have in general used statistics from the publications and reports of the time. They may differ from the statistics in the Appendix (p. 354) which are from the latest available sources. So I ask the reader's indulgence: where statistics differ none is necessarily wrong.

Similarly, or almost similarly, with people: with the passage of time some plain misters are revised upwards into Sirs and Lords. I have tended to use the title they enjoyed at the time; or no title at all. The Treasury is informal where names are concerned.

My thanks are due, and gratefully given, to a number of people and organizations: to Lindsay Hawkins, Jacky Hollylee, Jeanette Lodge, Alison Lyons, Jane Thompson and Michelle Wainwright; to Peter and Moya Rees, especially; to the Bank of England and the Central Statistical Office; and to those publishers and authors who have allowed me to quote from their works.

I am grateful to the Treasury for the provision of some factual material. They ask me to make it clear, and I am happy to do so, that although I am a former Treasury official this book is a private initiative and must in no way be regarded as an 'official' Treasury history of the period. The views expressed are my own, as are all the mistakes.

Ashley Green, Bucks
May 1985.

Acknowledgements

We are grateful to the following for permission to reproduce copyright material:

Bank of England for tables A4, A5, A8, 12.2; Basil Blackwell Ltd for an adapted diagram from *Getting and Spending* by L Pliatzky (1982); Andre Deutsch for extracts from *Inside the Treasury* by J Barnett; Faber and Faber Ltd & Harcourt Brace Jovanovich Inc for an extract from *The Family Reunion* by T S Eliot Copyright 1939 by T S Eliot Renewed 1967 by Esme Valerie Eliot, an extract from 'Little Gidding' in *Four Quarters* by T S Eliot Copyright 1943 by T S Eliot Renewed 1971 by Esme Valerie Eliot and an extract from 'The Hollow Men' in *Collected Poems 1909–1962* by T S Eliot Copyright 1936 by Harcourt Brace Jovanovich Inc Copyright 1963, 1964 by T S Eliot; the author's agent for extracts from *In My Way* by Lord George Brown; the Controller, Her Majesty's Stationery Office for various extracts from Crown copyright sources; the editor for extracts from *The Observer* (various issues); Times Newspapers Ltd for extracts from *The Times* and *The Sunday Times* (various issues).

Parties, Prime Ministers and Chancellors of the Exchequer 1964–1985

Date†	Party	Prime Minister*	Chancellor of the Exchequer
16 Oct. 1964	Lab.	J.H. Wilson	Leonard James Callaghan
1 Apr. 1966	Lab.	J.H. Wilson	Leonard James Callaghan
29 Nov. 1967	Lab.	J.H. Wilson	Roy Harris Jenkins
19 Jun. 1970	Cons.	E.R. Heath	Iain Macleod
25 Jul. 1970	Cons.	E.R. Heath	Anthony Perrinott Lysberg Barber
5 Mar. 1974	Lab.	J.H. Wilson	Denis Winston Healey
10 Oct. 1974	Lab.	J.H. Wilson	Denis Winston Healey
5 April 1976	Lab.	L.J. Callaghan	Denis Winston Healey
4 May 1979	Cons.	Mrs M.H. Thatcher	Sir Richard Edward Geoffrey Howe
9 Jun. 1983	Cons.	Mrs M.H. Thatcher	Nigel Lawson

† Of Election, except appointment of Mr Barber in 1970 and Mr Callaghan's succession in 1976

* And First Lord of the Treasury

Permanent Secretary (PS)/Joint Permanent Secretary (JPS) to the Treasury

1964–68 (JPS)
Sir William Armstrong
Sir Laurence Helsby

1968–69 (JPS)
Sir William Armstrong
Sir Douglas Allen

1969–74 (PS)
Sir Douglas Allen

1974–83 (PS)
Sir Douglas Wass

1983– (PS)
Sir Peter Middleton

Second Permanent Secretaries to the Treasury

A Payment and Management

Sir P. Allen	1964-66
Sir L. Petch	1966-69

B Resources and Expenditure

Sir R. Clarke	1964-65

Public Sector

Sir R. Clarke	1965-68
Sir D. Serpell	1968-69
Sir S. Goldman	1969-72
Sir D.O. Henly	1972-75

Public Services

Sir D.O. Henly	1975-76
Sir L. Pliatsky	1976-77
Sir A. Rawlinson	1977-83

Public Expenditure

A.M. Bailey	1983-

C Finance

Sir D. Rickett	1964-68
Sir S. Goldman	1968-69
Sir F. Figgures	1969-71
Sir A. Neale	1971-73

D Overseas Finance

Sir D.J. Mitchell	1973-77
Sir K.E. Couzens	1977-83
J.G. Littler	1983-

E National Economy

Sir D. Wass	1973-74

Domestic Economy

A. Lord	1975-77
Sir L. Airey	1977-80
Sir W. Ryrie	1980-83

Economic Advisers to the Treasury

A   Economic Adviser

Sir A.K. Cairncross	1964–65
R.R. Neild	1965–67
M.V. Posner	1967–69

B   Chief Economic Adviser

Sir D. MacDougall	1969–73
Sir K. Berril	1973–74
Sir B. Hopkin	1974–77
Sir F. J. Atkinson	1977–79
Sir T. Burns	1979–

Part One

Seven Chancellors

'A pawn goes two squares in its first move, you know. So you'll go *very* quickly through the Third Square – by railway, I should think – and you'll find yourself in the Fourth Square in no time. Well, *that* square belongs to Tweedledum and Tweedledee – the Fifth is mostly water – the Sixth belongs to Humpty Dumpty – But you make no remark?'

'I – I didn't know I had to make one – just then,' Alice faltered out.

'You *should* have said,' the Queen went on in a tone of grave reproof, '"It's extremely kind of you to tell me all this" – however, we'll suppose it said – the Seventh Square is all forest – however, one of the knights will show you the way – and in the Eight Square we shall be Queens together, and it's all feasting and fun!'

Lewis Carroll   *Through the Looking-Glass*

1

Mr Callaghan, 1964–1967

Triumph of the bears

> Instead of maintaining the principle that the internal value of a national currency should conform to a prescribed *de jure* external value, it [the Bretton Woods plan] provided that its external value should be altered, if necessary, so as to conform to whatever *de facto* internal value results from domestic policies, which themselves shall be immune from criticism by the Fund.
>
> J. M. Keynes, *House of Lords, 23 May 1944.*

> Her Majesty's Government have made clear, not only with words but with deeds, our unalterable determination to maintain the value of the pound.
>
> Harold Wilson, *Speech to Economics Club of New York, 14 April 1965.*

1964

A question of devaluation

Those who did not live through the period and who now do live with a value of the pound that changes continuously and often considerably may find it difficult to understand the passions generated by the question of devaluation. The debate now moulders in the history of the day before yesterday; but since Mr Wilson's unalterable determination to reject the option provided by the Bretton Woods arrangements dominated and governed economic policy for the duration of Mr Callaghan's

Chancellorship; and since economic controversies once thought to be settled have a habit of coming back to life, the arguments may be briefly rehearsed.

Those in favour of devaluation were on the economic 'left' and included, eventually, all three of the economic advisers brought into Whitehall from outside.[1]

In favour of defending the parity were the Bank of England and, in so far as it may be said to have a collective opinion, 'the City'. The Treasury was aware of the arguments on both sides. The Department of Economic Affairs (DEA), being concerned with domestic policies (see below), probably had a majority for devaluation.

The governments and central bankers of the major foreign countries, especially the United States, were anxious not to see the first currency domino fall, and were ready to provide loans for the defence of sterling. In terms of the slightly pejorative labels that came to be used, the divide could be seen as between those who gave primacy to 'the real economy' and those concerned with 'symbols'.

The case for devaluation was straightforward: for years the British economy had struggled with the balance of payments. A huge deficit had now appeared again, the balance of payments was 'in fundamental disequilibrium' (an undefined concept) and the time had come to accept the verdict of the market and devalue. The only alternative was to deflate quite heavily, a policy which would, by definition, lower the rate of growth and reduce the amount of real resources available to the economy. Devaluation would stimulate exports, reduce imports and, unlike deflation, allow the full use of resources.

Against devaluation a number of arguments was deployed.

1. There was the purely legal matter of establishing that 'fundamental disequilibrium' existed, to conform with IMF rules. No one took this too seriously because it was believed that if Britain declared that such disequilibrium existed the IMF would not argue.
2. The pound was not overvalued. What was holding up British exports – which anyway were not doing all that badly – was not price and quality but long delivery dates stemming from a shortage of capacity. Devaluation was no remedy for this 'structural' problem.
3. Following from (2), devaluation would not, anyway, avoid deflation. If the economy was already fully stretched, and if devaluation was to boost exports, then it followed that home

demand would have to be curtailed to make room for the additional exports.

4. Devaluation would destroy confidence in sterling and in 'the City' as an international financial centre. It would be a betrayal of all those, including members of the Commonwealth, who held funds in sterling. (This was the 'morality' argument.)

5. It might not work at all, or would work only partially, because other countries would 'follow us down'.

6. Once the speculators had taken their (undeserved) profits on sterling they would turn next on the dollar, the foundation then of the international monetary system.

7. The political argument, which weighed heavily with the Prime Minister, that it would damage the Labour Government, a Labour Government having been in power at the time of the previous devaluation, in 1949: 'it would sweep us away'. This argument gained strength with the passage of time. In the speech from which the quotation at the head of this chapter is taken, Mr Wilson argued that if it were to have been done it would have had to be done 'on that first day, when the fault could clearly and unambiguously' be laid on the outgoing Government.

The argument against devaluation prevailed; and thereafter the unalterable became the unmentionable in Whitehall and, to a large extent, by tacit and patriotic agreement, in the Press. One reviewer observed that 'open advocacy of devaluation was still [in September 1965] the next worse thing to publishing obscene literature'.[2]

Marcia Williams[3] in her account of life inside No. 10 conveys the atmosphere of taboo.

> When he [Harold Wilson] was alone the dreaded word 'devaluation' was sometimes mentioned. (p. 161)

After discussion of devaluation had been brought into the open by the French (who were never very helpful in the matter):

> ... the whole atmosphere at No. 10 changed ... conversations had to be whispered especially if they related even remotely to 'the subject' and the rumours. Meetings were held quietly behind closed doors. There was no relaxation about whether or not the door of a room was left ajar. It was firmly closed as you went in so that conversation could not be overheard from the corridors. Everything was done by allusion, rather than direct reference. (p. 167)

George Brown[4] tells a similar story ' ... it was absolutely essential that nobody should know it was being discussed; and indeed, only now can *even part of the story* be told. The Prime Minister and the Chancellor were not unnaturally always terrified lest talking, or *even thinking*, about devaluation should alert the world to what was going on. ... '[5] Nevertheless, as we shall see, George Brown (as he then was) not only discussed devaluation but put his civil servants to work on a devaluation strategy and had the issue discussed in Cabinet. We shall also see that the iron rule that no one must know that the Cabinet had discussed it had the curious side-effect of making George Brown the Foreign Secretary. Once the devaluation announcement had been made, says Marcia Williams (1975), 'We ... were able to relax for the first time on this subject. No longer were there fears of mentioning the unmentionable. But so well schooled was everyone that even then it was difficult to use the dreaded word.' (p. 170)

On the day after devaluation there was, she says, a 'large and ugly crowd outside No. 10'. These days it is difficult to imagine that a crowd, even a small and handsome crowd, would gather if the effective exchange rate fell from, say, 82.0 to 70.3; or that a contingent of hooligan exporters from the Confederation of British Industry would foregather if that rate went up to 93.7.

There are stories that after 1964 papers submitted by senior officials putting the case for devaluation were ordered by the Prime Minister to be destroyed. In the atmosphere of the time this was probably prudent, although Whitehall 'moles' were less active then than later. But even had some mole of the day popped a perfectly sensible discussion paper on devaluation into the offices of the *Financial Times* newspaper it is doubtful whether it would have been printed, so thoroughly had the media been indoctrinated with their patriotic duty. (We shall see later what happened when the *Sunday Times* did publish a story about the exchange rate.)

But we have jumped ahead a little. Let us go back to the beginning.

The crises

When Harold Wilson addressed the Economics Club of New York in April 1965 his first crisis was behind him.

Ten days after assuming office on 16 October 1964, to 'open the books' and find a balance of payments deficit of nearly £700 m. (Mr Callaghan's 'bitter harvest'), the Government (having decided within the first two days not to devalue), introduced measures to reduce the balance of payments deficit. Foremost among these measures was an import surcharge of 15 per cent which caused an international outcry.

The new Chancellor's first Budget on 11 November 1964 was orthodox and mildly deflationary. It included an increase in income tax and 6d. a gallon on petrol. But it included also an increase in pensions and a proposal to introduce a Corporation Tax, and was badly received by the City and the foreign financial community. Heavy sales of sterling followed in the next two days. In a speech on 16 November the Prime Minister declared, in Churchillian terms, his determination to take whatever measures were necessary for the defence of sterling.

By now markets were expecting an increase in Bank Rate on the following Thursday, the traditional way (and day) of defending the pound; but the day passed with no change, and further large withdrawals of sterling took place. Over the weekend the Prime Minister and his economic ministers decided to raise the Bank Rate by 2 per cent and to do so as soon as the markets opened at 10.0 a.m. on Monday (23 November).

The raising of Bank Rate by 2 per cent *on a Monday* was seen as a panic measure and by the Tuesday morning an avalanche of sterling selling had developed. The UK authorities had given their best shot and the result had been perverse. All that day Lord Cromer, Governor of the Bank of England, and heads of the New York Federal Reserve Bank were on the telephone to the central bankers of Europe; by the evening a support package for sterling of $3 bn had been put together.

On 2 December the UK drew $1 bn from the IMF to repay the central banks. On the 16th came the Joint Statement of Intent on productivity, prices and incomes.

1965

The early months of 1965 passed with only minor alarms. In February the $3 bn credit with the central banks was renewed; and in May $1.4 bn was drawn from the IMF and used to pay off the credits. A $750 m. currency swap arrangement with the United States was renewed.

The April Budget increased both direct and indirect taxes. A Prices and Incomes White Paper in April set a pay norm of 3–3.5 per cent.

In September the pound again came under pressure but this time the Bank and the Treasury were ready. On 10 September the Bank of England announced a new support arrangement with eight European countries (not including France), the USA and Canada. The size of the support was deliberately left unspecified; and the authorities, instead of relying upon the psychological effect of declaring the availability of huge sums to defend sterling, went on to the offensive and bought sterling aggressively, in what *The Times* later called 'the most massive bear squeeze in the history of the foreign exchanges' with the Bank having 'the exquisite satisfaction of deciding when to let the market out'.[6]

It was a bold operation, cleverly presented, and sterling was saved for another day.

After the Prime Minister had announced a March election the Chancellor opened an economic debate on 1 March 1966 with a major 'state of the economy' speech in the course of which he announced certain measures including the decision to decimalize the currency, and a proposal for 'option mortgages'. He revealed interesting new information on the use of the swap facility with the Federal Reserve Bank of New York and on the resources then immediately available for the defence of sterling. Including the gold and dollar reserves these totalled $5 bn, in addition to the borrowing arrangements made with central banks in the preceding September.

The election later that month returned the Government with a majority increased from 3 to 99.

The most interesting feature of the Budget of 3 May, on the external front, was the measures directed at the capital account of the balance of payments. These included the 'voluntary programme' of investment in the developed sterling area, and a commitment to a thorough review of the government's own overseas expenditure, including and in particular, negotiations 'with a view to securing relief from the full foreign exchange cost of keeping our forces in Germany'. The Temporary Import Charge was to be removed in November.

On an objective assessment the situation in early May 1966 looked reasonably secure: some debt had been repaid, liquid reserves mobilized, measures directed at the capital account were having some effect and more were in train, the deficit on the current and long-term capital account of the balance of payments had been more than halved.

A seamen's strike began on 15 May and was to last until 1 July. In June further pressure on the pound developed and new facilities of $2 bn were provided by central banks, including provision for off-setting fluctuations in the sterling balances. The Treasury began putting together a new set of July measures. This provided the occasion for the last stand of George Brown, Secretary of State for Economic Affairs at the Department of Economic Affairs (DEA) (see below). By this time he 'was persuaded by my advisers, and by such friends outside as I dared to consult, that the case for devaluation was overwhelming and inevitable'. This view 'was shared by almost all the Government's economic advisers and not only those in the DEA' (Brown, p. 105). He put a few of his civil servants to work on a devaluation plan. Because of the taboo surrounding the subject the plan was neither typed nor put on file. He then, with the support of one or two other ministers, insisted on raising the matter in Cabinet and argued for devaluation rather than further deflation. He lost, and after the deflationary measures of July 1966 he told the Prime Minister he was going to resign, but was persuaded not to mainly because it would have been almost impossible for him to do so without revealing that the Cabinet was seriously split on the issue of devaluation, a revelation that would have triggered a further run on the pound. If George Brown was determined to quit the DEA but could not be allowed to resign from the Government, some other post had to be found for him. He became Foreign Secretary (Brown, pp. 104–7). The package of measures against which George Brown had argued was presented by the Prime Minister (not the Chancellor of the Exchequer) on 20 July. The measures were designed to reduce home demand by what was then a massive £500 m.; they included public expenditure cuts and a statutory 'Prices and Incomes Standstill' to the end of the year to be followed by a period of 'severe restraint'. The pound was reprieved once more.

The Department of Economic Affairs

There is a pleasing bit of folklore that has it that the DEA was conceived in a taxi conveying Harold Wilson and George Brown to the House of Commons. That is not entirely true: it was *born* on that journey but, as is customary, conception had occurred some time beforehand. The father – or possibly the midwife – was George Brown fortified by lengthy discussion with Harold Wilson, other Labour Party politicians, senior civil servants (with the permission of the Government of the day), economists, industrialists, trade unionists and commentators. Conception was multiple rather than immaculate.

Soon after the Labour Government took office the infant
Department was installed at the rear of the building that houses
the Treasury. George Brown records that 'Tommy Balogh warned
me strongly against allowing myself to be installed at the backside
of the Treasury, observing, "That's exactly where you will end up."
How right he was!' (Brown, p. 91).

The Department was to be responsible for a number of things
including prices and incomes policy, industrial policy and regional
policy. But above all, certainly in its early days, it was to be the
instrument through which the Government would pursue its plans
for growth: Mr Maudling's 'dash for growth' continued by other
means. The division of function between the new Department and
the Treasury was, broadly, that the DEA would look after the
'real' economy and the longer term while the Treasury retained its
responsibility for finance (the 'unreal economy'?) and the short
term. It was hoped that the existence of two major departments
each charged with different aspects of the management of the
economy would generate 'creative tension', like some economic
chest-expander.

Nominally, the DEA, headed as it was by the Deputy Prime
Minister[7], was 'in the lead', as Whitehall jargon has it, but the
Treasury retained effective control over the crucial short-term
management of the economy.

At working level, relations between the Departments were
good. For example, in my field, all information and guidance briefs
prepared by the Treasury Information Division were cleared
before issue with the DEA's Information Division. An insight into
working at the policy level occurred at one of Sir Denis Rickett's
meetings with his senior officials on the overseas side of the
Treasury, which I attended. 'How' Sir Denis asked a Deputy
Secretary, 'are the DEA arrangements working out?' The Deputy
Secretary (later to get his own Department and his Knighthood)
replied, 'Well, actually, Denis, not too badly. You see, they are
mostly our chaps.'   One of the first and major tasks of the DEA
was to produce a National Plan for the economy, a plan which
'would break the ancient Treasury tradition of making economic
policy and industrial activity subject to all the inhibitions of
orthodox monetary control' (Brown, p. 104). The Plan, all 492
pages of it, appeared on 16 September 1965 (Cmnd 2764). In its
third sentence the Plan acknowledged that 'The most serious
economic problem facing us at the present time is the balance of
payments', a sentence no doubt inserted by 'our chaps'. Alas, the
words were only too true: publication came six days after the

second major sterling crisis and the Plan was, for practical purposes, stillborn. It was abandoned after the July measures of the following year. George Brown left for the Foreign Office to be succeeded at the DEA by Michael Stewart. In August 1967 the Prime Minister announced that he would supervise the DEA himself with Peter Shore as Secretary of State. In February 1969 Peter Shore published *The Task Ahead: Economic Assessment to 1972.*

The creation of the DEA was the only serious attempt, in peacetime, to wrest (or rescue, as some might prefer) the economy from the exclusive control of the Treasury. The new Department was led by one of the most dominant and charismatic politicians of the day[8] who, without doubt, inspired his staff with his own enthusiasm. Why, then, did it end up in the dustbin of Whitehall's reorganizations?

So far as its growth plans were concerned, it failed, as the 'Maudling dash' had failed, because the visions of growth were not reconciled with the reality of the fragility of the British balance of payments; perhaps the two were, and remained, fundamentally irreconcilable. Be that as it may, the DEA did not, in any case, have the muscle to impose any solution other than that favoured by the Treasury and the Prime Minister. The Treasury's control of finance and short-term management proved decisive. George Brown wrote:

> Once the heady first days had gone and the novelty had worn off the Treasury began to reassert itself, and with its absolutely superb mastery of the government machine gradually either filched things back or – more to the point – made it rather difficult for us to effect the grand design we had in mind so that a coherent and continuous economic policy would emerge. (p. 92)
> ... the DEA and the Treasury were running two diametrically opposed policies. We were vigorously stirring things up to try to get the whole economy running ahead; the Treasury was constantly damping things down. If there were to be any validity in the establishment of the DEA, it had to be laid down that the DEA was the senior economic Ministry, and that the Treasury would have to take on something of the style of a continental Ministry of Finance. The Prime Minister never did this (Brown p. 104)

That is the nub of the matter: the DEA did not have overall control of the economy; the First Secretary in charge of it was not an economic overlord. The economy was run by a triumvirate of

the Prime Minister, the First Secretary and Deputy Prime
Minister, and the Chancellor of the Exchequer. A division of
responsibility intended to generate 'creative tension' created only
tension and extra work:

> ' ... in fact, all this internecine warring achieved was to
> make everyone work many times as hard and quarrel far
> more often than was necessary to secure an outcome that
> was practically no improvement on what had happened
> before.' (Brown, p. 105)

As early as January 1965 Crossman had noted in his *Diaries*:
(1979)

> Though George Brown is a great success, the division of
> power between the Treasury and the DEA is a
> development for which we are having to pay a heavy price
> in divided authority and dissension in central planning (p.
> 58).

And later

> ... our economic policy has been run by the system of
> having two Ministries permanently at loggerheads, the
> Treasury and the DEA, with the Treasury gradually
> gaining mastery over the DEA but sufficient tension
> remaining between them to cancel out both Departments'
> policies. Our big economic decisions have been made by
> Harold's arbitration between the Chancellor and the First
> Secretary. This system, which looked pretty crazy
> anyway, came completely unstuck this summer
> [1966] ... (p. 210).
>
> Owing to the creation of the DEA and the permanent
> rift between Brown and Callaghan, our Government has
> been riven with dissension ... (p. 219).

The DEA was wound up in October 1970 and the economic
management function reverted wholly to the Treasury who, in
May of that year, published *Economic Prospects to 1972 – A
Revised Assessment*.

Perhaps the last word should be allowed to George Brown:

> The story of the DEA is the record of a social revolution
> that failed ... It envisaged a wholly novel form of national
> social accounting to replace the orthodox financial
> accountancy by which the Treasury has always
> dominated British life.
> Some Government, some day, will re-create a department

on the lines of the DEA and limit the out-dated authority
of the Treasury. When that happens — and it is bound to
happen – the thinking that went into the DEA will be
acclaimed. (Brown, pp. 87, 113)

1967

By the final quarter of 1966 the 1964 deficit on the current account
of the balance of payments of £400 m. had been turned into a
surplus at an annual rate of £560 m.; the improvement continued
into the early months of 1967 and by the end of March all short-
term debt to central banks had been repaid. There was reason to
suppose that the economy might be in surplus in the year as a
whole. Internally the pressure of demand had been reduced. The
rate of inflation had fallen below 4 per cent and was still falling,
aided by the 'period of severe restraint' which had begun on 1
January.

The Budget of 11 April 1967 was described by the *Financial
Times* as 'the most neutral since the war'. In the knowledge of the
sort of figures we have since become used to it is fascinating to
read that the *Financial Times*, while generally approving the
Budget, thought that the Chancellor was 'taking risks on the side
of caution'. The risk was that if the economy did not achieve the
forecast growth of 3 per cent he would, with unemployment
running at 2 per cent, reflate 'too hard and too late'. He should be
'ready to reflate mildly and selectively as soon as it appears
necessary'.[9]

The bright beginning to the year was not maintained. Exports
fell away, largely because of weak demand in the main markets.
Imports continued to rise. Confidence in sterling weakened after
the middle of May and was further damaged in June by the
outbreak of war in the Middle East and the closure of the Suez
Canal. Some large wage awards were made following the end of
the six months of restraint. In the first half of August there was
some quite heavy selling of sterling and the currency continued
weak throughout September. In October the EEC Commission, in
its report on the UK's application to join the Community,
published a damaging verdict on the UK economy. Trade figures
released in mid-month were bad. From mid-September to end-
November dock strikes affected different ports.

On 10 October the Government unwisely accepted a loan of
£37.5 m. for twelve months from three Swiss banks. The amount
was trivial in relation to what would be required if a full-blown
crisis developed and was seen as at best irrelevant and at worst as
a desperate scraping from the barrel of foreign banking credit
facilities.

Pressure on the pound built up in mid-autumn and around 10
November the Treasury's contingency plan for devaluation was
activated and the countdown began for a statement on Saturday
18 November. Much had to be done in the interval including,
especially, discussions with the IMF and the Americans and
discreet enquiries among other governments and central bankers
on what size of devaluation – if we did devalue – would be
acceptable. If the devaluation were too small it would be
ineffective and followed by further pressure on the pound; if it
were too large other countries would not accept it and would
negate it or partially negate it, by themselves devaluing. In the end,
and with the support of calculations made by a small number of
Treasury economists working in great secrecy, a figure of 15 per
cent was decided upon.

Security was tight, and the secret held. The devaluation could
have been brought off with a minimum of loss to the British
reserves but for a private notice question put down by Mr Robert
Sheldon MP, Chairman of the Labour backbench Economic
Committee, on Thursday 16 November, the day on which the
Cabinet had ratified the decision to proceed with the devaluation.
The question concerned a report by the BBC's economic
correspondent that Britain was negotiating a loan of $1 bn in Paris.
It was exceedingly embarrassing and the Cabinet sent the Chief
Whip[10] to try to persuade the Speaker not to accept the question,
but he refused. The Chancellor's response to the question was
seen as equivocal and when it appeared on the agency tapes,
sterling began to pour out of London. Devaluation could not be
brought forward, and the loss of reserves continued. It was an
expensive question and answer.

The devaluation announcement had to be made at a time when
foreign exchange markets throughout the world were closed. At
9.30 p.m. on Saturday 18 November the Chancellor of the
Exchequer announced a lowering of the exchange rate of the
pound by 14.3 per cent,[11] from $2.80 to $2.40 to the pound. The
bears had won. Mr Callaghan resigned the Chancellorship eleven
days later.

Public expenditure

The Callaghan regime was marked by a determined effort to make the Plowden system of public expenditure planning (see Ch. 10) operationally effective and to integrate it with the National Plan. This was an area of particularly close collaboration between Treasury and DEA officials. But the results were disappointing.

In the National Plan, GDP was to grow at about 4 per cent per annum and public expenditure slightly faster still. In the event GDP grew more slowly and public expenditure much faster so that in 1966–67 public expenditure grew three times as fast as GDP, and in 1967–68 five times as fast. Public expenditure was thus absorbing an increasing proportion of total resources at a time when resources should have been moving into the balance of payments.

This failure to keep the growth of public expenditure in line with the actual – as distinct from the hoped-for – growth of resources was one that was to recur repeatedly in the years that followed.

Monetary policy

There was a credit policy that relied heavily on the administrative control, by the Bank of England, of the amount and direction of bank lending, but no monetary policy as we now know it. No one was yet paying much attention to any of the monetary aggregates.

Mr Callaghan

The first thing to record about the Chancellorship of James Callaghan is that despite the unpopular things he had to do, he inspired an extraordinarily sympathetic response from the common people, not something that Chancellors of the Exchequer customarily do. The Treasury received hundreds of letters from ordinary people enclosing small sums of money 'to help the balance of payments' or to 'help pay the national debt'. This placed the Chancellor and his advisers in some difficulty. He could not reject outright gifts which seemed in many cases to have been ill-afforded; nor could he accept them. It was decided that the only solution was to return them, with thanks, and the advice that the sender could best help the economy by putting the money into national savings.

Mr Callaghan has been caricatured as a Chancellor uncertain of his economics and dominated by the Prime Minister and by his Treasury officials. This is too simple an interpretation. In itself it contains something of a contradiction for it is by no means obvious that the advice he received from the Treasury always accorded with the views of the Prime Minister. And for most of the time Treasury views had, anyway, to take account of the views of the DEA. Mr Callaghan was quite prepared to take the hard road where this appeared to him to be necessary to defend the parity of sterling. But because of the creation of the DEA, headed by the number two in the Government hierarchy, he was not wholly master in his own house. The Prime Minister, the First Secretary and their economic advisers believed that there was a third way between devaluation and deflation, that the economy could be manipulated more directly by an assortment of controls and fiscal measures. The Chancellor had to listen to these voices, and he may not have disagreed with what he heard. But what emerged was a compromise. Tough measures were taken but they were not tough enough: the degree of deflation imposed was not enough to maintain the parity. There were times when the middle way looked like succeeding but in the end it failed and the Government and the Chancellor gained neither the immediate relief of devaluation nor the longer-term rewards of maintaining the parity. Mr Callaghan was caught up in that failure. He had done his best in the circumstances of his time, circumstances which included for the first and so far only time an attempt to take economic management away from the sole control of the Treasury and the Chancellor of the Exchequer. That is not to suggest that control by the Treasury alone is best; only that divided control is likely to be worse.

Diary of events 1964–67

1964

16 Oct.	Labour Government to office with majority of 5. Department of Economic Affairs (DEA) set up.
26	Measures to reduce balance of payments deficit, including 15 per cent temporary import charge.

11 Nov.	Mr Callaghan's first Budget. Heavy sales of sterling.
16	Prime Minister states he will defend the parity.
19	(Thursday) Bank Rate unchanged. Further sales of sterling.
23	(Monday) Bank Rate raised from 5 to 7 per cent. Sterling selling accelerates.
25	$3 bn credits from central banks.
2 Dec.	$1 bn from IMF to refund credits.
16	Joint Statement of Intent on productivity, prices and incomes.

1965

10 Feb.	$3 bn credit renewed.
11 Feb.	*Machinery of Prices and Incomes Policy* Cmnd 2577. A National Board for Prices and Incomes to be established.
22	Temporary Import charge reduced to 10 per cent.
6 Apr.	Budget.
8	*Prices and Incomes Policy* Cmnd 2639. Norm of 3–3.5 per cent.
12 May	IMF drawing of $1.4 bn.
29	$750 m. swap arrangement with US extended for a year.
27 Jul.	Further measures to strengthen balance of payments, following large sales of sterling.
10 Sept.	Announcement of new central bank support for the pound following heavy sales of sterling.
16	DEA publishes National Plan (Cmnd 2764).
11 Nov.	*Prices and Incomes Policy: an 'Early Warning' System* Cmnd 2808.

1966

31 Mar.	General Election. Labour majority of 99.
3 May	Budget. Temporary Import charge to end. Selective Employment Tax (SET) introduced.
15	Seamen's strike commenced. (Ended 1 Jul.)
13 June	Pressure on sterling. New central bank facilities of $2 bn arranged.
14 Jul.	Bank Rate raised 1 per cent to 7 per cent.
20	Measures to reduce demand by £500 m. Voluntary prices and incomes freeze for six months.
29	*Prices and Incomes Standstill* Cmnd 3073.
9 Aug.	National Plan abandoned. Mr George Brown goes to Foreign Office.
13 Sept.	US Fed. Swap increased from $750 m. to $1,350 m.

| 10 Nov. | Discussions on entry to EEC. |
| 14 | £50 foreign travel allowance introduced. |

1967

1 Jan.	Six months' severe restraint begins.
11 Apr.	Neutral Budget.
4 May	Bank Rate reduced to 5.5 per cent, the third ½ point reduction of the year.
11	Formal application to join EEC.
5 Jun.	War between Israel and Egypt. Suez Canal closed.
1 Jul.	End of severe restraint. No new norm.
18 Sept.	Dock strikes begin (finally ended 27 Nov.).
3 Oct.	News of adverse report on UK economy by EEC (published 6 Oct.).
10	Britain accepts £37.5 m. loan from three Swiss banks.
19	Bank Rate raised from 5.5 to 6 per cent.
9 Nov.	Bank Rate raised to 6.5 per cent.
12	Britain negotiates $250 m. credit through Bank for International Settlements (to refinance IMF debts).
16	Chancellor of the Exchequer makes non-committal reply to question on reports of a $1 bn loan. Massive withdrawals of sterling.
18	Pound devalued by 14.3 per cent to $2.40. Bank Rate raised 1½ points to 8 per cent. Public expenditure cuts.
22	*Prices and Incomes Standstill: Period of Severe Restraint* Cmnd 3150.
27	de Gaulle opposes UK membership of EEC.
29	Mr Callaghan resigns. IMF agrees $1.4 bn stand-by credit
30	Chancellor's Letter of Intent to IMF.

Notes and references

1. Nicholas Kaldor, Special Adviser to the Chancellor of the Exchequer 1964–68.
    Robert Neild, Economic Adviser to the Treasury, 1964–67.
    Thomas Balogh, Economic Adviser to the Cabinet, 1964–67.
2. Alan Day in *The Observer*, 26 Nov. 1967.
3. Williams, M. (later Lady Falkender) (1975) (new edition).
4. Brown, G. (1972) p. 104. Other quotations or paraphrases labelled 'Brown' are from the same source.

5. My italics. 'Even part of the story?' As was once remarked
    about a Foreign Office report on Guy Burgess's proclivities,
    'What else can they mean – goats?' A terror of even thinking
    about devaluation suggests a degree of fear of Orwellian
    proportions.
6. 'Pound firm and calm on crisis anniversary' *The Times*, 25
    Nov. 1965.
7. The title 'Deputy Prime Minister' is disputed. Upon the
    formation of the Labour Government, George Brown was
    appointed First Secretary of State as well as Secretary of
    State for Economic Affairs. He comments 'The title of First
    Secretary then was meant to indicate what it said. There is no
    provision in our constitutional system for a Deputy Prime
    Minister, and the First Secretaryship was a convenient way of
    indicating who was in fact deputy to the premier.' (p. 90–1) It
    appears, however, that it was not absolutely necessary to be
    styled First Secretary in order to be an unconstitutional
    Deputy Prime Minister; for, telling the story of his resignation,
    on 15 March 1968, he writes: 'although I was Deputy Prime
    Minister, Foreign Secretary and a member of the Economic
    Committee of the Cabinet ... ' (p. 162)
8. George Brown. His stock has slumped since then. But in
    January 1965 Richard Crossman, not given to encomia, had
    this to say of him: ' ... his leadership has been outstanding.
    He has created the new DEA and got a number of excellent
    people into it, ... there is no doubt that as First Secretary and
    Deputy Prime Minister he is absolutely dominant over poor
    old James Callaghan (the Chancellor of the Exchequer) who
    trails along as number three.' (*Diaries*, pp. 57–8). Poor old
    James Callaghan, of course, went on to become Prime
    Minister.
9. *Financial Times*, 12 Apr. 1967, p. 16.
10. Crossman says he knew this was a mistake; to please the
    Speaker they should have sent the Lord President, not the
    Chief Whip. *Diary* (1979), 16 Nov. 1967.
11. Sterling became 14.3 per cent cheaper in dollars. Dollars
    became 16.7 per cent dearer in sterling.

2

Mr Jenkins, 1968–June 1970

The climate of the Treasury ...
during most of my time there was
that of a long dark arctic winter,
only slowly melting into a
tentative spring.

Roy Jenkins[1]

When Mr Jenkins arrived at the Treasury[2] at the end of
November 1967 he could have been pardoned for believing that he
was better placed than his predecessor when he became
Chancellor. The devaluation that had been denied Mr Callaghan in
1964 had been forced upon us, opening the door into the rose
garden of an economy free from balance of payments crises. Mr
George Brown had departed from a Department of Economic
Affairs which was now much less powerful than formerly: Mr
Jenkins could be master in his house. Of course, the balance of
payments would not swing into surplus overnight, because of the
'J' curve effect,[3] and there would no doubt be other problems, but
for the moment the strategy was clear: the immediate task was to
deflate home demand to release resources for the growth of the
exports which would, in due course, flow from devaluation.

The shock of the devaluation of one of the two reserve
currencies was followed by upheaval and rumour in the foreign
exchange and gold markets. The London markets were closed on
Monday 20 November 1967. Those who had sold sterling they did
not have rushed to buy it at the new rate and an acute shortage
developed. The dollar came under pressure and gold was in
demand. Some foreign exchange came back to London but there
was a renewed outflow in December as the measures

accompanying devaluation were judged to be inadequate. Further measures were promised and these came in a statement by the Prime Minister on 16 January 1968 announcing public expenditure cuts of £700 m., including the postponement of the rise in the school-leaving age and the re-imposition of prescription charges. Next day the Chancellor announced that the Budget, brought forward to 19 March, would contain further measures to restrain consumption. Before then came the gold crisis.

At the end of February fears about US gold policy stimulated heavy and continuing speculation into gold. Early in March there were heavy sales of sterling and the exchange rate fell below parity to its lowest point since devaluation. On 7 March Mr Jenkins told the Cabinet that if the Budget did not restore confidence a second devaluation would occur within three months.[4]

On 9 March the governors of the major central banks meeting in Basle announced their determination to maintain the price of gold at $35 an ounce but despite, or perhaps because of this, speculation continued. The British were asked to close the London gold market and at a Privy Council meeting the Queen declared 15 March a Bank Holiday, closing not only the gold market but the Stock Exchange and the foreign exchanges. It had the incidental effect of 'closing' George Brown also, who resigned because he had not been consulted or summoned to the Privy Council meeting.

On 18 March after a meeting in Washington the members of the gold pool announced the end of the gold support arrangements and the establishment of a two-tier system for gold: central banks would deal only among themselves at $35 an ounce and the private market would be left to find its own level. The London market re-opened on 1 April with a free price of $38 an ounce.

The Budget of 19 March was severe, raising revenue by £900 m. in a full year.[5]

The day after the Budget a 3.5 per cent ceiling for pay and dividends, except for productivity agreements, was announced. The White Paper setting out the policy (Cmnd 3590) followed on 3 April.

The Budget restored confidence and the immediate crisis was over, but sterling continued in a somewhat disturbed state with heavy selling at times during May and June. In July the Bank for International Settlements and central bankers announced a $2 bn stand-by credit to offset fluctuations in the sterling balances. The White Paper giving details of the new arrangements was published on 14 October: *The Basle Facility and the Sterling Area* (Cmnd

3787). In October the Bank announced further measures to conserve sterling, in the form of regulations stopping the use of sterling for trade between non-sterling countries. On 1 November hire purchase restrictions were introduced. The balance of visible trade was improving, but only slowly; the seasonally adjusted deficit of £358 m. in the fourth quarter of 1967 had moved in successive quarters of 1968 to £217 m., £255 m. and £182 m.[6]

In the middle of November there began a massive movement of funds into the Deutschmark and out of other currencies, particularly the French franc. Sterling also came under heavy pressure. Between the 20 and 22 November the major foreign exchange markets were closed while ministers meeting at Bonn discussed the crisis, which was resolved without parity changes. Immediately upon his return from Bonn, Mr Jenkins introduced further measures including the activation of the Regulator at a rate of 10 per cent[7], a tightening of credit and the introduction of an import deposit scheme.

At the end of the year the UK's foreign borrowing reached a peak of $8.0 bn.

In November the manpower functions of the Treasury had been hived off to the newly created Civil Service Department.

Bank Rate was raised by one point to 8 per cent in February 1969 and the Budget on 15 April was contractionary. Early in May further heavy speculation in favour of the Deutschmark was followed by an official denial that it would be revalued.

An event of some significance occurred on 22 May when Mr Jenkins's Letter of Intent to the IMF introduced the concept of Domestic Credit Expansion (DCE). We shall have more to say about DCE in Chapter 12 but as this was the first occasion on which a Letter of Intent had acknowledged it and stated a limit for it, it is perhaps worth quoting from the Letter:

> 8. ... the Government attaches the greatest importance to monetary policy, which provides an essential support to fiscal policy. The rise in money supply in 1968 of £986 m. was broadly in line with the growth of GNP; but the increase in credit in the economy was too high, and the Government intends not to permit credit to be supplied to the economy on anything like this scale in 1969/70.
> 9. The Government will therefore watch closely the development of domestic credit expansion during the year. The Government's objectives and policies imply a domestic credit expansion for the private and public sectors in the year ending 31 March 1970 of not more

than £400 m., compared with some £1,225 m. in 1968/69.
It is the Government's policy to ensure that the course,
quarter by quarter of domestic credit expansion as a
whole, and of the Central Government borrowing
requirement within it, is consistent with the intended
result for the year as a whole, and to take action as
appropriate to this end.[8]

Note that the Government 'attaches the *greatest importance* to
monetary policy, which provides an *essential* support to fiscal
policy ... '. And there is a promise to control the Central
Government's borrowing requirement.

So obsessed had the British become with the balance of
payments that the release of the monthly trade figures had
become an event, and their presentation a matter for
correspondence in the serious newspapers. It therefore caused
quite a stir when the Board of Trade announced in June 1969 that
the export figures had been consistently under-recorded by some
£10 m. a month. Some extreme spirits wondered whether we had
devalued because of a statistical error. But not so: the under-
recorded exports were still there, in the errors and omissions,
known as the balancing item.[9] Still, it was gratifying to have our
export performance improved at a stroke by well over £100 m. a
year.

Early in August the French, in a surprise move, devalued the
franc by 11.1 per cent. There was renewed pressure on sterling
which in mid-month reached its lowest point ever. But the August
trade figures showed a surplus of £40 m. and, following the
discovery of the under-recording, exports for the first half-year
were revised upwards by £70 m.

Late September saw further heavy buying of the Deutschmark
and the German foreign exchange market was closed until after
the elections on 28 September, on which date the Deutschmark
was temporarily floated. On 24 October it was revalued by
9.29 per cent.

In the meantime the Department of Economic Affairs had been
abolished and parts of it re-absorbed into the Treasury.

At the year's close sterling rose above its parity for the first time
since April 1968. Balance of payments statistics published
subsequently showed a surplus on the current and long-term
capital account of £370 m. in the second half of 1969. Devaluation
had finally 'worked'.

In April 1970 Mr Jenkins introduced a 'neutral' Budget. In the
currency markets one more domino fell when the Canadian dollar

was floated at the end of May. In June the Conservatives won the General Election aided, it was thought, by their exploitation of some erratically bad trade figures published just before polling day.

Mr Jenkins

The struggle to establish sterling firmly on its new parity – Mr Jenkins's primary task – was more protracted than expected, even allowing for a tendency for the lags in the system to be underestimated. For more than a year after devaluation there was still a real fear in the Treasury and the Bank that we might suffer the 'humiliation' of a second devaluation. It was an anxious time.

The fears of central bankers and finance ministers that the devaluation of sterling would expose other currencies to speculation proved well-founded. The French franc and the Deutschmark were swept off their parities by the currency tides; the Canadian dollar was floated and central banks forced to concede a two-tier price for gold. In retrospect the devaluation of sterling can be seen as the beginning of the end of the Bretton Woods system of fixed exchange rates.

Domestically, policy objectives were still couched in impeccably Keynesian language – the movement of real resources away from consumption into the balance of payments. Yet, in the Treasury and elsewhere, particularly the IMF, increasing regard was being paid to the monetary numbers; for the first time since the Second World War a monetary aggregate, DCE, became one objective of policy.

Recent statistics show that between 1967 and 1970 the turnround in the balance of payments on current account was over £1 bn. Yet perhaps Mr Jenkins's major achievement was to bring public expenditure under control. So successful was he in this that growth was actually negative in 1968–69 and in 1969–70. As a result of this the Public Sector Borrowing Requirement (PSBR) fell from £1,860 m. in 1967 to *minus* £445 m. in 1970, i.e. a surplus, allowing debt repayment. This was the last time Britain had a negative PSBR.

If it is true that the Conservatives won the 1970 election on the case that Mr Jenkins and the Labour Government were mismanaging the economy and sterling was not safe in their hands, that must surely count as one of the great electoral ironies.[10] For Mr Jenkins handed over to his successor an economy in sounder shape than it had been for many years. For the first time since the War an incoming Chancellor inherited an economy with no balance of payments problem, public expenditure firmly under control, the public finances in good order and no industrial trouble.

What the incoming Government did with that inheritance we shall see in Chapter 4.

Diary of events 1968–June 1970

1968

16 Jan.	Prime Minister announces expenditure cuts of £700 m.; postponement of the rise in the school-leaving age; and re-imposition of prescription charges.
15 Mar.	Gold crisis. London Stock Exchange, foreign exchange and gold markets closed. Mr George Brown resigns as Foreign Secretary.
18	Two-tier gold market established; central banks to deal at $35 per ounce, private market to find own level (see 1 Apr.).
19	Contractionary Budget, raising revenue by £900 m. in full year.
20	3.5 per cent pay and dividend ceiling, except for productivity agreements (White Paper, Cmnd 3590, published 3 Apr.).
1 Apr.	London gold market re-opened. Free price $38 per ounce.
8 Jul.	Bank for International Settlements and central bankers announce $2 bn stand-by credit to offset fluctuations in sterling balances. (White Paper *Basle Facility and the Sterling Area*, Cmnd 3787, published 14 Oct.).
25 Oct.	Bank of England stops sterling finances for trade between non-sterling area countries.
1 Nov.	Hire purchase restrictions. Civil Service Department (CSD) comes into being and takes over manpower functions from Treasury.
20–22	Finance ministers meet in Bonn to handle crisis of huge inflows of funds into Germany from France and elsewhere. Major foreign currency markets closed for 3 days.
22	On return from Bonn Mr Jenkins activates the 10 per cent Regulator, tightens credit and introduces import deposit scheme.

31 Dec.   UK foreign borrowing reaches end-quarter peak of
           $8.0 bn.

1969

17 Jan.   Government publishes *In Place of Strife* (Cmnd 3888)
           proposals for legislation to reform industrial relations.

27 Feb.   White Paper on public expenditure (Cmnd 3936)
           Bank Rate raised one point to 8 per cent.

15 Apr.   Contractionary Budget.

29   Treasury Green Paper *Public Expenditure: a New
           Presentation* (Cmnd 4017).

May   Renewed speculation about revaluation of
           Deutschmark. An estimated $4 bn flows into
           Germany.

9   Official denial that Deutschmark will be revalued.

22   Mr Jenkins's Letter of Intent to IMF introduces limit on
           Domestic Credit Expansion (DCE).

12 Jun.   Board of Trade announces that exports have been
           undervalued by about £10 m. a month.

8 Aug.   French franc devalued by 11.1 per cent. Renewed
           pressure on sterling, which, on 14 Aug. closes at its
           lowest ever.

10 Sept.   Exports for first 6 months revised upwards by £70 m.
           August visible trade £40 m. in surplus.

24   Further heavy buying of Deutschmarks. German
           foreign exchange markets closed until after election on
           28 Sept.

28   Deutschmark floated temporarily.

5 Oct.   DEA abolished and parts re-absorbed into Treasury.

24   Deutschmark revalued by 9.29 per cent.

4 Dec.   White Paper *Public Expenditure 1968–69 to 1973–74*
           (Cmnd 4234)

30   Sterling above parity for the first time since April 1968.

1970

21 Jan.   Treasury announces formation of Economic Group
           under the Chief Economic Adviser (Sir Donald
           MacDougall).

10 Feb.   White Paper *Britain and the European Communities:
           An Economic Assessment* (Cmnd 4289).

14 Apr.   'Neutral' Budget.

31 May   Canadian dollar floated; renewed currency speculation.

15 Jun.   May trade figures show deficit of £31 m.

18   General Election. Conservative majority of 31.

19   Mr Iain Macleod becomes Chancellor of the
Exchequer.

Notes and references

1. *Sunday Times*, 17 Jan. 1971, p. 26.
2. Bringing with him, to the consternation of the Treasury, his
   own Principal Private Secretary from the Home Office. The
   Civil Service does not encourage Ministers to attract a
   personal entourage of civil servants, nor civil servants to
   become identified with particular Ministers and their policies.
   (It is well known that Sir William Armstrong subsequently
   became very close to Mr Heath but as Sir William was Head
   of the Civil Service at the time he enjoyed a certain latitude.)
   Moreover, although the Administrative class of the Civil
   Service is supposed to be omni-competent a Minister's private
   secretary, as the Minister's interface with the Department,
   does need to know his way around that Department.
   Accordingly, the sitting PPS remained in post and for a while
   we had two PPSs to whom minutes had to be addressed
   jointly.
3. Upon devaluation the price of imports rises at once while the
   increased volume and value of exports takes time to come
   through. Hence the balance of trade at first falls and then rises
   – the so-called 'J' curve.
4. *Crossman (1979)*, p. 405. On 17 March he records 'So I
   missed hearing Roy's exposition of the crisis which nearly
   brought us into catastrophe. Since then I've been filled in by
   Tommy Balogh. It looks as though the threat of another
   devaluation within four months had suddenly become a threat
   of devaluation within four days.'
5. The Budgetary concept of revenue in a 'full year' is, on
   examination, somewhat elusive. It must clearly depend on
   some estimate of the incomes on which the taxes are levied.
   But what 'full year' are we talking about? It seems to be an
   entirely notional one.
6. *Economic Trends*, No. 182, Dec. 1968.
7. The Finance Act 1961 as amended by the Finance Act 1964
   allowed the Treasury to impose a surcharge or rebate of up to
   10 per cent on the duties on tobacco, alcoholic drink,
   hydrocarbon oils, betting and other minor duties, and

purchase tax. The provision was renewable annually by Parliament and was known as the Customs and Excise Regulator. It had been used twice before, in July 1961 and July 1966.

8. The Letter of Intent was issued to support our application (granted) for a stand-by facility of $1 bn. There had been six previous Letters, one by Mr Selwyn Lloyd, three by Mr Maudling and two by Mr Callaghan, the second of which, on 23 November 1967, was the first to be published.

9. Special note on the recording of exports, *Board of Trade Journal* 18 June 1969; and 'Under-recording of exports', *Board of Trade Journal*, Sept. 1969. One journalist gave the credit for the discovery to the Polish commercial counsellor, Mr Tadeusz Wisniewski.

10. 'On 1 June Wilson's old *bête noire*, the former Governor of the Bank of England, Lord Cromer, said on television that any incoming government would find 'a very much more difficult financial situation than the new Labour Government found in 1964'. The most charitable thing that can be said about this absurd judgement is that it may have been actuated by ignorance as much as malice: Cromer's grasp of macroeconomic policy had never been of the strongest ... In reality, one thing that was definitely *not* wrong with the British economy in the summer of 1970 was the balance of payments.' Stewart (1977, p. 116)

3

Mr Macleod,
June–July 1970

Macleod's death was widely regarded as a tragedy for the
Conservative Government, a view which subsequent
events did nothing to dispel.

Michael Stewart (1977, p. 120)

Iain Macleod became Chancellor of the Exchequer on 19 June
1970 and died a month later, on 20 July. Pointless as it may be to
speculate on what might have been had he lived, one cannot resist
doing so, however superficially.

The Conservative Government of 1970 came to power with
plans well formulated in Opposition. They promised an economic
philosophy and economic policies not dissimilar from those of the
1979 Government: Heath's 'Selsdon Man' was Thatcher Man
without the full monetarist dogma. There was to be less State
intervention, lower public expenditure, lower direct taxation, no
incomes policy; in short, a clear change of direction towards a
more market-orientated economy in which, to encapsulate the
philosophy in metaphors popular at the time, 'lame ducks' would
go to the wall if they could not stand on their own feet.

In the very short time that he spent at the Treasury, Macleod
was less concerned to examine the entrails of the latest economic
statistics – an activity otherwise known as conjunctural analysis –
than to get on with the implementation of the longer-term
programme hammered out at the conference at Selsdon Park
Hotel.[1] Now it may be that Macleod was one of those fortunate
men who dies before his promise and reputation can be sullied by
the cruel passage of time and events. Nevertheless it is difficult to
believe, from what can be inferred from his political pedigree to
that time, that the wily, long-sighted and tough-minded Macleod

would have allowed economic and political affairs to take quite the course they did under his replacement. If that is so then the Government might not have been forced into an early and losing election, might have won at some other time, and Mr Heath would have continued as Prime Minister and Leader of the Party.

Notes

1.   For a useful two-page summary of the Selsdon programme see Stewart (1977) pp. 111, 112; see also Sewill (1975) p. 30.

4

Mr Barber,
July 1970–March 1974

> Looking back we can see occasions since the war when
> the authorities have stepped on the accelerator to
> stimulate home demand at a time when in fact the
> economy was beginning to expand on its own. Time and
> again the result was, after a little time lag, an overheating
> of the economy, the development of demand inflation and
> a balance of payments crisis. I hope we shall not risk
> another similar episode.
>
> Governor of the Bank of England, Oct. 1970[1]

After some four years when most of my professional life seemed
to have been dominated by a need to explain to anyone who
would listen that the balance of payments was not as bad as it
looked and would soon get better, the later months of Jenkins's
Chancellorship and the early years of Barber came as welcome
relief; and I suspect that the same could be said of officials on the
overseas side of the Treasury. For fourteen consecutive quarters
from the first quarter of 1969 to the second quarter of 1972, the
balance of payments on current account, seasonally adjusted,
showed a surplus. Investment and capital flows were also positive
in most quarters, adding to the total inward flow of currency.
Towards the end of this blissful period the Governor of the Bank
of England commented:

> We have been running a massive and unprecedented
> balance of payments surplus. This surplus as well as some
> very large inflows of short-term funds has enabled us to
> repay most of our outstanding external debt and add
> greatly to our reserves. However, I am afraid we cannot
> give this surplus an unreserved welcome, or take it at its

face value. It reflects in large part a level of unemployment at home which is by any standards much too high, and which all of us must wish to see reduced.[2]

In his first Budget, in October 1970, Mr Barber took 6d. off income tax and cut public expenditure; and followed with further tax cuts in his Budget in the spring of 1971. Six weeks before that Budget, the currency had been decimalized. The move to a decimal currency was sensible; the decision to do it on a 'heavy' coinage was less so; some argued that it could add to inflation.[3]

Currency crises

The fixed rate system of exchange rates established at Bretton Woods (see Ch. 1) rested on the dollar. Currencies were fixed in terms of the dollar and the dollar against gold. The system began to fall apart when there were more dollars in the world than there were willing holders of dollars at the going (fixed) rates of exchange. The unwilling holders of dollars tried to exchange them for other currencies, notably German marks and Swiss francs, and the currency upheavals of the early 1970s ensued, leading eventually to the revaluation of currencies in terms of the dollar and of the dollar in terms of gold.

Early in May 1971 heavy flows of dollars into Deutschmarks led to the Bundesbank's suspending its quotation for the dollar. On 9 May the Deutschmark and the Dutch guilder were floated and the Swiss franc and the Austrian schilling revalued. Sterling was not much affected.

Competition and Credit Control

The Budget speech of 1971 had foreshadowed important changes in the techniques of monetary control and in May two important steps along the road to reform were taken. On 14 May the Bank of England published a consultative document *Competition and Credit Control (CCC)* outlining the new proposals.[4] At the same time the Bank announced that as from 17 May it was restricting its operations in the gilt-edged market, withdrawing its offer to buy on demand gilt-edged stock of any maturity. It would still buy stock with a year or less to run, but otherwise it would buy only at its own discretion and on its own initiative.

This was a substantial change of practice. For many years the Bank had held the view that in order to maintain a firm market for gilt-edged sales it had to underpin the market. More recently this view had come into question as attention began to be focused more on the monetary aggregates and less on the rate of interest. With the new arrangements in sight, the practice of offering an assured buyer for unlimited quantities of gilt-edged stock became unacceptable. Thus the change of 17 May was an essential preliminary to the introduction of Competition and Credit Control on 16 September. The new arrangements abandoned the long-established system of quantitative restrictions on bank lending in favour of a system that relied more on flexible interest rates and competition between banks. The system as it developed created a great deal of credit but very little control. (A more detailed account of CCC will be found in Chapter 12.)

Unemployment continued to rise quite sharply and on 19 July the Chancellor announced a package of measures to encourage consumer spending and investment. A month later, on 15 August, President Nixon announced measures to stimulate the US economy, restrain inflation and protect the dollar, which was made temporarily non-convertible into gold. Foreign exchange markets in London and elsewhere were closed on 16 August. When the London market re-opened on 23 August it was announced that although the parity remained at $2.40 to £1, dealings would not necessarily be confined within the existing limits; the pound would be allowed to float up beyond $2.42 but not to fall below $2.38. By the close of business on 27 August it had risen to $2.47. Exchange control measures were imposed to stop it from rising too high. The French also partially floated the franc, with a two-tier system. Sweden, Denmark and Norway floated their currencies while the Netherlands, Belgium and Luxembourg established a joint float. The Japanese yen was floated five days later.

In the second half of November heavy sales of dollars began and continued until in mid-December President Nixon announced the devaluation of the dollar against gold. The finance ministers of the major countries (the Group of Ten) met in Washington on 17 and 18 December and agreed, in what became known as the Smithsonian Agreement, upon a realignment of currencies. All the major currencies except the Canadian dollar were revalued against the US dollar. The dollar price of gold was to be raised from 35 to 38 per ounce. The foreign exchange market in London was closed for one day on 20 December, the first working day after the agreement.

A new middle price for the pound was agreed at $2.6057 with buying and selling points some 6 cents either side of this, significantly wider margins than formerly. After some ups and downs, sterling settled at around its middle rate.

The Smithsonian Agreement marked the end of the Bretton Woods system. But there was worse to follow.

1972

The 5 per cent policy

At the end of 1971 the balance of payments appeared strong and the official reserves had doubled, although they were still far less than short-term liabilities. Early in 1972 when the headline (not seasonally adjusted) total of unemployment had risen to over 900,000, Mr Barber deemed it both desirable and safe to embark on a hugely expansionary Budget. The Public Sector Borrowing Requirement was planned to rise to £3.3 bn from £1.3 bn in the year just ended.

> The measures I shall put before the House are intended to ensure growth of output at an annual rate of 5 per cent between the second half of last year and the first half of next ... If my present expectations are correct output will have risen by 10 per cent over the two-year period from the first half of 1971 to the first half of 1973.

He followed with a statement with which we have since become familiar:

> The extent to which there will be a reduction in unemployment is bound to depend on our success in slowing down inflation. If particular groups insist on pricing themselves out of jobs and the nation out of business no Government can secure full employment.[5]

In fact by the end of 1973 unemployment had fallen to some 500,000 but inflation had resumed its rise and was again over 10 per cent. Perhaps that was because the money supply had risen well over 50 per cent. But his views on the relationship between wages and unemployment notwithstanding, Mr Barber was no monetarist:

> ... this Budget will entail a growth of the money supply that is also high by the standards of past years, in order to ensure that adequate finance is available for the extra

output. To proceed otherwise would reduce the growth of real output itself.

And so monetary policy will be used in the future, as it has been during the past year, as an integral part of the general management of demand. Because one of the main qualities of monetary policy is its flexibility, I do not propose to lay down numerical targets.[6]

Both fiscal and monetary policy were to be highly expansionary. The UK had embarked upon its last great dash for growth.

The early weeks of 1972 had seen strikes in the coal and electricity supply industries and the country was on a three-day week for the second half of February. The Budget was in March. In April unemployment fell and continued to fall throughout the year. Unfilled vacancies had risen in February, and continued to rise sharply. Given the usual lags in the economic system it seems likely that the expansionary Budget was imposed upon an economy that was already on the way up and a balance of payments on the way down. The balance of visible trade had deteriorated by £100 m. in the final quarter of 1971 and by a further £200 m. in the first quarter of 1972. Britain was committed to entering the European Community on 1 January 1973 and there was a widespread, although not unanimous, view among economists that membership would impose, through budgetary payments and the price effects of the Common Agricultural Policy, a severe strain upon the British balance of payments. To take that strain without devaluation we needed a *larger* surplus on our 'non-EEC' balance of payments. Yet the lesson of history, and of quite recent history, was that all attempts to grow fast weakened the balance of payments to crisis point.

Thus, to the impartial observer of the British scene Mr Barber's view that the economy was well placed to receive a quite massive fiscal and monetary boost would have seemed at best ill-judged.[7] But Mr Barber might have enjoyed the benefit of any doubt for some time had he not gone out of his way to declare in his Budget statement that he would not let the rate of exchange stand in the way of his 5 per cent growth target:

> ... it is neither necessary nor desirable to distort domestic economies to an unacceptable extent in order to maintain unrealistic exchange rates ... Certainly, in the modern world I do not believe that there is any need for this country, or any other, to be frustrated on this score in its determination to sustain sound economic growth and to reduce unemployment.[8]

In the Budget debate Mr Harold Lever made some prescient observations on the Chancellor's statement:

> ... the Chancellor's bold statement has inevitably been taken to mean that if, on reflating the economy to full employment, we meet balance of payments difficulties, he will blandly solve the problem by devaluation ... the Chancellor announces that he will carry on pumping up demand as required ... and if this produces balance of payments difficulties – hey presto! – he will devalue ... as a result of his statement and the attitude he has been taken to adopt, the run on sterling will arrive earlier and will be larger than if he had not done this. This must rank among the most foolish statements ever made by a Chancellor in this House.[9]

Given the traumatic struggles of the Treasury with a fragile pound in the years up to 1969, and the volatile state of the currency markets since then, it is puzzling to know why the open declaration of a readiness to abandon the sterling parity was included in the Budget Statement. The Chancellor more than most should have been alive to the effect that such a statement from such a source could have on the foreign exchange markets. It was, after all, no more than an equivocal answer by Mr Callaghan that had sent sterling flooding out in November 1967. Why, then, had the passage been included? One hypothesis would be that the Government knew that entry to the EEC would be insupportable at the existing parity and wanted to bring the pound down without being seen to do so and offending the Americans and our prospective partners in the EEC.[10]

For nearly two months after the Budget, sterling continued fairly steady; then, in the words of the Bank of England:

> There was growing uneasiness about prospects for the UK balance of payments in the light of persistent industrial strife and the continuing high rate of domestic cost and price inflation. These worries were crystallised on 15 June when a national dock strike seemed imminent. There was talk of devaluation, and a substantial move out of sterling began ... By 22 June purchases of sterling by the Bank and five partner central banks totalled £1,001 m.[11]

To save further loss of foreign exchange, intervention to preserve a fixed parity was suspended.

The float

As at the time of devaluation in 1967, the matter of the timing of any announcement about the sterling parity was important. The Treasury decided to announce the 1972 float at 7.45 a.m. on 23 June by an announcement to the news agencies to be followed by a Press notice and, of course, a statement in the House. One difficulty was that an announcement over the agency tapes at that hour would find the economic commentators still abed and be likely to throw the newsrooms into some confusion. The Treasury wanted the story on the 8.0 a.m. news bulletin and wanted it right. So we made it known to someone at the BBC whom we trusted that it might not be a bad idea if he were in the office before 8 o'clock. The announcement when it came said that 'as a temporary measure, sterling will be allowed to float.'[12] The London foreign exchange market was closed for Friday 23 June and Monday 26 June. A separate notice imposed exchange control over capital transactions with the Overseas Sterling Area (because Sterling Area currencies were no longer necessarily linked to sterling).

Mr Barber made his statement to the House. Mr Jenkins, who had laid the foundations for the large balance of payments surplus that had been built up, commented: 'It has been a remarkable feat of organization to produce an almost unprecedented speculative crisis within six months of the biggest balance of payments surplus we have ever had.'[13]

Those who subscribe to the conspiracy theory of 'look, no hands' devaluation will think that he spoke more truly than he knew, that it was in truth a remarkable feat of organization.

Industrial relations

If, in a brief account of the economic affairs of 1972, the spotlight must fall on the Budget and the float, the Industrial Relations Act and its consequences provide the supporting action. The Act had become law on 5 August 1971. In July 1972 the National Industrial Relations Court (NIRC) ordered three dockers to prison. As a result,

> A large number of dockers immediately decided to go on indefinite unofficial strike, an action which was prevented only by the dramatic intervention of a character no one had ever heard of, but who was undoubtedly the hero of the hour, if not of the whole play: the Official Solicitor.
>
> Unbeknown to the three dockers, this shadowy figure applied to the Appeal Court for the NIRC's verdict to be

set aside on the grounds of insufficient evidence; and the
Appeal Court obligingly agreed.'[14]

On 21 July five dockers (including two involved in the previous
case) were sent to prison under the Act, and this time the Official
Solicitor was silent. Widespread strikes followed. On 26 July the
House of Lords delivered a judgment on a previous case which
resulted in the release of the five.

A national dock strike which began on 28 July and lasted until
21 August led to the declaration of a State of Emergency.

The disturbed industrial scene resulted in sterling selling so that
the rate, which had settled at $2.45 following the float, closed at
$2.34 at the end of October. This represented a devaluation of
over 10 per cent on the middle rates agreed in December 1971
and brought into play the sterling guarantee arrangements made
in December 1968 and renewed in September 1971.[15]

The end of Bank Rate

Bank Rate had for many years been the minimum rate at which
the Bank of England would lend to the discount market. It formed
the fulcrum on which the authorities sought to lever interest rates
up or down, and movements in it were taken as market signals
under the arcane system of monetary semaphore used by the
Bank. With the introduction of Competition and Credit Control,
interest rates became more flexible and the Bank required, as it
were, a movable fulcrum to match.

Accordingly, from 13 October 1972 Bank Rate ceased to exist
and became Minimum Lending Rate (MLR), determined each
week by a formula related to the tender for Treasury bills. Thus
MLR followed rather than determined market rates; but there was
provision for the authorities to override the formula, introduce an
imposed rate, and suspend MLR until market rates moved into
line with the imposed rate.

1973

On 1 January the United Kingdom joined the European
Community, with the Common Agricultural Policy to apply from 1
February.

In the years when the UK sought entry to the EEC, and
particularly at the time of the referendum on whether to stay in,
much play was made with the notion that entry would expand our

domestic market from 55 to 255 million or some such figure. This, it was argued, would allow our manufacturers economies of scale, and through this, and by some unexplained process of osmosis, we could achieve Continental rates of growth. Less emphasis was placed on the fact that our domestic market would be open to these same efficient Continentals, even though this carried advantages. If European exporters were able, at the going rates of exchange, to provide British consumers with cheaper goods, this would have been a good thing for the consumers. But consumers' interests, it appeared, did not enter strongly into the considerations. For the major price to be paid for entry into the EEC was entry also into the Common Agricultural Policy (CAP), surely one of the most absurd economic policies ever invented by man and one which acted directly against consumers (and still does). Entry to the EEC imposed additional burdens, after a short while, upon the consumer, the taxpayer and the balance of payments; according to Crossman (*Diaries* 1979, pp. 186, 310) it was recognized, at least in 1966 and 1967, that entry to the EEC would require devaluation.

Currency crises

Late in January the Italians introduced a two-tier market for the lira, the Swiss withdrew official support for the dollar, and, following estimates of a $6–$7 bn balance of payments deficit, the US dollar fell sharply. These were the first stirrings of what was to become, in the words of the International Monetary Fund, 'the most intense disruption of the international monetary system to occur since World War II'.

Early in February, Germany imposed exchange controls to try to stem an inward flood of dollars. On the 6th, central banks bought $6 bn bringing their total purchases since 23 January to $8.5 bn. Over the weekend of 9 to 11 February finance ministers shuttled in and out of Paris, and central bankers to and from Basle in a series of emergency meetings. Foreign exchange markets closed on the 12th but re-opened following an announcement by the United States Government that the dollar was to be devalued by 10 per cent against the Special Drawing Right (and, therefore, against gold). The yen and the lira joined the pound in a floating state.

But the outflow of dollars continued and on 1 March the central banks mounted a further massive support operation, buying $3.6 bn in one day. On 2 March foreign exchange markets in London and major centres were closed again.[16]

The markets re-opened on 19 March following the institution of a joint float of the major European currencies except the pound and the lira. That was not quite the end of the matter. Speculation in favour of the Deutschmark continued and at the end of June European central banks sold an estimated DM1 bn to keep that currency within its agreed limits. Next day the Deutschmark was revalued by 5.5 per cent. The market had its way in the end.

The currency crises of the first half of 1973 brought into being the joint float of Community currencies (which the United Kingdom did not then and has not since joined) and hastened the reform of the International Monetary System. The reserve currencies, the dollar and the pound, could no longer form the basis of the system. It had been demonstrated moreover that, with huge amounts of highly mobile funds in existence, even the resources of the central banks operating together were not enough to sustain an exchange rate that had got significantly out of line with reality or what the market perceived as reality. Immovable exchange rates were no longer a viable proposition.[17]

The 1973 Budget

The aim of the 1972 Budget had been to raise the growth of GDP to an annual rate of 5 per cent between the second half of 1971 and the first half of 1973. This objective was nearly achieved: the out-turn was 4.5 per cent. By early 1973 unemployment had come down by 200,000, most of it in the last six months, bringing the percentage unemployed down to 3.0 per cent; the number of vacancies doubled. The Treasury agreed that this seemed to suggest that activity was rising fast. The objective of the 1973 Budget was to raise the rate of growth further, to an annual rate of 5.2 per cent between the second half of 1972 and the first half of 1974. The main instrument for this was to be a 50 per cent increase in the Public Sector Borrowing Requirement, from an estimated £2,855 m. to £4,423 m. Anticipating criticism, Mr Barber pointed out that

> The increase in prospective borrowing does not come about because the public sector is raising insufficient revenue to cover its current expenditure. Indeed the reverse is the case. The public sector is expected to have a surplus of revenue over current expenditure in 1973-74 of £3,223 million ... [18]

He also made a pre-emptive strike against any who might fear that the increase in the PSBR might lead to a yet higher growth in the money supply – the stock of money (M3) had risen by 25 per cent in the year to January. Very little of the previous year's PSBR had been financed through the domestic banking system

> ... the increase in money supply, broadly defined, was almost equal to the banks' lending to private-sector borrowers. I think it right to put the public borrowing requirement into its proper perspective and to scotch the idea that it, and it alone, was responsible for the large growth in money supply last year. That was not the case. Indeed in 1972 the public sector made net repayments of debt to the banks.[18]

As in 1972 he prudently refrained from giving any target for the growth in the money supply. With the economy growing at a rate substantially higher than the generally accepted rate of growth of productive potential (about 3 per cent), with unemployment falling and unfilled vacancies rising, with the money supply recently growing at a rate of 25 per cent and with the balance of payments moving into deficit (the balance in the second half of 1972 showed a deterioration at an annual rate of £1.2 bn over 1971), Mr Barber's 1973 Budget was certainly a bold one. The National Institute of Economic and Social Research did not disagree with him. Their verdict in May was:

> ... there is no reason why the present boom should either bust or have to be busted so long as the additional instruments of incomes policy and the floating exchange rate are retained. It is the existence of these instruments which differentiates the present expansion from the boom of 1963–64 ... there appears to be room for the expansion of output envisaged in the forecast and from this point of view the recent public expenditure cuts may seem to have been unnecessary.[19]

The 'recent public expenditure cuts' had been announced by the Chancellor of the Exchequer on 21 May; they amounted to savings of £100 m. in 1973–74 and £500 m. (at 1972 prices) in 1974–75. These, however, were no ordinary cuts, forced on us by some crisis, actual or impending: they were made to allow expansion elsewhere to continue: 'We have before us', said Mr Barber, announcing the cuts, 'the greatest opportunity our country has had for very many years – an opportunity to achieve a faster and lasting improvement in our national prosperity. The changes which I have announced will ensure just that.'

House prices were rising; to help them along the Government announced a £15 m. grant to the building societies to prevent the mortgage rate from rising from 9.5 to 10 per cent. 'Is there any longer *anything* this Government is not prepared to subsidize?' asked one MP.

In late July sterling fell to an effective depreciation of 19 per cent on the Smithsonian rate and Minimum Lending Rate rose to a record 11.5 per cent.

By Autumn 1973 symptoms of an overextended economy were evident.

The balance of visible trade was clearly deteriorating, with exports more or less flat and imports rising. The stock of money (M3) in August was 27 per cent up on August 1972, and rising. MLR had gone to 11.5 per cent at the end of July but with inflation running at over 9 per cent the real rate of interest was little more than 2 per cent.

One scarcely needed to be an economist to be aware that the economy was overheating: one had only to look at the pages of advertisements for skilled and semi-skilled labour that filled the newspapers. One measure, the most commonly used, of the pressure of demand is the relationship between the monthly series of unemployment and unfilled vacancies. By August unfilled vacancies had reached 330,000 (seasonally adjusted), the highest figure since the series began in 1958, while unemployment was moving steadily downwards. The Bank of England, conceded that the convergence of the two series pointed to a *rising* pressure of demand, but remained unconvinced that the *level* was too high: 'unemployment, at 2.5 per cent in August still indicates a low pressure by comparison with the peaks of past cycles, when it has fallen to half as much'.[20]

The economists at the National Institute of Economic and Social Research, placing their faith in incomes policy and the Treasury view, regarded the situation with even greater composure:

> In our view, the most important economic policy problem now is to devise an effective Phase III (of incomes policy) ... To say that ... is not to say, of course, that the demand management problem has ceased to exist. It is simply that at the moment there seems no need to suggest any policy change here. The evidence is accumulating that the view taken by the Treasury ... is being borne out; the rise in real demand is slowing down of its own accord without excessive pressure on the economy's capacity ... In our view, the continuing aim of demand management should be to maintain the present slow fall in unemployment for some time to come.[21]

From May onwards the Press had been aware that all might not be well, but reactions differed. *The Times* (Peter Jay) was in no doubt that the expansion, imposed on a weak and deteriorating balance of payments, was unsustainable. The *Financial Times*, the *Guardian* and the *Telegraph* were worried but prepared to wait a bit. The popular Press, that same Press that in the mid-1980s views recession with equanimity if not approval, was clear that there was a patriotic requirement to refrain from 'slamming on the brakes'; businessmen were exhorted to 'invest, invest, invest'. The Government should ignore the scepticism of Press and City.[22]

What did the Treasury make of all this? Treasury economists had an answer to everything: if public expenditure was too high, its rate of growth was planned to fall; the rapid fall in unemployment merely mirrored an earlier rapid rise, and unemployment was still high by past standards; the growth in the money supply reflected financial transactions that had no significance for the real economy; industrial surveys showed that firms planned to take on more labour, and this indicated spare capacity; and so on. In the Information Division the remit was to insist that the Chancellor was not to be deflected from his 5 per cent growth target.

In October came the Middle East War and the oil producers imposed the first oil price rise, of some 70 per cent, accompanied by a threat to cut production by a cumulative 5 per cent per month. The Treasury estimated the balance of payments cost at £500 m. a year, offset by some additional exports to oil producers.

Industrial action by electricity power engineers early in November was followed by an overtime ban by coal miners on 12 November. The next day the Department of Trade and Industry announced a record trade deficit for October of £298 m. Hidden in the small print of the announcement was the admission that industrial action at London Airport had resulted in the under-recording of imports, so that the actual deficit was well over £300 m. In a statement accompanying the announcement, the Secretary of State said there were 'special features', the 'first and most important' of which was 'the trade in precious stones'. This was exotic but lacked conviction. The Government, anyway, was sufficiently unimpressed to raise MLR immediately from 11.5 to 13 per cent and to make a call for a further 2 per cent of Special Deposits. In a speech two days later the Chancellor conceded that this amounted to 'a tough credit squeeze' but he had 'no doubt that we can sustain our economic expansion'.

The energy crisis, moving parallel to the difficulties with sterling, gathered pace. At the end of November a 3½-hour meeting between the Prime Minister and the National Union of Mineworkers failed to reach agreement and the overtime ban continued. On 5 December new measures to conserve energy were announced, including a 50 mph speed limit for all motor vehicles. On 13 December the use of electricity for most of industry and commerce was restricted, television closed down at 10.30 p.m. and a three-day week was to come into force from 1 January.

The two crises came together on 17 December when the Chancellor announced measures to cut demand and public expenditure by £1.2 bn. Interestingly, in the light of what followed very shortly, he devoted a large part of his speech to proposed measures for the taxation of property development. The cuts in public expenditure, which overtook the annual White Paper on Public Expenditure published that day, were 'the largest reduction for a succeeding year which has ever been made.'[23]

The cuts in public expenditure were accompanied by a further squeeze on bank credit in the shape of an announcement by the Bank of England of the immediate introduction of a system that became known as the 'Corset' (see Ch. 12). Consumer credit was also restricted.

If ministers and officials thought that the worst was over and they could now think about going home, slowly, of course, to a nice energy-saving Christmas, they were to be disappointed. Two days later the secondary banking crisis began to unfold (see Ch. 13); and on 22 December the oil-producing states more than doubled the price of oil, making a fourfold increase since October. There is not much more to tell about the final days of the Heath Government. But since the end was intimately concerned with Mr Heath's anti-inflation policy we should first show what that policy was.

Dealing with inflation

At the last election the Conservative Party won because of its repeated promises, on which Mr Heath himself laid great emphasis, to deal effectively with rising prices: it was the chief election issue so far as Conservative Party propaganda was concerned, and so far as the electorate was concerned.[24]

It was concern with the inflation issue that led Mr Heath to make his famous 'at a stroke' pronouncement. Since he was almost as badly misrepresented over this as Mr Wilson had been over 'the pound in your pocket', it is worth quoting the full text of the relevant passage of the Statement put out by Conservative Central Office under Mr Heath's name:

> That alternative is to break into the price/wage spiral by acting directly to reduce prices. This can be done by reducing those taxes which bear directly on prices and costs such as the selective employment tax and by taking a firm grip on public sector prices and charges such as coal, steel, gas, electricity, transport charges and postal charges. This would, at a stroke, reduce the rise in prices ... [25]

We may note in passing that this approach to inflation is somewhat different from that of Sir Geoffrey Howe who in his first Budget (in June 1979) acted directly to increase the rise in prices at a stroke by raising VAT from 8 to 15 per cent, an action which was seen by some to indicate a belief that a rise in prices was not the same thing as inflation, the latter being something related only to, and curable only by, control of the money supply.

The important things to note about the Heath Statement are that it did put forward a plausible recipe for moderating the rate of inflation in one area even if it did beg a number of important questions. Secondly, what he was promising to reduce at a stroke was not prices but the *rise* in prices.

According to Brendon Sewill[26] the Statement was a Conservative Research Department paper which 'in the confusion of the campaign got issued under the name of the leader of the Party'. Nevertheless Mr Heath read it and approved it.

While we are considering the Statement it is worth quoting another passage:

> The danger is that since this problem [inflation] has no immediate impact on the balance of payments, nothing would be done until it was too late. Then there would be no alternative, when faced with the crisis, but to adopt once again these old, discredited policies of high taxation, high unemployment and a compulsory wage freeze.

The Government's anti-inflationary strategy, as it emerged, seemed to have four main elements. First, there was an emphasis on the responsibility of *employers* to resist excessive wage claims. Early in August 1970 the Secretary of State for Employment and Productivity, Mr Robert Carr, and other

Ministers met the chairmen of the nationalised industries, and the CBI. The statement issued after the meeting with the chairmen reported: 'The main conclusion was that responsibility for negotiating pay settlements which take account of the national interest, must rest on individual employers; this applies to the nationalised industries just as to private industry and to the public service.' Note the reference to 'the national interest'.

Secondly, there was what came to be known as the 'N–1 formula': an exhortation, made in many ministerial speeches, that each settlement should be lower than the one before so that inflation was de-escalated; we had to bring about 'a progressive and substantial reduction in the level of pay settlements', to use a favourite phrase of the time. Thirdly, there was, at least until the Budget of 1971, a mildly deflationary – or at least non-expansionary – credit policy. Fourthly, on the negative side, the Government 'stressed' that it had 'no intention of re-imposing any statutory incomes policy nor to call for a wage freeze'.[27]

The policy had little effect and the level of settlements continued to rise.

At the end of December 1970 the Government appointed a Court of Inquiry under Lord Wilberforce to settle a long-running dispute in the electricity supply industry – the power workers who 'had their fingers closer to the nation's jugular' than most. Included in the Court's terms of reference was the instruction to take 'into account the industry's productivity record and the interests of the public and of the national economy'. These innocent words came to cause the Treasury some embarrassment. For the Court, presuming itself to be in ignorance of anything but evidence placed before it, wanted someone to tell it what *were* the interests of the public and the national economy; ministers decided, for understandable but not altogether convincing reasons, that none of them could appear before the Court and it was decided that Sir Douglas Allen and Sir Donald MacDougall, respectively the Permanent Secretary to the Treasury and the Chief Economic Adviser, should be the ones to appear. Quite sensibly, they viewed the prospect with something short of enthusiasm. This was before the days when Parliamentary Select Committees began enquiring into departmental policies, and officials were not accustomed to appearing in public to answer questions on policy. The Treasury submitted a Memorandum of Evidence[28] and in due course the two Knights appeared before the Court to answer questions.

The Treasury Memorandum laid great stress on the need to

relate pay to productivity. Cross-examining Sir Douglas, Mr Chapple, the electricians' leader, asked him how much his salary would be at the end of the year. Sir Douglas did not know. Mr Chapple did: it would be £15,000, having gone from £10,400 to £12,700 the previous July. Mr Chapple asked what were the criteria for 'such splendid increases'. What improvements in Sir Douglas's productivity had there been to justify them? Sir Douglas said he may have read a few more papers, had more meetings with ministers but, really, there was no way that his productivity could be measured. His award had been given to him by 'something like a court'. 'Can we get our claim before that court?' asked Mr Chapple. There was much more, in similar vein. 'Both Sir Donald and Sir Douglas', said *The Observer* (23 Jan. 1971) 'maintained a prim calm during this unprecedented public barracking of civil servants of their stature.' It was all enormous fun, except for Sir Donald and Sir Douglas. Mr Chapple certainly enjoyed it: 'it was better than the Palladium, wasn't it?' he said.

The miners' strike that began on 10 January 1972 and which was reinforced by picketing of power stations brought a restriction of electricity supplies and a three-day working week. Lord Wilberforce was again wheeled in and the strike settled with an award of £6 a week to underground workers, bringing their minimum rate to £25. The miners had tested their strength.

If we may use the newspapers as an indicator of the issue of the day, there can be no doubt that in the middle of June 1972 that issue was inflation. On 15 June the two tabloids, the *Daily Mirror* and the *Sun*, both ran front-page splashes and double-page spreads inside. The *Sun* in a leading article on page 2 (opposite an almost fully clothed girl on page 3) listed twenty-five dates on which it had called upon the Government to do something, and demanded a statutory incomes policy. The *Daily Mirror* had a 'shock issue' with a brilliant front page of a dustbinfull of pound notes and just eight words: 'Who wants this for a fair day's pay?'; and no less than three double-page spreads inside. The next day *The Times* leader 'How to fight inflation' ran to 36 column-inches and also called for a statutory incomes policy. On the 19th the *Guardian* leader ran to 30 (wider) column-inches. Next day the *Financial Times* gave Lord Robbins 50 column-inches on the subject.

In July there began an extraordinary series of meetings between the Government, the CBI and the TUC on ways to combat inflation. There were ten meetings in all, the earlier ones at Chequers and the later ones at Downing Street. After many of them there was a press conference in Whitehall, sometimes quite late in the night, usually attended by the Prime Minister, the Chancellor of the Exchequer, and the leaders of the CBI and the TUC. To those who attended these press conferences it was apparent that there was much goodwill among the parties and a determination, not least on the part of the Prime Minister, to get agreement. After the fifth meeting, at Chequers on 26 September, the Prime Minister tabled detailed proposals and these were discussed at further lengthy meetings, at Chequers in mid-October and later at Downing Street. The Prime Minister's proposals went far to meet the wishes of the TUC. At a final press conference in Whitehall at 10.15 p.m. on 2 November the Prime Minister announced that the TUC did not consider the proposals a basis for negotiation. The TUC wanted statutory control of prices but not of incomes. The Government preferred a wholly voluntary policy or, as a second best, a wholly statutory policy.

On 6 November the Government introduced Stage 1 of a statutory policy, a standstill on prices, rents, dividends and pay for an interim period of 90 days.[29]

Stage 2 was introduced on 17 January 1973 (Cmnd 5205). It extended the standstill on pay to the end of March and that on prices to the end of April. The new pay limit would be £1 per week plus 4 per cent of the pay bill for the group. A Price Commission and a Pay Board were to be set up to administer the new policy.

In October the Government published its proposals for Stage 3 (Cmnd 5444). The provisions for pay included increases of up to 7 per cent or an average of £2.25 a week per head for the group; and a threshold safeguard of up to 40p a week if the increase in the Retail Price Index reached 7 per cent plus another 40p per week for every 1 per cent rise above that. After consultations Stage 3 came into effect on 7 November.

Mr Heath was desperately anxious to get a workable incomes policy as the key part of an anti-inflation policy. As has been indicated, the proposals he made in the autumn of 1972 went a long way to meet the demands of the TUC; but clearly he could not concede the demand for statutory control of prices but not of pay, and was forced reluctantly into a wholly statutory policy. He put an immense amount of work into the negotiations and into the policy that emerged; he was concerned above all that the policy should be fair and be seen to be fair, not least to the low paid. He wanted this not only for its own sake but because he and his advisers knew that ultimately a statutory policy for prices and incomes is a gigantic bluff: it cannot be enforced if it is widely disregarded. It is doubtful whether any anti-inflation policy anywhere has been constructed as carefully and thoroughly as Stages 1, 2 and 3 of the Heath policy. It was perhaps precisely because so much thought, work and goodwill had gone into the preparation that in the end he refused to have the policy broken by anyone on any pretext.

To summarize, the anti-inflation policies of the Heath Government fell into three phases. There was first an attempt to appeal, over the heads of the unions, to the people, invoking 'the national interest'. This may have been naive but it was not ignoble; it credited the British people with an understanding of what was sensible and fair. Alas, it reckoned without the 'orange-box syndrome': if those in front stand on boxes, no one behind sees the procession; then everyone scrambles for a bigger box. In more formal terms it is the conflict between the social and the private good; even if the social good is clearly perceived, no one can afford to pursue it unless everyone does.

Phase two was an attempt to secure union co-operation; once begun it was sincere enough, but perhaps it came too late, after relations had been soured. Phase three was the statutory policy.

1974

The three-day week began on 1 January 1974. On the 9th, Government talks with the NUM about their claim for exemption from the pay policy ended in deadlock: Mr Barber summarily rejected a TUC pledge that anything granted to the miners would be treated as an exceptional case. Further talks with the TUC on 14th found no agreement and negotiations between the two sides finally broke down a week later. The Government refused to break Stage 3 for the miners. Selective strikes by the railwaymen began on 5 February and a miners' strike on the 10th. Mr Heath decided to let the country decide whether he or the miners should govern the country. The General Election on 28 February produced no majority. After much manoeuvring Mr Wilson formed a Government.

Mr Barber's Chancellorship

To say that the Barber years were eventful is perhaps an understatement. Externally they were years of almost continuous turmoil. Crisis succeeded crisis, the Bretton Woods system came to an end, floating rates returned, gold was replaced by the Special Drawing Right, the dollar was devalued against almost everything. Along the way the UK floated sterling and joined the European Community.

At home a revolutionary new system of credit control was introduced. It proved a lax system and the money supply grew at unprecedentedly high rates (25 per cent in 1972 and 27 per cent in 1973). The ease with which credit could be obtained coupled with the collapse of the property market led to a serious banking crisis. The Crown Agents, an agency for which the Treasury itself was partly responsible, was one of the casualties.

The Heath/Barber years were years of big government and big spending: expansion of the Health Service (Sir Keith Joseph); re-organization of local Government (Peter Walker), expansion of British Steel (Peter Walker), Concorde, planning for the Third London airport at Maplin and for the Channel tunnel. The system of public expenditure 'control' ensured that whatever the cost turned out to be, the money was provided. Public expenditure grew in real terms by 2.9 per cent in 1971, 6.9 per cent in 1972, 8.5 per cent in 1973, and 12.4 per cent in 1974. (Financial years commencing in the years stated.) In money terms it grew even faster. While public expenditure grew, taxes were cut, with the result that the Public Sector Borrowing Requirement rose from £4 m. in 1970, to £1,382 m. in 1971, £2,054 m. in 1972, £4,209 m. in 1973 and £6,437 m. in 1974.

All governments find that their Party manifestos, drawn up in Opposition by the party theorists, have to be modified to deal with the reality of the world and with events as they unfold. But probably no government has made so many major policy reversals as that of Mr Heath: if for nothing else, his administration was famous for its 'U' turns. The first of these was on intervention policy: the 'lame ducks' (no help for) declaration was followed by the rescue of Upper Clyde Shipbuilders and Rolls-Royce. Secondly, the public sector, so far from shrinking or being contained, grew: these were the years of big government. Thirdly, on incomes policy the Government moved from 'hands off' to statutory control. Mr Barber made a personal 'U' turn in floating sterling, having earlier been determined to 'defend the pound'. Other domestic landmarks were the move to a 'heavy' decimal coinage and the introduction of VAT.

Tax reductions, high public expenditure and a runaway money supply did succeed in generating real growth in the economy and in bringing down unemployment, but at a cost: inflation accelerated and the exchange rate gave way. It is true that in the fourfold rise in oil prices at the end of 1973 the Government suffered one misfortune not of its own making and one which was the proximate cause of the final 'U' turn, from 'full ahead' to 'reverse'. But it seems probable that the boom could not have continued for much longer anyway: the oil price shock was the occasion for, rather than the cause of, the reversal.

Mr Barber was the most fortunate of Chancellors. He came to office only because of the death of Mr Macleod and he inherited from the outgoing Labour Chancellor, Mr Jenkins, an economy in better shape than had any incoming Chancellor in the post-war years. He bequeathed one close to collapse. After the election Mr Barber left politics, was ennobled and became Chairman of the Standard Chartered Bank.

Is it fair to place the blame for the whole horrible mess on Mr Barber and Mr Heath? True, they were the politicians in charge. But what of the Treasury? Did it play no part, have no views, give no advice, provide no forecasts? Could it spread its collective hands and say 'We did only what we were told'? Professor Robert Neild, a former economic adviser to the Treasury, did not think so: 'He has not yet got over the performance of the Treasury under the Heath Government,' reported *The Observer* in November 1975. 'How they could', said Mr Neild, 'have told Barber to blow up the economy by budgetary expansion as much as he did – or alternatively how they could have failed to stop him blowing it up, if they disagreed with him – is quite inconceivable.'[30]

Diary of events June 1970–February 1974

1970

18 Jun.	General election. Conservative majority of 31.
19	Iain Macleod Chancellor, of the Exchequer.
16 Jul.	Dock strike (to 3 Aug.). State of Emergency.
20	Iain Macleod dies.

25	Anthony Perrinott Lysberg Barber Chancellor of the Exchequer.
27 Oct.	DEA wound up. Budget. 6d. off income tax and cuts in public expenditure.
4 Dec.	Import deposits abolished.

1971

4 Feb.	Rolls-Royce appoints receiver.
15	Decimalization of the currency.
23	Rolls-Royce nationalized.
30 Mar.	Budget. Big tax reductions.
31	Prices and Incomes Board dissolved.
5 May	Bundesbank suspends quotation for the dollar.
9	Deutschmark and Dutch gilder floated to stem currency inflows. Swiss franc revalued by 7 per cent.
14	Bank of England publishes consultative document *Competition and Credit Control* (CCC).
17	Bank restricts its operations in gilt-edged market.
15 Jul.	CBI initiative to limit price rises.
19	Package of economic measures to boost consumer spending.
5 Aug.	Industrial Relations Act comes into force.
15	Dollar made non-convertible into gold.
16	Foreign exchange markets closed.
23	Foreign exchange markets re-opened but the Government announced that dealings in sterling will not necessarily be confined to existing limits around $2.40. Sweden, Denmark and Norway floated their currencies. Netherlands, Belgium and Luxembourg established a joint float. France floated partially, with a two-tier system.
28	Japanese yen floated.
16 Sept.	New monetary arrangements – Competition and Credit Control.
14 Dec.	Nixon agrees to devalue the dollar against gold.
18	The Group of Ten (G10) meeting in Washington produces the Smithsonian Agreement, marking the end of the Bretton Woods system. New gold price of $38 an ounce. All major currencies, except Canadian dollar, revalued against the US dollar.
20	Foreign exchange markets closed.
21	Wider buying and selling margin for sterling.

1972

10 Jan.	Coal strike (to 25 Feb.).
20	Commons majority of 21 (298 to 277) for signing Treaty of Accession to EEC.
10 Feb.	Electricity supplies restricted on a rota basis (to 1 Mar.). State of Emergency to conserve power supplies.
14	Three-day working week (to 27 Feb.).
18	Wilberforce Report on coal dispute.
21 Mar.	Expansionary Budget, incorporating 5 per cent growth target.
28 Apr.	All UK obligations to the IMF discharged.
Jun.	Pressure on the pound.
22	Bank Rate raised 1 point to 6 per cent.
23	Pound floated. Controls on capital flows to Overseas Sterling Area (OSA). London foreign exchange market closed (to 27 June).
21 Jul.	National Industrial Relations Court (NIRC) orders five London dockers to prison.
28	National dock strike (to 21 Aug.).
3 Aug.	State of Emergency.
9 Oct.	Bank Rate to become Minimum Lending Rate (MLR) from 13 Oct.
3 Nov.	Series of tripartite talks on measures to combat inflation breaks down.
6	Government imposes 90-day statutory freeze on prices, incomes, rents and dividends.
21 Dec.	Government approves £3 bn investment programme for the British Steel Corporation (BSC).

1973

1 Jan.	UK joins the EEC. Common Agricultural Policy (CAP) to apply from 1 Feb.
17	Stage 2 of incomes policy announced (see Apr.).
22	Swiss franc floats following withdrawal of official buying rate for dollars.
29	US balance of payments deficit for 1972, estimated at $6–7 bn. Dollar falls to floor.
1–2 Feb.	US and European banks buy $1 bn.
2	Germany imposes exchange controls to stem flood of dollars.
6–9	Central banks buy $6 bn. Total support since 23 Jan. $8.5 bn.
9–11	Finance ministers of France, Britain, West Germany, Italy and the USA hold emergency meeting in Paris to discuss currency crisis.

12	Foreign exchange markets closed in the US and UK, European and Japanese central banks withdraw from market.
13	Dollar devalued by 10 per cent against its Special Drawing Right (SDR) value. New official gold price of $42.222. Markets re-open. Yen and lira float. Pound continues to float.
14	Foreign exchange markets re-open.
22	Gold price jumps to $90 an ounce.
1 Mar.	Central banks mount massive support for dollar, purchase $3.6 bn in one day.
2	Foreign exchange markets closed in London and major centres.
6	Budget. VAT and car tax introduced.
19	Markets re-open. Joint float of all EEC currencies, except pound and lira. Deutschmark revalued 3 per cent.
1 Apr.	Pay Board and Price Commission established. Stage 2 of incomes policy brought into effect: £1 + 4 per cent.
4	£15 m. grant to building societies to subsidize mortgages.
16 May	Gold reaches $111.
21	Public expenditure cuts.
28 Jun.	EEC central banks sell an estimated DM1 bn to keep DM within currency 'tunnel'.
29	DM revalued by 5.5 per cent.
1 Jul.	Mr Gordon Richardson replaces Sir Leslie O'Brien as Governor of the Bank of England.
19	Bank of England acts to force up interest rates and calls for further Special Deposits.
27	MLR rises to record 11.5 per cent.
11 Sept.	Governor's letter to banks requesting restriction of credit to persons and for property and financial transactions.
6 Oct.	Commencement of Arab–Israeli three-week war.
16–17	First oil price rise of 70 per cent. Cumulative cuts of 5 per cent per month in Arab oil production.
1 Nov.	Industrial action by electricity power engineers.
5	Arabs to cut oil to West by 25 per cent.
7	Stage 3 of incomes policy brought into effect. Threshold agreements.
12	Coal miners start overtime ban.
13	Sterling crisis. Bank of England calls for further Special Deposits, and MLR goes to 13 per cent. State of Emergency declared.
14	Restrictions on the use of electricity.

28	Meeting between PM and NUM fails, overtime ban continues.
5 Dec.	New measures to conserve energy. 50 mph speed limit.
13	Use of electricity restricted for most of industry and commerce. TV to close at 10.30 p.m.
17	Economic measures. Public expenditure cuts. Introduction of Supplementary Special Deposits ('the Corset').
19	Beginning of secondary banking crisis.
21	'Lifeboat' launched.
22	Oil prices more than doubled by producing states, making fourfold increase since Oct.

1974

1 Jan	Three-day working week commences.
9	Government talks with NUM end in deadlock.
14	Talks between the PM and TUC end in deadlock.
21	Talks between PM and TUC break down.
5 Feb.	Selective strikes by railmen.
10	Miners' strike begins.
28	General election. No majority.

Notes and references

1. At the Lord Mayor's dinner to the bankers and merchants of the City of London, 15 Oct. 1970. *BEQB*, Dec. 1970.
2. Speech to the Lord Mayor's dinner to the bankers and merchants of the City of London, 21 Oct. 1971. *BEQB*, Dec. 1971. Unemployment in mid-1971 was 700,000.
3. Older readers will remember what happened. For younger readers innocent of their pounds, shillings and pence tables, a reminder may be in order: the 'old' pound was made up of 240 pennies. The basis of decimalized currency was the one pence (1p). The logical approach would have been to make the new 'p' as close as possible in value to the old penny, and this could have been done by dividing the old ten-shilling note (worth 120 old pennies) into 100 new pence, so that 1 new pence equalled 1.2 old pennies. The new pence would then have been 'heavier' (i.e. worth more) than the old penny, but only by one-fifth. But the traditionalists at the Bank of England and elsewhere would have none of it: the old pound must be retained and *it* divided into 100 new pence. Thus 1 new pence became equal to 2.4 old pennies. For the average shopper in

the supermarket the result was confusing: something which last week had cost 2 shillings (24 old pennies) might now be priced at 11p. Even allowing for some rough conversion into new currenty, it looked cheap. In fact such a conversion would have concealed a price rise of 10 per cent. The new currency did include a half-p equal to 1.2 old pennies but the new currency was incapable of accommodating the old half-penny, a unit in which many price rises had hitherto been made: the minimum price rise under the new currency was 1.2 old pennies, nearly 2½ times what had been possible under the old currency. And the new half-p could not anyway be used in writing cheques.

4. Reproduced in the *BEQB*, Vol. 11, No. 2, Jun. 1971.
5. *Official Report*, Vol. 833, No. 84, Col. 1353.
6. *Official Report*, Vol. 833, No. 84, Col. 1347.
7. The perennially optimistic National Institute thought the Chancellor had not gone far enough and saw no danger to the balance of payments: 'So whilst we welcome the change in strategy incorporated in the Budget, and the adoption of a 5 per cent growth target, we doubt whether the Budget injection alone is large enough to achieve the target.' They forecast a surplus on current account in 1972 of £475 m. It turned out to be £69 m.

   If the National Institute was not wise at the event, neither can it be accused of being wise after the event: in August 1973, with all the ingredients of a first-class economic crisis present, it was unrepentent: 'Going back a year, the policy of cutting taxes substantially in 1972 has in our view been justified.' *National Institute Economic Review*, No. 60, May 1972, p. 14; and No. 65, Aug. 1973, p. 6.
8. *Official Report*, Vol. 833, No. 84, Col. 1354. This view seems to represent something of a conversion. In an article 'What Tony will try' in the *Guardian* of 24 Sept. 1970, William Davis reported him as believing that devaluation was 'unthinkable'. 'Mr Barber is, if anything, even more determined than Mr Wilson was in 1964 to defend the pound.' Mr Barber's view was that 'For a Tory Government to devalue as well [as to go into the Common Market] is not a political possibility.'
9. *Official Report*, Vol. 834, No. 88, Cols 146, 151.
10. The National Institute of Economic and Social Research, where economists had good contacts with Treasury economists, had seen no danger to the balance of payments when, in May 1972, it endorsed the 1972 Budget. In August

1973, however, it seemed to be saying that one of the reasons for welcoming, and continuing to welcome, the expansion of demand in 1972 was that it would bring down the exchange rate: 'There was no way in which an export stimulus could have been provided without some prior reflation of home demand. It would not have been internationally acceptable to devalue against a background of a current account surplus of some £1,000 m.; and if the pound had then been floated, it would have floated upwards.' *National Institute Economic Review*, No. 65, Aug. 1973, p. 6.

11. *BEQB*, Vol. 12, No. 3, Sept. 1972, p. 310.

12. It has floated, or more often sunk, ever since; but at the time the accent was on 'temporary'; Ministers repeatedly stated that it was their intention to return to a fixed parity.

13. *Official Report*, Vol. 839, No. 141, Col. 881. A full debate followed on 29 June and may be found in the *Official Report*, Vol. 839, No. 145.

14. Stewart (1977), p. 128. Mr Stewart's book provides a highly entertaining account of this and related episodes.

15. These arrangements, concluded under a regime of fixed exchange rates, meant, broadly, that sterling countries agreed to hold a minimum proportion of official reserves in sterling in return for a dollar guarantee by the UK, the guarantee to be implemented when sterling fell and remained below $2.3760, 1 per cent below the parity of $2.40 ruling when the agreements were made.

16. The excessively curious reader may wonder how foreign exchange markets can be closed, given that, in London at least, the market is telephonic and electronic and not a physical entity. In London there are two ways it can be done. One is for the Bank of England to issue exchange control notices to all authorized dealers; the other is for the Treasury to issue a press notice or make an announcement over the agency tapes. The second method is the simpler and is the one usually adopted. But the closure is largely symbolic: in practice banks are allowed to continue to transact essential business and the major effect is that all intervention by the central bank ceases until the market is re-opened.

17. One solution to the crisis that had been considered was the adoption of a system of two-tier exchange rates, as already instituted by the Italians. The idea underlying this is that the 'real' or 'proper' rate is, or should be, that determined by the current account. Essentially, the two-tier system aims to

separate the current from the capital account. Such a system is administratively difficult and, so far as the UK was concerned, was made impossible by the existence of the sterling balances. The Germans at the time were also opposed to it.

18. *Official Report*, Vol. 852, No. 71, Col. 253.
19. *National Institute Economic Review*, No. 64, May 1973, p. 6.
20. *BEQB*, Vol. 13, No. 3, Sept. 1973, p. 280.
21. *National Institute Economic Review*, No. 65, Aug. 1973, p. 6.
22. See for example, 'The boom that must go bust' Peter Jay, *The Times*, 7 May 1973; 'The seeds of a classic inflation' and 'Tax strategies needed to restore balance', Robert Neild, *The Times*, 19, 20 July 1973; 'Why the Government's economic strategy is a dangerous gamble', Wynne Godley and Francis Cripps, *The Times*, 5 Sept. 1973; 'Closing circle of a self-inflicted dilemma', Peter Jay, *The Times*, 25 Sept. 1973; 'Catch 22 in Heath's gamble', Robert Heller, *Evening Standard*, 9 Oct. 1973; and (after the credit squeeze) 'The price of growth pushed too near to capacity', Anthony Harris, *Financial Times*, 14 Nov. 1973; 'Five fallacies of economic management', Samuel Brittan, *Financial Times*, 22 Nov. 1973. The analysis, much of it highly sophisticated, varied; but the general thrust was that the economy could not sustain a high rate of growth *and* a balance in overseas payments *and* a decelerating or even stable rate of inflation; something had to give.
23. *Official Report*, Vol. 866, No. 35, Cols 952–66.
24. *The Times*, leading article, 28 Jan. 1971.
25. For an explanation of how the statement came to be issued see 'In place of strikes' by Brendon Sewill in *British Economic Policy 1970–74: Two Views*, Hobart Paperback No. 7, The Institute of Economic Affairs 1975.
26. Sewill (1975), p. 47.
27. Department of Employment and Productivity Press Notice 6 Aug. 1970.
28. Treasury Press Notice 14 Jan. 1971.
29. The proposals were later set out in Cmnd 5125 *A Programme for Controlling Inflation: The First Stage*.
30. *The Observer*, 16 Nov. 1975, p. 36.

5

Mr Healey,
1974–1979

The real cause of our downfall, both throughout the five
years and ultimately at the General Election, was the
issue of pay.

Joel Barnett[1]

1974

Running loose

Mr Healey became Chancellor of the Exchequer on 5 March 1974.
On 26 March, after what he described as 'the most exhausting
three weeks of my life', he presented his first Budget, and gave
notice of a second one later in the year. It was an impressive
debut. The statement, 'one of the most complicated and wide-
ranging of modern times', lasted two hours and twenty minutes
and was presented with 'clarity and lucidity' (Mr Heath,
responding).[2]

The economic situation facing the new Chancellor was not only
difficult but more than usually obscure — even the Treasury
forecasts presented with the Budget ran only to the end of the
year instead of, as is customary, to the middle of the next. At
home there was the uncertain effect on production of the three-
day week. Retail prices were rising at 13 per cent a year and the
money supply (M3) at double that rate. Externally, the deficit on
the balance of payments in the second half of 1973 had been over
£1 bn (seasonally adjusted), and this before the fourfold increase
in oil prices had come through. As well as an increase in the price
of future oil, a reduction in supply was threatened and expected.
In the face of much uncertainty Mr Healey's broad strategy was to

leave total demand little changed but to shift resources into the balance of payments to correct the underlying, i.e. the non-oil, deficit. He accepted the view of the OECD and IMF that it would be wrong to attempt to eliminate quickly the coming oil deficit. This, and the residual deficit on non-oil account, would be met by borrowing. He announced a $2.5 bn loan for 10 years arranged by the clearing banks.

Mr Healey's approach to the problem of inflation is interesting in the light of much that happened later. If one did not know, one could take his statements on the matter to be those of an incoming Conservative Chancellor taking over from a Labour Government. One should remember the background: there was an incomes policy in place, with threshold agreements built in; and further substantial increases in the price of oil were certain. Not much could be done in the short term about incomes; he could operate directly only on prices, through indirect taxes, subsidies, the rate of interest and the money supply. On indirect taxation his policy was to switch the burden from more essential to less essential goods, although he raised revenue by some £600 m. in the process. On subsidies he also did a switch but his approach here was more radical. It had been the policy of the Heath Government to subsidize heavily the prices of the nationalized industries. These industries were now asking urgently for price increases, or further subsidies. Mr Healey said 'We could not allow the existing state of affairs to go on. Costs had to be reflected more closely in prices. There is no other way of avoiding a heavy excess demand for the products concerned, the uneconomic use of resources, the collapse of all financial disciplines, and an unacceptable level of support by the Government.' So, the subsidies were cut from a potential £1,400 m. to £500 m. To offset the effect on retail prices the subsidies on food and housing were increased. In principle subsidies on one thing have a similar effect, and are no more justifiable, than subsidies on another, but the immediate need was to put a stop to a widening gap between costs and prices in the nationalized industries. Mr Healey himself had small faith in the efficacy of subsidies: 'But price controls and subsidies, even in alliance with the most perfect incomes policy which could be devised, cannot go far towards winning the battle against inflation if fiscal and monetary policy are pulling in the opposite direction.' The trade unions were less than enthusiastic over this article of faith.

So what was he going to do about monetary policy? Well, not a lot. He dealt with it in one sentence: 'I hope that the new monetary technique adopted last December will enable us to keep the growth in money supply at a much lower rate in the next 12 months.' And interest rates? The answer here could have come straight out of Howe or Lawson, early 1980s. The aim was to reduce interest rates, but 'There is no short-cut available here. It will depend above all on our success in reducing inflationary expectations, since without question they are a major cause of high nominal interest rates. It will depend on our ability to restrict the public sector borrowing requirement here at home, and it will also require international co-operation to bring down interest rates world-wide.'

There was, however, a short-cut on the interest rate at which building societies could borrow: in April the Government offered to lend them £500 m. at 10.5 per cent instead of the MLR rate of 12.25 per cent in exchange for a promise to keep the mortgage rate down to 11 per cent.

By July the rate of inflation was 16–17 per cent, the threshold had been triggered six times and further price rises were in prospect before the end of the year. Mr Healey decided to do something more about inflation. On 22 July he introduced a packet of measures, the main elements of which were a reduction in VAT from 10 to 8 per cent, rates relief, and further food subsidies. It was a holding operation, designed to take the top off the rise in prices until threshold agreements came to an end in October and import prices stabilized. It was reasonably well received by the serious press. Unfortunately, Mr Healey had included in his statement an announcement that had little relevance to his main purpose but which gave the anti-Labour press an opportunity to ridicule him and his policies. He said that he had not had to draw on the $2.5 bn loan arranged by the clearing banks but went on to announce, with something of a flourish, a line of credit of $1.2 bn granted by His Imperial Majesty the Shah of Iran.

Now the Shah may have been a friend of the West but he was probably not the British public's favourite despot at that time; he was, after all, foreign, tinted, and had put up the price of petrol.[3] 'The Shah bails out Healey' and 'Britain in pawn' shrieked the *Daily Express*; 'Denis and his magic carpet' said the *Daily Mail* – we were to be wafted to prosperity on a magic Persian carpet. Cartoons abounded: a 'Vote Labour' poster picturing the Shah; Healey kneeling at the Shah's feet; a flying carpet emblazoned 'British Socialism by Courtesy of His Imperial Majesty The Shah'.

Perhaps it should have been foreseen that a hostile and chauvinistic Press would pluck this colourful plum from the dreary details of rate relief and an increase in the needs allowance.

In August the Government published a White Paper, *The Regeneration of British Industry* (Cmnd 5710), which set out the Government's proposal for 'a closer, clearer and more positive relationship between Government and industry'. Two new instruments were to be created: a system of 'Planning Agreements' and a 'National Enterprise Board'.

In the run up to the General Election in October the Conservative Manifesto claimed that inflation was running at 20 per cent and that if this rate continued the pound would be worth 55p in two years. The first statement was incorrect; and even if it had not been, the second was wrong (it would require inflation at 35 per cent to produce such a fall). Mr Healey claimed that in the three months June, July and August, the rate had been 8.4 per cent. He was subsequently much taunted with this claim but it was perfectly correct as a statement of historical fact. That *was* the annual rate in those three months. The Retail Price Index, however, is one of the few indices that is not seasonally adjusted and in these months the index reflected the seasonal fall in food prices.

The election produced a majority of five for the Government and Mr Healey continued as Chancellor of the Exchequer.

Autumn Statement

With the Election behind him, and a Government majority, albeit a small one, Mr Healey turned to his promised Autumn Budget. The situation facing him, while less uncertain than in March, was still a difficult one. The balance of trade on non-oil account was improving but oil imports were adding an extra £2.5 bn a year to the deficit, which was bound to be large. There was, however, no immediate problem on this front since capital inflows, from a number of sources, were more than sufficient to meet the deficit. Sterling was reasonably firm. Nevertheless there remained a need to shift resources from domestic uses into the balance of payments to eliminate the non-oil deficit. A consensus was emerging that for *all* the oil-importing countries to try to eliminate their oil deficits by deflation could result only in a world-wide recession. Some longer-term, international solution would have to be found, involving the recycling of the oil-producers' surpluses (some of which were already financing the UK's deficit).

The major problem was at home. The measures taken earlier had sliced the top off the rate of inflation but it was still unacceptably high, about 17 per cent. To contain that part of the rise in prices generated by home costs, mainly wages, the Government relied on the 'social contract'. This was an agreement between the Government and the TUC that in return for the Government's doing certain things in the social field the TUC would follow agreed guidelines on wage demands.[4] Much of what the Government was required to do entailed public expenditure, and this would add to the Public Sector Borrowing Requirement (PSBR). And there was the rub. In the March Budget the PSBR for 1974-75 had been estimated at £2,733 m. Not for the last time the Treasury had got it badly wrong and by November the estimate had doubled, to £5,541 m. Of the increase, £1 bn was attributable to an increase in subsidies, including, despite Mr Healey's intentions, price-restraining subventions to the nationalized industries. Such a huge PSBR left the Chancellor little room for further concessions on the Government's side of the social contract, although he did find £285 m. for additional tax relief for the elderly. On the other side he raised the rate of VAT on petrol to 25 per cent. But there was a further problem: companies were in liquidity difficulties arising from the effect of inflation on stock valuation. Mr Healey granted them tax relief worth £775 m. which, with other minor reliefs, raised the borrowing requirement to £6,331 m., a figure that Mr Healey conceded was 'disturbingly large'. He justified it, in part, in a rather novel way. An economy may be conceptually divided into three sectors, the public sector, the private sector and the overseas sector. The borrowing and lendings of these three sectors must sum to zero. Mr Healey argued that since the private sector could not be allowed to go into deficit 'without grave consequences' and since a large surplus in the foreign sector (i.e. a deficit in the balance of payments on current account) was inevitable, it followed as a matter of arithmetic that the public sector had to have a large deficit.

Despite the huge borrowing requirement output was forecast to rise at only about 2 per cent per annum. 'This', said Mr Healey 'reflects a slight weakening in the pressure of demand and would mean some increase in unemployment.'[5]

We have noted that in March the outlook was so unclear that Mr Healey felt able to take his forecast of the economy only to the end of the year; and we have seen that eight months later the

forecast of the borrowing requirement was wildly wrong. As a
postscript to the November Statement we might record Mr
Healey's view of economic forecasts, as expressed in that
Statement:

> Like long-term weather forecasts they are better than
> nothing. But no one who has held office in the Treasury
> or, indeed, who has had the job of following Treasury
> activity from outside will deny that they are subject to
> wide margins of error.
>
> The numbers contained in the forecasts – specific to 0.5
> per cent in every case – give a spurious impression of
> certainty. But their origin lies in the extrapolation from a
> partially known past, through an unknown present, to an
> unknowable future according to theories about the causal
> relationships between certain economic variables which
> are hotly disputed by academic economists, and may well
> in fact change from country to country or from decade to
> decade. The current state of our economic knowledge
> allows of nothing better ...

On 10 December a Reuters' report of rumours that under a new
agreement with the Saudis the American Aramco Oil Group
would in future use dollars instead of sterling for all future
settlements, sent sterling sliding. The rumours were later
confirmed. Anything that set sterling on the slide caused the
adrenalin to flow in the Treasury and the Bank of England. This
particular slide did not turn out to be prolonged. The piquant thing
about it was that at the time the Chancellor of the Exchequer was
in Saudi Arabia on a goodwill visit and neither he nor his hosts
knew what was going on in London. It turned out to be a case
of the Saudi left hand not knowing what the right hand was
doing. As the Chancellor said on his return '... the Saudi
Ministers I met were as surprised and dismayed as I was by
reports which reached the capital on Wednesday that
companies were selling sterling to meet tax and royalty payments
in dollars. I was told that ... the decision was purely in order to
simplify matters.'[6]

On 18 December the Government put up £85 million to rescue
the Crown Agents from the results of its dabbling in the property
market. On the last day of the year it salvaged Burmah Oil, faced
with critical liquidity problems. Meanwhile, the 'Lifeboat'
continued with its support for the secondary banks.

As announced by the Chancellor in his November Budget, the
sterling guarantee arrangements expired at the end of the year.

1975

The £6 policy

By February 1975 the rate of inflation had reached the self-fulfilling 20 per cent foreseen by the National Institute (see note 4), and wage rates were rising at 29 per cent. These increased costs and prices, together with the cost of rescuing Burmah Oil and the Crown Agents, raised the Public Sector Borrowing Requirement for the year just ended (1974–75) from the £6.3 bn at which it had been estimated five months earlier, to £7.6 bn. On unchanged policies it was estimated to reach £10.3 bn in 1975–76.

The excess of the increase in wages and earnings over the increase in prices implied that real wages were rising sharply at a time when the adverse shift in the terms of trade, largely due to the higher oil prices, had reduced real national income by some 4 per cent. The difference – between what we were paying ourselves and what we were earning – was reflected in a balance of payments deficit of £3.8 bn, some 5 per cent of GNP.

Mr Healey's Budget of April 1975[7] was centred around these two related deficits. But whereas in 1974 he had argued that a large balance of payments deficit must necessarily be reflected in a large Government deficit (given no deficit in the private sector) he now argued that ' ... it is impossible to bring about a sustained and progressive improvement in the balance of payments over a period of years if at the same time the public sector financial deficit is increasing rapidly as a percentage of GNP'. (The financial deficit is smaller than the borrowing requirement, since the latter includes on-lending.)

Financially there was no problem. The money supply was under control, notwithstanding the large PSBR, and interest rates had fallen; inflows of capital were more than sufficient to finance the deficit on current account.

Mr Healey's strategy for correcting the borrowing requirement and the overseas balance was to raise taxes for the current year, 1975–76, by £1.2 bn, and to cut public expenditure next year, 1976–77, by over £1 bn (£900 m. at the prices of the plans published the preceding January). The Treasury estimated that the overall effect of the Budget would be to reduce the 1975–76 PSBR to just over £9 bn; but by this time Mr Healey was viewing the Treasury's forecasts with less than complete confidence. The very high rate of inflation raised Government expenditure much more than Government revenue and Mr Healey doubted 'the wisdom of planning public expenditure on the basis of constant prices'.

The Government's anti-inflation policy rested heavily on the social contract with the unions. The 1975 Budget increased married and single tax allowances at a cost of over £400 m. but raised other taxes by £1.6 bn. Subsidies were to be phased out or reduced as part of the public expenditure cuts. Unemployment was expected to rise. Aware that he would be accused of reneging on the Government's side of the contract, Mr Healey said

> We in the Government have honoured our side of the
> social contract by our programme of legislation on
> industrial relations, by fiscal legislation to secure a juster
> and more equitable distribution of wealth and incomes, by
> action on food subsidies and rents, and by generous
> provision for the pensioners and others among the under-
> privileged in our society ... the social wage now amounts
> to about £1,000 a year for every member of the working
> population.

He then came as close as he dared to saying that the trade unions, however, had not kept their side of the bargain. For a Labour Chancellor, and especially for one committed to a 'social contract', it was a tough Budget. But it could be argued that it got the worst of both worlds, tough enough to justify the unions in abandoning any further pretence of honouring the contract, but not tough enough to deal with the economic situation. It might have been better to acknowledge that the social contract was already dead.

In the *Sunday Times* of the following weekend the Economics Editor, Malcolm Crawford, had an article on the Budget in which he advocated a lower rate for the pound and predicted that a fall of 4 or 5 per cent was inevitable. In a separate 'news' story he reported, on what evidence was not clear, that 'Denis Healey and the Treasury are prepared to let sterling drop a few percentage points.' A fortnight later a Business Forecast in the *Sunday Telegraph* was headlined 'Failure of the Budget strategy. Coming – extreme pressure on the £.' The pound did come under some pressure but this came to an end in mid-May, when the rate stabilized at an effective devaluation of about 25 per cent on Smithonian rates (from 22 per cent at the time of the Budget). The unease over the pound continued and it fell again in mid-June.

By June the rate of price inflation was 26 per cent and basic hourly wage rates were up 32 per cent on the year. The

Government, the TUC and the CBI were consulting on a new anti-inflationary policy. Mr Healey trailed some of the new ideas in various speeches and interviews and on 1 July made a statement to the House[8] even though the new policy had not yet been finalized. The objective would be to bring down inflation to 10 per cent by the end of the next pay round (July 1976) and to single figures by the end of 1976. Historically, the statement is of interest only because it contains the first mention of cash limits: cash limits would be set for wage bills in the public sector, and 'I propose to employ the system of cash limits more generally as a means of controlling public expenditure in the short term'.

The new policy was unveiled in a statement to the House by the Prime Minister on Friday morning 11 July 1975, in a subsequent press conference by the Prime Minister and Chancellor, and was formally embodied in a White Paper, *The Attack on Inflation* (Cmnd 6151).

The Government and the TUC recognized that the policy of trying to limit pay increases to compensate for past inflation had failed, and this policy was, in fact, reversed: instead of past price inflation governing the rate of wage inflation, the rate of wage inflation would now govern the rate of future price inflation. This was to be achieved by a flat-rate wage increase of £6 per week, up to a limit of £8,500 a year (the TUC had wanted £7,000). In its own policy document the TUC said that the flat-rate approach 'would give £6 a week to all full-time adults' and 'there should be a universal application of the figure of £6 per week'. The White Paper, however, said 'The £6 is a maximum within which negotiations will take place; some employers may not be able to pay it.' Nevertheless, the policy had the full support of the TUC and the CBI.

The major problem was that to get the support of the TUC the policy had to be voluntary (and, as we have noted, statutory policies are probably unenforceable anyway if widely breached). But history showed that voluntary policies were not noticeably effective. So what to do? The Government's answer was to introduce a wide range of statutory and administrative sanctions on employers, and to threaten more. There would be 'further powers' to ensure compliance in the private sector together with the new cash limits on public sector pay. New legislation would restrict the payment of the rate support grant to local authorities who breached the limits. In the nationalized industries the Government would not 'foot the bill for excessive settlements ... through subsidies, extra borrowing, or by allowing increased price charges'. Any excessive settlements would 'affect employment in the industry concerned'.

The Government, as it admitted, had no control over pay in the private sector, although there was legal control over prices. So one weapon they would use would be to disallow *the whole* of any price increase related to an excessive wage increase. Employers would be relieved of any contractual obligation to pay more than £6 per week. The Government would also enforce its policy administratively through its powers of discretionary assistance to industry and through its (quite considerable) powers of public purchase. The use of these discretionary powers was subsequently much criticized. The Government hoped and expected that this battery of powers, along with voluntary support for the policy, would be enough to secure compliance: 'If however ... the policy needs to be enforced by applying a legal power of compulsion they will not hesitate to do this.' To make it clear that this was no idle threat they announced that legislation had already been prepared which they would ask Parliament 'to approve forthwith if the pay limit is endangered'. This legislation would 'make it illegal for the employer to exceed the pay limit'.

It was, altogether, an ingenious system. There were no penalties on the unions or trade unionists; so far as they were concerned it was a voluntary policy. But around the voluntary system of wage bargaining was erected a formidable fence of obstacles to stop the employers, including public sector employers, from being altogether too voluntary. Ministers had learned some lessons from history: it had been a frequent complaint of Labour ministers, privately expressed, that employers were far too ready to yield to excessive wage demands. Later, the monetarists were to apply a similar system of placing the onus for opposing excessive wage demands upon employers, except that the incentives for employers to act responsibly were not legal or administrative, but applied impartially by the market in conditions of a tight control over money and credit.

The £6 policy did not achieve its objectives but it was far from being a failure: the rate of inflation fell from 26.9 per cent in August 1975 to 12.9 per cent in July 1976. Then it began to creep up again.

In his Budget and in the July measures the Chancellor had made no attempt to pretend that unemployment would not rise, and it did; from 800,000 (3.4%) in April it rose month by month to 1.2 million (5.3%) in February 1976.[9] Beginning in August the Government introduced a wide range of micro-economic measures to slow down the rise. In August there were subsidies for employment; in September a package of measures including money for training, labour mobility, industrial investment and factory building; in October came a special package for the construction industry; on 17 December a much bigger package that included more money for job saving and job creation, selective restraint on imports (mainly textiles, clothing and television sets), and encouragement for counter-cyclical stockbuilding. Finally, a package of measures on 12 February 1976 included further help for job saving and creation and for the construction industry and more aid for industry including a scheme for the stockpiling of machine tools. Despite the spread and variety of the measures, the total sums of money involved were relatively small, and even smaller in net terms because of savings on unemployment pay, social security, and tax flow-back. Some derided the measures, comparing the sums allocated with the huge sums that would be required to reflate the economy.

This missed the point: the general injection of spending power takes time to work its way through the system; there are lags and leaks. The Government's 'micro' measures were, in many cases, directly related to job creation or preservation. In some of the schemes it was a case of 'no job, no expenditure'. No one knows how many jobs the scheme created or preserved. It may not have been many, but it was all the Government could do; and the expenditure was probably cost effective.

The 'missing millions'

In November 1975 the Treasury and the Chancellor were not a little embarrassed by a former employee. In evidence to the House of Commons Expenditure Committee, Mr Wynne Godley, a Fellow of King's College, Cambridge, and Director of the Cambridge University Department of Applied Economics, former professional oboist and former Treasury economist (he had done much of the secret work on devaluation in 1967), showed that public expenditure in 1974–75 was some £5 bn more in *real terms* (constant prices) than planned in 1971.

Mr Godley's evidence was extremely damaging, for a number of reasons. Firstly, there had been in the intervening period a number of highly publicized programmes of 'public expenditure cuts'. If public expenditure had, nevertheless, risen by a huge amount the implication was that the Treasury had lost control. Secondly, and reinforcing the impression of a loss of control, Mr Godley's increase was net of (i.e. after taking account of) 'announced policy changes'. Thirdly, the excess could *not* be attributed simply to inflation because it was at constant prices.

The story achieved notoriety as the tale of 'the missing millions' and the Treasury had to respond. It produced its own set of figures which showed an excess of expenditure at constant prices of £5.8 bn, but this included *announced* policy changes, excluded from the Godley figuring. Of the remainder £1.7 bn was attributed to unforeseen cost increases, mainly house and land prices and construction costs; £800 m. was debt interest and the balance was 'other' changes. These seemed to be mainly policy changes which it had not seemed worth while to announce specifically. None of these excesses, the Treasury argued, constituted 'valid evidence of loss of financial control'. It was less than wholly convincing, and it did not convince the House of Commons Expenditure Committee which, after considering the Treasury's evidence, reported that 'The Treasury's methods of controlling public expenditure are inadequate ... ' Public expenditure was a theme on which we were to hear much more in 1976.

The Treasury Return

In satisfaction of an undertaking given to Parliament during the debates on the National Loans Act 1968, the Treasury published every month in the *London Gazette* (usually on a Friday afternoon) an obscure document entitled *Consolidated Fund and National Loans Fund – Transactions in the period 1 April to [the latest month]*. It was known as *The Treasury Return*.

The *London Gazette* is not well known as a source of economic statistics and there was only one journalist, on the *Financial Times*, who ever read this return and questioned the Treasury about it. It became something of a joke that there was this conscientious fellow who telephoned once a month on Friday afternoon to enquire into the entrails of this obscure set of statistics to which no one else paid the slightest attention.

In the course of 1975 things changed. Greenwells, the stockbrokers, and others, discovered the *Return* and sought to obtain from it information about the course of the Central Government Borrowing Requirement. The *Treasury Return* achieved some sort of instant stardom. Since there was such interest in the *Return*, and since in its raw state it could be misleading (it did not contain all the data people sought) it was decided, in November 1975, to take it in hand, and commentators were provided with copies and an explanatory note. Six months later it was replaced entirely with a regular monthly Press Notice

Central Government Financial Transactions. The *Financial Times* welcomed the new *Return* as giving more information, giving it earlier, and in more comprehensible form.

1976

Public expenditure, the Press and the pound

In January the IMF had approved the UK's application for a drawing of £575 m. on the oil facility and a stand-by credit of £400 m.

In Jamaica on 7 and 8 January the Interim Committee of the IMF had reached agreement on an exchange rate regime (flexible rates) and on gold – its role as a central standard of value to cease and be replaced by the Special Drawing Right.

In the first quarter of 1976 things did not look too bad at all for the UK economy. The rate of inflation had fallen in every month since its peak of 26.9 per cent in August 1975 and by April was below 20 per cent. Average earnings (seasonally adjusted) had similarly fallen from a peak increase of 30.7 per cent in April 1975 to 17.8 per cent a year later. The deficit on the current account of the balance of payments (seasonally adjusted) was down to £60 m. in the first quarter (from £1,700 m. in the year 1975). The deficit on visible trade, which had been £5.3 bn in 1974 and £3.2 bn in 1975, was a mere £20 m. (seasonally adjusted) in March.[10]

On 19 February the Treasury published its annual White Paper on Public Expenditure, *Public Expenditure to 1979–80* (Cmnd 6393). Expenditure on programmes was to fall in real terms in every year up to 1978–79. There were to be improved methods of control, through cash limits, better monitoring of expenditure through the year and tighter control of the contingency reserve, which was to become a Cabinet-controlled fund rather than a bottomless purse that could be drawn upon for any 'unforeseen' expenditure. It cannot have been an easy programme for a Labour Cabinet to agree upon; as Peter Jay said in *The Times*,[11]

' . . . Ministers have been through one of the most searching and painful re-examinations of cherished commitments that any Government has ever undertaken in peacetime.'

Yet, as he went on to point out, not a penny had been saved: public expenditure in 1979–80 would actually be, on these plans, over £4 bn higher than in 1974–75, at constant prices. Why? Mainly because of debt interest, provision for which in 1978–79 was raised by £3.3 bn over previous plans. All that had been achieved, in effect, was a redistribution of expenditure away from education, health and social services, subsidies, etc., and towards the holders of gilt-edged securities. It was hardly the euthanasia of the rentier, but given the huge deficits built up during the Barber years and beyond it was unavoidable.

The *Financial Times*[12] thought the plan only 'Semi-credible, semi-adequate'. The growth assumption was 'more than questionable, and indeed fanciful'. The Left-wing press disapproved for quite different reasons.

When the House of Commons Expenditure Committee examined the White Paper it was sceptical. This was the fifth public expenditure White Paper to show a profile of declining or stable expenditure in *future* years (none of which profiles had been realized). 'The continual appearance of this type of profile and its non-fulfilment', said the Committee, 'seems to us to show that the risk of the credibility gap we mentioned is growing.' The Committee wished to point out 'that the achievement of the Government's objectives ... presupposes a substantial improvement in the performance of the economy – indeed, by UK standards, almost an economic miracle'.[13]

Following the debate on the White Paper the Government was defeated, but won a subsequent vote of confidence.

In a sense, with the publication of the White Paper, the lines were drawn for a battle over public expenditure that raged throughout the year, to much sound and fury.

The exchange rate

During February, Continental currencies had been disturbed but the pound had remained unaffected. On Thursday 4 March there was considerable demand for sterling until lunchtime; then there was a sudden change of 'sentiment' and sterling declined very rapidly and, at the time, mystifyingly. It emerged subsequently that the authorities were reluctant to see sterling appreciate much above its then level of just over $2.0; so when a substantial but short-lived demand for sterling appeared late in the morning the Bank of England dealers had sold sterling. By mid-afternoon the dollar was strengthening and the Bank's earlier sales of sterling were misinterpreted by the market to mean that the authorities were actively pushing sterling down. The market reacted and sterling fell below the psychological barrier of $2. The dealers at the Bank had no instructions to buy.

The authorities' traditional reaction to a run on sterling is to raise the discount rate, MLR (formerly Bank Rate). But the next day, Friday, MLR was *lowered*, and the market, understandably but incorrectly, took this as further evidence that the authorities wanted the exchange rate down. The lowering of MLR was a miscalculation on the part of the authorities, who acted in the knowledge of what they *knew* they were doing and took insufficient notice of what the market *thought* they were doing. The Treasury denied that the Bank was trying to engineer a fall in the sterling rate; but the disturbance went on for the next ten days during which the pound fell to $1.9065 before steadying at around $1.92. There was much worse to come. The episode illustrates the power of City rumour,[14] the volatility of the foreign exchange market, and how closely the operators watch, and seek to interpret, the actions of the authorities.

The Prime Minister

Mr Callaghan became Prime Minister on 5 April, in succession to Mr Wilson who, on 16 March, had announced his resignation.

The tax and pay bargain

The Chancellor's Budget Statement,[15] presented on 6 April, was another marathon performance, lasting just over two hours. In terms of demand management he had no room for manoeuvre. With unemployment running at well over a million, he could not deflate; with the balance of payments still in deficit and the rate of inflation still well into double figures, he could not reflate. The main constraint was financial: the Public Sector Borrowing Requirement for the year just ended, forecast at £9.1 bn, had turned out to be £10.8 bn. The error, while an improvement on some of the Treasury's other efforts, was still considerable. The estimate for 1976–77 on unchanged policies was £11.3 bn. After Budget changes this was raised to £12.0 bn.

Mr Healey's statement, and his strategy, concentrated on two things: industrial policy and the fight against inflation. It is the latter which is of greater interest, but there was one item on the industrial side which is worth noting because it illustrates the way in which industrial considerations can determine taxation policy. It was known that the Government had been considering abolishing vehicle excise duty on passenger cars and recouping the lost revenue by raising the tax on petrol. The Chancellor said that the change had 'appeared increasingly attractive'. But 'To abolish it and make a compensating increase in petrol would immediately encourage people to change their present cars for smaller

ones ... and it is among the smaller models that our car industry
is particularly vulnerable to imports. I cannot make a change,
whatever its merits on other grounds, which would further expose
us to imports of foreign cars. ... ' He decided against the change.

On policies to continue the fight against inflation the
Chancellor's proposals were revolutionary, in the sense that
nothing like them had ever been proposed before. His proposal
was simply that he would make certain reductions in taxation, in
the form of increased allowances against tax, in return for the
TUC's agreeing to voluntary wage limits which would halve the
rate of inflation by the end of 1977. For illustrative purposes he put
the allowable increase in wages at about 3 per cent. The argument
for tax cuts instead of an 'equivalent' increase in money wages
was simple: tax cuts did not add to industrial costs and, therefore,
to prices; moreover, tax cuts would be backdated to the beginning
of the financial year whereas wage increases would be effective
only from some date after the beginning of the next wage round in
August. It followed that a tax cut would yield a higher real take-
home pay than an 'equivalent' rise in money wages which would
itself be taxable. Detailed tables were provided to illustrate this.

The procedure would be that once the TUC agreed to an
acceptable limit to wage increases the Chancellor would authorize
the inclusion of the higher tax allowances in the Finance Bill.

Agreement was announced on 5 May. The pay limit was 5 per
cent for those in a middle band of earnings (from £50 to £80 a
week), a limit of £4 a week for those earning more, and £2.50 a
week for those earning less. It thus became known as the
£2.50/5%/£4 policy. The overall effect was to keep the increase in
wages and salaries down to about 4.5 per cent. There was
criticism that the 4.5 per cent was half as much again as the 3 per
cent Mr Healey had suggested. The Chancellor, who had probably
never expected to get 3 per cent anyway, argued that it was a very
tightly structured policy, and he was satisfied that it would do the
job. The TUC had wanted 5.5 per cent.

The policy was an ingenious but simple idea carried swiftly
through to a successful conclusion. Mr Healey, and the TUC,
never received quite the credit for it that was their due.

Tax avoidance

In his first Budget in March 1974 Mr Healey had said 'The time has
now come for a determined attack on the maldistribution of

wealth in Britain ... Nothing is more offensive to the vast majority of ordinary taxpayers, most of whom are subject to PAYE, than the knowledge that people far better off than themselves are avoiding taxation by exploiting loopholes in the existing law.' He proposed a wealth tax, a closing of loopholes and the introduction of a capital transfer tax. Some measure to close loopholes and end some abuses were included in that Budget. In August 1974 he published a Green Paper on the wealth tax and a White Paper on proposals to replace the (largely voluntary) estate duty by a capital transfer tax. In his November 1974 Budget and Finance Bill he introduced the capital transfer tax. He said he had been 'shocked by the volume and intensity of protest generated by my determination to ensure that the estate duty is no longer a voluntary and avoidable tax ... I can construe the protests only as testimony to the scale on which estate duty has hitherto been avoided ... .' In his April 1976 Budget he said 'The lengthy and acrimonious debates which have accompanied the introduction of the capital transfer tax revealed how important these avoidance possibilities have been, since despite the fact that the new tax is levied at far more moderate rates than the old estate duty, it produced far more hostility among those whom it affected.'

Mr Healey's attempts to make the tax system fairer did not endear him to the tax avoiders and evaders and their supporters in the Press. In his April 1976 Budget he angered them further. It was offensive 'that a small minority have scope for evading and avoiding taxation either through limitations in the powers of the Revenue or through loopholes in the law. I propose to take steps to deal with both these problems.' To counter tax evasion, 'and by that I mean tax-dodging which involves breaking the law', he proposed to strengthen the powers of the Inland Revenue. His proposals, he said, were the minimum needed to deal with evasion.

Mr Healey's 'minimum proposals' to stop people breaking the law sparked a virulent response from the *Daily Mail*. 22 April: 'The *Daily Mail* today launches a new campaign ... the most urgent it has ever fought. Healey's secret police: we must stop them now.' The tone of the article may be judged from a couple of extracts: 'The effect of the Bill ... would be to set up a para-police force that could easily be turned into a political tool ... The Trotskyist International Socialists are active in the Inland Revenue, as in other arms of the bureaucracy ... ' 23 April: Under the logo 'Stop the tax spies' (with a pair of staring eyes) '"No" to Snoopers' Charter'. 27 April: '*Mail* campaign finds them in sinister action.

Where the tax spies break people.' 'Midnight knocks on the door
to check personal documents.' The article turned out to be about
Sweden. 5 May: An article claiming a 'tactical victory' over
Healey's 'tax spies' included a personal smear upon the
Chancellor: 'Yet Healey is not to be trusted ... he has a distinctly
totalitarian streak in his make up ... he managed to belong for
many years to a totalitarian party without apparent discomfort.'

It was all rather nasty. It is ironic that Mr Healey, the bushy-
browed ogre of the tax-evading classes, never became Prime
Minister and leader of the Labour Party partly because he was
thought to be too Right Wing, a prisoner of Treasury orthodoxy.

In the latter part of 1975 the Press had called strongly for public
expenditure cuts but this campaign died away after the publication
of the Public Expenditure White Paper in the following February –
more, presumably, because the other shoe had dropped rather
than because of any dramatic cuts actually announced.

The *Sun* newspaper returned to the theme at the end of April
1976 with a front page 'Exclusive' that to save 'the plunging £'
'Healey is poised to slash spending'.

Early in May the Government had announced the TUC's
agreement to the new pay limits. This was surely good news for
the fight against inflation. Yet what was interesting was the way in
which the Press, in reporting the news, still insisted that the more
important issue was public expenditure. The *Guardian* thought
that 'the real danger ... the much more fundamental problem' was
the public spending plans. The *Daily Telegraph* said the only
effective weapon against inflation was cutting Government
spending. The *Daily Express* referred to 'the crucial business of
cutting public expenditure'; 'The Government knows it is going to
have to slash expenditure.'

The *Sun* said that 'public spending has to fall substantially';
'When, oh when, will we see the savage spending surgery we
need?' The *Daily Mail* said 'The Government still has to cut its
spending and to reduce its crippling burden of debt.' The
Government had to 'hack back at public expenditure'.

When the pound fell below $1.80 in the middle of May the right-
wing Press renewed its demands for public expenditure cuts. The
Sun called for the Government to take 'a big sharp axe to its own
spending'. The *Daily Telegraph* City Editor foresaw 'July crisis
measures' which 'would have the desired impact only if they
included a credible scheme for scaling down Government
spending'. The *Daily Mail*'s City Editor also wanted the Prime
Minister 'to take an axe to the root of our evil – the huge

Government spending'. He hoped that the IMF when considering
the conditions for our next loan would 'insist on us tackling our
real problem. This is the monstrous overspending and
overborrowing by the Government . . . .' The *Daily Telegraph* in a
leading article 'Waiting for the IMF' also linked salvation to the
IMF: 'Only painful cuts in public expenditure will convince the
world that we mean to live within our real income. Probably we
shall have to wait until the Government is forced to seek a major
loan from the IMF. Then there may well be stringent terms on
public spending.' The *Daily Express* said 'Until a detailed, wide-
ranging, list of public expenditure cuts is announced by the
Government . . . sterling will continue to slump.' The *Financial
Times* and *The Times* saw the solution to sterling's weakness
more in the money supply: the *FT* in a leading article 'Money is
the missing link' wanted a 'firmly announced and closely
monitored money supply target', while *The Times*, in a leading
article presumably written by Peter Jay, concluded, after 27
column-inches, that the answer was to set up a statutory
Currency Commission.

The pound continued to fall and on Thursday 3 June reached a
record low of $1.7025. Next Monday, 7 June, the rate improved by
2 cents; and the Chancellor announced a credit of $5.3 bn from
the Group of Ten Countries (although France and Italy did not
take part), Switzerland and the Bank for International
Settlements. Of the $5.3 bn, $2 bn was in the form of a swap
arrangement with the USA, split evenly between the Federal
Reserve Bank and the US Treasury.

There was no problem about getting the credit; indeed the
initiative came from the lenders. The Bank of England, who had
co-ordinated the credit, explained that the central bankers
providing the credit believed that the market had 'carried sterling
to an unjustified level'. In a speech on 18 June the Governor said
'This experience illustrated sharply the importance of confidence
or its lack . . . My fellow Governors . . . considered, as I did, that
under market pressure the value of sterling had fallen to an
unjustified level . . . .'[16]

The Chancellor, in announcing the stand-by credit made the
same point: 'There is no economic justification for the fall which
has taken place in recent weeks. It goes beyond anything required
to make good past differences in rates of inflation . . . Recent
pressures in the exchange markets carried sterling to a level which
cannot be justified.' 'This is not a situation in which any
responsible British Government could allow itself to be pushed

into hasty and ill-considered changes of policy on public expenditure.'

Whatever the central bankers thought, the anti-Government Press in the UK saw the credit only as a way of avoiding cutting public expenditure. The *Sun*, invoking the IMF again, said 'All the Chancellor has done is buy himself a little time before he has to make the swinging cuts in Government spending on which the IMF will insist.' The *Daily Telegraph* said the Government was happy to borrow to sustain its colossal overspending. The Government had borrowed 'a hot five billion dollars rather than make instant cuts in the Government's colossal spending bills'.

The Press had been very sceptical about the Chancellor's pay/tax deal, doubting whether the TUC could deliver. On 16 June a Special Conference of the TUC overwhelmingly endorsed the policy and the Press was properly impressed. Only the *Sun* could find little good to say: the 4.5 per cent would not save us. Big spending cuts would have to be made soon.

Despite the TUC's vote, the central bankers' support and the recovery of sterling (it was up to $1.77 at the end of June), the Press refused to let go of the public expenditure story. But now the story changed.

The Chancellor and the Prime Minister had said on various occasions that public expenditure was being carefully looked at in the current round of the annual Public Expenditure Survey. It became known that if the $5.3 bn credit could not be repaid by December the UK would have to go to the IMF for funds. It was believed, indeed it was an article of faith among the right-wing Press, that the IMF would insist on cuts in public expenditure before granting any loan; and this belief had been encouraged by public statements by senior American officials. Putting all this together, the Press argued along the following lines: the Chancellor could do nothing until the TUC Special Conference had agreed to the pay limit; now that they had, he could act, knowing that if he did not do so he would be forced to go to the IMF later in the year.

Several 'impending cuts' stories appeared at the end of June: 'Spending cuts up to £2,500 million in contingency plan' (*Sunday Telegraph*, 27 Jun.); 'Healey plans a £1,000 million axe on spending' (*News of the World*, 27 Jun.); 'Treasury bid to axe an extra £1,000 million' (*Evening Standard*, 28 Jun.); '£1,000 million new spending cuts planned to boost industrial aid' (*The Times*, 29 Jun.); 'Cuts of £1,000 million planned' (*Daily Telegraph*, 29 Jun.). There was also a story out of Puerto Rico, where a Summit

meeting was taking place, that Mr Callaghan had promised
President Ford spending cuts. This was denied. On 30 June the
Guardian reported a Treasury plan for cuts of up to £1,250 m. and
next day said 'there can no longer be any doubt that cuts are on
the way ... '. The Government would have to make cuts to
appease bankers abroad and the City. The stories differed in detail
(except where one paper picked up its story from another), some
were written by the industrial editor, some by the political editor,
some by the economics or City editor. The sources of the stories
thus differed. But the figure of £1 bn became firmly entrenched.[17]
And it all came true: on 22 July the Chancellor announced public
expenditure cuts of £1,012 m. in 1977–78 (at 1976 Survey prices),
just about what everyone, by that time, was expecting. But the
Chancellor had a surprise: he added 2 percentage points to the
employers' national insurance contribution to raise another
£1,030 m. in a full year. And to please the monetarists he included
a figure of 12 per cent for the growth of the money supply. It
wasn't exactly a target or a ceiling, more a forecast or
expectation; but at least a number, at last, had been attached to
the aggregate to which growing importance was being attached.

The £1 bn of cuts in public expenditure had been agreed only
after six Cabinet meetings and, given the revolt that had followed
the cuts in the February White Paper, it is easy to believe that
consent was not easily come by. Members of the Cabinet were
not a little aggrieved, therefore, when Mr Healey, very late in the
day, doubled the value of the package by adding 2 percentage
points to National Insurance contributions.[18] This was seen as a
Treasury bouncer delivered off a short run, in fading light and
after the close of play.

The Chancellor's announcement did not still the clamour of the
Press, even though the £1 bn of cuts was what had been widely
expected, and the total package was worth twice that. True, the
Daily Mirror thought the measures tough enough and fair enough;
the *Observer* thought the measures well designed for their
purpose, and there was grudging acceptance from *The Times* and
the *Financial Times*. But the *Sun* regarded the cuts as no more
than a start; and the *Evening News* thought it probable that
further reductions would have to be imposed 'later on this year,
possibly in November'. The *Evening Standard* thought that
' ... had we not had the inspired leaks designed to soften up and
disarm the far Left, Chancellor Healey's announcement yesterday
would have had a tremendous impact'. *The Economist* also
thought the package badly prepared; 'first lied about ... and then

leaked'. The cuts were ' . . . bogus cuts, and will be followed by more next year'. The *Sunday Times* declared the measures 'botched' and 'a mystery' and 'bewilderingly ill-judged'. The *Sunday Telegraph* said 'The foreigners won't be convinced.' The following week *The Economist* returned to the attack: the cuts were 'incompetent' and public expenditure 'running riot'. There would be another sterling crisis. 'This is a major crisis of Government for Britain.'

Given that he was not dancing to a tune played by the Press, why had the Chancellor presented this package? He had the pay agreement under his belt, the pound was stable and the money supply under control. There was no immediate crisis. The first reason he gave was 'to release resources for the growth of exports'. But this had been a major theme in his Budget of three months earlier and not much had changed in the prospective demands on resources since then. It may have been, as the cynics had it, that he was waiting to act until after the Special Conference of the TUC. The more likely explanation lies in two things: the $5.3 bn loan, and pressure from the Americans.

The loan had originally been said to have no strings attached. This was not entirely true; it emerged that the Americans had insisted that it must be repaid by December. If it were not the UK agreed to apply to the IMF for funds. For some time senior American officials (who are political appointees, not civil servants) were concerned about what they saw as the financial profligacy of the Labour Government and the likely effects of this upon sterling and, through sterling, on the stability of the international monetary system. They remembered what had happened after devaluation. They believed that the UK would not be able to repay the loan and would be forced into the arms of the IMF who would impose stringent conditions. The Prime Minister, the Chancellor and Treasury officials were well aware of the American views;[19] and they had no desire to have to go to the IMF. They believed that it would not be necessary, that the loan would see them over a temporary weakness of sterling and could be repaid out of the reserves before December. So, the July package was an insurance policy, a sort of pre-emptive strike against the IMF. It is noteworthy that it included a specific target of reducing the PSBR by £3 bn, to £9 bn in 1977–78, and put a number to the growth of the money supply, both matters to which the Americans and the IMF attached importance.

Friday 13 August was a bad day: the July trade figures released on that day showed a deficit on visible trade of £524 m., more than that for the whole of the first quarter. And this followed a bad second quarter in which the current balance had deteriorated from near balance in the first quarter to a deficit of nearly £600 m.[20]

Nevertheless, sterling continued through the month relatively untroubled and as in July, there were no drawings on the short-term credit ($1,030 m. had been drawn in June).

At the end of the first week of September heavy pressure developed following news of a possible seamen's strike, industrial unrest at British Leyland, balance of payments statistics showing a big outflow of sterling balances in the second quarter, and proposals by the Executive Committee of the Labour Party to nationalize some banks and insurance companies. Although over $4.0 bn of the short-term credit remained undrawn, the authorities withdrew support from the pound at its $1.77 level and it fell to $1.7350. Over the years a great deal of money had been wasted in trying to support the pound at unjustifiably high levels, against the views of the market. But, it will be recalled, the $5.3 bn credit had been offered precisely to stop the pound being forced to what the central bankers were convinced were unjustifiably low levels, i.e. levels below the high $1.70s. The Treasury's decision not to use the credit meant that either they no longer believed that $1.77 was a realistic rate and that foreign exchange used to support it at that level would be wasted; or, whatever their views about the rate, they were so inhibited by the knowledge that the credit would have to be repaid by December that they had decided not to use it at all; the credit had become unusable ($515 m. was used during September, presumably in the first week, before support was withdrawn).

The continued downward drift of sterling stopped the sales of Government debt, with adverse effects on the money supply, as the gilts market waited for a rise in interest rates. On 10 September MLR rose 1½ points to 13 per cent and credit was tightened further with a call for Special Deposits on 16 September. This stabilized sterling and enabled the Treasury to sell a substantial amount of stock. But the respite for both sterling and the Government broker was short-lived: on 27 September the pound fell below $1.70.

The retreat from Heathrow

On Tuesday 28 September the Chancellor was to fly to the meeting of Commonwealth Finance Ministers in Hong Kong and the IMF meeting in Manila. During the morning the pound continued to fall. The Chancellor drove to Heathrow with the

Governor of the Bank of England and Treasury officials. In the VIP lounge they immediately telephoned the Treasury and the Bank for the latest news. The pound had continued its fall, down to $1.63. Mr Healey marched his men (except Sir Douglas Wass) back to the Treasury.

The retreat from Heathrow was a humiliation for Mr Healey and fed the atmosphere of panic and crisis. It is difficult to understand how he or his advisers could have allowed it to happen: the pound was falling when he left the Treasury and he left half-believing that he might have to turn back. In the absence of intervention it was hardly to be expected that the pound would recover dramatically in the time it took to drive to Heathrow. The decision to go or stay should have been made in the Treasury. An announcement from there that the Chancellor had decided to postpone his journey to the Far East would have created less drama, and left him the option of travelling later (the IMF meeting was not until 3 October).

Back at the Treasury the Chancellor announced his decision to apply to the IMF for a loan of $3.9 bn. On Thursday he flew to the Labour Party Conference at Blackpool where, denied a place on the platform, he made a tough five-minute speech from the floor, a bravura performance, captured on television.[21] The *Daily Express* (1 Oct.) loved it all: 'The Government began dancing to the IMF's tune yesterday, like puppets on a string attached to the life-saving loan.'

Perhaps the most puzzling aspect of the whole episode was the decision, once again, to refrain from touching the almost $4.0 bn that was available for intervention. It may have been sensible not to defend the $1.77 line if that was judged indefensible. But by Friday 24 September the market was prepared for the authorities to step in and put a floor under the $1.70 level, which certainly *was* defensible, representing as it did a depreciation of 30 per cent from the $2.42 of February 1975 when the economic outlook was a good deal worse. Thirty per cent in 18 months is a very large depreciation indeed.

The events in the last days of September 1976 probably represented the low point, up to then, of the Treasury's performance. It had had a very wearing twelve months; there had been the affair of 'the missing £5 bn', the mishandling of the run on sterling early in March, the forecasts of the borrowing requirement that had become a joke, the unremitting criticism from the Press, and the overhanging fear of being forced into the clutches of the IMF. By the end of September it appeared to the observer that the

Treasury, and the Bank of England, had lost some of their confidence and touch. An article in *Business Week* on 7 March 1977[22] said ' . . . after what critics see as an especially dismal performance last year, the bank's image of independence and unsurpassed technical excellence has eroded dramatically. The unprecedented litany of complaints and criticism of the bank's performance covers many issues . . . '. The article quotes Professor Brian Griffiths of London's City University as saying 'If you take the record of the Bank of England over the last five years in terms of technical expertise, you have to say that it is incompetent.'

The money supply and the gilt-edged market

The Chancellor placed considerable importance upon keeping the growth of the money supply within his 12 per cent figure. He knew that the Americans, the IMF and the markets generally attached much importance to the monetary numbers and he believed that if he could get the monetary side of the economy right this would take some of the pressure off the fiscal side. In September the stock of money had begun to grow at a faster rate because of the expansion of lending to the private sector and because sales of gilts had dried up following the weakness of the pound. The rise of MLR to 13 per cent on 10 September stimulated sales and a substantial amount of stock was sold. But the renewed fall in sterling at the end of September again brought the gilts market to a halt. The only thing that would get it going again was a further rise in MLR. Accordingly on 7 October, in an operation code-named 'Draconis', the Treasury and the Bank announced that the interest rate formula was suspended and MLR raised 2 points to 15 per cent. This was the first time since November 1973 that there had been an administered change in MLR. At the same time the Bank made a further call for 2 per cent of Special Deposits. The Government were able to resume sales of gilt-edged stocks; but the growth of bank lending to the private sector continued. The raising of the interest rate to a record 15 per cent was seen as a crisis measure and drew predictable cries of pain; but as the rate of inflation was 14.7 per cent in October and rose to 15.0 per cent in November the real rate of interest, as conventionally measured, was zero.

The end of summer

Early in the evening of Saturday 23 October 1976, the night the clocks were to go back, Adam Raphael of *The Observer* telephoned the Chancellor's Press Secretary at his home to draw his attention to an article in the next day's *Sunday Times*, and to ask for guidance. The article was by Malcolm Crawford, the Economics Editor, and was headed 'The price Britain faces for IMF aid'. The first paragraph read 'The International Monetary Fund and the United States Treasury have now agreed on the main terms under which Britain will be offered the $3.9 billion loan asked for by Chancellor Denis Healey. As well as severe restraints on borrowing, credit and money supply, the terms will include agreement to a further "short sharp drop" in the exchange rate of the £.' The article continued 'The Fund thinks that sterling should be let down to about $1.50 to the £ (against to-day's $1.64) . . . .' Mr Raphael's early warning set the bells ringing in a number of Treasury homes, in the Foreign Office and in Washington, where the Ambassador was provided with the text of the article by telex.

When the exchanges opened on Monday morning the pound lost, at one time, 7 cents, and there was no doubt that the cause of the fall was the *Sunday Times* article. The story was denied in unequivocal terms by the Chancellor of the Exchequer, the IMF and the US Treasury. The Acting Managing Director of the Fund said the report had 'absolutely no basis in fact as to either the Fund's method of procedure or the particular nature and size of the terms'.

William Simon, Secretary to the US Treasury, said the report was 'irresponsible and patently untrue'; negotiations between Britain and the IMF were 'none of our business'. These denials were carried on the front page of the *Financial Times* on the Monday.

Malcolm Crawford was interviewed on BBC radio's 'World at One', on the BBC television 9 o'clock news and, with his Editor, Harold Evans, on the 'Tonight' programme. He defended his article and was supported by his editor.

The Chancellor made a statement in the House to shouts of 'resign' from the Opposition. The shadow Chancellor, Sir Geoffrey Howe, said it was 'another sorry, savage condemnation of the Chancellor's management of the economy . . . it's only by urgent and resolute action to cut public spending and abandon the partisan and gravely damaging measures which have been forced through Parliament, that confidence will be restored'. Mr Eric Heffer sensed a conspiracy 'by the Opposition and certain press barons to try to force this Government out'. Mr Healey, not unreasonably, declined to take any responsibility for an 'irresponsible' Press story that had been emphatically denied by all the parties allegedly involved.

Mr Peter Viggers, Conservative MP for Gosport, and a Mr William Shepherd referred the matter to the Press Council who, acting with commendable speed, delivered their adjudication in April 1977. They rejected the complaints on the grounds that the journalist had taken reasonable steps to check his story (a view with which the Treasury would not agree – he had not checked with the Treasury) and he and the Editor genuinely believed the story to be true. The Council did, however, agree that the article might have been misleading.

In the light of some things that have happened since, it is interesting to note that in its report the Press Council had this to say; 'In the profession it has long been a well-known and accepted rule that the sources of information which a newspaper publishes need not be revealed. And this practice the Press Council accepts: it is essential to the news gathering process.'

As we have noted there were differences of opinion between the newspaper and the Press Council on the one hand and the authorities in the UK, the USA and the IMF on the other, as to whether the story had been adequately checked out. If the denials that were readily forthcoming after publication had been elicited beforehand, there would have been no story. But perhaps the most remarkable aspect of the incident is the way in which an inherently implausible story, firmly denied on all sides, was so readily accepted by the markets. Given that the central bankers of Europe had publicly declared their belief only a few months earlier that the pound was significantly undervalued at $1.70, it was not plausible that the IMF and the Americans would seek to push it down a further 20 cents. It was known that the IMF and the Americans were increasingly adopting a monetarist framework of thought and part of that framework was that devaluation did not work because the effect was short-lived, the competitive advantage soon frittered away in money wages that rose in line with the higher import prices generated by the devaluation. And the Americans, remember, had contributed $2 bn to help raise the pound above $1.70. Remarkable, too, was the readiness with which the market accepted the assertion that the IMF negotiations with the British Government, which had not even begun, had already been fixed in prior agreement with the US Government.

Over the weekend the Government public relations machinery had been active to some purpose: we had stimulated the responses we required. But to no avail; the cargo had begun to slip, the pound fell on Monday and continued to fall, reaching a low of $1.5550 on 28 October, when it closed at $1.57.

Mr Callaghan and the sterling balances

The most significant fallout from the episode was that it moved the Prime Minister, Mr Callaghan, appearing on the 'Panorama' programme on the 25 October, to speak out publicly against the sterling balances and the role of sterling as a reserve currency. The Treasury and the Bank were not pleased.

What Mr Callaghan said on 'Panorama' is interesting. Both he and Mr Wilson, he said, would have liked to hold the pound at $2 – but by the time he (Callaghan) became Prime Minister it was already down to 'one-eighty-something-or-other'. Asked why the pound had proved so vulnerable to just one newspaper story, he launched immediately into his attack upon the sterling balances. He answered:

> Basically it's because we are a reserve currency and I must say I rue it. I would love to get rid of the reserve currency. I am not sure that everybody in the Treasury would or maybe in the Bank ... I see no particular advantage of being a reserve currency at all. And we have got these vast sums ... held in sterling and so if it starts to go down and anybody sells anything at all it tends to feed on itself ... it isn't necessarily related to what is happening in the economy at all. So I would very much like to see ... these liabilities of ours which we have as a reserve currency taken over in some form or other ... I think Germany and the United States and perhaps Japan have got some responsibility here. They have got vast reserves ... if ... the IMF were to try to force us into policies which would be so harmful to the economy that we would go into a downward spiral, then we would have to say to some of those countries 'Look, the IMF and you yourselves must accept the political consequences of what you are doing.'

Further on in the interview he said:

> ... the IMF will have to be very careful because they've got a great responsibility here. And they will have to say, is it right to try to force Britain into courses which, unless the sterling balances are met in some other way could be very harmful to the whole politics and the whole nature not only of Britain but of the West.

He concluded with further remarks about the sterling balances, the 'vast reserves' of others, and the need to get the whole thing 'on to a more rational basis'.

It is clear from this that Mr Callaghan considered the sterling balances not only the basic problem but more or less the only problem. He warns against being forced into deflationary policies to meet a problem that has nothing to do with the real economy. Carried to its logical conclusion this meant 'We don't need an IMF loan, at least not one with any conditions attached; all we need is some international arrangement for taking the sterling balances off our hands.' But the Americans and, ultimately, the Germans, would not let him off the IMF hook. He got his 'safety net' for the sterling balances, but only after the IMF had approved a package of measures related to the conduct of British economic policy.[23]

The IMF travelling salvation show

On 1 November 1976 the IMF team, headed by Alan Whittome, a former Bank of England official, checked in to Brown's hotel, London, under assumed names. The six weeks of negotiations which followed were probably some of the most remarkable of their kind ever seen – remarkable not least for the degree of publicity surrounding supposedly secret meetings. To set the scene it will be helpful to outline the opening position of the parties involved.

Mr Healey

Mr Healey had had a very rough year. In his policy against inflation, he had achieved a success with the £6 policy and the pay/tax agreement with the unions; the rate of inflation had been halved from its highest levels but further progress had been halted mainly by the fall in the exchange rate. He had attached a number to the growth in the money supply but growth had accelerated in the third quarter; this, and the high level of borrowing, had weakened market confidence in sterling. On the basis of Treasury forecasts of the PSBR, and with tax increases ruled out – he believed the level of taxation to be too high – he needed some further cuts in public expenditure. While he did not welcome having to go to the IMF, now they were here he saw them as a useful ally in getting further public expenditure cuts through the Cabinet. Moreover, if these cuts satisfied the IMF, as they would have to, this would place an impeccable seal of approval upon them so that, unlike the July cuts, they would be seen as adequate. But he did not want big cuts, for a number of reasons: he believed that with the help of Mr Pliatzky, the Second Permanent Secretary in charge, public expenditure was now under control, or much better control; with 1¼ million unemployed large cuts were inappropriate; and, with good reason, he had little faith in the Treasury forecasts of the PSBR, upon which the whole thing hinged.

Mr Callaghan

Mr Callaghan was 'finding the idea of further deflation quite intolerable'[24] and he distrusted the Treasury. And, as we have seen, placed great importance on removing the incubus of the sterling balances. He was quite prepared to allow open Cabinet discussion of alternative policies.

The Cabinet

The Cabinet began by being almost unanimous in its opposition to public expenditure cuts. At an early count only two members supported Healey. The 'alternative strategy' that his opponents espoused was a modified form of siege economy, concentrating on 'the industrial strategy', the social contract and import controls.

The Treasury

There is rarely a monolithic view of anything in the Treasury. On this occasion there were senior officials, mainly on the overseas side, who wanted £2 bn of cuts in public expenditure: this was not the view on the public expenditure side; among the more unreconstructed Keynesian economists there was the feeling that, with 1¼ million unemployed, any cuts at all would be out of order: like the Prime Minister, they found the idea of further deflation intolerable, and unnecessary; they did not regard the money supply and the PSBR as central to the argument.[25]

The IMF

The IMF cannot, strictly speaking, be said to have had any view prior to their examination of 'the books'. Given the Fund's monetary bias, however, and the influence of American thinking, it would not be unreasonable to suppose that they did begin with some presupposition that big cuts in government borrowing were likely to be needed. To them their visit was a technical, almost a routine, matter, their purpose to examine the state of the British economy before granting a loan under the provisions of the Fund.

It was what they always did for any application. They wanted, and tried to keep, a low profile.

The Americans

The Americans were not a party to the negotiations; but their weight in the IMF has always been considerable, and the IMF team were bound to be aware of American views. As we have noted, the senior officials in the Administration were monetarists who believed that something had to be done about the level of British borrowing and the money supply. In particular they were anxious that the British Government should not escape the disciplines of the IMF by arrangements to deal with the sterling balances. Any agreement on these had to follow agreement to the IMF's terms.

The Germans

The Germans come into the picture only because Mr Callaghan believed he could enlist their support for a safety net for the sterling balances. German opinion was important internationally because of the strength of their economy and of the Deutschmark.

The Press

To the popular Press, Alan Whittome's team was the IMF's 'travelling salvation show', come to redeem the British people from a sinful Socialist Government, from Mr Healey, and from bankruptcy. They were determined to make a circus of it. Television was hampered by the team's low profile and the lack of visuals. I recall one programme in which, in the absence of faces and pictures, television was reduced to showing a map of London and a long-shot of a black saloon car, allegedly containing the team, on the way to a meeting.[26]

The negotiations

These fell into two overlapping parts; the negotiations between the IMF and Treasury teams; and the negotiations in Cabinet. The negotiations with the Treasury got away to a slow start because the Treasury forecasts were not ready. When they were presented the IMF did not believe some of them, in particular the forecasts of the borrowing requirement and of unemployment, both of which they thought too high. Ministers also distrusted the PSBR estimates, but for opposite reasons: they suspected the Treasury of trying to frighten them into public expenditure cuts with horror stories of the likely PSBR. Indeed, the discussion in Cabinet was overlain with suspicion of the Treasury. Joel Barnett (1982, pp. 102–3) wrote:

> It seems they [the IMF] were genuinely flummoxed by our National Income Forecasts ... [Whittome] was certain we had increased the unemployment forecast to avoid having to deflate, and he refused to believe many of our other forecasts. He was not alone. Most of our Cabinet colleagues were, for different reasons, unwilling to believe the forecasts, and would not countenance further deflation ... John Pardoe publicly voiced a strongly-held view that Treasury officials were sabotaging the Government in Washington by saying that the Government's economic policy was in danger of collapsing unless the IMF imposed tough terms for its loan. At least one senior Minister felt he had evidence that this was true. It also became clear that some of the Prime Minister's advisers, if not Jim Callaghan himself, believed it.

The Times, in a front-page article on 8 November, said:

> But relations between Ministers and Treasury officials are not helped by the growing suspicion that some senior officials, though not actually sabotaging the negotiations with the IMF are trying to use the loan application as a lever to impose their own political values on the elected government of the country.
>
> There is no hard evidence to substantiate those suspicions, although some distinctly strange comments, particularly about the need or otherwise to fund the sterling balances, have been attributed to senior Treasury officials in recent reports.

Progress within the Treasury building was slow, both teams preparing their positions. Formal negotiations did not begin until 19 November, when the IMF suggested cuts in the PSBR of £3 bn in 1977–78 and £4 bn in 1978–79. The Cabinet met on 23rd and again on 25th. Little progress was made and, after nearly a month, four of the IMF team returned to Washington.

The swing away from deflation

Meanwhile, something quite unexpected was happening to the British Press coverage: the more serious newspapers began to question the need for massive cuts in public expenditure. It was

Peter Jenkins, in the *Guardian* of 3 November, who first doubted whether the Emperor would be wise to buy the fine suit of deflationary clothes being pressed upon him by the IMF. He drew a distinction between the balance between the public and private sector, a matter for adjustment over time, and the demand for 'instant and savage deflation'. He sought to explode 'the pernicious political myth that we are all monetarists now'.

On 8 November *The Times* had as its main news story on the front page a most curious piece, headlined 'Government seeking IMF advice on how to boost the economy'. Unusually, it carried no by-line except 'By our economic staff'. The article, sprinkled with phrases like 'the IMF is expected to agree', argued at length that it would not be constructive to cut the budget deficit of a country already in recession, and would be perverse to 'chase falling revenue with more and more destructive cuts in the social services'. The Fund was not in business 'to promote world depression or to push any particular member under the water'. The article read like a Ministerial lecture to the IMF: perhaps that is what it was, beneath the by-line. The article concluded with a hefty side-swipe at the Treasury: things were difficult enough for ministers 'without having the Treasury change all the key figures every few weeks'.[27]

Peter Jenkins returned to his theme on 11 November and concluded with a plea for a solution that included a credit facility to deal with the sterling balances. A worrying problem for the Government was 'the excessively deflationary expectations of the financial opinion-makers'.

If it was surprising to have the monetarist *The Times* putting the case against deflation, it was equally so to find the growing chorus joined by Samuel Brittan of the *Financial Times*. In an article on 15 November, 'The doubts of a dissenting monetarist', he began 'There is a danger of a wrong-headed financial package being forced on a shell-shocked Cabinet and House of Commons.' He argued for a steady and gradual approach to the problems of public expenditure and the money supply: 'In the short-term there is no case for any restrictive measures in view of the depressed outlook for activity and the probability that unemployment is already above its minimum sustainable rate.'

The same day Peter Jenkins came back to the theme of the sterling balances, and added ' . . . a modest deflation will be worse than none at all but a great improvement over some of the lunacies canvassed'.

Next day the *National Institute Economic Review* forecast a

PSBR of £8.2 bn in 1977–78 and saw no need for a deflationary package.

But perhaps the best evidence for how widely the orthodoxy of deflation was now being questioned came from a leading article in the *Evening Standard* on 26 November:

> ... What is now discernible is a movement among both economists and politicians towards a common view that really savage cuts in public spending at this juncture would do more harm than good ... To cut too much too quickly would send the economy into shock, increase unemployment and stem economic growth ... if the National Institute forecast has caused the extreme deflationists to pause, it will have served a valuable purpose.

The final stages

With the negotiations seemingly deadlocked, William Simon, Secretary to the United States Treasury, stopped off in London at the end of November on his way home from Moscow, to see what he could do. Some suspected that his main purpose was to stiffen the resolve of the IMF team.

Next to arrive, on 1 December, was Johannes Witteven, Managing Director of the IMF, who had decided that he must intervene personally. He had meetings with Mr Callaghan, described as 'acrimonious'.

The Cabinet had discussed the loan and the IMF's terms over seven meetings from the 23 November. Cabinet meetings are secret; and a detailed account, however fascinating, would be, anyway, beyond the scope of this book. But some indication of how the Cabinet came to its decision is in order, and a fair account of what took place can be pieced together.[28] Very briefly, two factions had emerged, one supporting Healey and the other, led by Anthony Crosland, in favour of 'the alternative strategy'. At one stage, towards the end of November, it appeared that the latter group might be in the majority if it came to a show of hands. Early in December the Prime Minister, who had been impartial in the prolonged debate, came down on the Chancellor's side, and Crosland reluctantly supported him, and so did his group. It had been made clear to Mr Callaghan by the Germans and the Americans that he could get the 'safety net' for the sterling balances that he so badly wanted only after agreement with the IMF.

The terms to which the Cabinet had, in the end unanimously, agreed, were presented to the House of Commons by the Chancellor of the Exchequer on 15 December.

On that day Mr Healey announced a package of measures approved by the IMF.[29] The PSBR before the measures was estimated at £10.25 bn in 1977–78 and £11.5 bn in 1978–79. He proposed to bring these figures down to £8.7 bn and £8.6 bn respectively, representing reductions of nearly £2 bn and nearly £3 bn. As the major element in these reductions public expenditure programmes would be cut by £1 bn in 1977–78 and £1.5 bn in 1978–79 (at 1976 survey prices). On the revenue side the Government proposed to raise an estimated £500 m. in 1977–78 by the sale of some of its shares in British Petroleum.

The other main element in the package was the establishment of a target limit to Domestic Credit Expansion (DCE), the monetary aggregate preferred by the IMF. This was to be £9 bn in the year to April 1977 and £7.7 bn in the year to April 1978.[30] No *target* was set for the growth of the money supply, sterling M3, but this was expected to be between 9 and 13 per cent in 1976–77. The definition of DCE was changed so that only bank lending in *sterling* to the private sector was included instead of, as formerly, lending including foreign currency lending. The Treasury stated that as 'a parallel change', 'greater official emphasis will be placed in future on the *sterling* component of M3, ... '.

Finally, to cover the short period until the IMF loan could be drawn, the Chancellor announced a swap facility of $500 m. offered by the US Treasury and the Federal Reserve, and a stand-by facility of $350 m. offered by the Bundesbank. The stand-by arrangements with the IMF would be for nearly $4 bn over two years, of which $1.15 bn would be immediately available and a further $1 bn before the end of 1977.

The Chancellor presented his package as part of a medium-term strategy leading up to the 1980s. Mr Powell asked him to confirm that the measures would have been necessary whether the IMF had existed or not. The Chancellor replied:

> I shall confirm ... that the Government have taken decisions because they believe them to be necessary. I do not mind saying that it took some time to persuade the IMF team that these decisions were the appropriate ones ... They are Government decisions. They would have been more necessary if we had not been able to count on the endorsement of our policies by the IMF ... '[31]

As the *Financial Times* said in its leader the next day, 'The first thing to be said about Mr Healey's latest mini-Budget is that it can in no way justly be called, as Sir Geoffrey Howe called it, an IMF Budget.'

The right-wing Press was not pleased. If leader-writers can be said to splutter with rage, that's what they did. 'Inadequate' was the politest word they used. 'Chicken Chancellor' headlined the *Daily Mail*; 'Britain's Shame' the *Sun*. The Labour Left did not like it either, for opposite reasons. Mr Healey had few friends on that day but he was entitled to feel well pleased, if not actually smug, about the outcome of his negotiations with the IMF. In return for cutting public expenditure plans by no more than £1 bn next year, with a further cut in 1978–79, which was a long way away, he had got the foreign exchange he needed *and* the IMF's seal of approval on his policies. Since he would have had to make the cuts anyway, he had got something for nothing.

But he got much more than that, as it turned out. For at the time of the 1977 Budget, in March, the PSBR for 1976–77, which the Treasury had estimated at £11 bn as recently as December, was then estimated at £8.8 bn; and that for 1977–78, before Budget changes, at £7.4 bn, well below the figure of £8.7 bn in the Letter of Intent to the IMF. And this was before most of the measures of 15 December had taken effect. So, far from having to take any further measures, the Chancellor actually had a lot of room for manoeuvre. With one bound – quite a few bounds, actually – Houdini Healey was free.

The crowning irony, after all the Press and Opposition hysteria about public expenditure, was that, when the figures eventually became known, public expenditure in 1976–77 had fallen, by nearly 2 per cent, for the first time since Mr Jenkins's last year, 1969–70. Two cheers, at least, for Mr Pliatzky.

Reflections on 'the IMF crisis'

'The horror of that moment,' the King went on, 'I shall never *never* forget!'
'You will though,' the Queen said, 'if you don't make a memorandum of it.'

Lewis Carroll *Through the Looking-Glass*

Mr Healey, as we have seen, emerged from the crisis of the last quarter of 1976, if not unscathed, at least in a stronger position than before. The recovery from the crisis was so rapid and complete that there are reasonable grounds for wondering whether there was in fact any real crisis at all, or whether it was not all something got up by the Press: and whether, if there was a crisis, it was not wholly or largely self-inflicted.

The year began in the shadow of Mr Godley's revelation, of November 1975, of the 'missing £5 bn' of public expenditure. This helped to set what we might call 'the theme of the year' – that public expenditure was out of control.

Then early in March came the sharp run on sterling, triggered by the market's misreading of the authorities' intentions, and the Bank and Treasury's failure to react quickly enough, so that the pound went through the psychological barrier of $2 and continued on down. Or, on another interpretation,[32] the Treasury-inspired strategy was to engineer a devaluation down to around $1.90, although the Bank of England, closer to the foreign exchange market, realized that this was a dangerous manoeuvre which could result in the pound's going much further down that was

Healey, 1974–1979

the Bank and the Treasury between them could have handled the affair better.

Since, at $2, the pound was undoubtedly overvalued, the fall below that was bound to come sooner or later, and the level of $1.78–$1.77 around which it later settled was probably about right – if any rate can ever be said to be 'right'. So in terms of its actual effect, the mishandling of March was not all that important. But it did have side-effects: it established, early in the year, a nervous climate for sterling; it created uncertainty about the authorities' competence and intervention tactics; and it left some distrust between Bank and Treasury which may have weakened the confidence of both in the handling of the foreign exchange market.[32]

In June came a further run on sterling and the central banks, largely on their own initiative, offered a $5.3 bn credit to support sterling because, as they believed, and said, at its new rate of around $1.70 the pound was undervalued. The problem was not weakness, but instability; if sterling could be stabilized, it would remain stable. This accorded with Treasury thinking, in line with the 'shifting cargo' theory of the foreign exchanges.

The theory was justified by events: after the announcement of the credit sterling did in fact stabilize at around $1.78–$1.77 and continued at that level for some months without intervention.

Stability had been achieved at a cost of barely a fifth of the available credit.

Early in September the pound began to fall because, it was believed, of a threatened seamen's strike. The authorities withdrew support, judging that the market pressures were too strong to resist. Both the market's action and the authorities' reaction were understandable: a seamen's strike has a quick and severe effect on the balance of payments. The authorities withdrew from the front line, husbanding their resources, one supposed, for a better day.

That day came when the threat of a seamen's strike vanished and with it the threat of a hard run on sterling. We were back into thin markets for sterling, but the rate continued to fall. Here were precisely the conditions in which intervention is cheap and effective, where the rate can be stabilized by a regular buyer (the Bank) coming in to mop up any residual sterling on offer. They were the conditions for which the $5.3 bn credit had been provided, and of which over $4.0 bn remained.

But the authorities did not intervene; they sat on their hands and the $4.0 bn and watched the rate go down. Realizing what was happening, or not happening, and, perhaps, remembering March, the market drew its own conclusions: there was no visible floor to sterling, it would go on down for a while yet; and if a rate is on its way down there is only one thing to do – sell.

As we have seen, on 28 September, the day the Chancellor of the Exchequer was due to fly to the Far East, the rate began to fall fast. The Chancellor, sitting in the Treasury, had a clear choice: either to stay there where he could monitor the situation and possibly take some action; or shrug it off, say 'What crisis?' and take flight to the Far East, leaving the markets to look after themselves.

The Chancellor dithered, marched his troops to Heathrow and marched them back again. Why did he march back? Because sterling was weak and falling. But he knew that before he set out. What did he learn at the airport that he did not know in Parliament Street, except that sterling had, predictably, fallen another cent or two?

That was the second mistake. To have cancelled his visit to the IMF would have been drama enough. To cancel it within ten minutes of take-off had the mark of panic and indecision. It left no one in any doubt that the Chancellor of the Exchequer at least, believed there was a crisis.

What choices were open to Mr Healey, back at the Treasury?

He could do nothing, always a much underrated option; mere activity should not be confused with action. If he did nothing the pound would continue to fall, but it would not fall for ever. It had stood at over $2 at the beginning of the year, and at around $1.78 for several months in mid-year; and it was now just over $1.60. Some things had changed in the course of the year, but not all of them for the worse; $2 and $1.60 could not both be realistic rates, and the probability was that neither of them was. At some point the markets would realize that the decline had gone too far, that sterling was cheap and that there were profits to be made by buying. At that point the rate would rise, and very quickly: no one would want to be left behind once it became clear which way the market was headed. On an objective assessment it seemed improbable that the pound, shortly to become a petro-currency, would be overvalued at any level below $1.60. If $1.60 was seen as somewhere near the bottom, and the pound bounced back to, say, $1.65, could we live with a rate as low as that? It would be bad for inflation but very good for exports; and the economic strategy was based on export-led growth. Our competitors would not have liked it but it would have been good for us, certainly in the short run, and in the longer run if domestic costs could be contained. If we did not intervene then the $4.0 bn of the credit that remained would be intact and only just over $1 bn repayable in December; and the reserves at the end of September stood at over $5 bn. So, all in all, there was much to be said for doing nothing and letting the markets sort it out.

The second option was to intervene to support the pound at some level, probably $1.60 or just below, and, the classical response, to raise MLR sharply, probably, in this case, by 2 points. This would have been a gamble but, if the above analysis is correct, not much of one. If it had failed, and we had lost our $4.0 bn, then we should have had to go to the IMF – which is what we did anyway. If it had succeeded, then, depending upon how much of the $4.0 bn was used, we could have avoided going to the IMF at all, or we could have gone in our own time, and not in an atmosphere of desperation.

Chancellor Healey adopted neither of the above options; instead he went straight to the IMF. Why? It did not make more money immediately available for the support of sterling, if that is what his intention was; although news of the application did lift sterling (subsequent, and incorrect, reports of what the IMF wanted had the opposite effect). It may have been that, knowing he would have to borrow to meet the deficit on the balance of

payments, he preferred medium-term debt to short-term debt;
and, anyway, that was what the IMF was there for. One theory
has it that he went to the IMF because the conditions the IMF
would impose would strengthen his hand against the left wing in
the Cabinet. That may have been in his mind but it is unlikely that
it was a primary consideration. He had all along played down the
probability of going to the IMF, saying that he hoped not to do so.
As recently as the preceding Sunday he said that no decision had
yet been taken. Talking of the balance of payments deficit in his
1975 Budget speech he had this to say:

> Behind all these particular reasons for closing our deficit
> more quickly lies one overriding and, to me, absolutely
> compelling argument. We in Britain must keep control of
> our own policy. We must keep ahead of events. It would
> be disastrous if we were forced, as some times in the past,
> into running desperately after events which we could not
> control ... we would run the risk of being forced to
> accept political and economic conditions imposed by the
> will of others. This would represent an absolute and
> unequivocal loss of sovereignty ...

These are scarcely the words of a man anxious to place himself
under IMF surveillance. But they do provide a clue as to why
events took the course they did. There was a respectable if not
overwhelming case for going to the IMF. This case existed in July
and August when the pound was untroubled. The charge against
Mr Healey is not that he went to the IMF but that he left it too late
so that he went in an atmosphere of crisis and panic, and let loose
a flood of speculation that went on for two and a half months,
about what was wrong with the economy that the IMF would want
to put right. A hostile Press was not slow to assert that Mr Healey
had made a mess of things and had been forced to call in the IMF
to sort things out for him – and a jolly good thing too. None of this
need have happened if the application had been made at a time of
the Government's own choosing, when the economy was looking
reasonably good.

The mistiming of the approach to the IMF, and the use, or non-
use, of the June credit leads to the conclusion that throughout
1976 the authorities were in a muddle and had not properly
thought through their exchange rate policy. As we have seen,
having got the central bank credit they did not use it in the
circumstance for which it was provided and in which it could have
been effective; they were prepared to let the rate go in the face of

any but the lightest pressure on sterling. If that was so then why did they accept the credit in the first place? What was the point of accepting a credit which they were not going to use? If the tactics were to do no more than a little smoothing of the market, then the reserves, at $5 bn, were entirely adequate for that purpose and, indeed, that, in part, is what reserves are for.

The authorities manifested no clear and consistent exchange-rate policy and seemed still to be thinking in terms of the fixed rates of four years earlier and seemed never to have seriously considered the possibility of not intervening at all. There was still a nostalgic feeling around that 'the authorities' knew best and ought to be able to control rates. Yet Germany's experience with the Deutschmark told them that this could not be done against the weight of the market. They wanted to intervene but were afraid to do so, with the result that sometimes they did and sometimes they didn't; and when they did they incurred debts that had to be repaid. They ended up with an exchange rate no higher than it would have been had they not intervened *and* a foreign debt to repay. The lack of a clear policy for the exchange rate was compounded by a failure to take an early decision on whether, and when, to go to the IMF. Policy had the appearance of being made up from day to day, or even, *vide* Heathrow, from hour to hour, in reaction to events rather than in control of them.

So, had there been, in any fundamental sense, a crisis at all? The balance of payments, so far from deteriorating, was improving, aided by a significant input from North Sea Oil; both the visible deficit and the current account deficit fell by some £200 m., seasonally adjusted, between the third quarter of 1976 and the first quarter of 1977.

There had been fluctuations in the growth of the money supply but action had been taken (before the IMF arrived) to fund government debt and restrain lendings to the private sector so that by April 1977 the 12-month growth of sterling M3 was 7.2 per cent, well below the 12 per cent guideline. Over the same period Domestic Credit Expansion (DCE) was £4.2 bn, less than half the ceiling agreed with the IMF. The PSBR for 1976–77 was estimated at the time of the 1977 Budget to be £8.8 bn, over £3 bn below the estimate made a year earlier and £2.25 bn below the estimate given to the IMF in December. Public expenditure in 1976–77, which it was alleged was out of control and which had been at the centre of the whole episode, turned out to have *fallen* by 2.7 per cent, while expenditure on programmes fell by 3.6 per cent (Cmnd 7049).

So, in all major areas, and especially in those of concern to the IMF, namely DCE, the money supply, government borrowing and public expenditure, the underlying position was very sound indeed. And it is not plausible to suggest that these results, covering, for the most part, the whole of 1976–77, were brought about solely, or mainly, by the 'IMF conditions' agreed at the end of 1976. Those conditions were focused on 1977–78 and 1978–79 and had very little to do with 1976–77.

It does appear, certainly in retrospect, that at the end of 1976 the UK economy was not a suitable case for treatment; and that all the fuss was little more than an 'expense of spirit in a waste of shame'.

1977

Into the rose garden

Mr Callaghan landed his safety net for sterling on 11 January 1977 when the Chancellor of the Exchequer announced a new arrangement between Central Bank Governors, to be administered by the Bank for International Settlements. The purpose of the arrangement was not only to shield sterling from the impact of a run on the balances, but to facilitate an orderly withdrawal of sterling from its reserve currency role. The Chancellor's statement made it clear that the new arrangements were contingent upon the UK's following the policies recently agreed with the IMF. The text added, mysteriously, that 'The Managing Director of the IMF has been associated with these discussions and has been asked to assist in implementing the agreement.' The MD's precise role was not made clear; presumably he was to certify that the UK was behaving as scheduled.

On 10 February the details were spelled out. Essentially, the UK could draw on the facility, totalling $3 bn, whenever the official sterling balances fell below £2,165 m., their level on 8 December 1976; provided the reserves were less than $6,750 m. There were to be discussions about the issue of foreign currency bonds in which holders of sterling balances might invest. Details of an offer of such bonds were published on 4 April.

To deal with the immediate problem of financing the balance of payments other than by short-term inflows, a group of UK and foreign banks in January arranged a medium-term loan of $1.5 bn.

The 1977 Public Expenditure White Paper[33] was published in two parts, in January and February. The plans, which took account of the measures of 15 December, showed expenditure on programmes unchanged in 1976–77 over 1975–76 and falling by 4.5 per cent, at constant prices, in 1977–78 over 1976–77. Including the contingency reserve and debt interest, total public expenditure in 1977–78 was planned to fall by 2.2 per cent. The Treasury had discovered that (gross) debt interest was met in large part by receipts of interest on lending and through prices, rents and charges paid for services provided by the public sector. A substantial proportion of debt interest did not, therefore, have to be financed by taxes or borrowing and should not properly be included in public expenditure. The new basis of calculation reduced debt interest in 1977–78 by £5.0 bn and public expenditure by nearly 9 per cent. It was expected that the new basis for debt interest together with cuts in programmes would bring public expenditure, as a percentage of GDP at market prices, down to 42–43 per cent in 1978–79. (The 1976 White Paper on expenditure had publicized a figure of 60 per cent.) Control of public expenditure had been strengthened and was to be strengthened further, by cash limits, by closer monitoring of departmental expenditure; and by developing the contingency reserve into more of an operational tool – the reserve could be drawn on only as a very last resort, when any additional expenditure could not be met from cuts or economies elsewhere.

Even those who had held all along that the IMF crisis was unreal, an economic nonsense, were surprised at the speed and strength of the recovery in 1977. By the time of the Budget at the end of March, the exchange rate had put on 16 cents from its low point in October, to stand at just under $1.72; the reserves totalled £9.6 bn, double what they were at the end of October (and only a small part of this came from drawing on loans); and MLR had come down 4½ points to 10.5 per cent. Moreover, as we have noted, the estimate for the PSBR was more than £2 bn below what it had been in December.

Mr Healey's Budget, for the most part rather dull, had two redeeming features: it was short – a mere 1 hour 23 minutes – and it contained substantial tax cuts. In broad terms, what he proposed was to cut income tax by over £2.25 bn (in a full year) and increase indirect taxes by £800 m. to give a net tax cut of £1.5 bn. As in 1976, part of the tax cut, in this case 2p off the basic rate of tax, was conditional upon the achievement of a satisfactory pay deal. In the face of Parliamentary pressure he subsequently

amended his proposals, taking only 1p off income tax but raising
allowances, to give roughly the same relief overall. Parliament also
threw out a 5½p a gallon increase in petrol duty.[34] Mr Healey was
not pleased.

The Budget was significant for its switch from direct to indirect
taxation. But the heart of it was, once again, the tax-against-pay-
restraint offer. The tax cuts, said Mr Healey, were worth a 4.5 per
cent pay rise. The offer was not tied to any specific limit to pay
increases. Not everyone approved. Joe Gormley, of the miners,
was reported as saying 'Blackmail of that kind is just not on'; and
Hugh Scanlon of the Engineers did not like it either. The *Sun*
newspaper said 'He should not have relinquished his fundamental
responsibility, for the second year running, to the Robber Barons
of the TUC.' *The Times*, more sedately, thought it 'objectionable
that negotiations with the trade union minority should determine
the taxes paid by the non-trade union majority of taxpayers'.

The Chancellor got his pay deal. He made a Statement on 15
July and published *The Attack on Inflation After 31st July 1977*
(Cmnd 6882). The deal was a much looser one than that of the
previous year; the TUC endorsed no percentage limit for pay
increases, although the Chancellor urged a limit to *earnings* of 10
per cent, implying *settlements* 2 or 3 points below that level
(because of wage drift). In addition to the cut in the basic rate of
tax of 1p and an increase, over Budget proposals, in personal
allowances, the Government offered a number of other 'measures
to maintain living standards' including a substantial increase in
child benefit. The major contribution by the TUC was an
agreement to adhere strictly to 'the twelve-month rule' under
which there would be a twelve-month interval between
settlements; and settlements due before 31 July 1977 would not be
deferred in the hope of securing better terms.

Both the Government and the TUC regarded the agreement as
part of a 'phased return to free and responsible collective
bargaining'. Ministers did not deny that the agreement was little
more than an act of faith. At his press conference Mr Healey was
challenged about what he would do if a powerful union decided
not to play. He gave reasons for believing this would not happen
and concluded: 'None of this is a guarantee that we will get the
result we want, but the essence of a return to free collective
bargaining is that you do the thing with some uncertainty about
the outcome, but you know, if you have got a better answer,
perhaps you would send it to me in a plain sealed envelope and I'll
have a look at it.' In the Parliamentary debate that followed on 20

July, the Prime Minister said 'What we have on our hands ... is a gigantic essay in persuasion ... .'

Given that it was operating a voluntary policy on wages and that the TUC had given a firm assurance on the important twelve-month rule, the Government had no option but to go ahead with the 'conditional' element in the tax cuts, especially as there was plenty of scope within the agreed ceilings for them to do so. To have withheld the tax cuts because they had not got a specific number attached to pay increases would have been worse than pointless. The Government had got the best deal they could in return for Tax cuts which they wanted to make anyway.

The TUC's statement, *The Economic Situation and Pay*, issued on 19 July was very firm on the twelve-month rule, on not re-opening negotiations already concluded, and on the importance of not looking back and trying to compensate for past inflation. But there was a warning in the concluding paragraph: 'The TUC', it said, 'has never equated the positive functions of the social contract with the negative features of wage restraint ... .' In September Congress endorsed the twelve-month rule.

The financial side of the economy continued to recover at an astonishing pace. The current account of the balance of payments moved into substantial surplus (£400 m. seasonally adjusted) in the third quarter. Money poured into the reserves: £3.2 bn in the first quarter, £1.2 bn in the second and £3.3 bn in the third. By the end of October the reserves stood at £20.2 bn, almost four times their level at the end of 1976. From January until towards the end of July the exchange rate remained steady at just below $1.72. The stability of sterling and the accretions to the reserves reflected a deliberate policy of intervention, i.e. sterling selling. On 27 July, however, the dollar weakened and the focus of intervention policy switched to the effective rate for sterling; the rate against the dollar was allowed to rise, and rose 2 cents immediately. By Friday 28 October it had reached $1.7772. Domestically, MLR had come down to 5 per cent in mid-October, Domestic Credit Expansion was well below the IMF ceiling and the growth of the money supply, sterling M3, despite the creation of sterling that was the concomitant of intervention policy, and because of heavy sales of gilts, was within its target range, although accelerating.

Against this background, and with unemployment at 1.4 million, the Chancellor introduced, on 26 October, a package of reflationary measures worth £1 bn in the current financial year and £2 bn in 1978–79, of which £1 bn was increased public expenditure. Most of the remaining stimulus came from increased personal allowances against tax.[35] The measures, brought in ten months after the IMF package of December 1976, were made possible because the PSBR, estimated in March at £8.5 bn (after Budget changes) for 1977–78, was now put £2 bn lower. (This implied that the pre-Budget forecast of £7.4 bn should have been about £5.5 bn, just about half the estimate given to the IMF in November.) The October measures raised the PSBR to an estimated £7.5 bn in 1977–78 and £7 bn in 1978–79.

The complete turnaround in the United Kingdom's external and internal position meant that Mr Healey could, if he wished, have kissed the IMF goodbye. He chose not to do so. He announced that the next drawing, available at the end of November, would not be taken up, but that the stand-by would be kept in place until its expiry date at the end of 1978.

The uncapping of sterling

'Give the Treasury mandarins a problem', said Joe Haines, 'and they will turn it into a crisis.'[36] In the late summer and autumn of 1977 the Treasury had a problem, a conflict between exchange rate and monetary policy. There had been massive inflows of foreign currency into sterling; because the policy was to maintain the exchange rate stable, these inflows were absorbed into the reserves, that is to say the foreign exchange was bought by the authorities with borrowed sterling; it was feared, particularly by the monetarist commentators and analysts, of whom the City took much note, that this creation of sterling threatened the monetary ceiling. The Treasury feared that if the market's fears were realized, that is, if the monetary ceiling were exceeded, this would weaken confidence in sterling and foreign exchange would flow out, and the exchange rate weaken. Therefore, some in the Treasury argued, it was necessary to 'take the cap off sterling', to cease creating pounds to buy foreign currency, and to let the exchange rate rise to its natural level as determined by the market.

Now while the potential – and it was only ever potential – conflict between exchange rate policy and monetary policy was unwelcome, it was clearly a problem that, left to itself would solve itself. For there were only two possibilities: if the monetary targets were exceeded then either confidence in sterling would weaken, or it would not. If it did not there was no problem. If it did, and sterling flowed out (or failed to flow in) then the exchange rate would fall, the need for intervention would disappear, no more pounds need be created, the money supply would cease to grow (all other things being equal) and the problem would go away.[37]

Although there was no real problem, the continued inflow of
currency and the strength of sterling had created a choice: we
could either keep the cap on sterling, which would have the
advantages of building up the reserves and keeping the exchange
rate more competitive than it would otherwise have been; or we
could take the cap off, which (if sterling did in fact rise) would
have the advantage of making imports cheaper and helping the
fight against inflation (which had been severely hit by the fall in the
exchange rate in 1976); it would also make the money supply
more easily controllable and take some pressure off interest rates.
It was a matter of deciding priorities.

On Monday 31 October the cap was taken off, but not without
controversy. *The Times*, in its leading article on the day following
the uncapping, referred to ' ... differences of opinion between
politicians of both main parties, between economists and between
officials, both in the Treasury and the Bank of England'. *The
Observer* (6 Nov. 1977) said the decision 'was taken only after a
major rift within the Treasury ... ' and it was ' ... being stressed
that, although the move was an agreed one in the end, it was
against the known position of Sir Douglas Wass, the Permanent
Secretary to the Treasury'. Quite who should want to stress this
and why was not made clear.

The story of the uncapping may be pieced together from the
newspaper reports of political and economic journalists quoting
the usual informed sources.[38] The money supply figures published
on 20 October (but known, in substance, a week earlier) showed
growth at an annual rate of around 13 per cent. The Governor of
the Bank of England, speaking at the Lord Mayor's dinner that
evening, noted the 'crucial importance' of monetary restraint and
said that there must be no wavering in the resolve to bring
inflation down well into single figures and 'this must require the
continued assurance and discipline of living within appropriate
monetary limits. I see it as one of my prime purposes and, indeed,
as a duty for me and the Bank to ensure that we continue to do
so.' This left little doubt which side of the debate the Governor
was on.

A Cabinet meeting on Monday 24 October to discuss the
package of economic measures to be announced on Wednesday
26 October rejected the idea of including in the package a
relaxation of exchange controls on outward investment. The
Financial Times (leading article 1 Nov.) saw this as 'the immediate
cause' of the decision to uncap. Uncapping was not discussed in
Cabinet, probably because of a fear of leaks, but the Prime

Minister may have consulted two or three senior ministers. With the exchange control option counted out, some contingency planning would have been necessary for possible action after the results of Wednesday's economic package had been seen.

Reports agree that the final decision to uncap was made on the afternoon of Friday 28 October at a meeting held by the Prime Minister and attended by Mr Healey, Mr Lever, Mr Gordon Richardson and senior officials, including Sir Douglas Wass. The decision was to remove the cap on Monday 31 October and to announce it once there was sufficient pressure on sterling to make it manifest.

On Sunday 30 October *The Observer* carried an 'Exclusive' by William Keegan and Adrian Hamilton saying that the Government was about to allow the pound to rise by perhaps 5 per cent (about 9 cents). In the early hours of Monday upward pressure on sterling developed in Far Eastern markets and the Bank of England withheld support. At 8.0 a.m. the Treasury released a statement to the news agencies which explained the situation and concluded, rather primly, 'In these circumstances the Bank of England's intervention policies will be adjusted accordingly.' Sterling rose by over 6 cents to close at £1.84, exactly one year and three days since, on 28 October 1976, it had fallen to its lowest ever level of $1.555. A year, as Mr Wilson might have said, is a short time on the foreign exchange markets.

On Monday morning (31 October) most of the London Press followed up Keegan and Hamilton's story. 'Sterling rate may go up' (*Daily Telegraph*); 'Pressure rises for early exchange rate decision' (*Financial Times*); 'Cabinet shift puts heat on sterling' (*Guardian*); 'A lift for the Pound?' (*Daily Express*); 'Perky £ set for a leap' (*Daily Mail*); 'Denis will take brakes off the £' (*Sun*).

After nearly four years in which Mr Healey and his policies had been under almost continuous abuse from sections of the Press it was unnerving, next day, to find his decision to let the pound rise greeted with almost unanimous approval. The *Daily Telegraph* so far forgot itself as to head its lead story 'A Wise Decision'. This was worrying. The one exception was the *Daily Express* which ran an implausible lead story – 'Healey Fury but £ Soars' – that Mr Healey had been 'voted down' by the Prime Minister and the Governor. The only serious criticism was that the move came too late.

The surge in sterling was short-lived; by the end of the week the rate was back to $1.80[39] and by the end of November it was below $1.82, over 2 cents down on the October close. But thereafter it rose, to average $1.920 in 1978, $2.122 in 1979, $2.328 in 1980 and $2.025 in 1981.

The uncapping of sterling was referred to by some as 'floating sterling', 'letting the pound go free'. This was a misconception. The Treasury had made it as clear as it could that it still preferred 'stability', and what it had specifically announced was that intervention policies would be adjusted. This did not mean that there would be no intervention; it was a compromise between stability and letting the market have more of its way – 'dirty floating', as the jargon has it.

The significance of the uncapping of sterling was not that sterling was allowed to rise but that the growth in the money supply was not. For the first time the monetary objective had become an *overriding* objective: it had overridden the other policy objective of export-led growth, the instrument for which was a competitive exchange rate. Whether this was because the authorities now acknowledged the sanctity of monetary numbers out of conviction or because they believed the markets believed in them, is another question.

If the decision to uncap had been controversial, the way in which that decision was taken became even more so. Brian Sedgemore (1980) tells how he learnt about the decisive meeting of 28 October from one of those present.

> The decision taken at that meeting was so important that I could hardly believe my ears when Tony Benn said he had not known about it, had not subsequently been told about it and that the Cabinet had not been informed of the decision that had been taken. In fact no members of the Cabinet other than those present were ever officially told that the meeting was taking place or afterwards that it had taken place ... The decision they took was that the devaluation strategy of earlier years was over and that in future economic policies should be aimed at allowing the pound to appreciate. The meeting in effect confirmed, unknown to the Cabinet, a complete U-turn in economic policy.

Mr Sedgemore listed the incident as an example of the secrecy of Government and the illegitimate use of power by the Civil Service. Accordingly the matter was put to Sir Douglas Wass (one of those present at the meeting) in the discussion that followed his 1983 Reith Lectures. He was asked whether it should have been a more widespread decision. He replied: 'In principle, it should. Here was an extremely important macro-economic decision which had very big implications for employment and inflation and, indeed, many would say, that although it was taken in 1977, its effects were felt in 1979 and 1980 and we all had to live with the consequences.' He went on to point out the need for secrecy and security in exchange rate matters and the danger of leaks from a Cabinet.

Sir Douglas's reply is interesting. It confirms (does not deny) the manner in which the final decision was made; and that it was indeed, as Mr Sedgemore believed, an extremely important decision. His remark that 'we all had to live with the consequences' might suggest that he may not have thought it a wholly wise decision.

The whole uncapping saga would, if the facts could be known, form an interesting case history of decision-making in Whitehall, or 'How Economic Policy is Made'. For once, there was a clear-cut choice between two conflicting policies; in the narrow sense between objectives for the money supply and for the exchange rate; and in the broader sense (and if you believed in monetarist theory) between inflation and export-led growth. There was, we are told, disagreement both within and between the Treasury and the Bank; it would be fascinating to know how these disagreements were resolved to the point where positive official advice could be given to the Chancellor by his Permanent Secretary. The Chancellor himself, having recently come through a traumatic year, had, so it may seem, his economic foot in one camp and his political foot in another, a stance perhaps not unfamiliar to Chancellors.

The Prime Minister was advised by a minister who wanted the cap off, yet, distrustful of the Treasury,[40] was not going to be rushed into anything; and would not let the Cabinet decide. From such evidence as we have from the Press it appears that in the end the Prime Minister was swayed by the alliance of Mr Lever, Mr Healey and the Governor. Sir Douglas Wass was personally, but not, apparently, professionally, against uncapping, and would support his Chancellor's position. Neither the Governor nor Sir Douglas would have a vote if, indeed, anything so formal as a vote were to be taken. The Cabinet, not having been consulted, voted against the one measure – the relaxation of exchange controls – which might have made uncapping unnecessary. One wonders how many of those who voted against relaxation knew the probable consequences of their action.

Splitting the Treasury

Early in 1977 the General Sub-Committee of the Expenditure

Committee conducted an inquiry into the Civil Service. One live issue discussed was the proposal to split the Treasury by hiving off the public expenditure side and combining it with the Civil Service Department into a separate Department, or Ministry, of the Budget. Not surprisingly the Chancellor and Treasury officials were opposed to this. The Chancellor was particularly annoyed by evidence seemingly in favour of a split given to the Sub-Committee by Sir John Hunt, the Cabinet Secretary. Mr Healey assumed he would not have done this without Prime Ministerial approval; and, indeed, the Prime Minister was not opposed to a split. Mr Healey made it known to the Prime Minister that, in the event of a split, he would feel unable to remain as Chancellor.[41]

An exodus of mandarins

Within a few months in the first half of 1977 the Treasury lost four of its top five mandarins. Derek Mitchell went to the City, Alan Lord into industry, Leo Pliatzky went to be Permanent Secretary at the Department of Trade, and Bryan Hopkin, who had been employed part time since September 1976, returned full time to his chair of economics at Cardiff. The Treasury was mildly embarrassed by speculation about the reasons behind the departure of so much top brass within so short a period; but the exodus did relieve a promotion block; and the waters quickly closed over the departing figures.

The economy in 1977

North Sea Oil came on-stream in significant quantities. The balance of payments on current account, which had moved into substantial surplus in the third quarter, continued in surplus in the fourth quarter, and for the year as a whole was all but in balance for the first time since 1972. At year end the reserves stood at $20.6 bn and the pound at $1.92. MLR was 7 per cent. Unemployment was 1.4 million (6%) but had fallen for three successive months. The rate of inflation had fallen in five successive months to 12.1 per cent in December (and was to fall below 10 per cent in January). Average earnings increased in December (year on year) by 10.7 per cent. In 1977 as a whole prices increased 15.8 per cent and earnings 10.2 per cent, implying a sharp fall in real personal disposable income, which had been static for three years; but it fell by only about 1.25 per cent, sustained by tax cuts.

1978

Towards winter's rages

The Public Expenditure White Paper published in January 1978[42] showed the full extent of the fall in expenditure in 1976–77. In that year expenditure on programmes excluding debt interest was less than in 1975–76 by nearly 3.5 per cent; and the out-turn of programmes was less than planned, at 1977 survey prices, by £2.25 bn or just over 4 per cent.

Expenditure in 1977–78 on programmes and debt interest was estimated to be 2.8 per cent down on 1976–77; and expenditure on programmes was estimated to be 4.5 per cent below plans. Debt interest was also estimated to be significantly below the provision.

Expenditure planned for 1978–79 (programmes, contingency reserve and debt interest) was only slightly above that for 1975–76; but, largely because of the underspending in the two intervening years, the 1978–79 total was 8.2 per cent up on the out-turn for the preceding year – an increase likely to alarm the financial markets. The figure does not appear in the White Paper. In a neat bit of sleight of hand the Treasury revised the definition of public expenditure (for quite respectable reasons) and then compared 1978–79 plans with 1977–78 *plans*, arriving at an increase of 2.2 per cent. However, expenditure on programmes alone in 1978–79 was planned to be marginally below the figure for 1975–76, and this was in line with the spirit of the Letter of Intent of December 1976 which had stated 'The planned level for 1978–79 will also be about 1 per cent below that for 1975–76.' Public expenditure figures do need to be looked at rather carefully.

On the day following publication the *Guardian* headlined 'Chaotic spending figures leave Treasury bemused', and said that the White Paper was 'a work of exemplary obfuscation'; it was hopelessly unclear which figures were real figures, which plans and which daydreams.

At the end of January the Chancellor announced the Government's intention to repay early $1 bn to the IMF. This had no bearing on the stand-by, on which no drawing had been made since August 1977 and of which over half remained undrawn.

Exchange control

Early in April the trial began at the Old Bailey of a Bank of England official, and others, all of whom pleaded not guilty to charges of conspiring to obtain money dishonestly by manipulating the exchange control regulations. 'The £1 million bank fiddle', the *Daily Mail* called it. The allegation against the Bank official was that he had provided a blanket authorization which constituted 'a licence to print money', declaring that certain non-existent securities qualified for the 'dollar premium'.

The Budget

Chancellors of the Exchequers now feel much more free than formerly to talk about their forthcoming Budgets. Talking to the Parliamentary Labour Party early in February, Mr Healey had thought aloud about what he might be able to do in his spring Budget. The Parliamentary press are not admitted to these meetings and rely on reports from those present. Mr Healey had obviously been somewhat ambiguous, for 'Chancellor planning big Budget stimulus' said *The Times*; and 'Healey paves the way for cautious Budget' said the *Guardian*.

In his Statement[43] Mr Healey declared that the 'first purpose' of his Budget was 'to encourage a level of economic activity sufficient to get unemployment moving significantly down'. Yet the central economic forecasts that accompanied the Budget showed GDP growing at an annual rate of 2.5 per cent from the second half of 1977 up to the first half of 1979. Given the conventional assumption that the underlying rate of productive potential was around 3 per cent, this was scarcely enough to move unemployment significantly downwards. However, an alternative forecast, called 'Variant with stronger trade performance' showed growth of 4 per cent from the first half of 1978 to the first half of 1979. No information was given of a 'Variant with weaker trade performance'. Tax reliefs of £2,585 m. in a full year were almost entirely concentrated on direct taxes, the biggest single item being the introduction under pressure from the TUC of a lower (25%) rate band of tax on the first £750, at a cost of £1,569 m. None of this was tied to a pay deal of any sort. The Chancellor expressed his belief that 'by using tax cuts to increase the real value of the pay packet during the coming year I can encourage further moderation in pay settlements ... '; and, for the third year running, he published detailed tables showing the effects of tax cuts on families in different circumstances. He also spelled out what was required: 'We shall be unable to prevent our rate of inflation from rising significantly next year unless we can achieve much lower levels of increase in wage costs than we have achieved this year.' There would be discussion with both sides of industry.

In addition to the tax stimulus the Chancellor raised public expenditure by £500 m.; this did not, however, *count* as an increase in public expenditure, since he took it all out of the contingency reserve, already included in the public expenditure total.

That the Chancellor was able to inject as much stimulus as he did and yet remain within the ceilings agreed with the IMF was because, once again, the Treasury had got its forecasts of the Public Sector Borrowing Requirement badly wrong. At the time of the 1977 Budget the forecast for 1977–78 was £8.5 bn. In 'Economic Prospects to end 1978' published at the end of October 1977, this was reduced to £7.5 bn. By the time of the 1978 Budget, and despite expansionary measures through the year, the estimate was down to £5.7 bn. In the Letter of Intent the Chancellor had said that he would take fiscal action to bring the PSBR for 1978–79 'down to £8.6 bn in nominal terms'. In the event he was able to take fiscal action to raise it by £2.8 bn to £8.5 bn.

The Statement was notable for the emphasis laid on monetary policy. Because the balance of payments had moved into surplus, the focus of policy was to be shifted from Domestic Credit Expansion (DCE) to sterling M3, for which a system of rolling targets would be introduced.[44] The target would be rolled forward once every six months. For 1978–79 it was 8–12 per cent, with DCE below the £6 bn in the Letter of Intent.

The run-up to the Budget had been accompanied by warnings from the monetarist commentators, notably Greenwells the stockbrokers, and *The Times*, about the growth of liquidity. Greenwells warned that we had already seen the beginnings of a monetary explosion like that of 1972. Tim Congdon, in *The Times*, argued for a *lower* Budget deficit on the grounds that a high deficit *and* monetary targets would starve the private sector of funds (the 'crowding out' thesis); the *Financial Times*, less extreme in its monetarism, warned that the Chancellor would be addressing a suspicious City audience and that he had to take account of market opinion. And he did; late in the day, after the major Budget decisions had been taken, he raised MLR by 1 point, to 7.5 per cent ('the formula' having been suspended in October) as a sort of insurance policy, or pre-emptive strike, against a bad reception of the Budget by domestic and foreign market opinion. The 1978 Budget was dominated by fiscal and monetary constraints. The post-Budget consensus, at least on the monetarist side, was that the Chancellor had had his way on the fiscal side and the Bank on

the monetary side; and that the two might not be compatible,
leading to higher interest rates.

The 1978 Budget may be used to illustrate the importance the
Treasury placed on monitoring and influencing media opinion. In
the ten days following the Budget the Press Office produced over
20 pages of Press analysis. As was customary, the Chancellor met
the Parliamentary Lobby in the House of Commons immediately
after his Statement, recorded a radio interview for North America,
and went on to make his Budget broadcast.[45] On Wednesday he
did a radio 'phone-in' in the morning, had lunch with *The
Economist* at No. 11, and drinks with the *Guardian* in the evening.
On Thursday he gave lunch to the *Financial Times* and evening
drinks to the *Daily Mirror*, both at No. 11. On Friday he appeared
on the 'Jimmy Young Show', had the *Sunday Times* to lunch and
The Observer to coffee.

The money markets

Over the first five months of the year 'confidence' weakened,
partly because the balance of payments on current account, which
had been in £1 bn surplus in the second half of 1977, had
unexpectedly moved into a £300 m. deficit in the first quarter. In
April the pound lost 5 cents, down to $1.825 (it had been $1.95 at
the end of January), despite very heavy intervention by the Bank
of England. Partly as a result of this intervention the reserves fell
by $.3.3 bn in April. The Treasury thought it prudent to steer the
Press to expect this and did succeed in modifying the effect of the
announcement. Between the end of January and the end of April
the reserves fell by $3.8 bn.

The main worries, however, were related to the money supply.
Early in the year it had seemed that the growth of the money
supply would be within the target range of 9–13 per cent but,
surprisingly and disappointingly, it reached 16 per cent in the year
to mid-April. Part of this excess growth was purely statistical,
arising from the Bank of England's annual revision of its seasonal
adjustments. It is difficult for the authorities to mop up excess
money which exists only in the minds of the seasonal adjusters.[46]
To meet the problem MLR was raised, as we have seen, to 7.5 per
cent in the Budget and, in two stages, to 9 per cent by 12 May. On
25 May the Bank of England announced that the formula for
setting MLR, which had been suspended, was to be abolished and
in future the rate would be determined entirely by administrative

decision. Announcements of the rate would be made, at 12.30 p.m. on a Thursday, only when the rate changed.

In the latter part of May the markets expected a further rise in MLR and the institutions withheld purchases of gilt-edged. This sort of action, known, in its extreme form, as 'a gilt-edge strike', makes life very difficult for the authorities.[47] It can occur at any time, but the publication of monetary targets makes it more likely. One can almost formulate a 'law' which says that if there is a monetary target to which the authorities are committed, then the nearer the growth of the money supply approaches the upper limit of that target, the more likely it is to overshoot. This is because it is known, and it is known that the authorities know, that if the growth of the money supply exceeds the target, there will be a loss of confidence; to prevent this the authorities will raise interest rates; therefore it is foolish to buy gilts until the interest rate does rise – and stockbrokers will, legitimately, give this advice to their clients. 'At times', said the *Financial Times* in a leading article on 16 June 1978, 'we appear to have government by brokers' circulars.' The result is that money which could go to the purchase of gilts remains in the bank accounts of the institutions and other potential purchasers and swells (or does not reduce) the money supply. Thus the fear that the growth of the money supply might exceed its target proves self-fulfilling. Published targets for the money supply are not neutral: once published they are distorted by market behaviour.[48]

To the anxieties about the money supply a new factor was added, in the shape of Opposition amendments to the Finance Bill which reduced revenue and raised the PSBR by £500 m.[49] On 8 June the Chancellor took action to correct the situation. To offset the fall in tax revenue and preserve the limit on the PSBR, the National Insurance Surcharge was raised 2½ percentage points from 2 October; and to bring the money supply back, MLR was raised to 10 per cent and the Supplementary Special Deposits Scheme re-activated.

The Chancellor was cross about the whole episode, feeling that he had been forced into an unnecessary mini-crisis by the perversity of Parliament and the fears of the money market. He reacted quickly, saying, in effect, 'Right, if you want to play silly beggars with my Budget, in which I did my best and made massive tax cuts, you must take the consequences. I am not going to have my overall strategy imperilled.'

The fact that he had secured his PSBR and confirmed his commitment to his money supply target was not by itself likely to

be enough to get the gilts market moving again; he had to let the
market have its way over the rate of interest.

While the Government's displeasure with the gilts market was
understandable, the episode does illustrate the vulnerability of a
policy that relied on heavy borrowing. With unemployment at
what was then considered the intolerably high level of 1.4 million,
the Government had little choice but to try to expand the
economy within the limits available to it under the Letter of Intent,
especially if it was to have any hope of another round of pay
restraint later in the year. This meant a high PSBR; but the
Government also had a monetary target. If both objectives were
to be achieved, a high level of sales of Government debt was
essential, and to that extent the Government was a prisoner of the
market. The only way out of this dilemma was to have a much
smaller PSBR – but this was not an option open to the
Government at this time. To put it another way, only a high rate
of interest could reconcile their borrowing and money supply
objectives (aided, in this case, by a restriction on the creation of
private sector credit by the re-activation of 'the corset'). Mr
Healey was not happy to see the interest rate 50 per cent higher
than it had been on Budget morning; but had he not acted
promptly the situation would have smouldered on and erupted
into a possibly worse crisis later in the year.

Pay policy

The previous year the Government had set a guideline of 10 per
cent in the growth of earnings. In the middle of 1978 average
earnings were rising at 13–14 per cent but, aided by a high
exchange rate, the rate of inflation had fallen to 7.4 per cent, from
17.7 per cent in the previous June. (As it turned out this was its
low point; it did not again fall below 7.4 per cent for over four
years, until September 1982. At that time (1978) the 'tax and price
index' had not been invented; when that index was constructed,
backdated and published, it showed an increase in June 1978 over
June 1977 of 1.5 per cent, reflecting the substantial tax cuts made
by Mr Healey. June 1978 proved to be the low point for that index
too. It has never since shown a year-on-year increase as small as
that.)

By the middle of 1978, therefore, earnings were increasing at
over twice the rate of retail prices and over ten times as fast as the
increase in prices-plus-taxes (although this was not demonstrated
by any index then available). Real take-home pay was increasing

substantially. Real personal disposable income in the second quarter was 7.5 per cent higher than a year before.

Against this background the Government published, in July 1978, its White Paper *Winning the Battle Against Inflation* (Cmnd 7293). It outlined the progress made, at some sacrifice, stated the need to build on success and reduce the rate of inflation further, and said 'The Government has therefore decided to adopt a pay policy to apply from 1 August 1978 in which the guideline will be set at 5 per cent.' The White Paper conceded that 'This may seem an ambitious objective.' It was too ambitious for the TUC, which, in September, rejected it.

In an interview in *The Observer* on 2 September 1984, TUC General Secretary Mr Len Murray blamed Mr Callaghan for the 'Winter of discontent' that followed. Mr Callaghan, he said, 'was over-impressed by the quality of the Treasury printout and started thinking with his head rather than his stomach'. Mr Murray insisted that the TUC could have held pay deals to around 8 or 9 per cent if the Government had been prepared to bargain.

Thinking with our head, let's see how it looked from the Treasury end. In its November Economic Statement the Treasury *assumed* that pay settlements would be around 5 per cent with earnings of around 7 per cent. It was made clear that this was a forecasting *assumption* and *not* a central forecast (which, by implication, was something different but undisclosed). On the basis of that assumption the Treasury forecast that the rate of inflation would be 'between 8 and 9 per cent in 1979', i.e. higher than it was in 1978, when settlements and earnings were much *higher* than the assumption. Now the Treasury's short-term price forecasts are among their better forecasts. So it followed that settlements very little above the 5 per cent assumption would push the rate of inflation back into double figures; and Mr Murray's 8 or 9 per cent would certainly have done so. It should be remembered that an earnings increase of 7 per cent on top of the tax reductions already made would have kept the increase in take-home pay ahead of the increase in prices. The Government's guidelines did not require a drop in real take-home pay.

The year end

At the end of October the Government announced a further prepayment of $1 bn to the IMF, bringing total prepayments by the public sector in 1978 to $3.5 bn. The pound ended the month at $2.08, having touched $2.10.

The raising of MLR to 10 per cent in June had enabled the

Government to sell large amounts of gilts; and there was an expectation that interest rates would fall. From September, however, they began to rise, in response to a rise in American rates and reflecting fears that the TUC's rejection of the Government's pay guidelines would force the Government to rely, in its fight against inflation, more on the monetary weapon. By the end of October market rates were well above the 10 per cent MLR, and the Government was obliged to act. On 9 November it raised MLR to 12.5 per cent, and, following its policy of rolling targets, extended the 8–12 per cent target for the money supply to October 1979. So large a rise in MLR was rather more than required to validate market rates; and it was not required for the purpose of controlling the money supply, for in the five months to the banking month of October (the latest figures then available) sterling M3 had grown at an annual rate of only 6.1 per cent, below the bottom end of the target range. The official explanation was that it demonstrated the Government's determination to adhere to its monetary targets, and it was prudent to err on the side of caution. The rate stayed at 12.5 per cent until 9 February 1979 when it was raised to 14 per cent.

It had been widely expected that Mr Callaghan would call an election in October, but he chose not to do so. In mid-December the Government was defeated on pay sanctions policy and announced that action would no longer be taken against firms in breach of the policy. Since the policy had all along been supported by sanctions against employers, not employees, the Government was left with a pay policy, rejected by the Labour Party and the TUC, which it had no means of enforcing in the private sector. The way was open for a return to that free collective bargaining advocated by the opposition on both sides of the House and demanded by the unions. Pay demands considerably above the Government's 5 per cent were made[50] and, if not at first conceded, were enforced by strikes and stoppages, many of them, unofficial, and by secondary picketing. The country entered upon the period that became infamous as 'the winter of discontent.'

1979

Snatching defeat

The White Paper *The Government's Expenditure Plans 1970–80 to 1982–83* (Cmnd 7439), published in January 1979, showed expenditure rising by 2 per cent per annum in volume terms over the next four years, within, or no higher than, the expected growth of GDP. Expenditure in 1976–77 and 1977–78 had fallen by, respectively, 2.6 and 7.2 per cent; and was estimated to have risen by 6.2 per cent in 1978–79.

Table 2 of the White Paper revalued the *planning* totals for 1977–78 and 1978–79 at the latest (1978) survey prices and compared them with estimated *out-turn* to show an underspending of £4.3 bn in the first year and £2 bn in the second. On the face of it, the actual, and accidental, fall in public expenditure in 1977–78 was five times the £1 bn (excluding the sale of BP shares) negotiated with the IMF after seven weeks of trauma at the end of 1976.[51] Forecasting and control errors of this magnitude make a nonsense of the whole laborious PESC exercise (see Ch. 10). A spending minister may be less than wholly convinced of the absolute necessity for a £25 m. cut in his own programme (which may represent a significant proportion of the whole) when he is aware that the whole thing may turn out to be several billions adrift.

The great gilts fiasco

On 9 February MLR was raised 1½ points to 14 per cent to get the gilts market moving again. A week later the Bank of England announced the sale of £1,300 m. of Treasury stock at £96 per £100 nominal to give a yield of around 14 per cent. It was a part-paid issue,[52] only £15 being payable on application.

When lists opened and closed on Thursday 22 February there occurred one of the biggest fiascos in the gilts market for many years. It was expected that the issue would go to an immediate premium and this would have attracted the stags[53] anyway. But to add to the attraction Government was in effect financing the stags by lending them £81 per £100 of nominal stock. The issue was ten times oversubscribed, that is, there were applications totalling some £13 bn. The trouble was that because it already had far more than it needed, the Bank closed its shutters one minute after they opened, leaving a queue of brokers' clerks and messengers clutching applications on behalf of their clients. The stock did, as expected, go to a premium of about £3, to yield a profit for the stags of some £40 m. on an outlay of £195 m. Pricing a new issue is a matter of judgement. In this case the Bank of England got it badly wrong, at a cost to the tax-payer, in terms of a higher-than-necessary rate of interest, estimated at between £30 and £50 m. annually for many years. The incident caused dissatisfaction not

only in the Treasury and the Bank and among leading
commentators, but even in the City itself, where some brokers
talked 'of the gilts market reduced to a disorderly casino in which
idiots can make money as readily as the sagest analysts'.[54] The
Grand Old Duke of York began to march his troops down the hill
again on 2 March when MLR was reduced to 13 per cent.

The *Guardian* '£800 million loss' story

On 28 February 1979 the *Guardian* carried a lead news story by
Jane McLoughlin, 'Explosive Treasury analysis shows seven
schemes sabotaging present and future economic growth. £800 m.
losses predicted for ('job') projects.'

The story was about a 'secret document' sent by Sir Douglas
Wass, Permanent Secretary to the Treasury, to Sir Peter Carey,
Permanent Secretary at the Department of Industry, with a copy
to Sir Kennett Beril, Head of the Central Policy Review Staff
(the 'Think Tank'). The essence of the letter, which invited
comments, was that on investment of £1.3 to 1.4 bn in seven listed
programmes there was a prospective loss, in national income
terms, of some £800 m. It was, therefore, an expensive way of
creating jobs. In his letter Sir Douglas said 'Either we must accept
the unsatisfactory macro-economic performance that goes with
the acceptance of the projects quoted; or we must try to find
some means of influencing the decision-making process so as to
ensure a higher rejection rate in the future.'

It was all most embarrassing for the Treasury and for No. 10.
Here was the head of the Treasury criticizing the policies of a
Labour Government and apparently inviting one of his colleagues
to join him in thwarting such policies in the future. It was just what
left-wing critics of the Civil Service, and of the Treasury in
particular, had always suspected. Sir Douglas met this allegation
head-on in his 1983 Reith Lectures: his correspondance with Sir
Peter Carey was 'only a skirmishing, a reconnaissance if you like,
as a preliminary to my submitting the issue to my own Minister to
whom I was able to give a conspectus of the sort of opposition he
would encounter from his colleagues if he decided to act on my
advice.' The critics might still enquire whether Sir Douglas's
'reconnaissance' required him to invite a colleague in a key
position to join him in finding ways to 'ensure a higher rejection
rate' of ministerial schemes of job creation. That evening (28 Feb.)
the Chancellor went on BBC television's 'Nationwide' to defend
the Government's support for loss-making industries; and the
Treasury took the unusual step of circulating the transcript of the

interview the next day (with the BBC's permission).[55] The Press
followed up the story the next day with the added suggestion that
the Treasury was boosting the PSBR estimate for 1979–80 to
frighten ministers into public expenditure cuts or tax increases.

The reserves and sterling

It had been decided to revalue the reserves annually at the end of
March in accordance with a formula that related the price of gold
to the free market price. The first revaluation at the end of March
1979 increased the reserves by $4.5 bn.

The pound had been gaining strength steadily from the end of
January and was particularly strong towards the end of March.
The Bank of England had been intervening fairly heavily to
moderate the rise, but early in April it changed its tactics and on
10 April the effective rate[56] rose to 68.0, its highest since April
1976, with the dollar at $2.1028.

At the end of April the Government announced the early
repayment of $1 bn to the IMF.

Defeat

The Government, having been defeated on a vote of confidence at
the end of March, introduced a 'care and maintenance' Budget in
April, and called a General Election for 3 May. The Conservatives
were returned with a majority of 43. It looked as if the unions were
going to be granted what they had so long demanded, a return to
free collective bargaining; and so it turned out. There would be no
more beer and sandwiches at No. 10.

Mr Healey

Mr Healey took over an economy that was in a dreadful state:
industrial strife, a three-day week, inflation running at 13 per cent
and rising. Most serious of all, the balance of payments on current
account was in deficit at an annual rate of £4 bn, ten times bigger
than that inherited by Mr Callaghan in 1964. And that deficit did
not yet reflect the fourfold increase in oil prices at the end of the
previous year. Domestic Credit Expansion was nearly £8 bn, and
the year-on-year growth in the money supply 23 per cent. The
Public Sector Borrowing Requirement was running at close to
£4 bn a year.

Between 1974 and 1978 the balance of payments in current

account moved from a deficit of £3.3 bn to a surplus of £1.2 bn despite a deficit on oil in those years of £15 bn. With the help of the trade union leaders Mr Healey brought the rate of growth of wages and salaries down from 30 per cent to 7.5 per cent in two years, partly by his innovation of linking wage settlements to tax relief. Real personal disposable income fell during this period but between the second quarter of 1977 and the first quarter of 1979 it rose by 17 per cent. Unemployment fell in 1978 and 1979. Mr Healey was probably the only Chancellor to devise an incomes policy that reduced both the rate of inflation and unemployment.

Mr Healey introduced monetary targets and brought the money supply and credit expansion back under control. He introduced cash limits for the control of public spending and (helped by shortfall) controlled it so successfully that in 1978–79 it was lower, in real terms, than it had been in 1974–75. As a proportion of GDP it fell from 46.5 to 41.5 per cent.

Budgets and 'measures'

It is part of the Healey mythology that he introduced a large number of Budgets and 'Mini-Budgets'. In five years as Chancellor he introduced seven Budgets, the last a holding Budget, and made eight other major economic statements. It was not, especially in the circumstances of the time, an excessive number. Details are below.

1.	26 March 1974	Budget (Finance Act 1974)
2.	22 July 1974	Economic Measures
3.	12 November 1974	Budget (Finance Act 1975)
4.	15 April 1975	Budget (Finance (No. 2) Act 1975)
5.	11 July 1975	First phase of pay policy: Cash limits
6.	19 February 1976	First of three batches of public expenditure cuts in 1976
7.	6 April 1976	Budget (Finance Act 1976)
8.	22 July 1976	Further public expenditure cuts
9.	15 December 1976	Further public expenditure cuts
10.	29 March 1977	Budget (Finance Act 1977)
11.	15 July 1977	Pay policy Phase 3, and other measures
12.	26 October 1977	Economic measures (Finance (Income Tax Relief) Act 1977. 2 clauses only)
13.	11 April 1978	Budget
14.	8 June 1978	Monetary measures. National Insurance Surcharge raised.
15.	3 April 1979	'Care and maintenance' Budget.

Given the magnitude of the task facing him when he took office Mr Healey's success in turning the economy round was very considerable. At the end of it there was not much joy for him; but perhaps he could take some comfort that he need

> Fear no more the heat o' the sun
> Nor the furious winter's rages;
> Thou thy worldly task hast done,
> Home art gone and ta'en thy wages:[57]

Except that it wasn't Mr Healey who had taken the wages; it was the shop-stewards and union militants who, in self-defeating pursuit of money wages, snatched defeat out of victory.

Diary of events March 1974–May 1979

1974

5 Mar.	Denis Winston Healey becomes Chancellor of the Exchequer.
9	Coal miners back to work. End of three-day week.
26	Budget.
19 Apr.	First tranche of £500 m. loan to building societies.
24 May	RPI triggers first three threshold payments.
13 Jun.	Oil facility established by IMF.
26	Herstatt bank collapses after heavy losses in foreign exchange dealing.
22 July.	Economic measures to counter inflation.
26	Pay Board abolished.
Aug.	Secondary banking crisis: criteria for 'Lifeboat' help tightened, and limit set to total.
8	Green Paper *Wealth Tax* (Cmnd 5704).
8	White Paper on *Capital Transfer Tax* (Cmnd 5705).
15	White Paper *Regeneration of British Industry* (Cmnd 5710).
2 Sept.	TUC accepts new pay guidelines.
10 Oct.	General Election. Labour majority of five. Healey continues as Chancellor.
12 Nov.	Second Budget.

20	RPI triggers final three threshold payments.
9 Dec.	Mr Healey visits Saudi Arabia.
18	Government rescues Crown Agents.
31	Government rescues Burmah Oil. Sterling guarantee arrangements expire.

1975

Jan.	Bank buys Burmah Oil's 21 per cent stake in BP.
30	*Public Expenditure to 1978–79* (Cmnd 5879) published.
28 Feb.	'Corset' suspended.
15 Apr.	Budget.
Jun.	Substantial pressure on sterling, especially during first week.
5–6	EEC Referendum.
11	First North Sea Oil, from Argyll field.
1 Jul.	'Cash Limits' introduced for the control of public expenditure.
11	White Paper *Attack on Inflation* (Cmnd 6151), £6 pay policy.
31 Aug.	The Group of Five (G5 – USA, UK, France, West Germany, Japan) agrees to abolish official gold price. IMF to sell 25 million ounces of gold.
24 Sept.	Measures to alleviate unemployment.
13 Oct.	Kuwait no longer to accept sterling for oil.
31	Measures to alleviate unemployment in the construction industry.
Nov.	Godley's 'missing millions'.
17 Dec.	Measures to alleviate unemployment.
31	Sterling ended year at $2.02 (from $2.34 on 3 Jan.)

1976

7–8 Jan.	Interim Committee of IMF agrees new regime for exchange rates, and gold.
13	Announced that IMF had approved UK credits of £975 m.
19 Feb.	White Paper *Public Expenditure to 1979–80* (Cmnd 6393).
4 Mar.	Sudden run on sterling, which falls below $2.
10–11	Government defeated in Public Expenditure debate but wins subsequent vote of confidence.
16	The Prime Minister, Mr Wilson, announces his resignation.
5 Apr.	Mr Callaghan becomes Prime Minister.
6	Budget. Broadly neutral. Some tax cuts made conditional on a reinforcement of pay policy. White Paper *Cash Limits on Public Expenditure* (Cmnd 6440).

22	Pound falls to $1.81.
end	Reserves down by over £1 bn following heavy intervention to support sterling.
5 May	Statement on pay policy, following agreement with TUC.
end	Pound closes at $1.76.
3 Jun.	Pound falls to record low of $1.7025
7	Chancellor announces £5.3 bn credit.
16	TUC Special Conference accepts pay policy.
17	Conditional tax reliefs formally implemented.
30	White Paper *The Attack on Inflation – The Second Year* (Cmnd 6507) (debated 6 Jul.)
22 Jul.	Public expenditure cuts of £1 bn in 1977–78 plus 2 percentage points on employers' National Insurance contributions from April 1977. Money supply expected to grow 12 per cent in 1976–77. PSBR to be cut to £9 bn.
1 Aug.	£2.50/5%/£4 pay policy into force.
end	No drawings on $5.3 bn credit during the month.
7–8 Sept.	Sterling under heavy pressure. Rate falls to $1.735 on withdrawal of support.
10	MLR raised by 1½ points to 13 per cent.
16	Call for Special Deposits.
27	Labour Party conference at Blackpool commences.
28	Pound falls to $1.63. Chancellor retreats from Heathrow.
29	Chancellor applies to IMF for $3.9 bn loan.
end	Pound recovers to $1.6675.
3–8 Oct.	IMF conference at Manila.
7	Formula suspended and MLR raised 2 points to 15 per cent. Further call for Special Deposits.
24	*Sunday Times* report that IMF wanted sterling down to $1.50.
25	Pound falls to $1.5950. Prime Minister on 'Panorama' speaks against sterling as a reserve currency.
28	Pound falls to record low of $1.5550 and closes at $1.57.
end	Pound closes at $1.5850.
1 Nov.	IMF team arrives.
5	Treasury presents short-term forecasts to IMF showing PSBR of £11 bn for 1977.
18	Bank announce re-introduction of Supplementary Special Deposit scheme (suspended 28 Feb. 1975).
29	Government withdraws from commitment to introduce Wealth Tax in this Parliament.

3 Dec.	Cabinet reaches agreement in principle to cut PSBR by £2 bn in 1977–78.
15	Package of measures, approved by IMF and reflected in Letter of Intent.
29	Pound rises to $1.7055, its highest for three months.

1977

11 Jan.	Agreement with BIS on sterling balances ($3 bn available from 8 Feb.).
24	$1.5 bn medium-term loan from group of British, North American and German banks.
27	*The Government's Expenditure Plans*, Vol. I (Cmnd 6721–I): the first to appear without an economic assessment.
25 Feb.	*The Government's Expenditure Plans*, Vol. II (Cmnd 6721–II).
17 Mar.	Government defeat leads to Lib–Lab pact.
29	Budget. Tax cuts of £1.5 bn of which about £1 bn conditional on pay agreement. White Paper *Cash Limits 1977–78* (Cmnd 6767).
4 Apr.	Details announced oif foreign currency bonds for holders of official sterling balances.
6	National Insurance Surcharge comes into effect at rate of 2 per cent.
5 May	5½p increase in petrol duty to be withdrawn (see 8 Aug.).
12	'Corset' extended for six months.
16	Treasury announce issue, on 27 May, of new variable-interest bond.
30	Bank to respond to bids for new variable-interest bond.
22 Jun.	TUC guidance to pay negotiators.
15 Jul.	Basic rate of tax to be 34 per cent. Stage 3 of incomes policy agreed.
27	Pound rises sharply to $1.7370 on change of intervention policy.
1 Aug.	Price Commission re-constituted.
8	Withdrawal of increased petrol duty becomes effective.
11	'Corset' suspended.
4 Oct.	Reserves in September rise by $2.32 bn to over $17 bn.
14	MLR down to 5 per cent.
26	Measures of increased public expenditure, and tax cuts.
31	Sterling uncapped, and rises 6 cents to $1.8405.
2 Nov.	Reserves in October rise $3.04 bn to a record $20.2 bn.

1 Dec.	Government not to take discretionary action against Ford for breach of pay code.
30	Sterling closes at $1.9185.

1978

4 Jan.	Pound rises to peak of $1.9933.
12	*The Goverment's Expenditure Plans 1978–79 to 1981–82* (Cmnd 7049 – I and II).
26	UK to make early repayment of $1 bn to IMF.
15 Feb.	Sir Douglas Wass, lecture to the Johnian Society, Cambridge.
17	January RPI shows inflation down below 10 per cent for the first time since October 1973.
21 Mar.	White Paper *The Challenge of North Sea Oil* (Cmnd 7143).
11 Apr.	Budget. Tax cuts. MLR up from 6.5 to 7.5 per cent. Rolling targets for money supply. *Cash Limits 1978–79* (Cmnd 7161) published.
end	Reserves fall by $3.3 bn.
8 May	Government defeated on Opposition amendment to Finance Bill.
25	MLR to be set by administrative action, instead of by formula.
8 Jun.	The 'Corset' reactivated. MLR raised to 10 per cent. National Insurance Surcharge raised 2½ percentage points.
5 Jul.	Government not to seek to reverse amendment to Finance Bill reducing basic rate of income tax to 33 per cent.
21	Government announce pay guidelines of 5 per cent for next pay round.
17 Aug.	The 'Corset' to be continued for a further 8 months.
6 Sept.	TUC reject 5 per cent pay policy.
30 Oct.	Early repayment of further $1 bn to IMF.
31	Pound rises to $2.10, closes at $2.0864.
9 Nov.	Chancellor announces 8–12 per cent monetary target for year from October. MLR raised from 10 to 12.5 per cent.
24	Green Paper *The European Monetary System* (Cmnd 7405).
5 Dec.	UK not to join proposed European Monetary System from 1 Jan. 1979.
13	Government defeated in debate on pay sanctions policy.
14	Action no longer to be taken against firms that breach the pay policy.

1979

16 Jan.	PM announces three developments in pay and prices policy: on comparability, price controls and cash underpinning for the low paid.
17	*The Government's Expenditure Plans 1979–80 to 1982–83* (Cmnd 7439) published.
9 Feb.	MLR raised to 14 per cent.
14	Joint statement by the Government and the Trades Union Congress *The Economy, the Government and Trade Union Responsibilities*.
22	The great gilts fiasco.
2 Mar.	MLR reduced to 13 per cent.
28	Government defeated on a vote of confidence.
end	Reserves to be revalued annually; end March revaluation adds $4.5 bn.
3 Apr.	'Care and maintenance' Budget.
6	Change of intervention tactics to stem currency inflow. Pound rises by over a cent. MLR reduced 1 point to 12 per cent.
end	Early repayment of $1 bn to IMF.
3 May	General Election. Conservative majority of 43.

Notes and references

1. Barnett (1982, p. 160).
2. For Budget Statement see *Official Report*, Vol. 871, No. 15, Col. 277.
3. In January 1974 Peter Snow interviewed the Shah for ITN. In the course of the interview the following exchanges took place:

   Snow:
   Have you anything in principle against the system in Britain and other Western countries?
   Shah:
   Not really against – but I have to tell you of my opinion, which is that if you continue this way – the permissive, undisciplined society – you are going to blow up.
   Snow:
   What do you mean, blow up?
   Shah:
   Well, you will go bankrupt. You work not enough. You try to get too much money for the little work that you are putting up ...

Snow:
How, particularly, would you like us to change?
Shah:
Discipline. More work.

Pressed by Snow, the Shah doubted whether his people
wanted democracy. In Iran ' . . . the people and their King are
so close that they feel as the members of the same family.
They have, I think, the respect that families, or children, used
to have for their fathers.'
On democracy, at least, he seems to have been right.

4. Essentially, these guidelines required unions to limit their wage
demands to compensate for *past* price increases taking
account of compensation already received through the
threshold agreements. If these guidelines were followed (and
import prices did not rise) the rate of inflation would fall. But,
as the National Institute of Economic and Social Research
pointed out in November 1974 ' . . . this rule . . . is not being
followed . . . many current settlements are for increases of the
order of 20 per cent, in *anticipation* of further price rises of
this order in the coming twelve months. 20 per cent inflation
thus becomes a self-fulfilling prophecy'.
5. For the Budget Statement see the *Official Report*, 12 Nov.
1974, Vol. 881, No. 15, Cols 241–80.
6. *Official Report*, Vol. 883, No. 38, Col. 984.
7. Budget Statement, *Official Report*, Vol. 890, No. 104, Cols
273–322.
8. *Official Report*, Vol. 894, No. 149, Col. 1189.
9. Seasonally adjusted total of unemployed excluding school-
leavers in the UK.
10. All figures from *Economic Trends*, No. 272, Jun. 1976.
11. 'The classic profile of national bankruptcy', *The Times*, 20
Feb. 1976, p. 14.
12. Leading article, 20 Feb., p. 18.
13. Fourth Report Session 1975–76, H of C No. 299.
14. The City is unusually prone to rumour. One of my regular
contacts at one of the news agencies used not infrequently to
ring me up with some story that was sweeping the City – the
Chancellor of the Exchequer was about to resign, or some
such – and enquire 'whether there was anything in it'. The
anti-Labour Press was sometimes, it seemed, not unwilling to
help a rumour on its way if it would weaken sterling and
embarrass the Government. On 18 May 1976, for example,
the *Daily Mail* carried a front page story 'One man and the

threat to the £' and, on the City page, 'Now Nigeria gives the pound the collywobbles'. Their story was that a fall in the pound on the previous day had been caused at least partially by a Nigerian threat to withdraw its (considerable) sterling balances if the British Government did not return to them General Gowon, former President of Nigeria and then a student at Warwick University. It is doubtful, however, whether Nigeria had anything to do with the pound's slide. *The Times* reported the Gowon story as purely a diplomatic row and said 'Rumours that the new fall in the exchange rate yesterday was caused by the Nigerian Central Bank selling its reserves were discounted in the City.' It was noted that leading European currencies all fell against the dollar. Moreover, if you read beyond the headlines and first few paragraphs of the *Daily Mail* City page story you found this: 'It was not, though, nearly as bad as it looked. What we were seeing was more a strong appreciation of the dollar against the best Continental currencies than a depreciation of the pound.'

15. *Official Report*, Vol. 909, No. 85, Cols 232–82.
16. *BEQB*, Vol. 18, No. 2, June 1978, p. 168.
17. *Tribune* (16 July) noted that the stories about public expenditure cuts 'were taking on the air of certainty before the subject was even mooted at Cabinet level'. 'The leaks are the secret briefings that Treasury officials have been giving to financial journalists, with or without Government knowledge.' The Treasury did, in the ordinary course of business, give non-attributable briefings to journalists; but, so far as I am aware, nothing was leaked on the cuts.
18. The National Insurance Surcharge came into effect on 6 April 1977 under the National Insurance Surcharge Act 1976. It is levied as an additional percentage on the same earnings as employers' National Insurance contributions and is collected through the same machinery; it does not apply to employees' contributions or to the self-employed. Churches and charities are exempt. The receipts from the Surcharge are paid into the Consolidated Fund like other taxes, not into the National Insurance Fund.
19. The Americans had embraced monetarism and balanced budgets rather earlier than we did. The key officials in the Republican Administration at the time were Arthur Burns, Chairman of the Federal Reserve Bank; William Simon, Treasury Secretary; and Ed Yeo, Under-Secretary for

Monetary Affairs in the US Treasury – hard-liners all.

20. The bad July news had been leaked beforehand in an effort to soften the impact. The Press loves a good leaker, and in an article 'Forewarned is disarmed', Anthony Harris in the *Financial Times* devoted 18 column-inches in praise of this 'encouraging example' without naming the source.

Leaking, in the Ponting sense, is forbidden. But constructive leaking is a standard part of Government public relations. In the fifth of his 1983 Reith Lectures, 'Opening up government', Sir Douglas Wass had this to say: 'The manipulation of the media by government chiefly takes the form of the deliberate and covert briefing of selected elements in a way calculated to influence or condition public opinion ahead of some announcement. In its least objectionable form, this briefing may be the provision of privileged information on a non-attributable basis. The effect of such briefing, if it is done skilfully, is to diminish the shock or impact of some disagreeable policy statement. Public opinion is carefully prepared so as to reduce the risk of an immediate adverse 'gut' reaction which might be prejudicial to the policy. No one can reasonably object to this in principle.'

Those who wish to learn more – a great deal more – about the manipulation of the media by government may care to consult Cockerell *et al.* (1984).

21. On the morning 28 September, before the Chancellor had turned back from Heathrow, the Prime Minister, Mr Callaghan, had made a speech to the (largely left-wing) Conference which has since achieved some notoriety as marking his conversion from Keynesianism and which some suspected was drafted by his monetarist son-in-law, Peter Jay. The relevant passage is as follows: 'We used to think that you could just spend your way out of a recession and increase employment by cutting taxes and boosting Government spending. I tell you in all candour that that option no longer exists and that in so far as it ever did exist, it worked by injecting inflation into the economy. And each time that happened the average level of unemployment has risen. Higher inflation, followed by higher unemployment. That is the history of the last 20 years.'

22. 'The Bank of England's Fall from Grace'.

23. For an interesting account of how Mr Callaghan pursued his quest for a deal on the sterling balances over the heads of the Treasury see 'The day the pound nearly died', three articles

by Stephen Fay and Hugo Young in the *Sunday Times*, 14, 21
and 28 May 1978, especially Part 2, 'The Callaghan offensive'.
24. Barnett (1982), p. 101.
25. Sam Brittan (*Financial Times*, 25 Nov. 1976) said 'A large
section of mainstream Treasury opinion (including most of the
economists) is indeed deeply hostile to the forthcoming
package.' And he did not mean that they thought it
insufficiently deflationary.
26. However, television subsequently produced one of the best
accounts of the political conflict over the IMF loan: Granada
Television's 'The State of the Nation; The Cabinet in Conflict.
The Loan from the IMF.' It took the form of a reconstruction
of Cabinet meetings in which the parts of Ministers were
taken, and their arguments presented, by journalists who
were as well informed as anyone outside the Cabinet could be
on what took place.
27. The absolutely key figure was the estimate of the PSBR.
Successive estimates are summarized in Table 5.1. Note that
the estimates for 1976–77 fell by some £2.25 bn between
December 1976 and March 1977.

Table 5.1   Treasury forecasts of the PSBR (£ bn)

	1976–77	1977–78	1978–79
Budget, Apr. 1976	12.0	—	—
Measures, 22 Jul. 1976		9.0 (max)	—
Estimates for IMF, Nov. 1976	—	11.2	—
Estimates for IMF, No. 1976, revised*	—	10.5	11.5
Measures, and Letter of Intent, 15 Dec. 1976	—	8.7	8.6
Industry Act Forecast, 15 Dec 1976	11.0	8.5	—
Budget, Mar. 1977	8.8	7.4†	—

* 'These forecasts embodied unrealisticaly [*sic*] favourable
assumptions on several important points.' *Official Report*, Vol. 922,
No. 16, Col. 1525.
† £8.5 bn after Budget changes.

28. For a well-researched account of the negotiations, including the Cabinet discussions, see Stephen Fay and Hugo Young 'The day the £ nearly died' in the *Sunday Times* of 14, 21 and 28 May 1978; and the Granada programme referred to at Note 26. See also Chapter 10 of Barnett (1982) and contemporary Press accounts, notably those of Peter Jenkins in the *Guardian*.

29. *Official Report*, Vol. 922, No. 16, Cols 1525–37.

30. This limit was subject to review. On 20 June 1977 Mr Healey confirmed that it was adequate.

31. There were those who expected the Prime Minister to go on television at the time of the Statement. To have done so would have been to play the media at their own crisis game; and if he had gone on television the Opposition, under the broadcasting rules, would have had the right of reply, something of a gift to them. The PM decided not to go on television.

32. See Fay and Young, op.cit. (note 28 above) 14 May 1978 p. 34; and Keegan and Pennant-Rea (1979), pp. 160–2. According to these sources the Governor was sceptical about the 'devaluation strategy'. When it went wrong 'the Bank was accused of incompetence and the Treasury of insidious domination'; and 'Accusations and recriminations were thick on the ground for the rest of 1976 as to whether the Bank of England had been maladroit, or given an impossible task.'

33. *The Government's Expenditure Plans*, Cmnd 6721 – I and II.

34. Under the Provisional Collection of Taxes Act 1968 Parliament passes without debate a motion bringing certain indirect tax changes, including in this case the petrol tax change, into immediate effect. The proposal to increase petrol duty was withdrawn on 5 May and became effective on 8 August.

35. What he did was to activate the 'Rooker–Wise–Lawson Amendment' to the 1977 Finance Act which obliged governments to increase tax allowances in line with inflation, unless they obtained Parliamentary approval not to.

36. Haines (1977), p. 41.

37. The only people for whom there was a problem were the strict monetarists, who believed that any increase in the money supply would inevitably lead to a rise in the rate of inflation. But the Government was not monetarist and nor was the IMF; there was no *target* for the money supply, only a ceiling for DCE. On the other hand, monetarists were against

intervention; without intervention an excess supply of sterling would leak abroad, weakening the exchange rate.

38. See especially Fred Emery, David Blake and Caroline Atkinson in *The Times*, 2 Nov. 1977; and Adam Raphael and William Keegan in *The Observer*, 6 Nov. 1977.

39. Largely, it was thought, because the miners had rejected a productivity deal. Kenneth Fleet in the *Sunday Times* of 6 November thought that this brought us down to earth and began his article 'Thank God for Arthur Scargill'.

40. The *Daily Mail* of 2 November carried a John Kent cartoon showing Robin Day questioning the Prime Minister: Day asks 'What was the final argument that clinched your decision to let the £ rise?' The Prime Minister replies 'The Chancellor of the Exchequer said he was against it.'

41. See Barnett (1982), pp. 112–13. Much later Mrs Thatcher moved in the opposite direction, abolishing the Civil Service Department and returning part of it to the Treasury.

42. *The Government's Expenditure Plans, 1978–79 to 1981–82*, Cmnd 7049 – I and II.

43. *Official Report*, 11 Apr. 1978, Vol. 947, No. 93, Cols 1183–208. The Statement lasted only 1 hour 8 minutes.

44. In his Mais Lecture on 9 Feb. 1978 the Governor had explained the difficulties inherent in sticking to a monetary target set once a year for the whole year. He saw rolling targets 'as a minor, but useful, technical change to our continuing policy of having publicly-announced targets ... '.

45. In my own view no Chancellor should ever do a Budget broadcast, because it is a gift to the Opposition. On Budget Day and afterwards the Government gets massive media coverage for what it has done, while the Opposition is left trailing. The Government doesn't need the broadcast. The Opposition does need a broadcast but, under the Broadcasting rules, it gets one only if the Government does one.

46. In the banking month of January 1978 the seasonal adjustment turned the growth in sterling M3 from +£98 million to +£982 million; and DCE from –£386 million to +£354 million. One of the justifications for introducing rolling targets is to take account of random or seasonal movements in the money supply. It may be argued that seasonal movements are eliminated by the seasonal adjustment. Quite so. But the seasonal adjustment can show a nominal rise where no actual rise exists. In the opposite case, where the seasonal

adjustment shows a nominal fall against an actual rise, people may choose to look also at the unadjusted figure.

47. For a useful discussion of the management of the gilt-edged market see *BEQB*, Vol. 19, No. 2, June 1979, pp. 137–48.

48. 'Goodhart's Law' (after Charles Goodhart, formerly Chief Adviser on Monetary Policy at the Bank of England) states, in relation to published monetary targets, 'that any statistical regularity will tend to collapse once pressure is placed upon if for control purposes'.

49. On 5 July the Government announced that it would not seek to reverse the amendments made at the Committee Stage of the Finance Bill which reduced the basis rate of income tax from 34 to 33 per cent and amended the higher rate bands.

50. Not all pay demands above 5 per cent were unjustified on economic (i.e. productivity) grounds. In November Ford workers accepted a 17 per cent pay deal after a 9-week strike, and Ford later undertook not to pass on more than 5 per cent of this in prices, indicating that productivity could take care of much of the rest. The trouble was that workers in other less efficient, even loss-making firms, would expect the same. This was a perennial problem with pay 'norms', usually solved by the inclusion of a 'productivity' exception; but experience showed that this escape clause was widely abused by management and unions.

51. Definitions of public expenditure change from White Paper to White Paper. But we must assume that the figures in Table 2 of Cmnd 7439 are internally consistent, i.e. are not only revalued to the same price basis but use the same definition. Since the planning total for 1977–78 incorporated the £1 bn cut negotiated with the IMF, the shortfall of £4.3 bn brought the total achieved cut, over 1976–77, to over £5 bn. However, if the same calculation had been made using the definition of the 1977 White Paper (Cmnd 6721), the result would, except by coincidence, have been different; but the shortfall would still have been very large.

52. Partly paid stocks were introduced in March 1977 to smooth the flow of funds by staging the instalments to correspond with the Government's funding requirements.

53. 'Stags' are speculators who buy in the expectation of an immediate rise in price.

54. *Financial Times*, 6 Mar. 1979, p. 19. A year later (3 Mar. 1980) in the Lombard column, Samuel Brittan referred to 'the Bank of England's archaic method of selling stock, which works by

creating crises and giving a free ride to gilt-edged
speculators ... ' Crises and speculation apart, ' ... gilt edged
trading has provided a very fat living for two jobbing firms and
perhaps half a dozen top brokers' (*Financial Times*, 5 Oct.
1984, 'Costly scramble to survive in the City Revolution'). The
gilt-edged market has been one of the main beneficiaries of
the huge increase in government deficits since the Barber
years. Even if those deficits decrease – and under the 1984
Medium Term Financial Strategy the PSBR is planned still to
be £7 bn in 1988–89 – there will remain a very large volume of
new issues just to finance maturities.

55. Mr Healey was very fond of drawing on the policies of other
    countries in support of his own, and he did so in this case. In
    his 'Nationwide' interview he said: ' ... the German
    Government, ... they're spending £800 million ... every year
    supporting uneconomic pits in their coal industry and its a
    perfectly sensible choice for any Government to make.' He
    made the same point in his interview with Independent Radio
    News, adding 'because they regard the social disadvantages of
    letting these pits go out of operation as unacceptable'.

56. The 'effective exchange rate index' is an index of the rate
    against a basket of other currencies. From October 1974 it
    has been known as the 'Sterling Exchange Rate Index' or
    'Sterling Index'. See *Economic Progress Report* No. 172, Oct.
    1984. For further details see *Financial Statistics Explanatory
    Handbook* 1985 edn., pp. 116, 117. HMSO.

57. William Shakespeare, *Cymbeline*.

6

A new language

For last year's words belong to last year's language
And next year's words await another voice.

T. S. Eliot   *Little Gidding*

The Conservative Government of 1979 fought and was elected on
much the same political and economic philosophy as inspired the
Heath Government of 1970. But it had an added ingredient, one
that could reach the parts the earlier philosophy could not:
monetarism.[1]

The narrative that follows will make more sense if we have an
understanding of the monterarist philosophy and, in particular, of
how monetarists see the economy working. There is not space
here to go very far into theory or history, on which there are a
number of recent texts.[2]

Monetarist theory

Monetarist theory has two main strands: one is that the price level
and the change in the price level, i.e. the rate of inflation, are
determined, and determined only, by the quantity of money and
the rate of change of the quantity of money. The other strand is a
belief in the efficiency of markets; specifically, that markets must
be allowed to work with a minimum of restriction and that if they
are so allowed they will allocate resources efficiently. The
underlying mechanism is the stability of the demand for money to
hold and the individual's or firm's desire to maximize his return on
all his assets. If a person (or firm) has more money than he wants

to hold, he will spend it on something: goods, services or assets of one sort or another. Conversely, if he feels his money holding to be inadequate, he will refrain from spending. Since the amount of money in existence at any one time is finite, the community as a whole cannot change its money holdings; so, the attemt to get rid of money, or not to get rid of money, will set in motion forces which affect first output and then, after a lag, prices. *Changes* in the quantity of money in existence will also affect prices and output, but in an indeterminate way. Thus, there is a direct relationship between changes in the quantity of money and total money output, or money GDP. With a given money GDP the amount of employment will depend upon the level of money wages: the higher the wage the less the employment, and conversely. Thus, with the money supply, and money GDP, limited, the level of employment depends not upon government policy but upon the level of wages as freely determined in the market for labour. The government has no power to determine the level of output and employment. The level of real, as distinct from money, wages, is determined by the money wage and the price level, which is governed by the quantity of money. The market freedom that the theory requires covers not only the markets in goods and labour but extends to the markets in money: interest rates and the rate of exchange must be left free to fluctuate with supply and demand. The external demand for a currency is an extension of domestic demand and the price (the rate of exchange) depends upon supply and demand. Given proper control of the domestic supply of money, the rate of exchange will look after itself.

The British case

The theory, as sketched in above, has, according to British monetarists, a direct relevance to the British economy, which is seen as suffering from two major problems, or defects: inflation and poor productive performance.

Inflation was a serious problem from the late 1960s to the early 1980s. It was at one time thought that there was a trade-off between the rate of inflation and the rate of unemployment, so that less inflation could be achieved by having more unemployment. But this relationship failed: in recent years both inflation and unemployment have been higher under each succeeding government (except the present one). The alternative method of dealing with inflation has been through prices and incomes policies. Many of these have been tried and have worked for a short while but quickly generated forces that led to their abandonment. Not only are prices and incomes policies inadequate as a permanent solution to inflation, they distort relative prices and lead to a misallocation of resources: because they interfere with markets they are economically inefficient. The only permanent solution to the problem of inflation is to control the money supply: inflation is always a monetary phenomenon.

There is no general agreement on why the British economic performance has been so poor relative to that of other advanced industrialized nations. But at least part of the answer, according to the British monetarists (and others), lies in the excessive size of the public sector. This has a number of consequences. The public sector is relatively inefficient, because it is not subject to market disciplines. There is a tendency to go on supporting and subsidizing ailing and outdated industries. The public sector, and public expenditure, have an inbuilt and very powerful tendency to grow: the demand for public goods and services is, literally, unlimited. Since public expenditure has to be paid for, this means that taxation has to rise or the government has to borrow more, or do a bit more of both. Either course is bad for the private sector. Taxation reduces incentives to work, innovate and take risks, and lowers after-tax profits. High borrowing raises interest rates and 'crowds out' private borrowing for productive purposes. Thus a large and growing public sector is inimical to the interests of the private sector, the sector that produces the basic wealth of the economy upon which everything else rests. If public expenditure is not constrained, taxes and/or borrowing will go on rising. Constraint is a matter of political control, of limiting the supply of public goods and services in the face of unlimited demand. In addition the boundaries between the public and private sector must be redrawn and as much as is feasible of the public sector returned to the private sector where it will be subject to market disciplines.

From this diagnosis of problems and solutions some propositions may be made:

- The growth of the money supply must be limited in order to control and eliminate inflation.
- A major source of money generation is the PSBR.
- Public spending must be reduced or at least stabilized at

present levels. Such spending must be limited by the amount
of money available from taxation and borrowing, neither of
which can be allowed to increase.

So, the PSBR is relevant to both major problems – inflation and
economic decline, but especially to inflation . Firm control of it is
central to the economic strategy.

If the PSBR is to be tightly constrained it follows that it cannot
be used as an engine, Keynesian fashion, to generate demand,
output and employment. This does not matter – it is, indeed,
irrelevant – since it is an article of monetarist faith that
employment cannot anyway be created by this route: additional
public expenditure financed by borrowing generates not growth
but inflation.

What, then, does generate growth? Mr Nigel Lawson, when
Financial Secretary to the Treasury, explained it as follows: ' ... it
is essentially the growth of the money supply in relation to the
inflation rate that will be the prime determinant of the overall level
of domestic demand and hence output in the economy, and not
the fiscal stance'.[3]

Such a brief and bald account cannot display the full range of
the monetarist case, a matter beyond the purpose of this book.
Nor, by the same token, is this the place to deploy the
counterarguments. But it seemed necessary to prepare the way
for the story that follows; for after 1979 nothing was the same, and
to understand what was going on it was necessary to discard old
frameworks of thought, or at least put them on the back-burner.
As Keynes (1936) wrote: 'The difficulty lies not in the new ideas,
but in escaping from the old ones, which ramify, for those brought
up as most of us have been, into every corner of our minds.'

Notes and references

1. It also had Mrs Thatcher; but it is debatable whether it is
   correct to count her as an independent instrument of
   economic policy.
2. For an exposition, in simple terms, of the basic theoretical
   issues the reader might consult Browning (1983); Keegan
   (1984) gives a good account of how the Conservative Party
   came to embrace monetarism. Other useful texts are in
   Gilmour (1983) and Riddell (1983).
3. Speech to the Institute of Fiscal Studies, 23 March 1981.

7

Sir Geoffrey Howe,
May 1979–June 1983

To reverse the long decline

Information policy

In the summer and early autumn of 1979 considerable effort at the
highest level in the Treasury and involving the Government's
political advisers went into the problem of how best to present the
Government's economic strategy. The major objective was to
change the framework within which people, including
businessmen, interpreted policy. Not unnaturally policy was still
being interpreted within the quite different policy frame of the
outgone Government. With the passage of time people would
come to understand the quite different approach of the new
Government, but to generate appropriate responses this process
of perception had to be speeded up. People had to realize, for
example, that the Government was not in the rescue business,
that it would not intervene, specifically or generally, to rescue
companies, relieve unemployment, and so on. Expectations had to
be changed. People had to understand that economic policy was
medium-term, extending at least over the life of one Parliament,
and would be followed through. Perhaps there was here the
shadow of a desire to lay the ghost of Edward Heath, 'lame ducks',
'U' turns, and all.

This particular exercise, which had some limited success, was
not unique. It is frequently alleged, particularly when things are
going badly for the party in office, that the government does not
do enough to 'get its policies across'. If that is so it is not, usually,
for want of thought. Ministers, their political advisers and officials,
especially information officers, do think about how to present
policy and do make plans. One result, usually, is a 'speech

programme' in which a theme or themes are established for major ministerial speeches outside Parliament in the months ahead.

Lest the suspicious or the purists should think that such an exercise means that civil servants are helping with party political propaganda, two points should be made: first, that it happens under all governments impartially; and, secondly, and more fundamentally, a distinction is drawn between Party and Government: it is the civil servants' job to execute as efficiently and effectively as possible the policies of the democratically elected government of the day. Making policies understood is part of that process and is, in the end, the *raison d'être* of the information function within Whitehall.

1979

First Budget

Sir Geoffrey Howe's first Budget, introduced on 12 June 1979, was based on four principles: the strengthening of incentives to reward hard work, ability and success; greater freedom of choice by reducing the role of the State; the reduction of the Public Sector Borrowing Requirement; and firm monetary and fiscal discipline to control inflation.

The new Chancellor's most dramatic proposal, in pursuit of his first objective, was to make a huge shift of taxation from direct to indirect. The main instrument of this shift was Value Added Tax (VAT), raised from 8 per cent (or 12½ in some cases) to 15 per cent. Overall, direct taxes were reduced by £4.3 bn and indirect taxes raised by £4.7 bn (full-year effect). The very big increase in VAT was expected to raise the retail price index by about 4 per cent, at a time when inflation was already on an upward trend and when the control of inflation was a major objective. It was almost as if a rise in prices in the shops was seen as something separate from the rate of inflation, the latter to be controlled only by monetary discipline.

In pursuit of monetary discipline the PSBR was reduced by £1 bn to £8.3 bn and the monetary growth target (sterling M3) from 8–12 to 7–11 per cent. The Supplementary Special Deposits Scheme was extended, and MLR raised 2 points to 14 per cent.

Public expenditure was cut by £1.6 bn in 1979–80, the effect of cash limits was expected to reduce planned programmes by a further £1 bn, and there would be receipts from the disposal of assets, estimated at £1 bn.

Exchange control

In his Budget the Chancellor announced some measures of exchange control relaxation and his intention to dismantle the controls further. In October, in a bold move, he removed all remaining controls. Exchange controls were one of the instruments used to sustain an artificial exchange rate. Their removal reflected the belief that the price of sterling must, like other prices, be determined by the market. The removal of this long-standing control[1] was, and is, controversial. The effect was that some funds that could have been invested in home industries were invested abroad as fund managers increased their overseas portfolios. The case for this is that it extends to capital the free movement that has hitherto, at least in theory, been enjoyed by the trade in goods and services. If the latter leads to a more optimal international allocation of resources, then so does the free movement of capital. It is true that investment abroad does not create employment at home: but that is a reflection on relative investment opportunities. It is probably the case that the constraints on UK domestic investment have been less related to shortages of cash than to shortages of viable projects.

Public expenditure

The new Government's first Public Expenditure White Paper, Cmnd 7746, published on 1 November, extended the plans for only one year, to 1980–81. Growth was to be zero in 1979–80 and 1980–81.

Monetary policy

By October (the October banking month) money supply growth was running at about 14 per cent, above the target range of 7–11 per cent. Once again, part of the problem was an inability to sell gilts and this, in turn, may have been influenced by the removal of exchange controls and the opening up of investment opportunities abroad. To bring money supply back under control the Chancellor, on 15 November, extended 'the Corset' for a further six months and raised MLR by 3 points to 17 per cent. He also rolled the 7–11 per cent target forward by six months on an unchanged base (mid-June 1979), thus avoiding building into the target the higher growth since then. It had long been known to monetary theorists that strict control of the money supply implied a willingness to allow interest rates to fluctuate more frequently and more widely. But the Prime Minister, who has a strong dislike of high interest rates, particularly because of their repercussions on the mortgage rate, was not pleased to see MLR go up by a further 3 points. The Chancellor said he had set in hand a review of methods of monetary control and promised 'a discussion paper for consultation'.

The external account

The exchange rate, which had stood at around $2.07 in May, strengthened and on 26 July exceeded $2.33. At the year's end it was $2.225. Between May and December the reserves grew by $1 bn to $22.5 bn. The balance of payments on current account, which had been in £900 m. surplus in 1978, fell into a deficit of £2.4 bn in 1979.[2]

1980

The Runcible Budget

On 17 January it was announced that the Chancellor would present his Budget on Tuesday 25 March. The Press was quickly on to the fact that this was the date set for the enthronement of Bishop Runcie as Archbishop of Canterbury. The official line was that it was not a mistake and that the decision on the date had been taken in full knowledge of the enthronement.

The choice of Budget Day is in fact fairly closely constrained, and oddly enough in this context, by the ecclesiastical calendar – the date of Easter. Budget Day is traditionally on a Tuesday. In 1980 Easter fell on 4–7 April, and the House would recess on 3 April till mid-April. The later in April the Budget is held, the more revenue is lost from any increase in indirect taxes. The Budget, therefore, had to be before Easter. To hold it on 1 April would not have allowed time for the four-day Budget debate, so the latest date it could be held (if it was to be a Tuesday, as tradition demanded) was 25 March. The Bishop and the Church were horrified: it would push the enthronement down the television coverage and off the front pages of next day's papers. Representations were made to the Prime Minister and following further discussion it was agreed that the Budget should be on Wednesday 26 March.

The Rt Hon. Norman St John Stevas informed the House on 22 January of the change; and the *Evening Standard* made it their front-page story: 'Date change as Government slips on ecclesiastical banana skin BISHOP BEFORE BUDGET.'

According to Robert Carvel, the Lobby man who wrote the story, the Chancellor had recommended the original date 'in the full knowledge that it would coincide with the Canterbury Cathedral ceremony ... However, there was discussion among senior ministers, including Mrs Thatcher and the Government's first decision was a collective one ... The Chancellor is understood to have written privately to Bishop Runcie to explain the reasons ... .'

Reuters' tape put a fitting seal on the whole embarrassing episode by reporting that Mr St John Stevas had 'told Parliament the Budget Day had been rearranged to avoid a clash of dates with the *enthroatment* of the new Archbishop of Canterbury on March 25'.

Monetary control

It was natural that a Government so heavily committed to the control of the money supply should re-examine methods of control. The Government undertook such an examination and in March 1980 published *Monetary Control* (Cmnd 7858), which included proposals for improving short-term control and concluded that the Supplementary Special Deposits scheme (the 'Corset') should be phased out. This was done in the following June. New monetary arrangements were announced by the Chancellor of the Exchequer on 24 November 1980.

Public expenditure

The annual public expenditure White Paper *The Government's Expenditure Plans 1980–81 to 1983–84* (Cmnd 7841), was published, for the first time, on Budget Day, 26 March, adding to the mountain of economic paper released on that day. The plans showed that expenditure was to fall (in real terms) in every year covered by the plan, so that in 1983–84 expenditure would be 4 per cent below the expected out-turn for 1979–80.

The Budget

In his second Budget Sir Geoffrey Howe went further in tilting the burden of taxation away from direct and towards indirect taxation. Direct taxes were reduced by £1.68 bn and indirect taxes raised by £1.30 bn. The retail price index was thereby raised by 1 per cent. The 25 per cent tax band was abolished; and a wide range of tax measures affecting capital taxation and small businesses was introduced. The Chancellor also announced the setting up of Enterprise Zones.

The Medium-Term Financial Strategy

But the focus of his Budget, to which he came early in his two-hour speech, was the Medium-Term Financial Strategy (MTFS). Introducing the MTFS he said 'The Strategy sets out a path for public finance over the next few years. At its heart is a target for a steadily declining growth of the money supply that is set alongside policies for Government spending and taxation which will underpin that objective.'

The heart, as we shall see later, proved distinctly fragile and in need of several transplants. But first, let us see what form the MTFS took, beginning with the arithmetic and the projections.

Growth of the money stock (sterling M3)

The 'target range' for the growth of the money stock, per cent per year, was to be as follows:

1980–81: 7–11;   1981–82: 6–10;   1982–83: 5–9;   1983–84: 4–8

This progressive reduction in the growth of the money supply was to be achieved *not* 'by excessive reliance on interest rates' but by 'a substantial reduction over the medium-term in the PSBR as a percentage of GDP'. So, the second component of the MTFS was a projection of Public Sector Borrowing, as shown in Table 7.1.

What does this mean? It is best to approach the table from both ends, the top and the bottom. The first two rows yield a balance of projected revenue over projected expenditure. The bottom two rows project a Public Sector Borrowing Requirement (PSBR) that is consistent with the growth of the money supply; and the General Government Borrowing Requirement (GGBR) is consistent with the projected PSBR. Thus, we end up with *two* GGBRs; and the difference between them is the 'implied fiscal adjustment'. Let us look at the projection for 1982–83, the first year in which these totals differ. In the top two lines expenditure exceeds revenue by £1.5 bn (£71 — 69.5 bn). But the 'allowable' GGBR is £4 bn. Thus, to bring the two into equality there is required a fiscal adjustment of £2.5 bn (£4 — 1.5 bn). This means that since the allowable GGBR exceeds the projected GGBR there is scope for a tax reduction and/or an expenditure increase of £2.5 bn. (We should note in passing that there can never be an implied fiscal adjustment in the current year because by that time the actual fiscal adjustment, bringing the two sides into balance, has already been made.)

The Treasury conceded, realistically, that projections of this nature, for several years ahead, were extremely fragile. But whatever changes became necessary to realize the strategy

Table 7.1　1978–79 prices (£ bn)

	1978–79	1979–80	1980–81	1981–82	1982–83	1983–84
Total expenditure	74	74.5	74.25	73	71	70.5
Total receipts	−65	−66	−67.5	−67.5	−69.5	−71
Implied fiscal adjustment	—	—	—	—	2.5	3.5
General Government Borrowing Requirement (GGBR)	9	8.5	7	5.5	4	3
PSBR	9.3	8	6	5	3.5	2.5
PSBR as per cent of GDP at market prices	5.5	4.75	3.75	3	2.25	1.5

'including changes in interest rates, taxes and public expenditure', there 'would be no question of departing from the money supply policy ... '. Thus, at this stage, the money supply was at the heart of the economic strategy. Everything else was to be made to conform to the growth of the money supply.

The foreign exchanges

At question time in the House on 3 June a question put to the Prime Minister concluded: 'What does she intend to do to help our manufacturing industry, faced with an overvalued pound and high interest rates?' The Prime Minister's reply began 'I have already seen my right honourable and learned friend the Chancellor of the Exchequer today, and we discussed just these problems.' There followed some more questions and answers, some related to the refund from the EEC; then in response to a further question from Mr Callaghan, the Prime Minister began her reply 'One relevant matter that has come up today is that the refund will go towards reducing expenditure, which will help to reduce interest rates.'[3]

Nothing very exciting, you might think, in any of that. Put into the context of total government spending, the refund was unlikely to have more than the most minimal effect on interest rates; and in any case it would not appear in the Government's accounts until the last quarter of the financial year, in the following spring. The City, however, in its hair-trigger way, put the two statements together and decided that a reduction in interest rates was imminent. There was panic in the foreign exchange markets and sterling fell by over 4.5 cents, to £2.2880 in half an hour. There was also a certain amount of panic in Whitehall and at the Bank.

The incident highlighted once again the Gadarene nature of the money markets and the sensitivity of the rate of exchange to interest rates and to interest rate expectations. It also illustrates a somewhat perverse aspect of opinion about the value of the pound. It might have been supposed that reduced expenditure would, if anything, strengthen sterling. But if lower expenditure meant lower borrowing and lower interest rates, that weakened sterling. The corollary is that a higher PSBR strengthens sterling. We have witnessed this phenomenon in the United States, where a massive government deficit has led to a strong dollar.

Monetary developments

Up to April 1980 the growth of sterling M3 remained within the target range of 7–11 per cent at an annual rate. By June there was

concern in the Treasury about the stance on monetary policy
where the problem was seen as maintaining a balance between the
benefits of monetary discipline and the costs in terms of
bankruptcies, lay-offs, and company failures. Companies were
being squeezed by a high exchange rate, high interest rates,
depressed demand and, to some extent, by wage demands.
Happily, the Governor of the Bank of England found himself able
to advise that a fall in interest rates would not be inconsistent with
the maintenance of monetary discipline. Accordingly on 3 July
MLR was reduced to 16 per cent, without undue involvement of
Ministers or any suggestion of a departure from the strict
discipline proclaimed in the MTFS.

The money supply grew by 5 per cent in July, largely reflecting
the removal of the 'Corset', and by a further 3 per cent in August,
carrying the cumulative growth way above the top end of the
target range.

Early in September the Treasury issued a 'Statement on
Monetary Developments' designed to reassure markets about the
growth of government borrowing and the money supply. The
Treasury found 11 points to make, including their estimate that
the underlying growth rate of sterling M3 in July and in August
had been 1 or 2 per cent, not the 8 per cent over the two months
shown by the statistics. They expected both private and public
borrowing to moderate in the second half of the financial year. By
November sterling M3 was growing at an annual rate of 24 per
cent. How did it come about that the authorities lost control of the
variable that stood at the centre of the Government's economic
strategy? The Treasury, in evidence to the Treasury and Civil
Service Committee, gave four reasons: the larger-than-expected
effects of the removal of the 'Corset' in June; the unexpectedly
rapid growth of the PSBR; the favourable movement in the
balance of payments on current account; and the high level of
bank lending. As the Committee rather exasperatedly pointed out,
'This list covers virtually all the possible sources of monetary
growth and is tantamount to saying that the money supply has
risen because the money supply has risen'.[4] In setting the
monetary growth target, the Treasury was aware that the 'Corset'
was to be removed, and was responsible for controlling and
forecasting the PSBR. The Bank of England, under Treasury
direction, was the source of, and responsible for, lending to and by
the banking system. Only the improvement in the balance of
payments could be accounted outside the authorities' control or
beyond reasonable expectation.

That the Treasury had once again got its forecast of the PSBR badly wrong perhaps surprised no one; and a wayward PSBR cannot quickly be corrected. But the provision of funds by the Bank of England to the banking system is something that is under day-to-day control; and that that provision took place, and on a substantial scale, was perhaps the most surprising of the elements of money supply growth in 1980. The Bank's explanation was that it was done to relieve 'unusual stringency in the money market and persistent pressure on banks' liquidity ... because of continuing heavy tax payments and large official sales of gilt-edged stocks'.[5]

The last six or seven of those words are worth a second look. Government policy was to finance as much of the PSBR as possible by sales of gilt-edged stocks, to contain the growth of the money supply. The agent for such sales is the Bank of England. So here was the Bank of England with one hand selling gilts as fast as it could to contain the money supply, and with the other feeding the banking system with cash to relieve the stringency thereby caused. A very odd state of affairs; and hardly the action of a central bank wholeheartedly committed to the control of the money supply, and nominally acting under the direction of the Chancellor of the Exchequer. It will be recalled that the Medium-Term Financial Strategy, launched a few months earlier, had concluded that, whatever else happened, 'there would be no question of departing from the money supply policy, which is essential to the success of any anti-inflationary strategy'. The Prime Minister was not pleased: 'Indeed,' wrote the *Financial Times* on 27 October 1980, 'one of Mrs Thatcher's favourite jibes in the current monetary discussion is to remark that the Bank of England is now the lender-of-first-resort, not just the traditional lender-of-last-resort.' But if the Bank of England had not relieved the liquidity shortage of the banking system, market interest rates would have gone through the roof; and the lady would not have liked that either. As the Bank explained, ' ... the authorities were faced throughout the period with the choice of allowing very short-term interest rates to rise, perhaps precipitously, with the possibility of associated sharp swings in the exchange rate, or of providing assistance ... the authorities considered it more appropriate to provide liquidity ... '.[6]

Not only did the Governor provide liquidity to prevent a precipitous rise in interest rates, he was able to advise that MLR should be lowered. What the Governor did in this period was more or less to ignore the monetary numbers in favour of keeping sections of industry from bankruptcy. The Bank did not regard sterling M3 as a reliable guide to the tightness of monetary policy.

Attitude to wages

That the Bank of England was not yet wholly converted to monetarism had been made clear in a lengthy section on 'Monetary policy and inflation' in their June *Bulletin*.[7] There was, said the Bank, 'an important – and difficult – question whether greater monetary restraint in 1977–78 would have affected the outcome of the 1978–79 pay round. This bears on the issue of how monetary policy is transmitted through the system to have an effect on inflation.' Retail prices were rising by nearly 22 per cent over the year to May 1980, from under 8 per cent in mid-1978:

> Much of the recent deterioration represents important special factors ... the sharp rise in oil prices through 1979 and the increase in VAT in the June 1979 Budget each contributed some three of four percentage points ... But though much of the acceleration in retail prices may have been initiated by special factors, the underlying rate of inflation has accelerated dramatically; this is because the current rate of inflation appears to have been quickly anticipated in labour markets with the result that the outcome of the present wage round is expected to be at a similar high rate ... pay rises may have been an independent source of price inflation.

May they indeed. All this talk of cost-push inflation generated by oil prices, VAT and, above all, pay rises, suggested that the Bank had not yet fully adapted to the new frame of thinking.

While the Treasury may not have wholly endorsed the Bank's unreconstructed analysis, there was, nevertheless, a change of tone in ministers' speeches on wages. In a series of speeches between May and November 1979 Sir Geoffrey Howe had spelt out the Government's approach, which was very much 'hands off': if unions chose to bargain for unrealistic wages the money just would not be available. There were warnings that excessive awards would lead to bankruptcies and unemployment, but little recognition that they could lead to higher inflation – something to be controlled by the money supply. By the middle of 1980, however, the emphasis had changed, as *The Times* and other newspapers were quick to notice: ' ... senior ministers from Mrs Thatcher downwards have been touring the country urging the necessity of smaller percentage increases in the next pay round'. And ' ... over the past few weeks references to a connexion between the level of pay settlements and the rate of inflation have crept into ministerial speeches'. (*The Times* 2 July and 26 June 1980). The strict monetarist line that trade unions cannot cause inflation (without the connivance or acquiescence of the monetary authorities) had been modified.[8] The plea now was that lower wage demands would help to bring down inflation faster and would make the transition to a lower rate of inflation less painful. But the central doctrine remained intact: the instrument for lowering the rate of inflation was control of the money supply, not an incomes policy. Other influences on the cost side, such as oil prices and VAT, were 'once for all' shocks that did not affect the underlying trend.

The November package

At the time of the 1980 Budget the PSBR for 1980–81 was set at £8.5 bn, equal to an estimated 3.75 per cent of GDP at market prices. By November it was estimated at £11.5 bn, 5 per cent of GDP. On 24 November the Chancellor introduced a major package of measures including £1 bn of cuts in public expenditure in 1981–82 and a 1 per cent increase in National Insurance contributions to raise £1 bn in 1981–82. Minimum Lending Rate was reduced by 2 points to 14 per cent.

The external account

From the middle of the year the current account of the balance of payments moved strongly into surplus. In the second half of the year the surplus was £3.3 bn (not seasonally adjusted) and £2.7 bn in the year as a whole – a swing of £4.4 bn from the (revised) deficit of £1.6 bn in 1979. The exchange rate also strengthened markedly. The dollar rate rose from $2.2250 at the end of 1979 to $2.4495 in October, a rise of 10 per cent, while the effective rate showed a rise of nearly 13.5 per cent by early November. Year on year both the dollar rate and the effective rate were some 10 per cent higher than in 1979.

Overview of the year

The misfortunes and miscalculations of 1980 reinforced each other: because government borrowing was so high, interest rates were high; because interest rates were high, foreign money flooded in, pushing up the exchange rate and adding to the difficulties of British manufacturing industry and reducing employment; because unemployment was so high, social security payments were high and tax receipts low, raising the amount the Government needed to borrow.

It had been a dreadful year. The economy had moved much more deeply into recession than expected, industry had suffered badly and even the CBI had been moved to protest at Government policies and plead for relief. Unemployment went above 2 million. The Chancellor's November Statement, offering little help, had been badly received. The Treasury had lost control of public borrowing, and the Bank of England, rather more deliberately, of the money supply. The Medium-Term Financial Strategy had got away to a poor start.

> Between the idea
> And the reality
> Between the motion
> And the act
> Falls the Shadow[9]

1981

On 18 February 1981 Mrs Thatcher and her Government made a U-turn. The hard-line *Sun*, ever alert for any backsliding, nevertheless approved: 'Of course, it is a major U-turn. But it is a U-turn that shows a flexibility born of political courage and common sense.'

What had Mrs Thatcher done that was so flexible, courageous and commonsensical? Well, actually she had totally surrendered to the miners over pit closures. The *Financial Times*, less approving that the *Sun*, said she had suffered a major humiliation and had surrendered without a struggle on three fronts: pit closures, coal imports, and financing limits for the Coal Board. What she and the Government had done was to 'give way to the miners at the first whiff of a confrontation ... In Tory Britain, miners rule.' Interestingly, in the light of events of 1984, the *Financial Times* conceded that there was 'a case, however slim, for keeping open uneconomic pits on social grounds in areas where there are few alternative chances of employment'. But this was an argument the Government had not used.

Public expenditure
The Public Expenditure White Paper published on Budget Day, 10 March, *The Government's Expenditure Plans 1981–82 to 1983–84*

(Cmnd 8175) showed that expenditure in the year just completing, 1980–81, which in the previous year's White Paper had been planned to fall by £0.6 bn, had risen by £1.4 bn, at 1980 survey prices. In cash terms expenditure had risen by £17 bn over the 1979–80 out-turn and was planned to rise in 1981–82 by a further £10 bn cash. At constant 1980 prices expenditure was planned to rise only slightly in 1981–82 and thereafter to fall. It was an oft-told tale in public expenditure White Papers, too much jam today but less promised for tomorrow and the day after. Even so, expenditure between 1980–81 and 1983–84 inclusive was planned to exceed the plans in the White Paper of a year earlier by £7.3 bn at 1980 prices.

The Budget

With the economy in deep recession and worse expected, Sir Geoffrey's 1981 Budget was awaited with considerable interest. There had been widespread pressure on the Government to change course – pressure from the press, from the leaders of industry, from the trade unions, from some of the Government's own supporters. It was argued that the monetarist 'experiment' had been a total failure: it had proved impossible to control the money supply, and the only tangible result of two years' monetarism was one of the highest rates of unemployment seen in the United Kingdom this century; and all independent economic forecasts agreed that unemployment was likely to go on rising for some time yet. So some stimulus was expected, to at least stem the rise in unemployment. The balance of payments was in hefty surplus and the exchange rate strong, so those traditional constraints on expansion were not operative.

Ten minutes into his Budget Statement, Sir Geoffrey made it clear to the doubters – and this included many in his own party – that so far from retreating from his former policies he was intent to 'unthread the bold eye of rebellion, and welcome home again discarded faith'. He raised taxes by £3.6 bn (£2.6 bn in a full year), of which £2.4 bn was, once again, to come from taxes on consumption.

The logic behind this apparently perverse action was simple. The PSBR for 1980–81, which had been planned to be £8.5 bn, had overshot by £5 bn to £13.5 bn and, on unchanged taxes, was forecast to be £14 bn in 1981–82. The Medium-Term Financial Strategy implied a PSBR for 1981–82 of £7.5 bn; but, it was estimated, the severity of the recession would add some £3 bn to

that, to yield a required PSBR of some £10.5 bn. So taxes had to
be raised sufficient to bring £14 bn down to £10.5 bn.

Unreconstructed Keynesians assumed that such a huge
increase in taxes must be contractionary. Not so, said ministers;
what mattered was not the fiscal stance but the relationship
between the rate of inflation and the rate of monetary growth, and
since the underlying rate of inflation was within the new monetary
target the Budget was not contractionary. In monetarist terms the
argument was logical.

The Medium-Term Financial Strategy

Scrambling among the wreckage on the floor, the Treasury set
about reassembling the MTFS. It came out looking, on the face of
it, almost as good as new. The money-supply path remained
unchanged: 6–10 per cent in 1981–82, falling in successive years to
5–9 and 4–8 per cent. But of course 6–10 per cent in 1981 was not
the same as 6–10 per cent a year earlier, because in the meantime
the monetary base had risen by some 20 per cent: the target range
incorporated, as they say, base drift. 'Nonetheless,' said the
Treasury, 'it is important not to disregard the past year's rapid
rise ... it is the Government's intention to consider clawing back
some of the past year's rapid growth of £M3 by permitting an
undershoot as and when the opportunity arises.'[10] The authorities
stuck to their chosen central measure of money although they
conceded that 'Taken on its own £M3 has not been a good
indicator of monetary conditions in the past year.' We have noted
that in discounting cost-push explanations of inflation, the
authorities explained that things like oil price rises and VAT were
once-for-all shocks that did not affect the underlying picture. But
what about the excessive growth of the money supply in 1980; did
that not have implications for future inflation? Well, no; because
'Some of the factors that have been identified as contributing to
the rapid growth of £M3 in 1980–81 mean that it should not have
the implications for future inflation which generally follow an
increase in money supply.' Whatever had happened to sterling
M3, 'monetary conditions remained tight' because of a high
exchange rate and high interest rates.

What about the other component of the MTFS, the PSBR?
That was modified, as shown in Table 7.2. Thus an ostensibly
unchanged path for the growth of the money supply was still
consistent with a higher growth path for the PSBR.

The MTFS had been reconstructed; but the experience of 1980
had left its mark. The MTFS concluded with the assurance that

Table 7.2   Public Sector Borrowing (£ bn and per cent)

	1980–81	1981–82	1982–83	1983–84
1980 MTFS at 1978–79 prices	6	5	3.5	2.5
1981 MTFS at 1979–80 prices	11.5	8	6.5	4
Per cent of GDP				
1980	3.75	3	2.25	1.5
1981	6	4.25	3.25	2

although the outcome might, in the nature of things, differ from the plan, ' ... the intention would be to hold firmly to the main thrust of the financial strategy ... '. Fair enough; but not quite the same as the ' ... there would be no question of departing from the money supply policy ... ' of a year earlier.

The exchange rate dilemma

In 1980 the exchange rate was much too high for the comfort of exporting industry. One of the reasons for this was high interest rates in the UK. The Government wanted both interest rates and the exchange rate lower but because borrowing and the money supply were running away could do little about it. One of the purposes of the 1981 Budget had been to pave the way for a reduction in interest rates, and indeed MLR was cut by 2 points to 12 per cent in the Budget.

The exchange rate declined; from $2.375 in January, it had come down to $2.08 by the end of May. It then fell sharply, losing 17 cents, to $1.91 by 5 June. That was tolerable; but when the rate fell further to a four-year low of $1.7565 on 10 August, a fall of some 25 per cent since January, the authorities were in a real dilemma. The effective exchange rate (against all currencies) had fallen less, by about 14 per cent; but a fall of between 14 and 25 per cent implied, given the UK's reliance on imports, a rise of somewhere between 3½ and 6 points in the price level, after a lag. The Budget forecast had been for the rate of inflation to fall to 8 per cent in the second quarter of 1982 (a rate, you will recall, within the target range for the growth of the money supply). But this forecast was explicitly based on the assumption that the exchange rate would remain unchanged. There was no objective for the exchange rate, because under monetarist theory it had to be left to market forces; so no one *expected* it to remain unchanged, but you have to base a price forecast on some assumption about the exchange rate. So there was the problem: whether to go into reverse on interest rate policy or to put at risk the central focus of economic policy – the reduction of the rate of inflation.

In mid-September the authorities organized a 2-point rise in bank base rates (the continuous posting of MLR having ceased the previous month) to 14 per cent; and a further 2-point rise occurred on 1 October. The authorities, according to Press reports, also intervened to support sterling in the foreign exchange market. It was an interesting lesson in the conflict of objectives, on the limits that events impose upon theory and on the general futility of worrying too much about an exchange rate that is too high: the markets will, more often than not, take care of that for you. Similarly, they will correct a rate that falls too low, as they might have done on this occasion, given time. Later, in 1984, under a different Chancellor, the authorities were to take a more relaxed view of a steeply falling exchange rate.

Monetary management

Even if monetarist theory is wholly correct it is useless as a policy instrument unless something called the money supply can be both identified and controlled. For identification the authorities at first settled on sterling M3 (£M3) but this did not prove entirely satisfactory. Speaking at the Lord Mayor's dinner on 16 October 1980 the Governor of the Bank of England, reviewing the events of that year had this to say:

> In reflecting on this whole experience my final observation is to emphasise the sheer erratic variability of the counterparts contained in sterling M3. The lesson, perhaps, is the need to avoid attaching undue importance to short-term developments in any single monetary aggregrate; it is sounder to take into account, as we in fact do, the underlying developments both in the aggregates as a whole and in the real economy.

Note the last five words. The Treasury, for once, agreed, conceding in the next MTFS that ' ... £M3 has not been a good indicator of monetary conditions in the past year'. One reason for the limited usefulness of sterling M3 was that it included interest-bearing deposits; and the instrument for controlling the money supply (or, rather, credit – not at all the same thing, according to Prof. Friedman) was the rate of interest. When interest rates were high because monetary growth was high, money naturally tended to flow *into* interest-bearing deposit accounts, inflating sterling M3. Thus, to some extent action designed to contain the growth of the money supply expanded it.

But whether policy is focused on one aggregate or several, the money supply still has to be controlled; and to this problem the Treasury and the Bank, acting in disharmony, turned their attention. The first results, as we have seen, had been published in *Monetary Control* (Cmnd 7858), in March 1980. There were proposals for improving short-term control, and the 'Corset' was to be phased out; this was done in the following June.

After consultation, the Chancellor of the Exchequer had announced in the House of Commons on 24 November 1980 the broad outlines of new arrangements, and the Bank of England had issued a background note *Methods of Monetary Control*. On 12 March 1981 came another Bank paper *Monetary Control: next steps*; and on 5 August 1981 the Bank published *Monetary Control: provisions* setting out new arrangements, some of them already gradually introduced, that were to come formally into effect on 20 August 1981. The whole exercise had taken some 18 months; given the wide range of views that existed, this was not excessive.

In broad terms the choice facing the authorities in seeking to improve control lay between a modification of existing methods, which relied heavily on interest rate movements, and a move to some form of 'monetary base control' (MBC). (In Friedmanian terms a choice between controlling credit [wrong] and controlling the monetary base [right].) The authorities came down on the side of credit control but pointed out that the modifications introduced ' ... would be consistent with a gradual evolution towards a monetary base system ... '.

In addition to the abolition of the 'Corset' (already done), the main features of the new arrangements were as follows:
1.   The practice of continuously 'posting' Minimum Lending Rate (MLR) was discontinued. (Bank base rate took its place.)
2.   In future the Bank would aim to keep interest rates at the very short end of the market within an undisclosed band. This it would do by open-market operations rather than by direct lending through 'the discount window.' (Open-market operations affect the banking system's assets and are thus 'consistent' with MBC.)

3.   The requirement that the banks maintain a minimum reserve ratio was abolished.

These new arrangements, it was said, represented 'a significant change' in the operations of the Bank of England in the money markets. The intention was that the markets should have a much greater influence on short-term interest rates. Interest rates were likely to fluctuate more widely; and the Bank would discount (buy) larger quantities of commercial bank bills instead of, as formerly, mainly government paper.

The new regime was a compromise, a reluctant move away from outright control of interest rates by the authorities and towards control of the monetary base. In terms of monetary theory it was a move away from controlling the *price* of money (the rate of interest) towards controlling the *quantity*. (As is well known, one cannot simultaneously control both price and quantity.)

It was a somewhat uneasy compromise. The authorities were reluctant to let go of the rate of interest instrument (the rate was to be held within an undisclosed band) and seemed still to regard this as their main or fall-back instrument. Yet this instrument was now outside their control except through open-market operations. The linkage had been extended. Nevertheless, as we have seen, when the pound came under pressure in September the Bank was able to organize a 2-point rise in bank base rate.

Civil Service Department

On 12 November the Prime Minister announced that the Civil Service Department would be abolished from 16 November. The Treasury would be responsible for the control of civil service manpower, pay and superannuation, the Central Computer and Telecommunications Agency, and the Civil Service Catering Organisation. Other functions would go to a new Management and Personnel Office in the Cabinet Office.

Autumn Statement

In his Autumn Statement on 2 December the Chancellor announced decisions on Public Expenditure in 1982–83. In cash terms (the new basis for public expenditure planning) expenditure in 1982–83 was raised by a net £5 bn over the plans in the previous White Paper (converted to a cash basis). Employees' National Insurance Contributions were to be raised by 1 per cent from the beginning of April 1982 to raise £1 bn. The economic statement published on the same day forecast that GDP, after falling 4 per cent in the previous two years, would rise by 1 per cent in 1982; but unemployment, which reached 2,940,000 in December, would go on rising.

1982

Public expenditure

The Public Expenditure White Paper *The Government's Expenditure Plans 1982-83 to 1984-85* (Cmnd 8494) published on Budget Day, 9 March, was the first to be presented entirely in cash terms. It showed, unusually, that the out-turn for the year just ending was very close to plans. As foreshadowed in November 1981, expenditure in 1982-83 was to be £5 bn more than planned and £10 bn more than in 1981-82. As a ratio to GDP, expenditure (including debt interest) was planned to fall slightly, to 44.5 per cent.

Public expenditure White Papers have always been fairly impenetrable. The switch from the 'funny money' of constant prices to cash did not seem to have improved matters: the Paper, said the *Financial Times*, was 'a virtually unintelligible heap of numbers.'[11]

The Budget

The Budget included substantial tax cuts overall although, continuing the pattern of switching the tax burden to consumption, indirect taxes were raised, by about £1 bn. Direct taxation was reduced by £2 bn in 1982-83 and £3.2 bn in a full year; and the National Insurance Surcharge reduced, at a cost of £1 bn gross. The Budget included changes in oil taxation, including the introduction of advance payment of Petroleum Revenue Tax. These proposals were amended on 9 June 1982. The economic forecasts showed GDP rising by 2 per cent in the first half 1983 over the first half of 1982. The PSBR for 1981-82 was on target at £10.6 bn and was planned to fall to £9.5 bn in 1982-83.

The Medium-Term Financial Strategy

For the third period running, the growth of sterling M3 had substantially exceeded the target, despite the fact that each new target, by starting from a higher base, discounted all previous excess growth. By February 1982 the base of sterling M3, after adjusting for the change in the monetary sector that took place in November 1981, was some 37 per cent higher than in February

1980. In the year to February 1982, growth was 14.5 per cent, against a target of 6–10 per cent.

To judge from the March 1982 MTFS, the Treasury was in some difficulty over the money supply. First it had to explain the excess growth, which it did on the basis of unexpected changes in the behaviour of money-holders and on institutional changes and banking behaviour – the banks going in to mortgage lending, for example.

But early on the Treasury made it clear that it was not at all happy with its chosen measure, sterling M3.

> In the short run ... the relationship between any one measure of money and money incomes may be influenced by a range of factors including the behaviour of the exchange rate, the level and structure of interest rates, changes in savings behaviour and the imbalance between interest rates and fiscal policy, as well as institutional changes.
>
> Both broad and narrow measures of money convey useful information about financial conditions.
>
> The case for looking at a range of measures is especially strong when the financial system is undergoing rapid change.

Quite so. Yet *Monetary Control* had come down firmly on the side of having a single aggregate:

> The Government believes that its monetary policy can best be formulated if it sets targets for the growth of one of the aggregates ... This gives the clearest guidance to those concerned in both financial markets and domestic industry, on which to assess the direction of Government policy and to formulate expectations.

To have targets for several or all aggregates

> ... would make it much more difficult for the market and the public to appraise the determination of the authorities to meet their monetary objectives. In the short run, the various aggregates respond differently and with different speeds to changes in interest rates so that seemingly inconsistent measures might be needed to meet the various targets. The Government therefore believes that targets are best set in terms of a single aggregate.

Despite the risk of confusion the Treasury decided that the target range should in future apply not only to sterling M3 but to a narrow definition of money, M1; and to a broad definition, PSL2. (See Fig. 12.1) Since these different aggregates moved differentially it was a fair bet that *one* of them would hit the target range. What about M1?

> Sustained progress in reducing inflation and interest rates may lead to some shift back into non-interest bearing forms of money. In such circumstances a more rapid growth of M1 than indicated, might, for a time, be acceptable. On the other hand further changes in the terms offered on transactions and savings deposits could affect the relative size and significance of different measures of money. The size and timing of these effects is inevitably uncertain, but they will be taken into account in assessing the performance of the monetary aggregates ...

That seemed to cover most possibilities.

Not only had the Treasury increased the number of goal posts, it had made them wider: the new range for the growth of the aggregates in 1982–83 was 8–12 per cent, from 6–10 in 1981–82 (when the range for 1982–83 had been 5–9, on, of course, a much lower base).

Moreover, the objective now was not so much to hit the monetary targets as to 'maintain monetary conditions that will bring about a further reduction in inflation'. And 'Interpretation of monetary conditions will continue to take account of all available evidence, including the behaviour of the exchange rate.' The general intention, the Treasury concluded 'would be to hold firmly to the central purpose of the strategy by steady but not excessive, downward pressure on the monetary variables. The key to sustained recovery lies in moderating the growth of costs ....'

The growth of costs? How did costs get into this? The MTFS, 1982 version, may have been all very sensible and pragmatic but it bore only a passing resemblance to monetarism.

The other component of the MTFS, the PSBR, had also been loosened, but not very much: the objective of getting the PSBR down to 2 per cent of GDP was shifted back one year, to 1984–85. It was the PSBR rather than the money supply that now appeared to be at the heart of the MTFS.

The Autumn Statement

In November 1982 the Autumn Statement became a formal part of the economic year. Since the Industry Act of 1975 the Treasury had been obliged to publish a set of economic forecasts in the autumn and this had sometimes been the occasion for a Statement by the Chancellor. Now the procedure was formalized and expanded. The Treasury published a printed document containing the forecasts, an outline of public expenditure plans for the next financial year, details of changes in National Insurance Contributions and in the National Insurance Surcharge, and tables showing the revenue effects of illustrative tax changes. In addition the Chancellor made a fairly brief Statement to the House. Since the Statement included a cautious assessment of possible tax changes in next spring's Budget, what was presented in total was a sort of mini-Budget.

In 1982 the content of the Chancellor's Statement was in fact fairly unexciting; but then, almost anything Sir Geoffrey Howe announced *seemed* fairly unexciting.[12] There were some public expenditure changes, the biggest of which was £622 m. to cover extra costs following the Falkland Islands action. For the first time since 1977 public expenditure in the next financial year was to be lower than planned on Budget Day. Spending on programmes actually increased but this was accommodated by using £2.5 bn from the contingency reserve. The National Insurance Surcharge was reduced by a further 1 per cent to 1.5 per cent.

On the financial front, the PSBR and the money supply were deemed to be more or less on target. The GDP, estimated to have grown 0.5 per cent in 1982, was expected to rise 1.5 per cent in 1983. The year-on-year change in the retail price index, already down to about 6 per cent from 12 per cent in January, was expected to fall to 5 per cent. Thus, in terms of its strategy and its declared priorities the Government could fairly claim some success. But the economy was still deep in recession. The headline total of unemployment had passed 3 million in September and, with only modest growth of GDP, was likely to rise further.

The money markets

The rate against the dollar declined throughout the year but the effective rate remained remarkably steady, at around 90.0, until mid-November when both rates fell sharply. In the course of the year the dollar rate declined by some 15 per cent, from $1.91 to $1.62, and the effective rate by about half that, from 91 to 84. Despite the weakening rate against the dollar, the authorities did not resist a steady fall in nominal interest rates: base rate fell from 14.5 per cent in January to 9 per cent in November.

When, towards the end of November, the rate fell below $1.60 the market waited for the authorities to signal a rise in interest rates, but they remained silent. On 26 November Barclays Bank took the matter into their own hands and took everyone, including apparently the Bank of England, by surprise by raising its base lending rate by a full point to 10 per cent. The pound immediately jumped 4 cents, back to above the $1.60 level.

Further heavy selling developed in the week commencing 6 December and the Bank intervened heavily and continuously to support sterling; unofficial estimates put the amount spent at $800 m. At the same time it provided generous assistance to the money market to restrain the rise in interest rates. This was somewhat paradoxical. The Bank appears to have taken the view that the pressures on sterling were likely to be temporary and it did not want to see interest rates go higher unnecessarily.

Although the nominal rate of interest had fallen substantially through the year until November, the rate of inflation fell even faster so that the real rate of interest rose slightly. This, in conjunction with lower inflation expectations, enabled the authorities to sell large amounts of gilt-edged stocks and keep the money supply under control.

1983

Public expenditure

For a long time there was a lobby which pressed for the public expenditure figures to be published at the same time as the Budget so that the revenue and expenditure plans of the Government could be seen together. This was done for three years commencing in 1980. In 1983, following proposals by the Treasury and Civil Service Committee of the House of Commons in their report on Budgetary Reform, the Public Expenditure White Paper was published *before* the Budget, on 1 February.

The Government's Expenditure Plans 1983–84 to 1985–86, (Cmnd 8789), published in two volumes and, as in the previous year, in cash terms, showed that the estimated out-turn for 1982–83, at £113 bn, was well within the plans of the March 1982 White Paper. And the plans for the two succeeding years were also slightly below the totals planned in 1982.

This was undoubtedly commendable but, as usual with public expenditure White Papers, it was wise to look beneath the headline figures thrust before our wondering eyes. Further examination revealed that expenditure on programmes in 1982–83 was way above plans and the total was only brought back to below planning level by a £1 bn under-use of the contingency reserve and another near-billion of shortfall. The plan had been undershot because the Government had, through the contingency reserve and not allowing for shortfall, made an over-generous provision in the first place.

This might be an election year; and since any scope for tax reductions would depend upon public expenditure estimates for 1983–84 it would be prudent not to inflate the expenditure plans for that year. Accordingly, the provisions for 1983–84 made in the 1982 plan were altered downwards by reducing the contingency reserve by £2.5 bn and inserting £1.2 bn for shortfall. Without these adjustments, planned spending, so far from being below 1982 plans, would have been some £2.5 bn above.

Although public expenditure in 1983–84 was within plans it was still planned to rise, both in cash and in inflation-adjusted terms. The White Paper contained one table (Table 1.14) in prices adjusted for past and expected inflation which showed that public expenditure had risen by 4.4 per cent between 1979–80 and 1982–83 and, on present plans, would rise by a further 0.8 per cent in 1983–84.

The Budget

On 15 March, in what was to be his final Budget, Sir Geoffrey Howe reduced taxes overall but continued the switch from direct to indirect taxation. Direct taxes were reduced by £2.3 bn (£2.9 bn full year) and indirect taxes raised by £370 m. (£205 m. full year). These changes included the indexation of allowances and duties that was now expected so that the 'additional' changes were somewhat lower. A further 0.5 per cent was taken off the National Insurance Surcharge. Largely because of a windfall on oil revenues the estimated PSBR for 1982–83, at £7.5 bn, was £2 bn below forecast. For 1983–84 it was raised to £8.2 bn. The economic forecasts showed that output in 1982 had risen much less than expected, 0.5 per cent instead of 1.5 per cent; and so had prices, 6 per cent against 9 per cent. In 1983 GDP was forecast to rise 2 per cent, not enough to lower unemployment; and the rate of inflation was forecast to stay at around 6 per cent.

The Medium-Term Financial Strategy

After two disastrous years the MTFS came good in 1982–83. All six of the monetary aggregates, including the three targeted in the MTFS, were, up to February, within the target range of 8–12 per cent. The central aggregate, sterling M3, at 10 per cent, was in the middle of the range. For the future there was to be no change, with the range at 7–11 per cent in 1983–84 and falling to 6–10 and 5–9 per cent in the next two years.

Following the undershoot of the PSBR in 1982–83, its path was lowered and flattened (see Table 7.3).

Table 7.3

	1981–82	1982–83	1983–84	1984–85	1985–86
PSBR (£bn cash)					
1982	10.5	9.5	8.5	6.5	
1983	8.7	7.5	8	8	7
As % GDP					
1982	4.25	3.5	2.75	2	
1983	3.5	2.75	2.75	2.5	2
Money GDP, market prices					
1982	255	280	307	336	
1983	254	275	296	322	346

Money GDP had been included in the MTFS tables since 1982. This seems to reflect an aspect of the strategy that is important but not spelled out, namely that with a given path for money GDP, composed of an unknown combination of prices and quantities (and with a growth of the money supply consistent with it), a fall in prices, including wages, will leave room for higher quantities, i.e. for real growth. Or, to look at it from another angle, with a given nominal money supply a fall in the price level will increase the *real* money supply, and generate growth.

The Budget – postscript

It used to be customary to hold the spring Budget in April, after the end of the financial year, but in recent years it has been moved forward to March. This means that all the figures relating to the financial year just ending are estimates, but with less than a month to go, these estimates are not expected to differ greatly from the final out-turn and are used, as they have to be, as the basis for estimating what the PSBR would be in the financial year about to begin before Budget changes. Upon this figure the Chancellor bases his Budget judgement, i.e. whether he has to raise taxes to reduce the projected PSBR or can reduce taxes to increase it. In March 1983 the estimate for the financial year 1982–83 was for a PSBR out-turn of £7.5 bn, £2 bn below the forecast in the 1982 Budget of £9.5 bn. This, as we have seen, enabled the Chancellor to cut taxes and still remain within a PSBR of £8.5 bn for 1983–84 as projected in the MTFS. Had the Budget taken place in April the Chancellor would have been in some difficulty; for within a month of the Budget the Central Government Borrowing Requirement for 1982–83 was revised upwards by £1.3 bn and the PSBR by £1.7 bn to £9.2 bn, with consequent implications for the PSBR in 1983–84.

The exchange rate

The fall in sterling that had begun the previous November continued into the new year. The pound fell sharply early in January, and, once again, it was Barclays Bank that took the lead in raising base rate by one per cent to 11 per cent. The Bank of England validated the rise in market rates but did not intervene in the currency market. After their heavy intervention in December the authorities seem to have decided that enough was enough and that for the time being the market must have its way.

The fall continued, in something of a crisis atmosphere. A number of causes were cited: the possibility of a general election, a statement by Mr Peter Shore that the Opposition would devalue by 30 per cent in two stages, and, most importantly, turmoil in the oil markets and an expectation of a significant fall in the price of oil (which would damage the UK, an oil producer, relatively more than oil importers).

By the end of March both the rate against the dollar and the effective rate had fallen to all-time lows: $1.4515 and 77.9, falls of nearly 13 and over 15 per cent respectively. In contrast to earlier bouts of weakness, in, say, 1976 when the flight from sterling was attributed to high government borrowing, the growth of the money supply, inflationary expectations and so on, this all-time low was reached only two weeks after a firm Budget in which all these aspects of the economy appeared to be in order. After March the rate recovered, wobbled a bit in early May on the announcement of a General Election, but strengthened again

when polls predicted a Conservative victory. By the end of May
much of the earlier loss had been regained.

Exchange rate policy

The Opposition had declared in favour of a deliberate and
substantial devaluation; and the Government, in the later stages at
least, had argued the futility of intervention to prevent a
depreciation brought about by the market.

This, therefore, may be an appropriate point for a short
digression on the virtues, or otherwise, of a low exchange rate. It
is well known that to lower the exchange rate has one major
advantage and one major disadvantage. On the one hand it
improves competitiveness in overseas markets, and on the other it
raises the price of imports in sterling. This latter raises the
domestic price level and may, depending upon the circumstances
of the time, stimulate secondary rises through higher money
wages. Thus, it is better, if possible, to improve competitiveness
without lowering the exchange rate, i.e. by lowering domestic
costs. It is easier and less painful to lower the exchange rate than
to lower domestic costs and hence the former course is known as
'the soft option'.

A second, and less obvious consequence of lowering the
exchange rate is that, generally speaking, it worsens the terms of
trade. We trade on worse terms because we are providing our
goods and services at a lower price in foreign exchange. We either
earn less foreign exchange (which will buy fewer foreign goods and
services); or to earn the same amount of foreign exchange as
formerly we need to export a greater quantity of goods and
services. Since a higher volume of goods and services exported
(or a lower volume imported) reduces the amount available for
home consumption, the national standard of living is reduced.
Thus the soft option carries hard consequences. The alternative –
to lower domestic costs – may not have such hard consequences.
If we assume that costs are reduced not only in exporting
industries but across the board, then *prices* will fall also, so that
real incomes may not fall or may not fall much.

But if the domestic economy is severely underemployed and the
only route to increased employment is via exports, then to lower
the exchange rate may be a sensible option. The effect would be
to increase the total quantity of goods produced (including,
through secondary effects, goods for home consumption), and this
would in some degree offset the deterioration in the terms of
trade. The net effect would be that those formerly unemployed

would be much better off and the rest would be slightly worse off; there would be some redistribution of real income.

International policy

At the end of April the Finance Ministers of the UK, USA, West Germany, France, Italy, Japan and Canada journeyed to Washington to consider the report of a Working Group on exchange market intervention. They concluded that intervention had only a limited role to play, that exchange rate stability was a major objective, that it must be achieved by compatible policy mixes, that countries must look at the exchange rate as a possible guide to policy and have regard to the effect on other countries. They were against sin.

Election

At the general election in June the Conservative Government was returned with an increased majority.

Sir Geoffrey Howe

Sir Geoffrey Howe, kindly, soft-spoken, hard-working, was not quite the 'dead sheep' of Denis Healey's famous barb.[13]

Given that it was his task to implement the new regime, with all that that implied in the way of changing entrenched practices and modes of thought, he would probably have chosen to start at a time other than 1979. There were, immediately, two major problems: the huge rise in oil prices in the second half of 1979; and the backlash from previous incomes policies including the Government's election promise to honour the findings of the Clegg Commission on public sector pay. The oil price rise had two effects on trade: it depressed the world economy, upon the state of which British exports depend quite heavily; and, because we had our own oil, it raised the exchange rate, adding to exporters' difficulties. (But it also improved the terms of trade and helped to bring down the rate of inflation faster than expected.) Pressure from wage awards and the exchange rate helped induce a sharp fall in output and employment. But to have delayed the implementation of the new policies, and in particular the anti-inflationary policy, would have been damaging to credibility. Sir Geoffrey pressed ahead.

After considerable deliberation and consultation he took the risk of publishing a Medium-Term Financial Strategy and, in its first two years, he, and it, were blown right off course by the factors cited above, by the Treasury's failure to forecast or control public spending and borrowing (itself partly due to the unexpected depth of the recession), and by the Bank of England's inability or reluctance to control the money supply. By the time of the 1981 Budget Sir Geoffrey was under severe pressure to abandon the strategy but, not unreasonably, since it was a *medium-term* strategy, he declined to do so; and the world obliged by turning up roughly the numbers in the strategy.

Some Chancellors of the Exchequer are, by common consent, a success; others, by equal consent, a failure, even a disaster. It is a matter of weighing their successes and their failures against the difficulties they faced, largely a question of judgement. In so far as success can be measured objectively it can be done only by matching achievement against declared objectives.

Sir Geoffrey Howe's objectives were limited. Unlike Mr Callaghan and Mr Jenkins he had no objective for the balance of payments which in any case, with North Sea oil flowing, more or less looked after itself. Between 1980 and 1983 the net trade in oil was worth nearly £15 bn to the balance of payments on current account. Nor, again like those two Chancellors, did he have any objective for the exchange rate, which was floating and, under monetarist doctrine, was to be determined by the market. Unlike Mr Callaghan and Mr Barber, he had no objective for economic growth, no National Plan or 5 per cent growth policy. Unlike every other Chancellor since the War he had no objective of full employment since, under the monetarist philosophy, this was not something within the control of government.

What he did have objectives for were public expenditure and taxation, public sector borrowing, the rate of growth of the money supply, and the rate of inflation, all of which were to be reduced. He did not achieve the first two: both public expenditure and the burden of taxation grew. Public sector borrowing he reduced from £10 bn to £8.9 bn (although it rose to £12.7 bn in between). But beside this achievement must be set the fact that over the four financial years ending in 1982–83 the Government received well over £20 bn in revenue from the North Sea (before that, *total* revenue had been under £1 bn). The rapid and huge increase in North Sea revenue was the major factor in reducing the borrowing requirement.

Over the whole period the money supply grew by some 67 per cent. This was rather worse than the performance of Mr Healey, who, in a Chancellorship lasting a year longer than Sir Geoffrey's, saw the money supply grow by some 65 per cent. The control of the money supply was the instrument through which the rate of inflation was to be brought down. Despite the failure to control the declared instrument, the rate of inflation did come down, to 3.7 per cent. Sir Geoffrey Howe achieved his primary and overriding objective. But there was a cost, part of which was a rise in unemployment from 1.2 million (5.1%) when he took office to 3.0 million (12.5%). In the nature of macroeconomics, possibly in the nature of life itself, the more objectives there are, the harder it is to achieve any of them. Sir Geoffrey was not unduly beset by this problem since his objectives were so limited. It might be argued that any Chancellor allowed the luxury of 3 million unemployed could have brought down the rate of inflation. There is nothing exclusively monetarist in curing inflation with depression. It may be debated whether the one objective that was secured was not secured at too great a cost; but the objective itself was an important one, from which benefits will flow.

Sir Geoffrey's longer-term objective was to reverse the relative decline of the British economy, and for a verdict on that we shall have to wait longer.

Diary of events, May 1979 – June 1983

1979
5 May   Sir Richard Edward Geoffrey Howe becomes Chancellor of the Exchequer.
15   Price Commission to be abolished.
12 Jun.   Budget. VAT raised to 15 per cent. Exchange control eased.
18 Jul.   Exchange control further relaxed.
31   Pound falls 6.5 cents to $2.2480.
17 Aug.   New 'Tax and Price' Index published.
23 Oct.   Remaining exchange controls lifted.
1 Nov.   White Paper *The Government's Expenditure Plans 1980–81* (Cmnd 7746) published.
15   Monetary measures. MLR up 3 points to 17 per cent. 'Corset' extended. Target for sterling M3 of 7–11 per cent.

1980
17 Jan.   Date of Budget announced: 25 March.

22	Date of Budget changed to 26 March.
20 Mar.	Green Paper *Monetary Control* (Cmnd 7858).
26	Budget; and Public Expenditure White Paper, *The Government's Expenditure Plans 1980–81 to 1983–84* (Cmnd 7841). Medium-Term Financial Strategy (MTFS) launched. Announcement of Enterprise Zones.
27 May	Pound closes at $2.3705, highest since March 1975.
3 Jun.	Pound falls 4.5 cents in half an hour after PM's answer.
18	The 'Corset' abolished. During 1979 and the first half of 1980 OPEC oil prices rise from around $13 to $32 per barrel ($2.70 in Sept. 1973).
3 Jul.	MLR down 1 point to 16 per cent.
Aug.	Bank changes methods of intervention to allow markets more influence on interest rates.
27 Aug.	Unemployment reaches 2 million.
9 Sept.	Treasury 'Statement on Monetary Developments'. Removal of 'Corset' has exaggerated growth of sterling M3.
17 Nov.	First issue of index-linked National Savings Certificates.
21	£250 m. for special employment measures.
24	£1 bn cuts in public expenditure 1981–82. MLR down 2 points to 14 per cent. National Insurance contributions up 1 per cent in 1981–82. Changes in monetary management; Bank background note *Methods of Monetary Control*.

1981

6 Jan.	Mr Leon Brittan replaces Mr John Biffen as Chief Secretary to the Treasury.
18	Government surrenders to miners over pit closures.
27	New 20p coin in 1982, new £1 coin in 1983.
2 Feb.	Effective exchange rate index rebased on 1975, with new weights.
18	NCB withdraws pit closure plans; Government to provide extra funds.
5 Mar.	Highly critical report from Treasury and Civil Service Committee, *Monetary Policy*, House of Commons Paper 163-1.
10	Budget; and White Paper *The Government's Expenditure Plans 1981–82 to 1983–84* (Cmnd 8175) Indirect taxes up by almost £2.5 bn, total taxes by £3.6 bn. No increase in personal tax allowances. MTFS updated. MLR cut by 2 points to 12 per cent. Sterling

	M3 target unchanged at 6–10 per cent. Public expenditure to fall to 1983–84.
	Next (1981) expenditure survey to be in cash terms.
12	Bank published *Monetary Control: next steps* (see 5 and 20 Aug.).
23	Lecture on *The Budget Strategy* by Nigel Lawson to Institute of Fiscal Studies.
27	First issue of index-linked Treasury stock.
12 May	Sir Geoffrey Howe gives Mais Lecture on 'The fight against inflation'.
4 Jun.	Sterling falls by 7 cents in the day, to $1.94 ($2.38 in Jan.).
2 Jul.	Tobacco, betting and gaming taxes to be raised to offset halving of proposed Budget increase in derv duty.
27	Special employment measures.
5 Aug.	Bank paper *Monetary Control: provisions*. To come into force 20 Aug.
10	£ falls to 4-year low of $1.7565 but quickly recovers.
20	New arrangements for monetary control into force. MLR no longer to be continuously posted.
24	£ reaches $1.8790.
14 Sept.	£ falls to $1.7671. Bank base rate raised 2 points to 14 per cent.
1 Oct.	Base rate raised 2 points to 16 per cent.
21	Government to buy BP shares acquired by the Bank of England in the Burmah Oil rescue.
12 Nov.	Civil Service Department to be abolished from 16 Nov.
18	'Monetary sector' to replace the more narrowly defined 'banking sector'.
2 Dec.	Statement on public expenditure – to be increased by £5 bn cash over plans. National Insurance contributions to be raised one percentage point in April 1982.
15	Special employment measures.
16	Green Paper on alternatives to domestic rates.
31	Pound closes at $1.9110.

1982

7 Jan.	Green Paper *Corporation Tax* (Cmnd 8456).
9 Mar.	Budget; and White Paper *The Government's Expenditure Plans 1982–83 to 1984–85* (Cmnd 8494 – I and II). Substantial tax cuts overall but indirect taxes raised.
	National Insurance Surcharge reduced. PSBR on target. Money supply targets relaxed.

end	Reserves reduced by $4.2 bn on annual revaluation.
2 Apr.	Falklands invaded.
Jun.	Bank to introduce new monetary aggregate, M2.
9	Chancellor announces changes to Budget proposals on oil taxation, especially Advanced Petroleum Revenue Tax.
mid	End of Falklands fighting.
25	Chancellor announces new arrangements governing borrowing by the corporate and public sectors.
7 Jul.	Report of the Committee of Inquiry into Civil Service Pay (the *Megaw Report*) (Cmnd 8590).
26	All remaining controls on HP removed.
27	Measures to alleviate unemployment.
8 Nov.	Autumn Statement. National Insurance Surcharge cut by 1 per cent from April 1983. National Insurance contributions for employers and employees increased by 0.25 per cent from April 1983. Public expenditure for 1983–84 reduced.
end	Pound falls 6.5 cents against dollar in latter part of November. $1.6175 at year end ($1.9110 at end 1981).

1983

Jan.	Rate of inflation (RPI) falls to 4.9 per cent, lowest for 13 years.
11	Green Paper on trade union reform.
28	10p increase in prescription charges from April 1983.
1 Feb.	*The Government's Expenditure Plans 1983–84 to 1985–86* (Cmnd 8789).
15 Mar.	Budget. Tax cuts.
Apr.	Mortgage Interest Relief at Source (MIRA) introduced; and a new £1 coin.
May	Rate of inflation 3.7 per cent.
9	General Election announced for 9 June. Progress of full Finance Bill halted, replaced by Shorter Finance Act.
13	Parliament dissolved.
28–31	Williamsburg Economic Summit.
9 Jun.	General Election. Conservative majority.

Notes and references

1. The controls were imposed by Defence (Finance) Regulations under the Emergency Powers Act 1939; and continued after

the end of the Second World War under the Exchange
Control Act 1947. The controls were largely operated by the
Bank of England under powers delegated by the Treasury.

2. *Economic Trends*, No. 317, March 1980.
3. *Official Report*, 3 Jun. 1980, Oral Answers, Cols 1243, 1244.
4. *Second Report*, 1980–81, H of C 79, para. 39, Dec. 1980.
5. See *BEQB*, Vol. 20, No. 3, Sept. 1980, pp. 266, 283, 284.
6. *BEQB*, Vol. 20, No. 3, Sept. 1980, p. 266.
7. *BEQB*, Vol. 20, No. 2, Jun. 1980, pp. 120–2.
8. This line continued to be modified. In a speech on 26 June
   1981, the opening shot in a campaign to influence the pay
   round commencing on 1 August, the Chancellor of the
   Exchequer pleaded for considerably lower pay rises. Next day
   the *Financial Times* in its leader wrote 'The present
   Government came to office with the view that pay was no
   concern of ministers, and should be left to market
   forces ... we have now reached the stage ... when ministers
   decide that pay is after all a political issue. The Chancellor,
   the Bank of England, a whole parade of junior ministers, and
   in the end, we may be sure, all the Queen's horses and all the
   Queen's men are praising the virtues of restraint.'
9. T. S. Eliot, *The Hollow Men*.
10. This and following Treasury quotes from the 1981–82
    Financial Statement and Budget Report.
11. Leading article 17 Feb. 1984.
12. As Alan Watkins observed, 'Those who are acquainted with
    him know him to be a kindly and decent soul, with no side at
    all: but, if the Government had decided to set up a
    concentration camp in the Western Highlands for, say,
    dissident elements who had incurred Mr Bernard Ingham's
    disapproval, there would be no one more suitable to make the
    announcement than Sir Geoffrey.' *The Observer*, 29 Jan.
    1984.
13. Denis Healey had likened an attack by Sir Geoffrey to 'being
    savaged by a dead sheep'.

8

Mr Lawson, June 1983–

Custodian of the strategy

Protecting the PSBR

When Mr Nigel Lawson, former Financial Secretary to the Treasury and author, in large part, of the Medium-Term Financial Strategy, became Chancellor of the Exchequer following the Conservative victory in the June Election, he was soon in action to defend the PSBR and the MTFS. As we have seen, the Budget forecast for the PSBR had been quickly invalidated, and the markets were nervous. On 7 July the new Chancellor introduced a package of additional sales of assets, worth £500 m., and public expenditure cuts of a similar amount in 1983–84 which together were planned to reduce the 1983–84 PSBR by about £1 bn. Later (25 July) the Chancellor announced that he would raise his £500 m. from the sale of BP shares.[1] To cut public expenditure within a month of the election was brave but the markets were not entirely happy, partly because of press reports that the prospective overshoot of the PSBR was greater than £1 bn.

1983

The exchange rate

After the Election the pound lost 8 cents in 5 days, falling to $1.5117 (83.5 effective). It recovered slightly and was then fairly stable until early August when it fell below $1.47. At the end of August it was still below $1.50. The weakness was variously related to interest rate expectation, poor trade figures and the strength of the dollar.

The Autumn Statement

The Autumn Statement of 17 November confirmed the view that the PSBR was running above the Budget plan. In the first seven months of the year it was £7 bn, against a forecast for the whole year of £8.2 bn. The Statement raised this to £10 bn for 1983–84. The MTFS was amended accordingly for the current year but the projection for 1984–85 remained unchanged with a PSBR of £8 bn, 2.5 per cent of GDP (raised marginally from £322 to 329 bn). However, the amendment to 1983–84 reduced the 'implied fiscal adjustment' (tax changes) from an implied £0.5 bn tax cut to a £0.5 bn tax increase. Money supply targets remained unchanged.

When in earlier years the Treasury had underestimated the PSBR this had been blamed mainly on the unexpected depth of the recession. This explanation was not now available. In the Budget forecasts of GDP it had been shown to grow 0.5 per cent in 1982 over 1981 and was forecast to rise 2 per cent in 1983 over 1982. By November the basis of the constant price estimates of GDP had been moved on to a new base (1980 instead of 1975) but the effect of this was said to be 'probably fairly small'. This, and new information, raised the estimate for 1981. Despite this, growth in 1982 over 1981 was now put not at 0.5 per cent, but 2 per cent. And, on this higher estimate for 1982, growth in 1983 (and 1984) was expected to be not 2 per cent but 3 per cent. So over the two years 1982 and 1983, growth was to be about double what it had been expected to be when the 1982–83 PSBR had been estimated. Yet the Treasury still managed to underestimate the PSBR by £2 bn.

The underestimate proved extremely fortunate for Sir Geoffrey Howe in his last Budget before the Election. If the forecast for 1983–84 had been the £10 bn now projected (after Budget changes), he might have felt unable to reduce direct taxes by £2.9 bn in a full year.[2]

The year end

The exchange rate, which had been fairly steady around or just below $1.50 since August, dipped to $1.4551 at the end of November and came under persistent and widespread selling pressure in the first half of December, falling to $1.41 (81.8 effective) on 14 December. It recovered to end the year at $1.4540 (83.0).

The balance of payments on current account for the year fell to a surplus of £2.0 bn from £5.6 bn in 1982. Visible trade was in deficit by £500 m. compared with a surplus of £2,384 m. in 1982 – a swing of £2.9 bn. An increase in the surplus in trade in oil of £2,446 m. was more than offset by an increase in the deficit in other goods, mainly in manufactures, of £5,330 m. Overall, oil showed a surplus of £7.0 bn and non-oil a deficit of £7.5 bn. The trend in non-oil trade was disturbing, the balance having moved since 1980 as follows: +£1.2 bn, +£0.5 bn, —£2.2 bn, —£7.5 bn. Our historical surplus in manufactured goods had finally disappeared.

The headline total of unemployed stayed over the 3 million mark throughout the year (except for one month, June) and ended the year only 18,000 below the level of the previous December.

Over the year average earnings grew by 8 per cent and retail prices by 5.3 per cent.

The index of the average estimate of GDP at 1980 prices showed an increase of 3 per cent in 1983 over 1982. For the first time GDP had risen above its level in 1979.

1984

The exchange rate

On 10 January the pound fell to an all-time low of $1.3865, reflecting dollar strength rather than sterling weakness. It recovered quickly, rose to $1.49 at the end of March, but drifted down during April to end just below $1.40 (effective 79.7). After fluctuating it fell to a new all-time low of $1.37 on 24 May. The annual revaluation at the end of March lowered the reserves by about $1 bn.

Public expenditure

The White Paper *The Government's Expenditure Plans 1984–85 to 1986–87* (Cmnd 9143), published on 16 February, showed negligible changes from either the 1983 White Paper or from the 1983 Autumn Statement, an indication that cash planning was working well and that the Government had a grip on public spending. The expected out-turn in the year just ending, at £120.3 bn, was only marginally above plans of £119.6 bn. Planned totals for the next two years were almost unchanged from the 1983 White Paper. The rate of growth of expenditure over the next three years was planned to fall, in line with the rate of inflation: 5.0, 4.5 and 3.5 per cent, implying that expenditure was to be held roughly constant in real terms. The Government had abandoned, at least for the short term and probably for the longer term, any attempt actually to cut expenditure in real terms. But, provided expenditure was contained, it would fall as a percentage of GDP as, and if, GDP rose.

The low totals for later years were much assisted by a very sharp drop in the external financing needs of the nationalized industries, the provision for which was to fall from £2,500 m. in 1983–84 to £90 m. in 1986–87. This seemed optimistic. In 1984–85 the Coal Board and British Rail needed about £1 bn each, while the electricity industry was expected to *contribute* £740 m. The House of Commons Select Committee on Energy was strongly critical of this, arguing that a rise in electricity prices was being used, like a tax, to subsidize the coal and railway industries. 'The Treasury', it said, 'should not seek to cloak a largely fiscal policy in the impenetrable garb of economic pricing jargon.'

In this White Paper the nature of the reserve was changed. From being a contingency reserve it was now to 'cover *all* changes in expenditure for whatever reason they arise'; including, that is, not only policy changes, but estimating changes.

Capital spending

The White Paper included a table of capital spending designed to meet the 'widely-held belief that such spending had been drastically cut since 1978–79'. It was an odd table. Logically and in conformity with national income accounting conventions, it included all spending by the main nationalized industries, not just the small proportion paid for by borrowing and government grants (the part included in public expenditure). On the other hand, sales of council houses and other assets, which are counted as a deduction from public expenditure, were not deducted. Defence capital expenditure was included and in 1983–84 constituted the largest single category of the total, having more than doubled since 1979–80 and risen, as a proportion of capital spending on goods and services, from 17 to 24.5 per cent. Under United Nations national accounting conventions, defence expenditure is counted as current expenditure, a convention followed in the national income acounts of the UK and by the Treasury in its other public expenditure tables. The Treasury's defence of its inclusion was rather quaint: 'Defence spending on equipment such as ships, lorries, tanks and aircraft is included as capital spending, as it would be in most business accounts.'

So, the table bore only a tenuous relationship to capital

spending as defined for public expenditure totals; and it is the
proportion of capital spending within those totals that has been
the focus of criticism. When critics complain that public
expenditure cuts customarily fall relatively too heavily on capital
expenditure, what they have in mind is the need at least to
maintain, if not to improve, the economic and social infrastructure
– roads, railways, hospitals, and so on. It is doubtful whether
defence expenditure, necessary as it is, can properly be counted
as contributing to that.

The Budget

The theme of Mr Lawson's first Budget, on 13 March, was radical
tax reform. But before we come to that let us see what he did with
existing taxes. In any Budget there is a bias towards an increase in
indirect taxation and a fall in direct taxation for the simple reason
that, under law and convention, both personal tax allowances and
excise duties are raised in line with inflation. The first lowers direct
taxation and the second raises indirect taxation. In 1984 the
withdrawal of postponed accounting for VAT on imports further
increased indirect taxation by a once-for-all £1.2 bn. Overall, direct
taxes were reduced by £2.4 bn (£2.9 bn full year) and indirect
taxes raised by just over £2 bn (£6.5 bn full year) to give an overall
change of –£0.3 bn (–£2.3 bn full year). Within the total the
abolition of the National Insurance Surcharge accounted for
–£335 m. in 1984–85 and –£865 m. in a full year.

But by far the most important and radical element in the new
Chancellor's Budget was the reform of company taxation. It is an
essential part of the philosophy of the Conservative Government,
and of Treasury ministers in particular, that the economy must
become more efficient, to arrest, and reverse, the relative decline
of many past years. Governments themselves cannot bring this
about: all they can and must do is to create the right environment,
an environment in which markets can work, an environment – in
this context – undistorted by the tax system.

One of the major distortions, argued the Chancellor, was the
system of generous investment grants allied with a high rate of
corporation tax. Investment grants distorted investment decision
by basing these decisions on post-tax, rather than pre-tax returns,
with the result that there was a bias towards investment with a low
pre-tax return. Investment was largely governed by tax rules.
Taking advantage of these rules, one-third of companies never
paid any corporation tax at all, with the result that rates of
corporation tax were higher than they need otherwise have been.

What needed to be done was to divorce, as far as possible, investment decisions from the tax rules; and to lower the rate of corporation tax. In the long run what companies lost (and the fiscal balance gained) from the phasing out of investment grants would be offset by lower corporation tax. But it was more than an offsetting exercise: the important result would be that investment decisions would be taken more efficiently, the return on investment would rise (having been very much lower in the UK than elsewhere), with a resultant general improvement in the efficiency of the British economy. As an incidental result, any bias that the investment grants had introduced towards the use of capital rather than labour would be eliminated.

Accordingly, the first year allowances on plant, machinery and assets were to be phased out and abolished after March 1986; and the rate of Corporation Tax was to be cut from 52 to 50 per cent and then in 5 per cent steps to 35 per cent in 1986–87. There were other measures to help industry, including the abolition of the National Insurance Surcharge, but those relating to investment allowances and Corporation Tax were the main tax reforms, and radical they were. Like the financial strategy, the tax strategy was medium term.

The Medium-Term Financial Strategy

A number of changes was made in the MTFS. Projections for the borrowing requirement, compared with those made in March 1983 were as shown in Table 8.1

The projections were extended for a further two years, to 1988–89. The overshoot of the PSBR in 1982–83 and 1983–84 was quickly corrected so that borrowing in the target year, 1984–85, is actually below the earlier estimate. This early lowering of the path is because high asset sales in later years are 'unlikely to make a large contribution to reducing interest rates'; and because North Sea oil revenues may peak in 1984–85. Otherwise, the paths are much as before and much as might be expected. Projections into the distant years are obviously subject to considerable uncertainty and are 'illustrative' only. The GDP projections assume real growth of 2.25 per cent a year on average, and the rate of inflation falling to 3 per cent by 1988–89. Another assumption is that 'there is no major change in the effective exchange rate from year to year'. This is a large assumption; but some assumption has to be made.

The behaviour of the monetary aggregates in the year up to

Table 8.1

	1982–83	1983–84	1984–85	1985–86	1986–87	1987–88	1988–89
PSBR (£bn cash)							
1983	7.5	8.0	8.0	7.0	7.0	7.0	7.0
1984	9.2	10.0	7.0	7.0			
As % GDP							
1983	2.75	2.75	2.50	2.00	2.00	1.75	1.75
1984	3.30	3.25	2.25	2.00			
Money GDP, market prices							
1983	275	296	322	346	371	392	412
1984	281	304	328	350			

February 1984 was satisfactory with only PSL2, at 12.25 per cent, outside the range of 7–11 per cent.

In the 1983 MTFS the monetary targets had applied to M1, £M3 ('sterling M3') and PSL2, one narrow and two broad measures of money. M1 and PSL2, it will be recalled, were called in because £M3 by itself was not considered satisfactory. Now it was the turn of M1 to fall into disfavour; its behaviour was 'becoming increasingly more difficult to interpret'. The Treasury seems to have had a hankering after the new measure, M2, but it was too new. So, for 1984–85 at least, M0 was to be the target for narrow money (see Fig 12.1). For broad money £M3 was retained and PSL2 discarded, perhaps for bad behaviour in 1983–84; but it would still be taken into account in looking at broad money, as would M2 for narrow money. The target range for broad money was to be as before, extended; but narrow money was to have a path two points lower, as set out in Table 8.2.

Broad and narrow money were to have equal importance in the assessment of monetary conditions; and, as before, the authorities would 'take into account all the available evidence, including the exchange rate'.

The ultimate objective was stable prices, so the trend of borrowing and monetary growth would need to go on declining beyond the MTFS period.

Table 8.2   Per cent change during year

	1984–85	1985–86	1986–87	1987–88	1988–89
Narrow money – M0	4–8	3–7	2–6	1–5	0–4
Broad money – £M3 (new definition)	6–10	5–9	4–8	3–7	2–6

The longer term

One of the Government's other major objectives was a reduction in taxation. On Budget Day the Treasury published, along with the other mountain of paper released late on that day, its much-leaked Green Paper *The Next Ten Years: Public Expenditure and Taxation into the 1990s* (Cmnd 9189). The Paper, an interesting document containing some unexpected statistics, made the case that for there to be any chance of reducing taxation, public expenditure would have to be 'held broadly at its present level in real terms right up to 1993–94'. The Paper is discussed in Chapter 10.

The pound, the dollar and the rate of interest

In the summer and early autumn a number of factors led to troubled conditions in the money markets: the dollar went from strength to unexplained strength.[3] US interest rates were high, there was the miners' strike and its unfolding developments, a threatened dock strike, and, from time to time, poor money supply figures.

At the end of June the Bank issued a statement saying that it saw no need for a rise in interest rates; but early in July, in the face of heavy selling of sterling which carried the rate down to $1.31, and renewed pressure for a rise in interest rates, the Bank endorsed a rise to 10 per cent, hoping that this would stabilize the situation. It did not. The pound went below $1.30, and base rates rose to 12 per cent on 11 and 12 July. Very reluctantly, the Bank endorsed this. The Bank's attitude seemed somewhat ambivalent: at the same time it declared that it had no exchange rate target (which was probably true, and meant that it would not want to raise the rate of interest simply to arrest a run on sterling) *and* that domestic monetary conditions did not justify a rise in interest rates. Thus, there was no objective reason for a rise in interest rates. Nevertheless, the Bank validated a big rise. It seems that in the end market realities, or market sentiment, got the better of theory and judgement and a rise was conceded because to deny it would have caused confusion and loss of confidence. The Bank may have taken the view that if it was right, rates would soon come back anyway, and so they did, to 10.5 per cent. In the meantime, on 1 August, the pound fell to a new all-time low of $1.2956 in the Far East, but thereafter steadied.

The pound had ended 1983 at $1.45 and 82.8 on the effective. The levels of $1.31 and 77.9 reached in July, representing depreciations of around 10 and 6 per cent, looked extremely low: in retrospect they looked rather strong.

By mid-September the dollar rate had touched a trading low below $1.24 and the effective rate had dropped to an eight-year low of 77.0. On 21 September the pound reached an all-time trading low of $1.2065, reflecting dollar strength. At this point the Bundesbank intervened heavily to stem the dollar's rise; the British Chancellor of the Exchequer departed for Washington saying 'Crisis? What crisis?'; and the Treasury stepped in to divert media attention away from the dollar rate towards the effective, or 'sterling', rate, which had fallen much less than the dollar rate.

In the mid-October the strength of the dollar and the weakness of sterling re-emerged, with the pound falling below $1.20 for the time time and reaching an all-time trading low of $1.1820.

The Autumn Statement

Mr Lawson's mid-term report on 12 November contained few surprises: most of the major aggregates were on course, and the prospect for growth good. But for the miners' strike, growth of GDP would have been 3.5 per cent in 1984 and 2.5 per cent in 1985; the strike reversed these estimates, reducing them to 2.5 per cent in 1984 and, from the lower base, 3.5 per cent in 1985.

Within the Medium-Term Financial Strategy, the targetted money supply aggregates were within the target ranges and the future ranges remained unchanged. The only change of any significance was in the PSBR for the current year, 1984–85, raised from £7 bn to £8.5 bn: a windfall of £2.5 bn on oil taxes, arising from the stronger dollar, was insufficient to offset overspending by local authorities, the budgetary cost of the miners' strike and higher-than-expected interest rates that increased the cost of the national debt. The implied fiscal adjustment for 1985–86 was lowered from £2 to 1.5 bn.

The planning total of public expenditure in 1985–86, £132 bn, was held close to the £131.7 bn at the time of the spring Budget; but this statistical achievement was helped by raising the estimate for special sales of assets (which count as a negative item in public expenditure) by £500 m., and by reducing the Reserve by £750 m. Within the total public expenditure the external financing limits (EFLs) of the nationalized industries were raised by £180 m. over White Paper plans. This increase would have been greater but for an increase of some £0.5 bn in the *negative* EFLs of the electricity and gas industries which, together, were expected to contribute some £1.5 bn to the Exchequer in 1985–86.

The Treasury itself was to contribute £3 m. to savings by ceasing to issue £1 notes after 31 December 1984.

Withdrawal of ½p coin

The ½p coin ceased to be legal tender after the 31 December 1984. It is an appropriate and salutary comment on the times that our period should end with the pound note transmuted into small change and the withdrawal, from loss of value, of a coin that was 2½ times (well, 2.4) as valuable as the ha'penny we started with.

The pound sterling

At the year's end sterling weakened sharply in the face of a
stronger dollar and fears of lower oil prices. On each of the three
days 18, 19, 20 December it touched new trading and closing lows,
closing at $1.1655 (73.0 effective) on 20 December. Next day it
gained a cent but weakened further after Christmas to end the
year at a new record low of $1.1590 (73.0).

The rates at the end of 1984 represented depreciations during
the year of 20 per cent against the dollar and 12 per cent on the
effective rate. The 1967 devaluation which, it will be recalled, had
caused ugly crowds to gather in Downing Street, was of 14.3 per
cent, to $2.40.

Since 1964, when the rate was $2.80, the pound sterling had lost
43 per cent of its dollar value.

1985

Public expenditure

The Public Expenditure White Paper (Cmnd 9428) published in
January 1985 – 320 pages in 2 volumes costing £19.10 – showed
the estimated out-turn for the current year to be £1.75 bn above
plans; but expenditure on programmes alone had exceeded plans
by £5.1 bn (4.1%). For 1985–86 and 1986–87 the planning totals
were unchanged from the 1984 White Paper but this stability was
achieved in part by a reduction in the provision for the Reserve by
£0.75 bn in each of these years. Expenditure on programmes was
planned to rise, by £1.3 bn in 1985–86 and £1.0 bn in 1986–87.
Expenditure on net debt interest, not included in the planning
total, showed a substantial increase: from a previously planned
£7.5 bn in each year from 1984–85 to 1986–87 to £8.5 bn in 1984–
85 (estimated out-turn) and then by £0.5 bn a year to £9.5 bn in
1986–87 and £10 bn in 1987–88 (when gross interest would be
£18.0 bn, the same as planned expenditure on health and personal
social services in that year and not far short of planned
expenditure on defence, respectively the third and second largest
programmes).

In real ('cost') terms the planning total was planned to fall by 1.5
per cent between 1984–85 and 1987–88; and the planning total
plus net debt interest was planned to fall to 39.5 per cent of GDP
by 1987–88, from 42.5 per cent in 1984–85.

On the evidence of the White Paper, the Government, in pursuit of its public expenditure goals, was running hard to stand still, failing, marginally, in cash terms but hoping for some success in real and relative terms.

The Budget

The 1985 Budget on 19 March was coloured by the sterling crisis from which the country had just emerged (see p 190). The Chancellor depicted by the Press as a now somewhat chastened figure, was expected to do nothing that might disturb the confidence of the money markets.

In 1984 Mr Lawson had received plaudits for his tax reforms and raised expectations that he would be a reforming Chancellor, sweeping away fiscal privileges and moving towards a neutral and more widely based tax system. These hopes were not fulfilled in the 1985 Budget which, so far from moving further towards major reforms – except in one respect to be noted below – closed the door on some changes for the duration of the present Parliament.

The Budget was billed as a 'Budget for Jobs'. The major justification for this description lay in a major reform of the structure of National Insurance contributions, where contributions payable by those on lower earnings, and their employers, were sharply reduced, and the cost partly offset by abolishing the upper earnings limit for employers' contributions, raising the cost of employing higher-paid workers. The purpose was to make it both cheaper for an employer to employ a low-paid worker and to raise the take-home pay of that worker. The full-year cost of the measures, to come into force in October, was put at £450 m. The Treasury calculated that 'a single youngster on just under £90 a week will pay about £1.80 less in National Insurance contributions on top of a reduction in his income tax bill of £1.15 a week – an overall increase in take home pay of about £3 a week'. They did not add that unions should take this into account when framing wage demands, but the formulation did carry distinct echoes of Mr Healey *circa* 1976 and the Treasury's efforts then to explain the arithmetic of the true value of the tax-against-pay proposals.

In fiscal terms the Budget was unexciting. The PSBR had overrun by an estimated £3.25 bn, to £10.5 bn, but this year there was a valid reason – the miners' strike, which accounted for all but £0.5 bn of the excess. As had been widely expected, the tax reduction was less than implied by the 'fiscal adjustment' and amounted to £0.75 bn in 1985–86 (£1 bn in a full year). This was in addition to the cost of the changes in National Insurance contributions. The net reduction in taxes masked a £1 bn (full year) increase in indirect taxes and duties.

GDP was forecast to rise by 3.5 per cent in 1985, and the rate of inflation to fall to 4.5 per cent in the second quarter of 1986.

Public expenditure

In 1984-85 the public expenditure planning total had overrun by £3.5 bn, of which over two-thirds was attributed to the miners' strike. In a somewhat surprising move the Chancellor added £2 bn to the Reserve, and hence to the planning total, in 1985-86 and in each of the following three years. This, as he pointed out, was not an addition to expenditure on programmes. It appeared to be a precaution against future overruns, on the grounds that it was better to have a larger total that was not overrun than a smaller one that was. Between 1983-84 and 1988-89 general government expenditure was planned to rise by £33 bn (23½%) in cash terms, an average of £5.5 bn a year. From 1984-85 to 1988-89 expenditure was planned to be on average nearly £6.5 bn a year higher than the plans in the 1984 Financial Statement and Budget Report (FSBR).

Oil and gas revenues

On the revenue side the estimates of North Sea oil and gas revenues were revised upwards as follows (in £bn).

	1984-85	1985-86	1986-87
1984 FSBR	10	9.5	9.5
Autumn Statement	12	12	..
1985 FSBR	12	13.5	11.5

These very substantial increases were attributed to higher estimates of both output and the sterling value of that output.

The Medium-Term Financial Strategy

With these and other changes in expenditure and revenue the PSBR was put at £7 bn in 1985-86 and 1987-88 and £7.5 bn in 1986-87 and 1988-89, much the same as in the 1984 MTFS.

The target ranges for the money supply were unchanged from 1984, the ranges for M0 and sterling M3 falling by 1 percentage point a year up to 1988-89. Targets were set for the yearly percentage growth in money GDP.

Thus, on the face of it, the MTFS was much as before. But there was some subtle relaxation. On the PSBR the MTFS said, as in the 1984 version, that figures beyond the current year were illustrative only, and decisions about the appropriate PSBR in particular years would be taken nearer the time. In his Budget speech the Chancellor said 'there is nothing sacrosanct about the precise mix of monetary and fiscal policies required to meet the objectives of the Medium-Term Financial Strategy'. But perhaps most significant was what he said about maintaining money demand: 'A policy for demand expressed unambiguously in terms of money provides a further important advantage, for it ensures that wage restraint will provide more jobs ... the Medium-Term Financial Strategy is as firm a guarantee against inadequate money demand as it is against excessive money demand.' As we have noted the table showing the targets for the money supply included also percentage rates of growth for money GDP, indicating that they too enjoyed the status of targets.

The MTFS had moved a further step away from being a strategy for the PSBR and the money supply, towards being a policy for money GDP. In place of ceilings for money GDP (which might be undershot) we now had targets which it was intended should be hit.

In other words, if effective demand fell short because of a lower growth of money wages (or presumably for any other reason) the Chancellor would compensate through fiscal or monetary relaxation. Would Keynes have found anything to quarrel with in what?

The exchange rate

The exchange rate, lifted from its former status of an indicator of monetary conditions, was no longer to be benignly neglected.

Monetary policy, 1985

By the spring of 1985 the exchange rate crisis and the authorities' uncertain response to it had left the money markets in a state of some confusion. Lending rates, which had been hoisted to 14 per cent during the exchange rate scare, came down ½ a point following the Budget but the Bank indicated firmly that it wanted no further fall. When, however, two of the major banks (but not the other two) cut rates by a further ½ point to 13 per cent eight days later, the Bank endorsed the lower rate. On 12 April the other two banks dropped their rates from 13.25 to 12.75 per cent but the Bank declined to endorse this move, forcing the discount houses to borrow at 13.25 per cent. A week later the two banks who had been leading the downward movement again cut their rates by ½ point to 12.5 per cent, and the Bank endorsed this but again indicated that it wanted no further fall. So, with grudging approval from the Bank, rates had leapfrogged down 1¼–1½ points. The authorities justified the lower rates on the basis of the new strength of sterling; but their earlier insistence on maintaining higher rates had been based on their alleged concern for the monetary aggregates and the future rate of inflation. So what indicators *were* the authorities looking at?

Well, several, it appeared. On 1 April the Chancellor, in a speech to the American Chamber of Commerce, said there was no mechanical formula for deciding the appropriate combination of exchange rate and growth of the money supply for keeping financial policy on track. The Governor of the Bank of England, in evidence to the Treasury and Civil Service Committee, welcomed the Chancellor's restatement of the importance of the exchange rate as an indicator of monetary policy. So far as the monetary numbers were concerned, the Governor would prefer them in the middle of the range, but even if they were at the top interest rates could come down if there were no worries about the exchange rate. So far, so good: there was an unspecified trade-off between the position of the monetary aggregates within their target ranges, and the exchange rate. But the Governor added that in looking at the prospects for inflation he was also concerned about the acceleration in wage costs and the rapid increase in bank lending.

In monetarist theory wage costs have nothing directly to do with the price level, which is determined, at least in the longer terms, by the money supply. On wage costs, however, the Governor had an ally in Mr Gavyn Davies, chief UK economist of stockbrokers Simon and Coates: 'Econometric analysis shows conclusively that changes in unit costs are still the best lead indicator of inflation – far better than any of the monetary aggregates.'[4]

Too much should not be made of all this, for the Chancellor had made it known before that in judging monetary conditions he would look at a number of indicators, including the exchange rate. But, taken in conjunction with his remarks in the Budget Statement, it did indicate that the exchange rate had become *relatively* more important, and the monetary aggregates, therefore, relatively less important; a conclusion, so far as the broader aggregates were concerned, acknowledged by the Treasury in the 1985 MTFS: ' . . . the significance of the broad aggregates as monetary indicators has somewhat diminished'. This did not go quite as far as the *Financial Times's* verdict that 'the relation of broad money to anything in the real economy is still largely a mystery ... '.[5]

In June Barclays and the Midland Bank fell into line with Lloyds and the National Westminster and brought their base rates down to 12.5 per cent. As sterling strengthened during July, pressure built up for lower interest rates and the authorities allowed base rates to come down in two stages to 11.5 per cent by the end of the month. While the exchange rate during the summer was, with a few wobbles, strong, the money supply figures in the shape of sterling M3 were, month by month, showing excessive growth. (The unsatisfactory money supply figures sometimes had the paradoxical effect of pushing up the exchange rate as operators expected the authorities to respond with higher interest rates). The authorities, looking both ways, trod a cautious path, on the one hand resisting exchange rate pressures for lower interest rates and on the other disregarding the excess growth of broad money. By the autumn the authorities had publicly abandoned any attempt to contain sterling M3 within its target range; and the technique of overfunding directed to that end was declared at an end. Henceforward the short-term interest rate would be used – vigorously, it was implied – to ensure the ultimate aims of policy. (For a detailed account see Chapter 12, p. 264).

The pound in 1985

Towards the one dollar pound
The weakness of sterling which had been apparent in December 1984 continued into the new year and there ensued weeks of extreme turmoil in the foreign exchange markets and considerable confusion among the British political and monetary authorities. The collapse of sterling during this period was variously attributed, with the emphasis shifting from time to time, to a number of factors: the continued and largely unexplained strength of the dollar, which affected all currencies, not only sterling; worries about the weakening price of oil which, it was believed, not entirely logically, would affect the UK, as an oil producer, more than it would oil-importing countries; concern about the monetary aggregates and public borrowing allied to a suspicion that the Government had relaxed its anti-inflationary policy; a belief, fuelled by some inept Lobby briefing from the Prime Minister's office, that the Government 'had no policy for the exchange rate' and was prepared to see the pound continue in free fall; and finally, although this was probably of minor importance, the continuance of the miners' strike into March.

On 6 January the *Sunday Times* carried a story reflecting

Lobby briefing by the Prime Minister's Press Secretary that the Prime Minister had 'firmly rejected interest rate increases to defend the pound'. This was in character: the Prime Minister's antipathy to high interest rates, and especially to high mortgage rates, was well known. On 9 January the pound touched a new low of $1.1370 in the Far East; and late in the morning of 10 January came under heavy selling pressure. On Friday 11 January National Westminster Bank raised its base rate 1 point to 10.5 per cent, the other banks followed, and the Bank of England, the Prime Minister notwithstanding, endorsed the rise. The market, however, had already discounted the rise and the pound fell further to close at $1.1185 in New York.

Incredibly, the Prime Minister's Press Secretary, in his briefing that Friday of the Sunday Press, declared, no doubt in an attempt to dispel any suggestion that the rise in base rates represented a reversal by, or for, the Prime Minister, that the Government was not going to throw money at the pound in order to defend any particular parity. Headlines in the Sunday papers, with the notable exception of *The Observer*, who had a contrary story, reflected this briefing. The *Sunday Times* reported that the Prime Minister was prepared to see a one-dollar pound. According to *The Observer* (20 Jan.), 'When the BBC's political correspondent telephoned the duty press officer at No. 10 to check the conflicting stories, he was told that any talk of a U-turn was rubbish, *The Observer's* story was wrong, and the other stories were broadly right.' On this basis the BBC broadcast that the Government remained unconcerned by the pound's fall and was prepared to see a one-dollar pound. For the markets this meant only one thing: sell sterling.

On Monday 14 January the Bank of England and the Treasury moved quickly to limit the damage: sterling was supported in early dealings in the Far East, and MLR was re-introduced for one day, at 12 per cent. The pound, which had fallen to a new low of $1.1020 in the Far East, closed at $1.1130.

How did it come about that the press secretaries of the Prime Minister and the Chancellor of the Exchequer, intelligent men, whose job it was to manage the Press, presided over such a muddle? The most charitable explanation is that each, in his way, had been trying to play down the crisis (if crisis it was) and to calm the markets by displaying unconcern. But the Prime Minister's Press Secretary it appears, on the evidence, was overemphatic, not understanding, perhaps, that there is a very great difference between having a policy of non-intervention and *saying* that you have such a policy. Whether the Treasury and the Bank *did* have a policy of non-intervention is another matter: as the fall in sterling continued they gave the impression of making up policy as they went along.

Three days later, on 17 January, the Group of Five Finance Ministers and central bank governors meeting in Washington re-affirmed their commitment to undertake collective intervention in the foreign exchange markets as necessary. A week later it emerged, by courtesy of senior French officials, that Mrs Thatcher had made a personal appeal to President Reagan to smooth the way for a joint intervention agreement by the Five. It was embarrassing to discover the great apostle of market disciplines and non-intervention urging her colleagues to throw dollars at the exchange rate. Downing Street declined to comment on the French report. The European central banks did intervene jointly to sell dollars on 22 January, but on a comparatively small scale, a reported $100 m. Next day the pound fell to a record closing low of $1.1105 and fell to $1.080 in New York a day later. On 28 January, 'Black Monday', the pound went down to $1.1065 when an OPEC meeting seemed likely to break up in disarray; and the clearing banks raised their base rates to 14 per cent, a move endorsed by the Bank.

The pound touched new all-time closing lows on 11 and 12 February and again on 21, 22 and 25 February. The bottom was reached on 26 February when the pound closed at $1.0420, 70.2 on the effective rate, after touching $1.0357 and 70.0.

On 27 February the central banks of Europe, in a well-planned and well-timed move led by the Bundesbank, intervened heavily to sell dollars. It was subsequently confirmed that in intervention in late February the central banks spent nearly $11 bn between them. The effect on the pound was to force it briefly above $1.10 and it close the month at $1.0820 (71.3).

Early in March the pound slipped back again, to $1.0555 (70.8) on 5 March, but went no lower. On 18 March, the day before the Budget, it gained 2.25 cents to close at $1.1065 (73.0) and on Budget Day itself it gained another 3 cents and 1 point on the effective index. Recovery continued and on 27 March, in the face of dollar weakness, the pound rose above $1.20 to close at $1.2390, its highest since November, while the sterling index reached 77.6, its highest since September. The month closed with the pound at $1.2375 (77.2).

What are we to make of this extraordinary episode in which the pound fell to below $1.04, from an average of $1.34 in 1984; and to

70.0 on the effective index, from an average of 78.8 in 1984; and then quickly recovered most of the loss? The first point to note is that, as the figures suggest, it was as much a story about the strength of the dollar as of the weakness of the pound. The pound's value against all currencies, as measured by the effective rate index, did fall, but it has to be remembered that the dollar itself has a weight of 25 per cent in that index. Leaving aside the question of *why* currencies took the course they did at different times – we have given some broad explanations – let us return to a question hinted at earlier: what *was* the Government's exchange rate policy? Or, to put it more precisely, what was that policy on 1 January, before the worst of the trouble?

Exchange rate policy
The official word was that there was no policy for the exchange rate, or at least no floor to the rate, which is not quite the same thing. Like the level of unemployment, it was something outside the Government's direct control although the Government, no doubt, could create 'the right conditions'. The exchange rate would be determined by the general strength of the economy and by proper control of the money supply and the rate of inflation. Intervention in the exchange market by the UK acting alone, apart from a little smoothing here and there, was a waste of foreign exchange if designed to support sterling, and a threat to the monetary numbers if designed to keep sterling down. The exchange rate was, however, one of the indicators, and an increasingly important one, to be used in judging 'monetary conditions'. This concept, of the exchange rate as an indicator, is not devoid of ambiguity. Suppose that on all other evidence, notably the monetary numbers, monetary conditions appear to be satisfactory yet the exchange rate is falling. What then? Are monetary conditions to be tightened? If they are, this comes close to a policy for the exchange rate, for it implies that there is a level for the exchange rate which is appropriate. On the other hand, it can be sensibly argued that it is not the level of the exchange rate that matters but the direction and speed of change. Either way, there seems to be an implicit assumption that, given the monetary conditions, there is some state of the exchange rate that is appropriate and should be maintained.

In the early stages of the crisis these aloof attitudes to the exchange rate were paramount, as evidenced by the official briefings referred to above. These attitudes quickly changed as the pound continued to fall. One reason for the change may have been the Prime Minister's reaction for, as the *Financial Times* observed she seemed 'to have taken the descent of sterling towards parity as a personal insult'.[6] Interest rates were raised first by a modest 1 point, then by a further 1½ points as MLR was resurrected, and then by 2 more points, to 14 per cent, at which point the *real* rate of interest stood, by rule-of-thumb calculation, at a huge 9 per cent, a level far in excess of anything justified by domestic monetary conditions as measured by the monetary aggregates. It appeared that the Prime Minister had appealed personally for intervention to stem the rise of the dollar. It became quite clear that there was, after all, a policy for the exchange rate. It is worth considering whether there should have been.

In 1980 when, as the Government would be the first to claim, the economy was in a much worse state than in 1985, the pound averaged $2.33 and 96 on the effective index. True, both rates declined after that; but did anyone seriously consider that a rate of one dollar to the pound was a realistic and sustainable rate in 1985? Moreover, did it matter if it was? As has been argued earlier, there are advantages and disadvantages in a low exchange rate; but it is by no means clear that the disadvantages of a one-dollar rate would have greatly outweighed the advantages.

Let us consider the possibilities. Either a rate of around one dollar to the pound was a realistic rate that would be sustained, reflecting the relative strengths of the American and British economies; or it was not. If it was not, then it would correct itself, probably quite quickly, without any, or much, action on our part. If it was, then there was conferred upon us, by the grace of the market, a huge competitive advantage in a strong economy, namely the United States. Since our effective rate had also fallen, there was a similar, but smaller, competitive advantage in third countries. The assumed continued strength of the dollar would offset any fall in the price of oil, denominated in dollars. The weak rate of the pound against the dollar would increase the *sterling* value of North Sea oil and the sterling tax taken from that oil. In the absence of any necessity to raise interest rates to defend the parity, these rates could have remained low, with advantages to investment, mortgage rates and the retail price index (offsetting to some extent the inflationary effects of a low exchange rate). The Treasury gives considerable weight to low interest rates as an engine of growth, and they are an important objective of policy.

None of this is to argue that a one-dollar pound would be, or would have been, an unqualified blessing; it would, as we have noted, have had unfavourable implications for the rate of inflation, and for the terms of trade. Rather, it is to argue that it would have been by no means an unqualified disaster and that, since it was in any case unlikely to happen (or if to happen, to be sustained), the panic that set in as one dollar approached was unnecessary and somewhat unseemly. It would have been interesting to have seen a more resolute application of the policy of benign neglect with which the year had opened – but with less Lobby briefing.

The middle months

Sterling recovered to touch $1.30 in the Far East on 18 April but ended the month at $1.24 (78.1). By the end of the first week in May it was down to $1.1770 but by 20 May it was close to $1.30 again and it ended the month at $1.2865 (80.3).

By the end of June sterling had established itself above the $1.30 mark and at the end of July stood at $1.4160 (83.5). August and September provided something of a switchback ride. By 7 August the rate was down to $1.3262 but a week later it was back to $1.40 and it ended the month only marginally below that level. Again the early days of the following month saw a sharp reaction, to $1.3050 on 9 September followed by a recovery to $1.37 by 20 September.

Bringing down the dollar

The United States had asked for a special meeting of the Group of 5 (G5), a meeting which took place over the week-end of 21–22 September in New York. Unusually for G5 the meeting was given a high profile. Its purpose was to agree on a policy, initiated and supported by the United States Government and the Federal Reserve Bank, of intervention to bring down the rate of exchange of the dollar against the major currencies with the primary objective of improving the trading position of the United States and so head off Congressional demands for protectionist measures. Next day, 23 September, President Reagan made a strong policy statement in favour of free trade. On that day the pound gained 5.70 cents and closed at $1.4270 having gone as high as $1.4470. The following day the Bank of Japan, one of the G5 participants, reportedly sold $1 bn. Over the next ten days the central banks of the G5 plus Italy sold nearly $3.5 bn. This declared policy of concerted central bank intervention was treated by commentators with some scepticism, the view being that one would have to wait and see whether the central bankers, and the Federal Reserve in particular, were going to continue to put their dollars where their mouth was. After the initial phase of fairly heavy intervention, which did bring the dollar down, the central bankers – whose actions are usually revealed only some time after the event – appeared to be playing something of a cat and mouse game with the markets, intervening spasmodically on a relatively small scale, trying, it seemed, just to keep reminding the markets that the policy of intervention was still in place. The tactic seemed to achieve some success in that it kept the markets guessing and at least stopped the dollar from developing any upward momentum. The pound stayed above $1.40 and at the end of September stood at $1.4090 and 80.2.

During the first nine months of 1985 the range of fluctuation of sterling against the dollar was huge – between $1.0420 and $1.4470. Between the end of the first quarter and the end of the third the rate against the dollar appreciated by 14.5 per cent while the sterling index rose by no more than 4 per cent. This strengthening of sterling was helpful for the future rate of inflation but, despite the relatively small rise in the sterling index, was probably still rather too much for the Confederation of British Industry who on 25 September, when rates were somewhat higher than at the end of the month, had pleaded for a lower exchange rate. But they were spared a rise in interest rates: the strength of the exchange rate convinced the authorities that despite the excessive growth of sterling M3 monetary conditions were tight, or tight enough, and no corrective action was necessary.

The Autumn Statement

In the economic forecasts for 1986 accompanying the Statement GDP was forecast to rise by 3 per cent, the growth of exports to fall from 7 per cent to 2 per cent and the growth of imports to rise from 3½ per cent to 4 per cent; the deficit on manufactures would increase. The surplus on the current account of the balance of payments was, nevertheless, forecast to rise from £3 bn to £4 bn. The rate of inflation was expected to fall to 3¾ per cent by the end of 1986.

Public expenditure, excluding Special sales of assets, was planned to rise by 5.2 per cent in cash terms in 1986–87. In real terms its path was to be more or less flat up to 1988–89. By 1986–87 general government expenditure as a proportion of GDP would have regained its level of 1978–79. Estimated expenditure in 1985–86 on the Intervention Board for Agriculture and the Common Agricultural Policy, at £1.9 bn, was equal to the expenditure on the whole of the Foreign and Commonwealth Office (including Overseas Development Administration) and more than expenditure on the Department of Trade and Industry (£1.65 bn), all the Chancellor's Departments (£1.8 bn), and the Department of Energy (£1 bn). The estimate of the PSBR for the current year, 1985–86, was raised £1 bn to £8 bn mainly because of lower oil revenues.

The general impression of the policy stance was of a modest fiscal relaxation, financed by asset sales, supported by a monetary policy that, despite the abandonment of control over sterling M3, looked tight on the evidence of the exchange rate and interest rates.

Mr Nigel Lawson

Of all recent Chancellors of the Exchequer Mr Lawson is the most economically literate, well able to fight his corner with (or against) the Treasury mandarins. As Financial Secretary to the Treasury under Sir Geoffrey Howe he had been by far the Government's most effective and articulate expositor of the new economic philosophy; and the begetter of the Medium-Term Financial Strategy. Indeed, Mr Lawson may go down as the 'medium-term Chancellor', not only for the strategy but for his proposals for tax reform and his work on the future of public spending. He, and his predecessor, may be said – we shall have to wait for a final verdict – to have moved the focus of economic policy back from the short to the medium and longer term. It has been argued many times that for a number of reasons – political ambitions, political horizons, the pressure of events – ministers and civil servants are unable to plan much for the future, to take the longer view; that their philosophy, perforce, is that if they look after the short term, the long term will look after itself, the long term being nothing but a lot of short terms strung together. It may be that Mr Lawson intends to reverse this, to look after the medium and longer term in the belief that the short term will look after itself. This would be consistent with the monetarist view that, given the appropriate framework, the markets know best. If this is so, economic management will become much less exciting (and books like this much shorter); we shall have come to the end of management by crisis. We shall move into the 'eighth square, where it's all feasting and fun'

Diary of events June 1983

1983

9 Jun.	Mr Nigel Lawson becomes Chancellor of the Exchequer.
11	Departments of Trade and of Industry to merge.
16	Abolition of Central Policy Review Staff ('Think Tank') announced.
1 Jul.	Mr Robin Leigh-Pemberton becomes Governor of the Bank of England. Summer Finance Bill introduced.
7	Measures. Asset sales of £0.5 bn and public expenditure cuts of similar amount to bring the PSBR back within plans.
19	Bank modifies monetary control arrangements with effect from 18 Aug.
25	Statement on measures not included in Summer Finance Bill. Chancellor announces sales of BP shares, to raise about £500 m.
27	Revised Cash Limits published.
27 Sept.	*Financial Management in Government Departments* (Cmnd 9058) published.
Nov.	Treasury and Central Statistical Office to issue joint monthly statement of the PSBR.
17	Autumn Statement.
20 Dec.	Government published Rates Bill to limit local authorities freedom to raise rates.
end	Pound closes at $1.4520.

1984

10 Jan.	Pound falls to all-time low of $1.3865.
10 Feb.	Changes to definition of PSBR and sterling M3.
16	*The Government's Expenditure Plans 1984–85 to 1986–87* (Cmnd 9143).
13 Mar.	Budget. Radical tax reforms in company sector. National Insurance Surcharge abolished from 1 Oct. 1984. Tax cuts neutral in 1984–85, reduction of £2.3 bn in full year. MTFS extended to 1988–89. Monetary targets for M0 and sterling M3. *The Next Ten Years: Public Expenditure and Taxation into the 1990s* (Cmnd 9189).
7–9 Jun.	Tenth Annual Economic Summit, London.
26	Bank of England statement – no need for rise in interest rates.
5–6 Jul.	Pound falls to $1.31, base rates rise to 10 per cent.

11	Pound falls to $1.2970 in the Far East.
11–12	Base rates rise to 12 per cent.
23	Treasury Green Paper *Building Societies: A New Framework* (Cmnd 9316).
25	*Progress in Financial Management in Government Departments* (Cmnd 9297).
1 Aug.	Pound falls to $1.2956 in the Far East.
8–10	Base rates down 0.5 point on 8th and 10th, to 11 per cent.
17	Base rates down 0.5 point to 10.5 per cent.
31	Pound closes at $1.3098 (78.1 effective).
5 Sept.	Pound at $1.2795.
17	Pound at trading low of $1.2393. Effective at eight-year low of 77.0.
18	Pound at trading low of $1.2160 (76.0).
20 Sept.	Pound at all-time closing low of $1.2210.
21	Pound at all-time trading low of $1.2065. Bundesbank intervenes to stem dollar rise.
1 Oct.	Bank of England rescues Johnson Matthey Bankers.
16	Pound falls below $1.20, in North America, for first time. All-time trading low of $1.1975 (75.9).
17	Pound at all-time low of $1.1905, and closes below $1.20 for first time in London.
18	Pound at all-time trading low of $1.1820 and all-time closing low of $1.1875 (75.2).
19	Effective rate at record low of 74.0.
7 Nov.	Bank of England issues discussion paper *The Future Structure of the Gilt-edged Market*.
12	Autumn Statement. PSBR for 1984–85 raised to £8.5 bn. No major changes in MTFS or public expenditure. No more pound notes to be issued after 31 Dec. The ½p coin no longer legal tender after 31 Dec.
21	Bank of England announces revised supervisory arrangements for the discount market.
18 Dec.	Treasury drops its request for official sterling balances to be held to 'working levels'.
31	The ½p coin ceases to be legal tender after today. Pound closes at $1.1590 (73.0).

1985

6 Jan.	*Sunday Times* story that the PM had 'firmly rejected interest rate increases to defend the £'.
9	Pound touches new low of $1.1370 in the Far East.
11	Base rates rise 1 point to 10.5 per cent.
13	Some Sunday papers reflect briefing from No. 10 that

the Government was not going to defend any particular parity for sterling.

14   Pound falls to new low of $1.1020 in the Far East. MLR re-introduced for one day, at 12 per cent. Pound closes at $1.1130 (70.8).

17   PSBR figures for December published, showing cumulative PSBR for the first nine months of 1984/85 of £10 bn (£8.5 bn for the full financial year in the Autumn Statement).
Group of Five finance ministers and central bank governors meeting in Washington re-affirm their commitment to undertake collective intervention on the foreign exchanges as necessary.
FT ordinary share index rises about 1000 for the first time.

19   December RPI shows annual rate of inflation 4.6 per cent.

22   Publication of *The Government's Expenditure Plans 1985–86 to 1987–88* (Cmnd 9428 – I and II).
European central banks intervene jointly to sell dollars. Intervention comparatively small, about $100 m.

23   Pound falls to a record closing low in London of $1.1105. Effective rate falls 0.6 to 70.7.

25   Pound closes at $1.1140 (70.6); and falls to $1.080 in New York.

28   'Black Monday'. Pound drops to $1.1065, base rates raised 2 points to 14 per cent.

30   Pound improves following OPEC agreement, and firm speech by Chancellor of the Exchequer.
Treasury publishes *The Relationship Between Employment and Wages*.

31   Unemployment in January rises to record 3,341,000, 13.9 per cent, seasonally adjusted 3.13 million, up 18,200. Pound closes at $1.1297 (71.6).

11 Feb.   Pound falls to all-time trading low of $1.0940 and record closing low of $1.0965 (71.1). In New York it touches $1.092.

12   Pound falls to all-time trading low of $1.0845 and record closing low of $1.088 (71.0).

13   Pound reaches an all-time low of $1.0835 and closes in London at $1.088 (70.9).

21   Pound falls to new closing low of $1.0830.

22   Dollar soars after President Reagan speaks against

	intervention. Pound closes in London at record low of $1.0770, and falls to $1.0735 in New York.
25	Pound closes in London at an all-time low of $1.0545 (70.9) after touching $1.0525.
26	Pound closes at record low of $1.0420 (70.2) after touching $1.0357 and 70.0. Paul Volcker, Chairman of the US Federal Reserve Board, questions whether intervention has been forceful enough.
27	In concerted action, central banks sell dollars heavily. Sterling touches a peak of $1.1070 and closes at $1.0875 (71.6). Subsequently confirmed that central banks between them spent nearly $11 bn intervening, mainly in later February.
28	Pound closes at $1.080 (71.3).
	Chancellor closes the tax loophole of 'bond-washing'.
1 Mar.	Further intervention by central banks, estimated at up to $1.5 bn, fails to bring the dollar down. Pound closes at $1.0725 (70.8).
3	Miners decide to end their year-long strike and return to work on 5 Mar. (The strike was triggered on 1 Mar. 1984 when the NCB announced it wanted to close Cortonwood Colliery. On 6 Mar. 1984 the Yorkshire NUM called an indefinite strike.)
4	Pound closes down at $1.0685 (70.9).
5	Miners return to work. Pound closes at $1.0555.
6	Dollar drops sharply after testimony to Congress by Paul Volcker. Pound closes at $1.0725 (70.7).
	Fifth Report of Treasury and Civil Service Committee, *Exchange Rate Policy*, is critical of the Chancellor's exchange rate policy.
7	Pound closes at $1.0665 (70.8).
	Seasonally adjusted unemployment rises to a record 3.148 million (13%). Unadjusted 3.324 million. At the end of January there were 647,000 people covered by special employment measures, estimated to have reduced the registered unemployed by 465,000.
	Two papers published by the Bank of England's Panel of Academic Consultants (*Panel Paper No. 24*) are sceptical of the link between high wages and unemployment (see 30 Jan.).
18	Pound rise 2.25 cents on Friday's close (15 Mar.), to close at $1.1065 (73.0).
19	Budget.

	Dollar weak, pound closes at $1.1365 (74.0), up 3 cents on the previous day.
20	Pound closes at $1.1515 (74.0) after peak of $1.1745. Banks lower base rates by ½ point to 13.5 per cent. Bank of England indicates that it wants no further reduction.
21	Building societies raise mortgage rate by one point to between 13.875 and 14.125 per cent.
27	Dollar falls sharply, pound rises above $1.20 to close at $1.2390, its highest since November. Sterling index rises to 77.6, highest since September.
28	National Westminster, followed by Lloyds, cut base lending rate ½ point to 13 per cent; Barclays and Midland fail to follow, but Bank of England endorses the move. Government publishes White Paper on employment policy, *The Challenge for the Nation* (Cmnd 9474).
29	Dollar continues its fall, and pound closes at $1.2375 (77.2). Bank of England and two dozen other financial institutions sign an indemnity agreement of £150 m. to cover losses of Johnson Matthey Bankers above £170 m. Half of the indemnity borne by Bank of England.
6 Apr.	March unemployment figures show 56,000 fall to 3.27 million (13.5%). Seasonally adjusted total rises to 3.15 million.
12	Barclays and Midland Banks cut base lending rates from 13.25 to 12.75 per cent. Bank of England does not endorse and forces discount houses to borrow from it at a penal 13.25 per cent. Bank of England publishes *The Future Structure of the Gilt-Edged Market*. US Government offers to host a meeting on the working of the international monetary system.
17	At IMF meeting in Washington, Group of Ten hold informal discussion on future of IMF in securing greater international monetary co-operation and exchange rate stability.
18	Sterling touches peaks of $1.3000 and 79.9.
19	National Westminster and Lloyds Banks cut base rates by ½ point to 12.5 per cent. Bank endorses but indicates it wants no further fall. Annual rate of inflation in March rises sharply to 6.1 per cent.

22	Pound falls 1.65 cents to $1.2775 (79.3).
23	Pound falls 2.55 cents to $1.2520 (78.8).
24	Pound falls 2.70 cents to $1.2250 (77.3).
25	Pound falls 2.05 cents to $1.2045 (76.6), bringing the fall against the dollar in four days to 7 per cent.
26	Record visible trade deficit of £900 m. in March. Deficit on non-oil goods nearly £1.27 bn.
	Pound falls below $1.20 in trading, closes higher on the day at $1.2165 (77.0).
30	Pound ends month at $1.2425 and 78.1.
	The headline total of unemployed in April rises 4,973 to 3.273 million. Seasonally adjusted total rises 29,200 to 3.177 million (13.1 per cent).
17 May	Annual rate of inflation in April 6.9 per cent.
12 Jun.	Barclays and Midland Banks cut base rates by 0.25 per cent to 12.5 per cent, bringing them into line with National Westminster and Lloyds.
14	Annual rate of inflation in May 7 per cent. (It is the May rate that governs the rise in pensions and benefits in November.)
20	Statement by Chancellor of the Exchequer on Banking Supervision and Johnson Matthey Bankers, presenting the recommendations of the Review Committee. White Paper to be published and Banking Bill to be introduced.
	Bank of England's Annual Report includes the Bank's account of the rescue of JMB.
8 Jul.	Sterling rises 1.75 cents to $1.3450, highest for a year; and closes above DM 4.00 for the first time since September 1983.
9	Sterling M3 rises by 2 per cent in 5 weeks to mid-June, 12 per cent up on June 1984. £ rises to $1.3655 (83.2) on expectations that interest rates will remain high.
10	Sterling reaches a peak of $1.40 (84.4) and closes at $1.3865. Against DM, 4.0811, best since November 1982.
11	Bank of England cuts its dealing rates by 0.25 per cent and then by a further 0.25 per cent. £ closes down at $1.3820 (83.4) and DM 4.0275.
12	Commercial banks fail to lower base rates in response to Bank's signal of yesterday.
	Rate of inflation 7 per cent in June.
15	Commercial banks cut base rates ½ point to 12 per cent.

17	$ falls sharply, £ rises to a peak of $1.42 and closes at $1.4125 (83.8). Bank of England acts to dampen expectations of further fall in interest rates.
	Chancellor of Exchequer announces that the City of London police are to investigate Johnson Matthey Bankers to establish whether criminal offences lay behind the collapse.
	Government limits the scope of wages councils, and removes workers below the age of 21 from protection.
18	Government announces very large pay increases for top people – senior civil servants, top military officers and the judiciary. Head of the Home Civil Service to get increase of 46 per cent, from £51,250 to £75,000 by March 1986.
19	Lira crisis. Milan foreign exchange market closed.
20	Lira devalued by an effective 8 per cent within EMS.
23	Chancellor of the Exchequer to be sued by Arthur Young, auditors to Johnson Matthey Bankers, for statements made on radio and television.
26	Bank of England cuts dealing rates by ½ point but again acts to discourage expectations of further falls.
29	Clearing banks cut base rates by ½ point to 11.25 per cent. £ rises 2.05 cents to close at $1.4290 (84.7).
1 Aug.	Unemployment in July rises to 3,235 thousand, 3,175 thousand seasonally adjusted (excluding school-leavers), 13.1 per cent. Unfilled vacancies rise to 179,700, highest for five years.
	£ falls 4 cents to $1.3732 and closes 2.5 cents down on the day at $1.3845 (82.1).
2–7	£ falls, to $1.3262 on 7 August.
8–13	£ recovers, to $1.40 on 13 August.
15	Building Societies reduce mortgage rate 1¼ points to 12.75 per cent. Bank of England continues to resist pressure for lower interest rates.
16	Rate of inflation in July falls to 6.9 per cent. £ closes at $1.4005 (82.2).
30	Unemployment in August rises to 3.18 million seasonally adjusted (excluding school-leavers).
6 Sept.	Dollar strong. £ falls to $1.3200 and closes at $1.3255 (81.0), a fall of 3.95 cents on the day.
9	£ falls to $1.2940 and closes 2.05 cents down at $1.3050 (79.9).
10	£M3 rises 2 per cent in August to give annualized increase of 16.75 per cent over 6 months (target 5–9).

13	Annual rate of inflation in August falls to 6.2 per cent. £ rises to close at $1.3410 (81.0).
16	Government launches $2.5 bn floating rate note to bolster reserves.
20	$ falls, £ rises to $1.3700 (82.0).
21–22	US calls sudden meeting of G5 Finance Ministers and Central Bankers. Meeting given unusual publicity. Purpose to step up intervention and bring the dollar down to head off calls for protection within US Congress.
23	President Reagan makes strong policy statement in favour of free trade. £ gains 5.70 cents to close at $1.4270 (83.1) having touched $1.4470 and 83.9.
24	Reported that Bank of Japan intervened heavily against the dollar, spending more than $1 bn. £ closes at $1.4320, best since April 1984. Sterling index down, at 82.8.
25	Announced that Mr George Blunden to be new deputy governor of the Bank of England. Also announced, new high level Committee on supervisory policy. £ closes higher against the dollar at $1.4400 but sterling index down at 82.6. CBI pleads for lower exchange rate, especially against D-mark.
27	£ falls to $1.4065 and DM 3.77 on rumours that UK is to join the EMS currency system.
3 Oct	Unemployment in September rises to a record 3.35 million, 3.18 million (13.1 per cent) seasonally adjusted and excluding school-leavers. Dollar falls sharply on rumours of intervention by the US Federal Reserve. £ rises to $1.4260. Cabinet sets up 'Star Chamber' on public expenditure, presided over by Viscount Whitelaw.
4	Dollar falls against D-mark. Speculation of Federal Reserve intervention. Announced at IMF meeting in Seoul that intervention 'in 10 days' had been as follows: Bank of Japan $1.3 bn (see 24 Sept.); the Federal Reserve about $300 million; the Bundesbank about $250 million; the Bank of France about $400 million; and the Bank of England about $200 million. This totals about $2.45 bn. In addition the Central Bank of Italy (not a member of G5) sold about $1 bn.

8	In banking month September sterling M3 again rises excessively to give growth of 14.5 per cent over 12 months and an annual rate of 18.5 per cent since April. M0 rises 4.5 per cent over 12 months, within target range (3–7 per cent).
16	Report by the House of Lords Select Committee on Overseas Trade on the causes and implications of the deficit in the UK balance of trade in manufactures attracts a lot of attention and an immediate Government response.
	Central banks intervene to sell dollars. Reported that the Federal Reserve sold $350 million. Nevertheless the dollar rises against major currencies.
17	Chancellor of the Exchequer's Mansion House speech. Sterling M3 no longer to be controlled by overfunding. Dollar falls after further central bank intervention.
21	£ rises to $1.44 and closes at $1.4340 (81.0).
24	Pound falls 1.25 cents to $1.4215 (80.7)
31	Unemployment in October seasonally adjusted and excluding school leavers falls 4,000 to 3.175 m, 13.1 per cent.
	Pound ends month at $1.4451 and 80.9
1 Nov.	Pound falls to $1.4275 on oil worries
8	Bank of Japan and Bundesbank intervene to halt rise in dollar. Pound falls to $1.4080 in New York.
12	Autumn Statement
22	Pound recovers to $1.45
29	Pound ends month at $1.4904 and 81.3
2 Dec.	Pound reaches $1.50 ($1.5020) for first time for over 2 years but closes at $1.4875 and 81.4
5	Seasonally adjusted unemployment in November falls to 3.165 m, 13.1 per cent. Unadjusted total 3.259 m, 13.5 per cent.
9	OPEC countries meeting in Geneva agree, in effect, to risk a fall in oil prices in pursuit of higher output (although official selling prices and output quotas remain nominally in force). Pound closes nearly 1.9 cents down at $1.4585 and 80.3
10	Oil prices fall sharply. Pound touches a low of $1.4290 and closes at $1.4350, 2.35 cents down on the day. Sterling index falls below 80 to 78.9
11	Pound falls to $1.4060 and closes a further 2 cents down on the day at $1.4150 and 77.9

JMB report loss of £210 m in 15 months to 30 June 1985.
Bank of England's loss is £39.15 m, £26.65 under the indemnity and £12.5 m as shareholder.

12 Pound recovers to $1.4395 and 78.6
13 Rate of inflation in November rises to 5.5 per cent.
17 Government publishes White Paper *Banking Supervision* Command 9695. Main recommendations are establishment within the Bank of England of a Board of Banking Supervision; and distinction between recognized banks and licensed deposit takers to be abolished.
end Pound ends year at $1.4485 and 77.9.
Unemployment, seasonally adjusted, 3.181 m
Growth of money supply during the year: sterling M3 15.1 per cent, MO 2.4 per cent.
Base rate 11.5 per cent.
Rate of inflation 5.7 per cent.

Notes and references

1. There had been three previous sales of the Government's interest in BP: June 1977, 67 million shares, raising about £564 m.; October 1979, 80 million shares, raising about £290 m.; 1981, a rights issue entitlement sold for £14 m.

   In its Report on the Autumn Statement the Treasury and Civil Service Committee of the House of Commons criticized the practice of counting asset sales as a reduction in public expenditure. The Treasury argued that since asset purchases counted as public expenditure it was symmetrical for sales to score as a reduction in expenditure. While recognizing the force of this argument, the Committee nevertheless thought it misleading to count asset sales as an offset to overspending. Since sales affect interest rates in much the same way as sales of gilts, it would be more appropriate for them to count as a financing item. With this and other adjustments the Committee estimated that public expenditure in 1984–85 would be 8 per cent higher than in 1980–81 in constant terms, not 6 per cent as suggested by the Government. The Committee included a table showing that receipts from the sale of assets and housing between 1979–80 and 1983–84 totalled £9 bn at 1983–84 prices.

Not counting asset sales as a reduction in public expenditure has implications for the MTFS since it raises the PSBR.

2. The uncharitably minded may say that that is not the way Chancellors work: that what they do is to decide on the tax changes first and work backwards from that to arrive at a compatible PSBR, the PSBR being such a malleable and uncertain magnitude that no forecaster can summon up his integrity, place his hand upon his heart and assert that *any* PSBR is inviolable.

3. The conventional wisdom was that the huge US Budget deficit was sucking in the world's savings, thus putting the dollar in such demand as to more than offset the deficit on the US current account. This seemed at odds with the other conventional wisdom that the weakness of sterling at various times had been entirely due to an excessively large public sector deficit (PSBR).

4. *Financial Times*, 11 Feb. 1985.

5. Leading article, 1 Apr. 1985.

6. Leading article, 18 Apr. 1985.

Part Two

Themes

All his professional life, it seemed to Smiley, he had
listened to similar verbal antics signalling supposedly great
changes in Whitehall doctrine; signalling restraint,
self-denial, always another reason for doing nothing.
He had watched Whitehall's skirts go up, and come down
again, her belts being tightened, loosened, tightened.
He had been the witness, or victim – or even reluctant
prophet – of such spurious cults as lateralism, parallelism,
separatism, operational devolution, and now, if he
remembered Lacon's most recent meanderings correctly,
of integration. Each new fashion had been hailed as
a panacea: 'Now we shall vanquish, now the machine will
work!' Each had gone out with a whimper, leaving behind
it the familiar English muddle, . . .

John le Carré *Smiley's People*

Part Two

Themes

9

The Treasury

There are only three Departments of State which are
strong both in tradition and in power ... only the
Treasury, the Home Office and the Foreign Office occupy
roughly the same relative positions in 1970 as they did a
hundred years ago.

Roy Jenkins[1]

The Treasury is one of the oldest Departments of State and, in
terms of numbers, one of the smallest, because it is a policy-
making department with few executive duties that bring it into
contact with industry or the public. Its contacts with the financial
markets are conducted mainly through the Bank of England, as
agent. Historically, its primary duty has been to control the
expenditure of public funds; but nowadays one of its main tasks is
to 'manage the economy of the United Kingdom so as to achieve
the economic objectives laid down by Ministers and approved by
Parliament'.[2]

Formally the heads of the Treasury are the Lords
Commissioners: the First Lord of the Treasury (now always the
Prime Minister), the Chancellor of the Exchequer and five junior
Lords. In practice, the Lords Commissioners never meet as a
board and their responsibilities are carried by the Chancellor of
the Exchequer assisted by the Chief Secretary to the Treasury (a
Cabinet Minister), the Financial Secretary and, at present, a
Minister of State and an Economic Secretary.

The Junior Ministers

The Chief Secretary is responsible for public expenditure; the
Financial Secretary looks after the Inland Revenue, Parliamentary

financial business, and privatization; the Minister of State's main responsibilities are for Customs and Excise, public-sector pay, civil service manpower, and a number of smaller government organizations (including HMSO and the Central Office of Information); the Economic Secretary's remit includes monetary policy, banks, building societies and other financial institutions, international financial issues and institutions, European Community business, the Royal Mint, the Department of National Savings, the Friendly Societies and the National Loans Office.

The Permanent Secretaries

At the top of the official Treasury are the Permanent Secretary, the Second Permanent Secretaries (at present two in number) and the Chief Economic Adviser. These are the Treasury Knights.

The work of the Treasury

The work of the Treasury falls into four main blocks: public expenditure, finance, economics and – before 1968 and after 1981 – the civil service.

Public expenditure

As we have noted, it is the traditional function of the Treasury to control the public purse, that is to say the expenditure of the departments of central government. No department can ask Parliament for funds without prior Treasury approval. But for many years now the Treasury has been responsible not only for the expenditure of central government but for that of the whole of the public sector including the public corporations (largely the nationalized industries) and the local authorities. Public expenditure is by far the largest of the four main sectors within the Treasury.

Finance

The financial side of the Treasury is concerned with fiscal policy (in conjunction with the Revenue departments) and with financial transactions, markets and institutions in so far as these have a bearing on government policies. The work includes the management of the money supply, interest rates, the exchange rate, and government debt, in all of which the Treasury works closely with the Bank of England. On the overseas side the

Treasury has an interest in aid, exports, commercial policy, and
the Government's own transactions with overseas countries
including the European Community. In this field the Treasury
works in touch with the Foreign and Commonwealth Office and
the Bank of England.

Economics

The economic sector's central concern is with short- and medium-
term forecasting and policy analysis. But it has strong links with
many other aspects of Treasury work. Many of the Treasury
economists are 'bedded out' to work in the policy divisions.

The civil service

Since the disbandment of the Civil Service Department the
Treasury has been responsible for civil service manpower, pay and
superannuation.

Other functions

There are three functions that do not fall within any of these four
sectors and which report directly to the Permanent Secretary.
These are Establishments and Organisation, Information, and the
Central Unit, which has a co-ordinating role.

The organization of the Treasury

The organization of the Treasury is governed by its functions, and
changes as the functions change; or, as the Treasury puts it,
rather more elegantly, 'The Treasury is a living organization which
adapts itself continuously to changing needs.' There was a major
re-organization in 1962 following the Treasury's implementation of
the 'Plowden system' of public expenditure management (see Ch.
10), and between 1964 and 1985 further changes occurred.

In 1964 the Treasury was still running the civil service and had
two Permanent Secretaries, one for the pay and management side
and the other for the financial, public sector, and economic side.

After the Government re-organization that followed the 1964
Election, the Treasury lost its responsibility for the co-ordination
of overseas aid policy to the new Ministry of Overseas
Development; and most of its longer-term responsibilities in the
economic sphere were transferred to the new Department of
Economic Affairs. These included responsibility for long-term
economic forecasting, for growth and for incomes policy. The

Treasury's major responsibilities, for the public sector, for finance, and for short-term management of the economy and of the balance of payments, remained with it. In March 1965 the Treasury looked as in Fig. 9.1.

In November 1968 the pay and management side was hived off to form the new Civil Service Department; and at the end of the following year the Treasury absorbed parts of the disbanded Department of Economic Affairs. A reorganization of the Treasury followed and this established a third major group (Public Sector, and Finance were the other two), the National Economy Group, to be managed by the Chief Economic Adviser, the Deputy Chief Economic Adviser and a new Deputy Secretary National Economy. The new group had responsibility for short- and medium-term forecasting, for the formulation of economic strategy, for fiscal policy and for those aspects of economic policy which were mainly the responsibility of other departments, notably prices and incomes policy and industrial policy.

By 1973 the development of the Government's counter-inflation policy and of the work on domestic and international monetary matters including those stemming from membership of the EEC necessitated further changes. A new Deputy Secretary Command was established within the National Economy Group to co-ordinate at official level work on prices and incomes policy; and work on domestic monetary matters (Home Finance) was transferred from the Finance Group (which became the Overseas Finance Group) to the National Economy Group. In 1975 the structure at the top of the Treasury was as in Fig. 9.2.

A major internal management review took place in October. Under the new arrangements, set out in Fig. 9.3 the work of the Treasury was regrouped into four Sectors, three headed by a Second Permanent Secretary and the other by the Chief Economic Adviser. (There was a change of terminology: what had been 'Groups' were now 'Sectors'.) The function of the new Domestic Economy Sector was to

> bring together under a new Second Permanent Secretary two major areas of responsibility, each supervised by a Deputy Secretary. The Deputy Secretary (Industry) will be in charge of developing a more active and coherent Treasury approach to industrial problems and policies. The Treasury intends to widen and deepen its contacts with industrialists to achieve a better understanding of the effects on decision-making in industry of Government economic policies.[3]

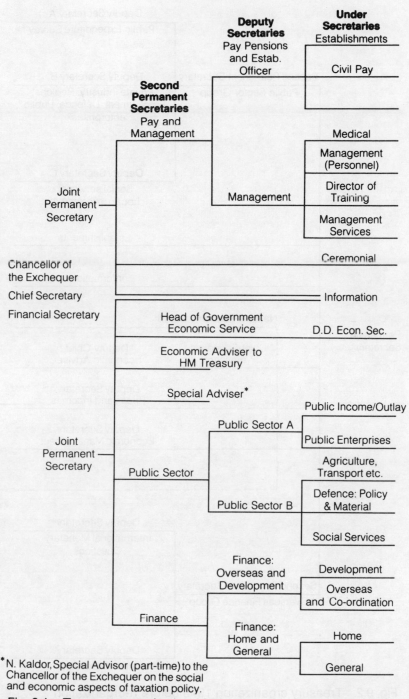

*N. Kaldor, Special Advisor (part-time) to the
Chancellor of the Exchequer on the social
and economic aspects of taxation policy.

Fig. 9.1   Treasury organization 1965

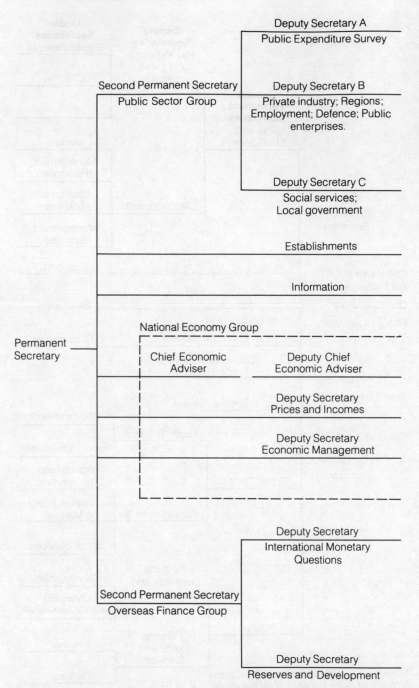

Fig. 9.2   Treasury organization 1975 before reorganization

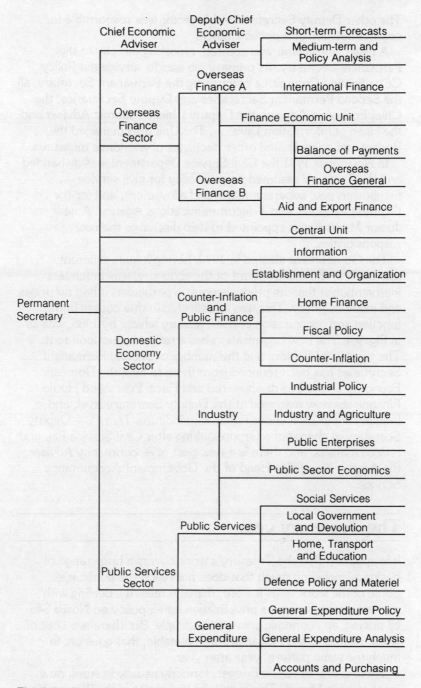

Fig. 9.3 Treasury organization 1975 after reorganization

The other Deputy Secretary in this sector was responsible for counter-inflation and public finance.

A new Central Unit was created, reporting directly to the Permanent Secretary. Its primary job was to service the Policy Co-ordinating Committee comprising the Permanent Secretary, all the Second Permanent Secretaries and Deputy Secretaries, the Chief Economic Adviser, the Deputy Chief Economic Adviser and the Head of Information Division. The Unit also managed the Budget and co-ordinated other packages of economic measures.

In November 1981 the Civil Service Department was disbanded and the Treasury assumed responsibility for civil service manpower, pay, superannuation and allowances, and for the Central Computer and Telecommunications Agency. A new Junior Minister was appointed to help discharge the new responsibilities.

The Government elected in 1979, having a quite different approach to the management of the economy, was much less interventionist than its predecessors; in particular, it had no prices and incomes policy. This was all reflected in due course in the function and organization of the Treasury which, by 1985, was as in Fig. 9.4. The new organization has a rather leaner look to it. The number of Sectors and the number of Second Permanent Secretaries has been reduced from three to two; the Domestic Economy Sector has disappeared and Fiscal Policy and Home Finance are now managed at the Deputy Secretary level; and Industry is paraded under Public Expenditure. There is a Deputy Secretary in charge of a Group looking after Civil Service Pay and related matters; and there is a new post of Accountancy Adviser, the Adviser being also Head of the Government Accountancy Service.

The Treasury year

It is apparent that the Treasury's work covers a huge range of business, including much that does not reach the public eye. Some of the work is, as it were, demand related – dealing with matters as they arise – a privatization issue, policy on North Sea oil pricing, an economic crisis, for example. But there is a core of work, related to the Parliamentary timetable, that goes on, in much the same pattern, year after year.

There is first of all the Budget, formerly usually in April, now most often in March. This is still the high point of the Treasury's

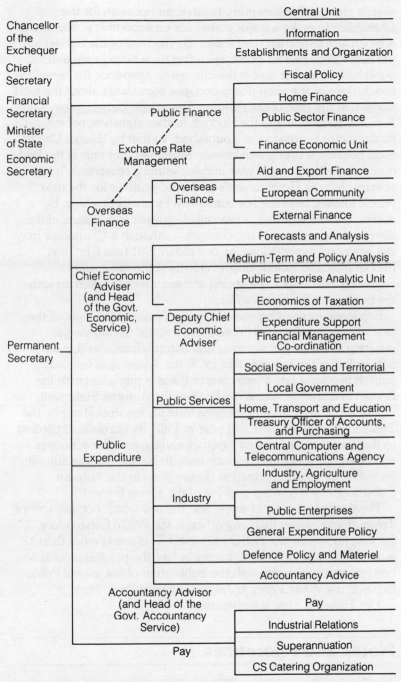

Fig. 9.4   Treasury organization 1985

year, a piece of Parliamentary theatre, an occasion for the Chancellor to make a major statement on economic policy. But it is much less important than it was. By the time of the Budget all the major decisions on public spending have been taken and published. Indeed, it is now the custom to announce the broad conclusions of spending policy *and* give some hints about the next Budget, at the time of the Autumn Statement. Between the Autumn Statement and the Budget, further statistics, notably on public sector borrowing, are published, so that by Budget Day the fiscal position is pretty well known. Moreover, not only is the likely outcome for the current year known, within a reasonable margin of error, but the Government's preferred position for the next year is known, from the Medium-Term Financial Strategy. By putting the two together, a reasonable guess can be made of the direction and amount of tax changes – although a Chancellor may still confound expectations, as one did in 1981 (see Ch. 7). A Budget may also include major reforms of the tax system. Following the Budget, the spring and summer are taken up with the passage of the Finance Bill.

Economic forecasting goes on in the Treasury throughout the year. There are three full 'forecasting rounds' during the year, resulting in the winter, summer and autumn forecasts. Under Schedule 5 of the Industry Act 1975, the Treasury is required to publish two forecasts a year; one of these is published with the Budget and another forms the basis of the Autumn Statement.

The Autumn Statement became formally incorporated into the Treasury (and Parliamentary) year in 1982. Its purpose, according to the Treasury, 'is to bring together and expand the economic and other announcements which have to be made in the autumn.'[4] As noted, so much information is now given in the Autumn Statement that it forms a preview of the spring Budget.

The third main cycle of work, and the one which occupies more Treasury manpower than any other, is the Public Expenditure Survey, known as 'the PESC exercise'.[5] This spans more than 12 months, because one round begins before the previous round is brought to a conclusion with the publication of the annual Public Expenditure White Paper in January or February.

The Treasury Year is summarized in Fig. 9.5.

Notes and references

1.   *Sunday Times* 17 Jan. 1971, p. 25.

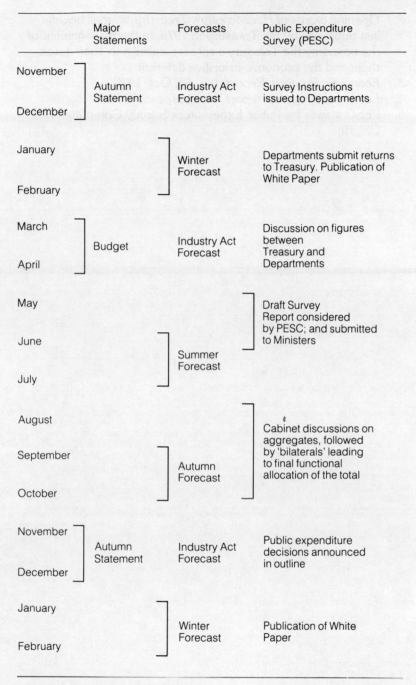

	Major Statements	Forecasts	Public Expenditure Survey (PESC)
November / December	Autumn Statement	Industry Act Forecast	Survey Instructions issued to Departments
January / February		Winter Forecast	Departments submit returns to Treasury. Publication of White Paper
March / April	Budget	Industry Act Forecast	Discussion on figures between Treasury and Departments
May / June / July		Summer Forecast	Draft Survey Report considered by PESC; and submitted to Ministers
August / September / October		Autumn Forecast	Cabinet discussions on aggregates, followed by 'bilaterals' leading to final functional allocation of the total
November / December	Autumn Statement	Industry Act Forecast	Public expenditure decisions announced in outline
January / February		Winter Forecast	Publication of White Paper

Fig. 9.5   The Treasury year

2. *Opening words of Her Majesty's Treasury*, a small booklet last published by the Treasury in 1976. In the management of the economy the Treasury's role is smaller now than it was then; and the economic priorities different.
3. *Economic Progress Report*, No. 67, Oct. 1975.
4. *Economic Progress Report*, No. 153, Jan. 1983.
5. PESC stands for Public Expenditure Survey Committee (see Ch. 10).

10

Public expenditure: planning, control, cost

This task of allocating public funds to Departments, and
ensuring that they keep within their allocation, is the most
long standing of all the duties of the Treasury.

Sir Richard Clarke[1]

The Plowden system

As Sir Richard Clarke and other historians of the Treasury have
noted, the control of the Exchequer, of the public purse, is the
earliest of the Treasury's functions. It is also one of the oldest and
constitutionally most important tasks of Parliament;[2] and it was
Parliament that set in motion the process that led, in the mid-
1960s, to a fundamental change in the system of control.

The years following the Second World War saw a great
expansion of the role of government. It became accepted that the
State ought to make more comprehensive provision for the
education and social welfare of the people. The acceptance of the
ideas of Maynard Keynes, ideas developed and consolidated –
some would say proven – in the forcing-house of rearmament and
war, had placed upon government general responsibility for the
management of the economy and particular responsibility for the
level of employment. To these forces, powerful in themselves,
were added the commitment of the post-war Labour Government
to the provision of a universal health service and the
nationalization of large sectors of industry.

Parliament became increasingly dissatisfied with the machinery
at its disposal for scrutinizing and controlling the growing sums of

money that now, in one way and another and for one purpose and another, passed through government hands and required authorization. In the 1957–58 Session the then Estimates Committee produced a Report *Treasury Control of Expenditure* (H.C. 254, 1957–58) which led to the appointment of the *Committee on the Control of Public Expenditure* under Lord (then Sir Edwin) Plowden in the summer of 1959. The Plowden Committee concluded and recommended that 'Decisions involving substantial future expenditure should always be taken in the light of surveys of public expenditure as a whole, over a period of years, and in relation to prospective resources.'

These recommendations were quickly adopted and from 1961 annual surveys of public expenditure were prepared for ministers, and some were published in white papers.

The changes between the 'old' system and the new 'Plowden' system were considerable. The old system was centred on Parliament's control of 'supply', that is to say the granting of cash, for one year ahead, for the expenditure of the departments of central government. It was, as the Estimates Committee had realized, a piecemeal and inadequate system. It did not bring together expenditure for the same purpose made by different spending authorities (central and local government); it paid no regard to the total resources available to the nation and hence no regard to relative priorities; and it could not accommodate the fact, already well recognized, that expenditure decisions made now had major implications for expenditure years hence. Indeed, many expenditure planning decisions simply could not be made on a one-year basis. In defence, for example, a new weapons system might take ten years to develop; in education, planning needed to take account of the birth-rate (with its 'bulges') and the future need for teachers, teachers' training, school and college building.

To make good these deficiencies the new surveys introduced the following features:

1. The *total expenditure* of the public sector was shown, transactions within the sector being eliminated to avoid double counting.
2. Expenditure was analysed *by function*, regardless of who spent the money; i.e. all expenditure on education was grouped under one head.
3. Expenditure was also analysed *by economic category* (current expenditure, capital expenditure, transfers) on a basis consistent with the National Accounts and expressed *at constant prices*. This was essential if the effects of public

expenditure on the national economy were to be analysed in relation to the prospective demand in resources, as it was intended that they should be.

4. Each survey looked *five years ahead*. Early surveys looked only at the first and fifth years; later surveys at the intervening years as well.

5. Each survey was considered in the light of a parallel *economic survey* showing the prospective availability of resources.

Once the new system of surveys was established, the next step was to formalize it and introduce it into the arrangements for Parliamentary scrutiny and control of expenditure. This latter process was begun in April 1969 with the publication of a 'Green Paper' *Public Expenditure: A New Presentation* (Cmnd 4017). In essence the Government proposed to present to Parliament an annual White Paper on public expenditure embodying the features (1) to (5) above and including also projections of public sector revenue. The first such White Paper was presented to Parliament on 4 December 1969, *Public Expenditure 1968–69 to 1973–74* (Cmnd 4234). Two years later Parliament adapted its procedures by replacing the Estimates Committee with an Expenditure Committee to scrutinize the whole of public expenditure.

The presentation of a White Paper to Parliament was, and is, the final act of the survey process. That process has been improved and refined over the years but remains unchanged in its essentials.

The first stage, conducted by the Treasury early in the calendar year, is a detailed analysis of existing expenditure plans, programme by programme, and of the scope for changes. (A 'Programme' is a functional category of expenditure, e.g. 'Defence', 'Housing'. There is a separate programme for Northern Ireland.) The collection and analysis of this quite vast amount of data is co-ordinated by the Treasury through the Public Expenditure Survey Committee (PESC) – an inter-departmental committee chaired by a Treasury Deputy Secretary.

The outcome of this process of collection, analysis, discussion and horse-trading emerges around the end of June in the 'PESC Report'. The purpose of the PESC Report (which also includes information on the spending plans of local authorities and public corporations, and an economic assessment) is to provide Cabinet ministers with the basic information they need in order to decide on the total and composition of public expenditure. It bears the imprimatur of the Chancellor of the Exchequer; but that does not mean that it embodies final decisions on expenditure. For there now begins the crucial stage of the survey procedure: the discussion in Cabinet and bilateral discussions between Treasury ministers (usually the Chief Secretary, although the Chancellor may be called in in stubborn cases) and spending ministers. This is nearly always a difficult business, under governments of all complexions. The theory is that the Cabinet takes the broad decisions and then leaves it to the individual Departmental Minister to settle the details (or 'fight it out') with the Treasury. Issues that cannot be resolved in this way go back to the full Cabinet or to the Prime Minister. An alternative solution, and one adopted by Mrs Thatcher, is to appoint a Cabinet Sub-Committee (MISC 62 but known as the 'Star Chamber' Committee) of senior ministers (usually from non-spending Departments) to adjudicate. The final decision may depend as much on the amount of political clout carried by a minister as on the merits of the case. These procedures occupy the late summer and autumn and, when resolved, culminate in the publication of the Public Expenditure White Paper – a somewhat movable feast.

That, in barest outline, is the system of public expenditure planning that became known as the Plowden system. We now move on to see how it evolved into the system that we have today; and how much of it remains.

The evolution of Plowden

The scope and definition of public expenditure may be altered from one White Paper to the next for various reasons: perhaps to reflect more clearly the extent to which a service makes a call on taxation or government borrowing; perhaps because a recurrent item is taken into account for the first time, or because an activity previously undertaken by the government is taken over by the private sector (or vice versa).[3]

The theology of public expenditure accounting is so impenetrable that the real overall significance of a major statement ... frequently eludes all observers, except perhaps a tiny handful in the bowels of the Treasury.[4]

The place identified by Mr Jay as the locus of the Treasury's public expenditure experts is perhaps unfortunate; but that the public accounts are labyrinthine and less than unambiguous is not to be doubted. One reason for this is that the definition and coverage of 'public expenditure' are constantly changing. Let us consider some of the problems that have made a stable definition so elusive

1. *Changes stemming from the need to make the public expenditure accounts consistent with, or at least reconcilable with, the national income accounts.* The White Paper Cmnd 8789 notes (Part V, para. 11) that 'The definitions are intended to reflect the role of public expenditure in the national economy and for this reason are based on the concepts of the national income accounts which are used to describe the economy as a whole.' Now the national income accounts are themselves exceedingly complex and subject to continuous development, so it may follow from this that changes in national accounting methods would require consequential changes in public expenditure accounting. Or it may not; for para. 31 goes on to say 'The definitions used for public expenditure have been modified to reflect methods of control and differ from those used for the national income and expenditure accounts.' There are then listed eleven adjustments that have to be made to move from *General government expenditure* in the national accounts to the corresponding total *public expenditure on programmes* in the public expenditure accounts.

2. *Considerations of purpose.* For what purpose do we need a definition of public expenditure? Do we want it for Parliamentary control; or for economic management; or for some other reason? The appropriate definition will depend to a large extent on the purpose for which it is required. If there is more than one purpose, we shall require more than one definition.

3. *Changes of concept.* For example, the capital expenditure of the nationalized industries was at first included, later excluded. Should sales of public sector assets be counted as negative public expenditure or as a financing item?

4. *Should expenditure be shown gross or net?* If, as is sometimes the case, public expenditure gives rise to a charge or a flow-back of revenue in some form, should we show that as revenue or as a deduction from expenditure? What about the income from fines and fees collected in magistrates' courts? Should they be treated as negative expenditure? (They were, from 1983.)

5. *Policy changes.* The problems here are similar to but conceptually different from, the 'gross or net' problem. For

example, if, as a matter of policy investment aid to industry (of which there has been a vast amount) is changed from investment *allowances* (against tax) to investment *grants*, then the grants are an immediate and obvious charge on the exchequer. But the abolition of tax allowances would result in an increased tax flow to the exchequer. Should this be deducted from the cost of the grants to give a truer picture of the cost to the exchequer? And if so, for how long?

6. *Changes related to changes in the machinery of government.* Changes in the organization of government departments and the responsibilities of departments, mean changes in 'votes' (the procedure by which Parliament authorizes expenditure); and votes have to be reconciled with public expenditure categories. Suppose, to take a hypothetical example, responsibility for school buses were transferred from the Department of Education to the Department of Transport. Should the expenditure be transferred from the functional category of 'Education' to 'Transport'? And where should it have properly been in the first place anyway? Borderline cases such as this – and there are many – cause much distress to statisticians and administrators. There is really no 'correct' solution. The re-allocation of items between heads of expenditure affects the composition of public expenditure but not usually the total.

7. *Statistical refinement.* For example the March 1981 White Paper, Cmnd 8175, notes (p. 231) 'In this White Paper there has been a change in the definition of survey prices in order to improve their consistency.' ('Survey prices' was the main price basis of the statistics until 1981.)

So much for some of the difficulties. For an early definition of public expenditure we can turn to Mr Peter Rees, then Chief Statistician at the Treasury.[5]

> Since public expenditure directly or indirectly represents such a large claim on the output of the economy and is a powerful instrument by which the government can influence economic development, it is essential when it is looked at in relation to available resources that it should be measured in accordance with the principles and definitions used in the national accounts. Accordingly public expenditure in its widest sense is defined as the current and capital outlays of the central government (including the national insurance funds) and of local authorities, together with the capital expenditure and debt

interest of the nationalised industries and other public corporations (mainly New Towns). All transfers within the public sector, such as central government grants and loans to local authorities and public corporations, are eliminated.

For planning and control purposes public expenditure is defined with a more limited coverage. Debt interest is excluded because it is a function of other expenditure, largely in the past, and is not subject to independent control as a programme; forecasting the future level of such payments also involves assumptions about the future levels of taxation and borrowing. Since 1965 the capital expenditure of the nationalised industries has also been excluded from the control total on the grounds that these industries are essentially enterprises producing goods and services for sale, and the size and composition of their investment have been considered in relation to the industrial needs of the economy and the financial obligations laid on the undertakings.

We may note that the primary definition was of public expenditure 'in its widest sense' and that already a distinction was made between the definition appropriate for measuring the use of available resources and that appropriate for planning and control purposes. Debt interest and the capital expenditure of the nationalized industries were excluded from the latter total. Debt interest was excluded because it 'is not subject to independent control as a programme'. That has proved convenient for the planners, because debt interest is a very large item. In the White Paper of February 1983, Cmnd 8789, for example, gross debt interest for 1982–83 at £14,750 m. cash, exceeded every programme except social security (£32,473 bn). It was greater than the expenditure on defence, and nearly six times greater than expenditure on housing; and exceeded by £2.5 bn the programmes for Scotland, Wales and Northern Ireland put together.

While it may be legitimate to exclude debt interest from public expenditure *plans* (because it is held to be unplannable), it should be included in *actual* (achieved) public expenditure because it *is* expenditure and has to be financed.

With the framework of the Plowden, or PESC, system established, we can move on to see how it developed and was presented, by looking at the annual White Paper, the public face of public expenditure.

The presentation of public expenditure: the White Papers

The White Paper *Public Expenditure: Planning and Control* (Cmnd 2915), presented to Parliament by the Chancellor of the Exchequer in February 1966, was thirty pages long, contained seven tables, relegated to appendices, cost 2s.3d. (11½p) and weighted under 50 grams. The White Paper *The Government's Expenditure Plans 1983–84 to 1985–86* (Cmnd 8789-I and 8789-II) presented in February 1983 was not so much a White Paper as a Blue Book in two volumes and printed in two colours. Each page was two-thirds bigger than in the 1966 version and there were 148 of them, containing 134 tables and 2 charts. The two volumes together cost £14.85 and weighed 450 grams (1 lb). The cost of public expenditure information, per gram, had risen by some 1,400 per cent. But look at the quality, feel the width.

The evolution of presentation was continuous, but not smooth. In every White Paper the statistics were not only on a new price basis but were ordered differently, so that rarely was it possible to move directly from the main table of expenditure in one White Paper to the corresponding table in the next.

Early White Papers were simple. The main table in the 1966 version merely listed the programmes and added a contingency allowance. Estimates were given for the current year and a year four years ahead. The February 1969 paper, Cmnd 3936, looked only one year ahead.

By the early 1970s things had become more sophisticated and the main tables included items for debt interest and shortfall; and they gave projections for each of the four years ahead. The figures were given in both volume terms and 'cost' terms (then called 'outturn prices'). The 1972 and 1973 editions contained 'use of resources' tables which set public expenditure claims in the context of other claims and the likely resources available to the whole economy. These latter were based on projected rates of growth distinctly on the optimistic side: 3.5 per cent, 4.5 per cent and 5.0 per cent. But rates of this order were required to justify the high rate of growth projected for public expenditure, 3.2 per cent. With something of an air of whistling in the dark, the 1971 White Paper explained (para. 8):

> Such a rate is close to that of the productive potential of the economy over the past decade and more, which has been around 3 per cent a year. But a projection of this

trend will understate the future growth in resources. First there is the increase in output that will result from the taking up of spare capacity. Second there is the likelihood that the recent improvement in productivity will be found to have made some permanent addition to the level of productive potential.

One may speculate on what projections of growth might now (1985) be made on parallel reasoning, bearing in mind claims that the economy is now more efficient and that, as measured by the numbers unemployed, 'spare capacity' is four times what it was in 1971. On the other hand, it could be argued that the recent slow growth of measured production and the rusty and obsolescent state of many silent factories make a high rate of future growth improbable. The wonderful thing about economics is that you can always find plausible arguments and statistics to support almost any proposition.

The Expenditure Committee welcomed the 'material relating to resources and claims' but was highly critical of the spending proposals:[6]

> The most striking feature of the new programmes ... is the very large additions to the expenditure now planned, not only in 1972-73 and 1973-74, but for the later years as well ... We are strongly critical of these decisions taking them as a whole ... Our major conclusion is that the expenditure decisions taken during the past year, unless they are now modified, will make it essential to constrain the growth of real personal disposable income and consumption to a rate significantly below that of total output, and this could well adversely influence the acceptability of any form of incomes policy.

And this was *even if the economy expanded at 5 per cent per annum.*

In March 1975 the Expenditure Committee[7] returned to its anxieties about the compatibility of the expenditure plans with other objectives, in particular the Treasury's expressed objective of eliminating the balance of payments deficit:

> Your Committee feel bound to consider whether the resources will be available to provide for the level of public expenditure projected in the White Paper. ... we do not wholly understand how this target [of a balance in the balance of payments] will be achieved. It involves assumptions about changes in exports, imports and the

> terms of trade ... we gravely doubt the likelihood of
> anything remotely approaching a 10 per cent per annum
> increase in exports being achieved ... we cannot see how
> the Treasury's balance of payments targets and the White
> Paper's assumed 3.5 per cent rise in output can be
> achieved simultaneously.

The Committee proved right. The balance of payments came to
near-balance in 1977; but GDP grew by only about 1.25 per cent
per annum between 1974 and 1977; and public expenditure fell in
the last two years.

Public expenditure and GDP

The White Paper of February 1976, Cmnd 6393, contained the
following statement (para. 25): 'The ratio of total public
expenditure to GDP at factor cost has grown from 50 per cent in
1971–72 to about 60 per cent in 1975–76.' It is difficult, certainly in
retrospect, and in the context of the times, to conceive of a more
unfortunate statement, following, as it did, the Godley revelations
of overspending. It fed not only the belief of *The Times*
newspaper, and other less responsible observers, that public
expenditure was out of control, but the paranoia of those who
equated a growth of public expenditure with a passage into
serfdom; and it provided a fairly hefty shillelagh for those seeking
an instrument with which to beat a Labour Government, in the
forefront of whom we might fairly place the *Sun* newspaper (see
Ch. 5).

The statement was totally misleading, and the figure of 60 per
cent became a factoid[8] and passed into the mythology of public
expenditure.[9]

As we have seen, 1976 was a year of crisis for the Government,
characterized by a Press campaign against public expenditure of
quite extraordinary virulence. The Treasury, encouraged by
ministers, took a fresh look at its public expenditure methodology.
The results were seen in Cmnd 6721, published in January 1977,
in which three major changes were made. The first was to score
as public expenditure on the nationalized industries only
government loans and capital grants instead of, as formerly, the
whole of their capital expenditure. The effect of this was to reduce
public expenditure in 1976–77 by £3 bn. The rationale of the
change was that the capital expenditure of the nationalized
industries could be met from three sources: internally generated

funds, borrowing from the market or overseas, and borrowing from the government; only the last of these was in any sense a call on the public sector.

The second change was in debt interest, which was now to exclude interest payments which were balanced by receipts of interest on money lent or by provision for interest from the profits (including subsidies) of trading activities in which public money had been invested. Under the revised presentation only that debt interest was included which had to be met either out of taxation or by fresh borrowing. Formerly the whole of the debt interest paid by the public sector had been included; but the major part of this was met by the community at large through the prices, rents or charges which it paid for goods and services provided by the public sector. Grants paid by central government to local authorities included sums to enable local government to pay interest on housing loans: to score as public expenditure both the grants and the interest was to double-count. The revised presentation reduced public expenditure in 1976–77 by £4.7 bn.

Thus two definitional changes that with hindsight looked no more than common sense had reduced total public expenditure by some £7.7 bn at a stroke.

The third change was to measure GDP, when calculating the ratio of public expenditure to it, on the same basis as public expenditure, namely, market prices, instead of, as formerly, at factor cost. As GDP at market prices is higher than at factor cost, the effect was to enlarge the denominator and lower the ratio.

These changes reduced the ratio of public expenditure to GDP in 1975–76 from 60 per cent to 46 per cent. Of this fall of 14 percentage points about half (7½ points) was attributable to the change to market prices. Nothing in the real world had changed at all.

And, anyway, the ratio of public expenditure to GDP, however measured, is not, as the Treasury carefully put it (Cmnd 6721-I, para. 52) 'a wholly reliable indicator of the importance of the public sector in the economy as a whole', because transfers and loans to the private sector finance private, not public, consumption and investment. If we eliminate all such transfer payments, which account for nearly half of all public expenditure, and count only direct expenditure on goods and services by central and local government we obtain a ratio to GDP of 26.5 per cent in 1975–76.

The White Paper Cmnd 6721 looked only two years ahead, to 1978–79. The restructured main table of that Paper set, with modifications, the basic presentation for future years:

Table 1. Public expenditure plans
Public expenditure by:
    Central government (including government loans
        and capital grants to the nationalized industries)
    Public corporations other than the nationalized industries
    Local authorities
    Total expenditure on programmes
    Contingency reserve
    Debt interest
    Total public expenditure

The next White Paper, Cmnd 7049 of January 1978, modified
this as follows:

Title: Public expenditure plans
Expenditure on programmes
Central government
Local authorities
Total general government
Certain public corporations (not including
    nationalized industries)
Total expenditure on programmes
Contingency reserve
Total
Debt interest
Total public expenditure
Total programmes, contingency reserve and net overseas
    and market borrowing of nationalized industries.

For the first time we had a sub-total for 'general government'.
'Total public expenditure' was the same as in Cmnd 6721 but we
now had, below the 'total' line, an 'adjusted total' that *added* the
net overseas and market borrowing of nationalized industries and
subtracted (did not include) debt interest. The market and
overseas borrowing of the nationalized industries is hardly public
expenditure but it was included, on the recommendation of the
Select Committee on Expenditure, because its exclusion would
distort the year-to-year path of government lending to the
nationalized industries as they switched into and out of overseas
and market borrowing and out of and in to borrowing from the
National Loans Fund (NLF). There is little harm in having an
alternative total; but if the logic of the reasoning was that it is only
government grants and loans that properly score as public
expenditure, then it would seem to follow that variations

('distortions', as the White Paper calls them) in that borrowing should be displayed rather than masked. But really it would be preferable to exclude borrowing by nationalized industries entirely since this is a financing item only. It belongs in the Public Sector Borrowing Requirement (PSBR) but not in public expenditure.

The White Paper Cmnd 7049 included (paras 48–56) an economic assessment in general terms. The Expenditure Committee was not satisfied with this and asked for a 'more quantified assessment of the medium-term prospects.' To this request the Treasury replied:[10]

> The Government has not thought it appropriate to include medium-term economic projections in the last two White Papers because of the very great uncertainties involved and the likelihood that more weight would be placed on the figures than would be justified. Experience has illustrated the risk, in present circumstances, of linking firm planning decisions too closely to highly uncertain projections of the economy over a number of years.

Rather more boldly, reflecting concern with the fiscal dimension of public expenditure (and anticipating in some respects the projections of the later Medium-Term Financial Strategy), the Treasury included a table of projections of general government receipts and expenditure to 1979–80. The projections, which were on a different statistical basis from the main tables, showed the General Government Borrowing Requirement (the GGBR, not the PSBR) falling from £7.3 bn in 1976–77 to £4.3 bn in 1979–80, at 1976–77 prices.

Cmnd 7049 provides an interesting example of the way in which the numerous and differing totals generate that impenetrability for which the Treasury's public expenditure White Papers became famous. Let us try to discover, from Cmnd 7049, the growth of expenditure in 1976–77 and 1977–78 and the planned growth in 1978–79.

There are two main tables of public expenditure: Table 1 right at the front of the book (the one we are supposed to look at) and Table 9 in the statistical section at the back. From each table we have a choice of five totals: total general government expenditure; total expenditure on programmes; programmes plus contingency reserve; programmes plus contingency reserve and debt interest (defined as total public expenditure); and an adjusted total of public expenditure, defined as 'Total programmes, contingency reserve and net overseas and market borrowing of nationalized industries'. By implication, debt interest is excluded from the adjusted total. Each of the five totals has some validity as a measure of public expenditure and its growth – why include it, otherwise? But, to be fair, we shall look at only the totals defined as total public expenditure. The results are shown in Table 10.1.

So, according to taste and which table we look at (and if we work out the percentages, which are not given), public expenditure in 1978–79 was planned to rise by between 2.2 and 8.2 per cent.

But these are plans. We should be able to say with some certitude what had actually happened in the year that had ended some nine months earlier, 1976–77. According to Table 9 it had fallen 2.6 or 2.7 per cent. But paragraph 11 of Cmnd 7049 informs us that at out-turn prices it was 11 per cent up; although in volume terms and excluding debt interest the total of programmes was 3.5 per cent down. All clear? Good; because paragraph 12 tells us 'The outturn of programmes in 1976–77 was less in volume terms than the Cmnd 6721 plans for that year, by just over 4 per cent, or £2.25 billion at 1977 survey prices.' Well, yes, that's different but I understand that we now have a different base, not what actually happened but what the plans in Cmnd 6721 had intended to happen. But wait: what does paragraph 14 say? 'The aggregate outturn in 1976–77 in volume terms on all programmes other than the nationalised industries was about 3 per cent below the planning figure in Cmnd 6721.' Sir Leo Pliatzky, who was in charge of these figures at around the relevant time, subsequently had a consistent series prepared for him by the Treasury and this showed that expenditure fell by 1.9 per cent in cost terms. Oh

Table 10.1 Per cent change in public expenditure (from Tables 1 and 9 of Cmnd 7049)

	1976–77	1977–78	1978–79
Table 1 total	..	..	+2.7
Table 1 adjusted total	..	..	+2.2
Table 9 total	–2.7	–2.8	+8.2
Table 9 adjusted total	–2.6	–4.8	+6.7

Note: In Table 1 there are no figures for years before 1977–78; and the 1977–78 figures are of *plans* as in Cmnd 6721. In Table 9 the 1977–78 figures are of estimated *out-turn*.

well; at least everyone got the sign right. (The 11 per cent rise
does not count: that was in real money.)

In the following year, Cmnd 7439, published in January 1979,
made further changes in the main tables:

Title: Public expenditure 1973–74 to 1982–83
1.   Central government
2.   Local authorities
3.   Certain public corporations
4.   Total expenditure on programmes (1+2+3)
5.   Contingency reserve
6.   Debt interest
7.   Total public expenditure (4+5+6)
8.   Total expenditure on programmes and
          contingency reserve
9.   Net overseas and market borrowing of
          nationalised industries.
10.   Planning total for future years (8+9)
11.   General allowance for shortfall (–)
12.   Outturn and projected outturn (8+9+11)

The sub-total for general government has disappeared. The
'adjusted' total of the previous White Paper is now called the
'planning total'; the first use of this nomenclature. There is a
specific allowance for shortfall; and this is deducted from the
planning programme for future years to arrive at a projected out-
turn. (Shortfall is expressed as a minus quantity.) The White
Paper explained: 'Some continuing difference is to be expected
between planning figures and outturn, and the Government allow
for this in taking decisions both about expenditure plans and
about taxation.' Thus, the *planned* outturn (line 10) was not the
same as the *projected* out-turn (line 12). And remember that the
planned total already included a contingency reserve (for 1980–81
the contingency reserve was £1.4 bn and the allowance for
shortfall was —£2.0 bn).

This was the last Public Expenditure White Paper published by
the Labour Government. The next, Cmnd 7746, published in
November by the new Government, was a short, interim affair and
followed the style of its predecessor with the addition of a new
item 'Special Sales of Assets'. There was, however, one other
change, recorded in the Notes, which is worth noting for its
general bearing on the 'gross or net' problem. The Notes recorded
that now that the transition to child benefits was complete, the
cost of those benefits were shown gross instead of net of the tax

flowback arising from the reductions in child tax allowances. Clearly when child benefits were introduced it was sensible to show the net cost to the exchequer of the changeover; and this was the gross cost less the increased tax take. But as time went on it would become increasingly unrealistic to continue to offset the cost by some notional tax flow accruing because at some time past there had been child tax allowances and now there were not.

The White Paper of March 1980, Cmnd 7841, was not only the first public expenditure presentation by the new Government, it was also the first published on Budget Day with the *Financial Statement and Budget Report* (FSBR). From a purely practical standpoint this was not a development that I welcomed, for the Budget Day Press operation was already complicated enough, with a huge mass of documentation to be shifted late in the day to a waiting Press. And it added considerably to the weight of facts and briefing to be mastered by the Press Office before the curtain went up, or, to be more precise, before the telephone lines were opened. On the other hand, the media would be faced with similar problems of absorption: it was unlikely that they would be able to enquire deeply into both the Budget and the public expenditure statistics in the short time available to them on the day. That apart, there was much to be said for linking public expenditure with the Budget. From the early days of the new presentation it had been argued that projections of expenditure must be accompanied by projections of revenue and by an assessment of the course of the economy. The revenue projections were attempted only briefly and abandoned; and the economic assessment varied in quality and the amount of detail. Publication with the Budget obviated entirely the need for a separate economic assessment, since the Budget Statement always included an economic review, and quantified economic forecasts were published in the FSBR for a period some twenty-one months ahead. The FSBR had not, however, in the past projected revenue beyond the financial year just started, or about to start, and for the 'first full year' (a not unambiguous concept). But the 1980 Budget and FSBR saw the introduction of something new, the 'Medium Term Financial Strategy', which did give projections for government revenue as well as expenditure (see Ch. 7).

In other respects the presentation of Cmnd 7841 did not differ markedly from that of its predecessors: there was a total for public expenditure (before shortfall and special sales of assets) and two planning totals, one before and one after shortfall. Plans were given for four years ahead, 1980–81 to 1983–84.

The next White Paper, Cmnd 8175 of March 1981, was again

published with the Budget. It made a number of changes, which can be best seen by looking at the main table:

Table 1.1 Planning total
      Public expenditure programmes
1.   Central government (including finance for nationalized
      industries)
2.   Local authorities
3.   Certain public corporations' capital expenditure
      Adjustments
4.   Nationalized industries' net overseas and market
      borrowing
5.   Special sales of assets (net)
6.   Contingency reserve
7.   General allowance for shortfall
8.   Planning total
9.   Percentage change on previous year
      Memorandum items
      A.   Debt interest – gross
                           – net
      (Not included above.)
      B.   Nationalized industries' total net borrowing (included
            in lines 1 and 4.)

The title of the table was not 'Public expenditure' but 'Planning total' and nowhere in the table was there any total described as 'public expenditure'. Nor was there a total for 'programmes'. Only one 'planning total' was given, after shortfall. Two new pieces of nomenclature were introduced: the 'non-programme' items were titled 'Adjustments'; and two 'Memorandum' items appeared: debt interest gross and net (not included in the planning total), and a total for all nationalized industries' borrowing (included in the planning total). The forward planning period was shortened by one year, i.e. it went only to 1983–84, as in Cmnd 7841 of 1980.

Movement towards a cash basis

But more significant than these rearrangements was the inclusion of a column in the table showing planned spending in 1981–82 on a cash basis. Cash limits for the coming year were also, for the first time, published in the Public Expenditure White Paper. The White Paper noted that although, following past practice, plans were in volume terms at constant prices,

> ... the Government's policy is that all volume plans are to
> be regarded as no more than indicative working targets;

their attainment is dependent on the availability of
finance. It is actual cash expenditure which must be
considered in relation to, and made consistent with, the
Government's objectives for taxation, the borrowing
requirement and the money supply. . . . in future, the
Government intend to give more weight to prospective
cash costs in expenditure planning. (pp. 2–3).

This notice of a move to cash planning came as no surprise but
it is worth spelling out just how big a departure this was from the
early conceptions of the way public expenditure should be
planned. It was a matter of what were to be regarded as the
constraints. The Plowden system was rooted in Keynesian
thinking and implicitly assumed full employment or, to put it
another way, the absence of any significant margin of unused
capacity. It followed that any increase in public spending, implying
an increase in the public sector's absorption of resources, could
be realized only if total resources increased or if other users of
resources took less. This was clearly expressed in the 'Use of
resources' tables of some earlier White Papers. In short, the
constraint on the growth of public expenditure was the availability
of real resources. In the early 1980s with considerable spare
capacity, represented by over 3 million unemployed workers, this
constraint clearly no longer had effect. The constraint now was to
be 'the availability of finance'. But there are, in both theory and
practice, no limits on the amount of finance available to
government, except limits imposed by the government itself.
These limits the Government, in the early 1980s, imposed by
setting, in its Medium-Term Financial Strategy, objectives for
taxation, borrowing and the money supply. These objectives, it
should be added, were themselves *intermediate* objectives
designed to achieve a primary policy objective of a sustained
reduction in the rate of inflation. It is interesting to note in passing
that the Government achieved its primary objective without, for
the most part, achieving the intermediate objectives that were
supposed to be essential to it.

As foreshadowed, the next White Paper, Cmnd 8494, of March
1982 was couched entirely in cash terms. To mark, perhaps, the
occasion, it was in a new, larger format; and tables and charts
were prettily printed in two shades of blue. The only change in the
main planning table was the disappearance of the identified
allowance for shortfall. As in the previous year the forward plans
covered only two years beyond the year just beginning.

The White Paper of 1983, Cmnd 8789, published in February,

money supply total, such as monetarists might have preferred, would not have served. The aim was still to control credit, not money as such. But the public incorporation into the economic management armoury of a specific ceiling for a monetary aggregate of sorts did seem to indicate acceptance of the view that money did matter, at least a bit.

DCE was a useful indicator or monitor to be used by the UK authorities and the IMF with the former committed to take action if DCE departed from its agreed path. The precise corrective action to be taken would depend upon which component of DCE had got out of line.

Subsequent developments

The definition of DCE was changed slightly on 15 December 1976, to exclude from lending by the banks to the private sector all lending in foreign currencies and to include only lending in sterling. At the same time it was announced that in future greater official emphasis would be placed on the sterling component of M3; and that a new statistical series of sterling M3 would shortly be published. The effect of this change was, for the most part, to lower both DCE and the growth of M3.[6]

DCE retained its importance until 1979. But from the end of 1981 a change in the format of monetary statistics meant that DCE could no longer be directly calculated, although it continued to be shown as a memorandum item. In June 1983 even this was discontinued. For a number of reasons, including the growth of sterling lending to overseas residents, the removal of exchange control, and a relatively freely floating exchange rate, the concept was now less relevant than when introduced (when exchange rates were fixed). The Bank of England doubted whether it ever had been particularly appropriate to the UK and concluded that 'none of the conditions propitious to a straightforward interpretation of DCE hold at present in the United Kingdom'.[7]

1970

In April 1970 the Treasury and the Bank of England resumed, in Washington, their Monetary Seminar with the IMF. The Bank participants were concerned mainly with fundamental theoretical issues related to the alternative Keynesian and monetarist approaches to money and income. The Treasury's interests were more practical, related to the problems of incorporating monetary factors into the short-term forecasts and into policy advice. The IMF presented evidence drawn from many countries.

The results of the Bank of England's research into monetary matters, largely the work of C.A.E. Goodhart, that had been presented to the IMF Seminar, were made public in a forty-page article, 'The importance of money', in the *BEQB* of June 1970. In so far as the results of a long and carefully researched article can be fairly and briefly summarized, the conclusions may be said to have been that neither the extreme Keynesian nor the extreme monetarist position was tenable, that there was a good deal of common ground, and

> Monetary policy is not an easy policy to use. The possibility of exaggerated reactions and discontinuities in application must condition its use. We are not able to estimate the effects of such policy, even in normal circumstances, with any precision. Such effects may well be stronger than some studies undertaken from a Keynesian approach, relating expenditure to changes in nominal interest rates, would suggest, but weaker than some of the monetarist exercises may be interpreted as implying.
>
> As there will always be multiple objectives ... no single statistic can possibly provide an adequate and comprehensive indicator of policy. And basing policy, quasi-automatically, upon variations in one simple indicator would lead to a hardening of the arteries of judgement.

In the August issue of *Economic Trends* the CSO gave notice that it would, from September, be introducing two new monetary aggregates, M1 and M2, both narrower than the existing official definition, M3. These new, narrower definitions, were intended to relate more closely than M3 to money as a medium of exchange. The narrowest one, M1, comprised notes and coin plus all chequeable current accounts of private-sector residents denominated in sterling. The intermediate definition, M2, comprised M1 plus sterling deposit accounts (time deposits) of private-sector residents with the deposit banks and with the discount houses. (M2 on this definition was discontinued in December 1981.)

In his annual speech to the Lord Mayor's dinner in October 1970, the Governor of the Bank, Sir Leslie O'Brien, discoursed on the serious problem of inflation. His approach was not noticeably monetarist:

I know that some feel I should limit my public
pronouncements to reporting on the movements in the
money supply and our efforts to influence it. It is my
belief, however, that for a lasting solution to the problem
of inflation we must look much wider than the bounds of
conventional monetary and fiscal policy. I do not see how
we can expect to maintain a fully employed, fully informed
and increasingly well-off democracy, in which the
development of wages and prices is left entirely to the
operation of market forces ... If we try to rely on the
market place and on the strict operation of fiscal and
monetary policies, we shall find, I think, that we can
achieve price stability only at the cost of unemployment
that might be on a very large scale indeed.

   ... I do not accept either that the monetary authorities
can exercise a precise control over the rate of increase in
the money supply from month to month, or that in
regulating the course of the economy overwhelming
priority should be given to trying to influence movements
in this particular magnitude. Real life is too complex and
the objectives of policy too many and various for us to be
able to rely on any simple rule.

Two months later Sir Leslie delivered the Jane Hodge Memorial
Lecture and took as his subject 'Monetary management in the
United Kingdom'. Although he conceded right at the beginning
that 'Monetary policy has an inescapable part to play in pursuit of
these aims' (full employment, growth, relatively stable prices and
external balance), he remained sceptical: ' ... changes in the
amount of money may have some consequences for money
incomes but ... in the short run the relationship is neither strong
nor predictable'. The relationship between money and incomes
told us nothing about causation. Aggregates such as money
supply and DCE could be useful indicators;

But to focus solely on the money supply or DCE among
the financial, let alone the economic variables is not
enough. It cannot be emphasised too strongly or too often
that attacking a severe inflation simply by holding down
the growth of the money supply means reducing real
activity: or in more homely terms a lot of bankruptcies
and unemployment ... it should be recognised that
excessive reliance on monetary policy is bound to place
severe strains on financial markets and the financial

position of companies and may have serious effects on the nation's productive investment and housebuilding.

Not surprisingly, perhaps, from a Governor of the Bank of England, Sir Leslie devoted much of his lecture to the existing institutional framework and the difficulties that this posed for monetary policy. He looked forward to the end of quantitative restrictions on bank lending and hoped that ' ... credit allocation could come to be determined more by price than by physical rationing throughout the banking sector', and that there might be ' ... a greater use of such mechanisms as special and cash deposits, buttressed perhaps by the acceptance of greater variability of short-term interest rates'. He emphasized the distinction between nominal and real interest rates. This part of his speech was seen as a distinct shift in the Bank's position.

The year 1970 was a busy year in the Bank's thinking about monetary policy. But it was moving cautiously, still believed in the 'incomes policy' approach to inflation, but was prepared to accord a bigger, if limited role, to monetary policy, and to countenance more flexibility in interest rates.

1971

The system of ceiling controls on bank credit that had been in force almost continuously since 1965 was effective in its main purpose but it introduced rigidities, inequities, and inefficiencies into the banking system; and it encouraged the growth of financial institutions outside the control and supervision of the Bank of England. The Bank was not happy with the state of affairs that had developed, and worked to construct an alternative. In early 1971, with the balance of payments in surplus and lending conditions easier, the climate was considered right to bring in the new system. In May the Bank published a consultative document 'Competition and Credit Control' and, after consultation with the banks, the discount market, the finance houses and all those affected, and with the approval of the Chancellor of the Exchequer, introduced the new system on 16 September.

Competition and Credit Control (CCC)

Under the new arrangements, ceiling control of lending (the assets side of the Bank's balance sheet) was abandoned in favour of control, at least nominally, of liabilities by means of the imposition of a uniform minimum reserve ratio (the ratio was lower for certain finance houses). To maintain the ratio, of 12.5 per cent, banks could be required to place Special Deposits with the Bank. The reserve ratio, however, was not the cutting edge of control, which was intended to be interest rates.

The aggregate to be controlled was 'eligible liabilities', defined as the sterling deposit liabilities of the banking system as a whole, excluding deposits having an original maturity of over two years, plus any sterling resources obtained by switching foreign currencies into sterling.

The 'eligible reserve assets' which had to be 12.5 per cent of 'eligible liabilities' were defined as balances with the Bank of England (other than Special Deposits), British Government and Northern Ireland Government Treasury bills, company tax reserve certificates, money at call with the London money market, British Government stocks with one year or less to maturity, and local authority and commercial bills eligible for re-discount at the Bank of England. Notes in tills were not included.

The clearing banks were to give up their interest rate cartel. The London Discount Market was little affected except that members were required to hold 50 per cent of their funds in public sector debt. On 19 July 1973 this requirement was dropped in favour of a more flexible control.

One of the most significant aspects of the new arrangements came into force not in September but in May, when the CCC proposals were first publicized. This was an immediate restriction on the Bank of England's operations in the gilt-edged market, in particular:

1. The Bank no longer responded to requests to buy stock outright, except in the case of stocks with one year or less to run to maturity.
2. The Bank reserved the right to make outright purchases of stock with more than a year to run solely at their discretion and initiative.
3. The Bank prepared to undertake, at prices of their own choosing, exchanges of stock with the market except those which unduly shorten the life of the debt.
4. The Bank prepared to respond to bids for the sale by them of 'tap' stocks and of such other stocks held by them as they may wish to sell.

In short, the Bank had retracted its long-cherished and almost unconditional support of the gilt-edged market; support was now at the Bank's choosing, rather than quasi-automatic. The Bank's explanation of this change was that:

> ... it will help to limit, further than can be achieved solely by alterations in the Bank's dealing prices, fluctuations in the resources of the banking system arising from official operations in the gilt-edged market ... More generally it is considered appropriate to accompany changes in credit control intended to allow greater freedom of competition in the banking system with lesser intervention by the authorities in the gilt-edged market so as to leave more freedom for prices to be affected by market conditions and for others to operate if they so wish.

In his Sykes Memorial Lecture in November 1971 the Chief Cashier explained further:

> Some time before the reappraisal of monetary policy which led up to 'Competition and Credit Control' had been completed, the conclusion had been reached that the Bank's operations in the gilt-edged market should pay more regard to their quantitative effects on the monetary aggregates and less regard to the behaviour of interest rates.

The Bank's tactics had already become more flexible, but did not go far enough for CCC:

> So long as monetary policy was closely concerned with the total of bank lending, the banking system's operations in the gilt-edged market were not of critical importance for monetary policy. Under the new arrangements the ability of banks – and others – to deal in large quantities at moments of their own choosing at prices not far removed from those ruling in the market at the time would clearly be unacceptable.
> ... this part of the change ... was designed to help the effectiveness of a restrictive monetary policy.

In his Munich speech of 28 May 1971 the Governor too referred to the monetary aggregates: ' ... we have increasingly shifted our emphasis towards the broader monetary aggregates ... the money supply under one or more of its many definitions, for example, or domestic credit expansion'.

But the Bank had only loosened its control over interest rates, not abandoned it; nor had it abandoned its interest in the assets side of the banks' balance sheet; for in the same speech the

Governor went on to say: 'It is not expected that the mechanism of the minimum asset ratio and Special Deposits can be used to achieve some precise multiple contraction or expansion of bank assets. Rather the intention is to use our control over liquidity, which these instruments will reinforce, to influence the structure of interest rates.'

Thus the Bank was hoping to have it both ways: to give more emphasis to the money supply *and* to influence interest rates. It is not, as the Bank was aware, possible to control absolutely both the money supply and the rate of interest. But that was not the Bank's intention: rather it was a matter of 'emphasis' and 'influence'; and it is not inherently contradictory to switch the emphasis between the two as circumstances appear to require. The test would come when it was seen just how far the Bank, or, perhaps more importantly, the Government, would allow interest rates (and gilt-edged prices) to fluctuate with the aim of controlling the monetary aggregates.

Finally, the Bank was not going to abandon its other weapon: 'Notwithstanding the abandonment of quantitative ceilings, and the adoption of the above proposals, the authorities would continue to provide the banks with qualitative guidance as may be appropriate.'[8]

So, there were ambiguities in the new arrangements, reflecting perhaps, uncertainties and disagreements among the authors of the scheme within the Bank and the Treasury. But CCC was without doubt a revolution in post-war British banking practice, a revolution which the banks were quick to exploit.

Bank Rate and MLR

Bank Rate was retained under the new arrangements, but with experience, certain contradictions emerged between the traditional use of Bank Rate and the role of interest rates in the new system. As we have seen, before CCC, monetary policy was orientated towards the management of the gilt-edged market, with the Bank standing ready to buy stock at prices that reflected the authorities' wishes about the rate of interest. Within this system Bank Rate had two main functions: it was a 'penal rate' applied by the Bank of England as lender of last resort; and it was the focal rate of the whole banking system, determining the borrowing and lending rates of the clearing banks. Because Bank Rate stood, rock-like, at the centre of the banking system, it became understood that it was a rate not lightly to be moved; so that if the authorities did move it, it signalled something important in the authorities' view of things and what they wanted to happen. In short, Bank Rate was something more than a technical matter; it was a policy instrument that carried with it an 'announcement effect'.

Under CCC the authorities relinquished, in part, their control over interest rates, which were to be allowed to fluctuate more freely, and did. In theory there was nothing to prevent the authorities from making frequent changes in Bank Rate to keep it in line with market rates; but it was feared that the market, still thinking in the traditional way, would interpret these essentially 'trailing' changes as 'leading' changes, signalling something that was not in fact being signalled. So Bank Rate was *not* moved flexibly with the result that it moved out of line with market rates and ceased, on occasion, to be a penal rate, thereby causing some difficulties with money market management.

The authorities resolved the dilemma in October 1972 by abandoning the practice of posting Bank Rate at midday on a Thursday and replacing it by an ostensibly market-determined 'last resort rate'. 'What is needed' said the Chancellor of the Exchequer, 'is a rate which can respond more flexibly to the changing conditions of the money market and one whose week-to-week movements are not interpreted as signalling major shifts of monetary policy.'[9]

The 'last resort rate' was normally to be set at 0.5 per cent above the average at each Friday's Treasury Bill tender, rounded to the nearest 0.25 per cent above. Since it was above the Treasury Bill rate, it became a penal rate. The authorities retained the right to set the rate independently of this formula on occasions when they wished to give a definite lead to rates. When this happened the announcement would be made at midday on Thursday (changed to 12.30 p.m. in March 1974) and the formula would remain suspended until market rates moved into line. In his Statement announcing the change, the Chancellor did not use the term 'Minimum Lending Rate' but that is what the new rate became known as.

The system certainly worked well in that it induced, or allowed, frequent changes in the rate of interest; and it was acceptable to the authorities so long as the market turned up roughly the rate, or the direction and amount of change in the rate, that the authorities wanted. But from about 1974 there was a growing tendency for it not to do this, despite the fact that the Bank became increasingly explicit in letting the market know what it wanted. One problem was that while the discount market, in its privileged position, was quite prepared to play ball with the Bank, the increasingly large outside tenderers were not, with the result that the rate fell more than the authorities wanted. The situation was somewhat curious: on the one hand MLR was, ostensibly, a market-determined rate and – if you believed in the efficiency of markets – the market rate must be, in some sense, the 'right' rate. If it wasn't, there was something wrong elsewhere. On the other hand, the authorities has always been careful to retain ultimate responsibility for the rate, with the capability to override the market-set rate. So, if the authorities acquiesced in the rate set by the market it could, by default, be said to approve it. If the authorities insisted that their view should prevail they could have suspended the formula, week after week if necessary. But this would have been tantamount to returning to a fully administered rate – a solution which some in the Bank of England would probably have preferred. In the end the Treasury and the Bank decided on a compromise which gave them more control on the downside. On 11 March 1977 the Bank announced that in future in cases where the normal operation of the formula would bring about a reduction in MLR, they reserved the right, exceptionally, either not to change the rate or to change it less than the formula indicated.

A little over a year later, on 25 May 1978, the market formula was abandoned and MLR became a fully administered rate to be announced, normally, at 12.30 p.m. on Thursdays. The Treasury's explanation ran as follows:

> The Chancellor of the Exchequer has approved a proposal by the Bank of England to discontinue the present system for determining the Bank of England's Minimum Lending Rate. This system has generally worked reasonably well but experience – particularly during the last year – has shown that the very close and automatic link with the Treasury Bill discount rate can on occasion lead to undesirable erratic movements in interest rates and to confusion as to the views of the authorities. Since the authorities already in practice bear the main responsibility for the level of MLR, despite the operation of the present formula, the Chancellor has concluded that the proper course would be to recognise this explicitly.

The notice[10] went on to say that MLR would continue to be adjusted flexibly, taking account of market developments; and reminded readers that 'as with administered changes under the present rules, future changes in MLR will require the Chancellor's approval'. So, in a sense, we were back to Bank Rate, expressing 'the views of the authorities'. The difference was that in the mean time the markets had become used to frequent small changes in the official rate so that changes now did not have quite the drama of old.

1972

Our discussion of the evolution of Bank Rate and MLR under the system of Competition and Credit Control has taken us ahead of the main story, to which we now return.

Speaking about CCC in January 1972 the Governor said 'I believe that we have now devised a system which will enable the authorities to exercise appropriate influence over monetary conditions at all times, without stifling competition.' In this he proved to be over-optimistic; but note that he did not talk about 'control of the money supply' only 'influence over monetary conditions', a phrase we were to hear more of later in different circumstances.

The Chancellor of the Exchequer made his views quite clear in his Budget Statement of 21 March 1972:

> Monetary policy will be used in the future, as it has been during the past year, as an integral part of the general management of demand. Because one of the main qualities of monetary policy is its flexibility, I do not propose to lay down numerical targets. The policy will be geared to the needs of the situation, and will change as those needs change.[11]

The 'needs of the situation' demanded 5 per cent growth and it is noteworthy that when Mr Barber made his statement in October abolishing Bank Rate he went out of his way to say that the recent rise in interest was not intended to stand in the way of that. Nor was the exchange rate which, in June, was floated.

1973

'Does the money supply really matter?'

If we are to understand the development of monetary policy we have to look not only at what happened but why it happened. For this the speeches of the Governor and senior officials of the Bank of England are an invaluable source. They may not reveal the state of the Bank's very latest thinking but they do articulate the conclusions that the Bank is sufficiently confident about to make public. Treasury ministers and officials were less forthcoming.

In April 1973 the Deputy Governor spoke to the Lombard Association on the subject 'Does the money supply really matter?'[12] His short answer was 'Yes' but he spent the rest of his speech in qualifying that. There was the intractable question of definition: 'There is no abolute answer to the question "What constitutes the money stock?"'; there was the problem of establishing stable relationships between money – in one or other of its definitions – and other variables such as economic activity and the rate of interest. There was the practical problem of measurement: 'no matter what concept of money we adopt it cannot in practice be measured direct'. There were the difficultis of seasonal adjustment 'as much an art as a science'.

His conclusions on the practical uses of a money supply figure were, unsurprisingly, cautious: 'We have never, of course, suggested that it could or should be our only indicator; but we have regarded it as one, and potentially an important one, among the whole range of financial indicators. . . . Knowledge is never perfect; and in the meantime we have to live from one month, or indeed from one day, to the next . . . '

The difficulties of 'defining, measuring and interpreting the money supply' were substantial and 'while the money supply does really matter, they have to be faced and largely overcome before we can put more than limited weight upon any particular measure of money supply as a practical guide to policy . . . What I am certain about is that there are limits to what – in the real world – can be achieved by monetary policy alone.' The Deputy Governor applied his general agnosticism to specific results: 'I would share in . . . the general feeling that last year's [1972] rise in M3 of 26 per cent was excessive . . . '; but ' . . . we are not able to say with any precision what rise would have been "appropriate" or, in other words, by how much the rise has exceeded that "appropriate" figure.'

The high rate of expansion of the money supply continued into 1973, with growth at an annual rate of 22.5 per cent in the first half of the year, accelerating to over 38 per cent (annual rate) in the third quarter. The Bank no doubt shared the view that this was excessive. Close to 90 per cent of the growth came from bank lending to the private sector, including continued lending to the property and financial sectors. One of the more bizarre features of banking practice inflated the money supply in an unusual way: it was possible for certain borrowers to borrow from the banks on overdraft at rates that allowed them to re-lend the money at a profit, thus inflating both the assets and liabilities of the banking system. This became known as 'interest arbitrage' or, colloquially, as 'the merry-go-round'. The Governor wrote to the banks in September 1973 asking for credit restraint and, specifically, for 'further restraint on lending for property development and financial transactions'. Referring to the merry-go-round, he encouraged 'all banks to be on the watch for, and active in combating, this misuse of their lending facilities'. Minimum Lending Rate was raised 1 points to 13 per cent in November and further calls were made for Special Deposits.

The Supplementary Special Deposit Scheme

In the fourth quarter the money supply (M3) continued to rise at an annual rate of over 30 per cent and the Bank decided to take action to 'improve their control over the money supply and bank lending'. The Government did not want interest rates to go any higher nor to restrict credit to industry because it was 'a period of unusual uncertainty for business, and the financial effects of the three-day working week could lead to a temporary exceptional demand for credit. There is no intention of preventing the banks from accommodating industry's needs of this kind ... '

Since the creation of credit is the major source of the growth in the money supply, this posed something of a problem for the Bank. They solved it by introducing in December 1973 the Supplementary Special Deposit Scheme, which became known as the 'Corset'. What it aimed to do was to control the growth in banks' liabilities, and therefore of the money supply, by imposing an incremental penalty to a three months' moving average of the increase in interest-bearing eligible liabilities above an allowable rate of growth. Specifically, if eligible liabilities grew by 1 per cent or less faster than the allowable rate of growth the penalty would be 5 per cent of the excess; between 1 and 3 per cent excess growth it would be 25 per cent; and thereafter 50 per cent. The purpose was to prevent the banks bidding aggressively for deposits. 'The arrangements', said the Bank, 'should restrain the pace of monetary expansion ... without requiring rises in short-term interest rates and bank lending rate to unacceptable heights.'[13]

It was an ingenious device which seemingly achieved what had hitherto been thought to be impossible, namely to control at one and the same time the money supply, credit creation and the rate of interest. Like many other forms of direct control, it had some initial success and played a part in turning round the monetary excesses of 1972 and 1973, but in the longer term the banks learnt how to anticipate and avoid its effects. Since they were not limited in the amount of deposits they could take (mainly big deposits from the wholesale market) without incurring penalty, these deposits, after a learning process, found a home without passing through the banking system, a process that became known, somewhat inelegantly, as 'disintermediation'. By the end of the 1970s the 'Corset' had turned out to be, as some had suspected it would and as its name implied, no more than a cosmetic device, making the money supply look slimmer by squeezing the bulges out of the monetary numbers. The numbers looked better but the Bank had lost control of part of the money supply because it had passed outside the bits of the banking system controlled by the Bank. The Supplementary Special Deposits Scheme was periodically suspended and re-introduced until its final abolition in June 1980 when the money reappeared in the statistics, much to the embarrassment of the Government of the day.

No further changes of a technical nature were made in the arrangements for monetary control until 1981; but there was a progressive shift in the policy stance.

1974-79

The watershed between demand management and monetarism, if we may, for shorthand, use these omnibus terms, may be dated at 1974. From then on the authorities gave a much higher priority to the monetary aggregate, even though they did not commit themselves publicly to a number for the growth of the money supply until 1976. (It was not, when first announced by Mr Healey, a target, although it quickly assumed the status of one.)

In October 1976 the Governor spoke in favour of monetary targets. He took the 'simple view' that since we lived in inflationary times ' . . . it must be right to aim publicly for a growth in money supply which will accommodate a realistic rate of economic growth but not accommodate, more than in part, the rate of inflation . . . monetary policy becomes a powerful weapon in the fight against inflation. . . . Monetary and fiscal policy – and I would add incomes policy – each have their part to play . . . '[14]

In January 1977 the Governor dealt with monetary policy at length in a speech to the Institute of Bankers in Scotland. We should be 'more precise about our monetary aims'. Monetary targets were the best way to give 'a clear indication of the thrust of monetary policy'. But 'I do not take the view that monetary targets can sensibly be fixed for all time in accordance with a predetermined formula . . . the true objective of policy is not to keep monetary expansion at a particular level; but to bring about a reduction in inflation and a recovery in employment, growth and the balance of payments.'

He returned to monetary policy in his 1977 speech to the Lord Mayor's Dinner. Perseverance with monetary targets would

> require a changed perception of monetary policy. Monetary targets have hitherto tended to be seen as providing essentially flexible support for other tools of economic management. But if monetary targets are to provide, as I believe they should, a continuing and long-term constraint on the inflationary bias which our economy has been shown to possess, it would follow that the availability of monetary instruments for other purposes would, over time, be significantly reduced. This seems to me to be a logical and desirable extension of the course we are now on.

The Governor was given an opportunity to expound his views at length in the Mais Lecture in February 1978, for which he chose as his subject 'Reflections on the conduct of monetary policy'.

> The achievement of a monetary target is not an end of policy in itself. The real objectives of policy include economic growth . . . sufficient investment . . . adequate employment opportunities . . . and price stability.

Targets for one policy instrument might introduce too much rigidity; on the other hand, there was a danger of being overactive in economic management. But

> To eschew demand management entirely would involve tenacious faith in the self-correcting properties of the private sector of the economy, for which the evidence is not strikingly clear.

The Governor anticipated aspects of monetary policy that were to become much more familiar after 1979: to announce a commitment to a target

... is to serve notice on all those concerned with wage
bargaining how far the authorities are prepared to finance
inflation. It will be said that those involved in wage
bargaining pay no heed to the size of the monetary
targets. This may be so – though I would think it better if
it were not. Yet, over time, perseverance with a policy of
the sort I have outlined will, I believe, have an increasingly
pervasive effect. As it becomes clear to all that faster
growth can only be had with less inflation, will there not
be more pressure to see how this can be done?

The essence of monetary management, as I see it, is to
act to offset divergences from forecast in these sources of
monetary expansion ... as soon as it becomes reasonably
clear that inaction is likely to undermine achievement of
the monetary target.

'These sources' include the PSBR; and we have seen how Sir
Geoffrey Howe and Mr Lawson acted to bring this into line to
protect their monetary targets.

The Governor concluded his lecture:

We have not, it is plain, adopted a wholeheartedly
monetarist philosophy. But what we do is likely to give a
monetarist a good deal of the prescription he would
recommend ...

The language throughout, from 1973 to 1978, is cautious,
balanced, undogmatic; but there is a progression from a view of
the money supply as a useful indicator which it may be prudent to
control, to a view of the money supply as a policy weapon capable
of producing powerful results. Early on the question 'Does the
money supply really matter?' had been answered in the
affirmative, but hedged about with practical difficulties; later that
question would no longer be asked; the question by then was not
whether or how much the money supply mattered but how best to
use it, allied to such practical questions as which was the best
measure to use and whether targets should be rolled forward. The
question was no longer whether God existed, but which church to
belong to.

Perhaps the clearest evidence of the authorities' conversion to
pragmatic if not to theoretical monetarism had come in the
autumn of 1977 when the sterling exchange rate was uncapped
and the exchange rate objective overridden by the monetary
objective.

1979–85

With the advent in 1979 of a Conservative Government
committed to the monetarist philosophy, monetary policy became
the focus of economic policy. We might note in passing that it is
an exaggeration to say that 'the Government' was committed to
the monetarist philosophy; for the first Thatcher administration,
drawn from the Shadow Cabinet, contained many who were not
so committed and others whose grasp of the matter was
understandably limited and who did not, therefore, fully appreciate
the implications of what was intended. This, however, need not
have limited their commitment: lack of understanding has rarely
been an impediment to faith and may, indeed, be a necessary
condition for it.

The Medium-Term Financial Strategy

> But if we are to persist with medium-term analysis we
> have I think to recognize explicitly and completely the
> limitations to which it is subject.
> And, as of now, these limitations are considerable; so
> much so indeed that I have serious reservations whether
> the production for the medium-term of single projections
> of the future path of key variables does not do more harm
> than good (Sir Douglas Wass[15])

From the time of the 1980 Budget the Government set its
monetary policy within the framework of the Medium-Term
Financial Strategy (MTFS), the key elements of which were a
target range for the growth of the money supply as measured by
sterling M3, for four years, and 'a projection of the course of the
PSBR based on the assumed growth of GDP and present public
expenditure plans that should be broadly compatible with the
monetary objective'. Limits for the PSBR and the growth of the
money supply had formed the basis of the financial policy of the
previous Government. The difference was that the Strategy was
medium-term but even this distinction became blurred as the
strategy was progressively modified and its component parts
annually revised and rolled forward. The purpose of the Strategy,
according to the Governor of the Bank of England,[16] was 'to
provide some reassurance and guidance to the market about
future developments and to constrain the authorities themselves
from taking short-term soft options'. Mr Healey's purpose in
setting targets and limits had been much the same.

As we have seen, for the first two years the strategy was in disarray, with the Treasury and the Bank unable, between them, to control its two major components. It was modified year by year, the emphasis moving from control of the money supply to influencing monetary conditions. The number of monetary targets was increased while their relative importance decreased as more attention came to be paid to the exchange rate as an indicator of monetary conditions; there was scepticism about the effectiveness of the authorities' instruments for controlling the money supply; and the growth of money GDP was elevated to the status of a target. This was pragmatic rather than doctrinaire monetarism; but while the MTFS had been significantly changed from its original conception its usefulness as a framework for policy and a platform from which to conduct the attack upon inflation was not wholly lost.

The control of the money supply and the PSBR were intermediate, not ultimate, objectives. But had ministers been operating within a broadly Keynesian framework they would have had to declare objectives for output and employment. It would have been politically difficult to announce that, in pursuit of a low or zero rate of inflation, output would have to fall, or rise very slowly, and unemployment rise. Concentration instead on the money supply, the PSBR and money GDP relieve them of this obligation and enabled them to distance themselves from the consequences of bringing down the rate of inflation. Economic expansion was now up to (or down to) the operators and decision-makers in the economy: if they could bring down wages and prices in conformity with 'monetary conditions', then the *real* money supply would expand and of the permitted, later targetted, growth in money GDP more would be in the form of output and less in the form of wages and prices.

The debate on monetary control

The belief, strongly held by some, that it was essential to hold the growth of the money supply within a fairly narrow path over a period of years, in conjunction with the apparent inability of the authorities to do this, led to a search for better methods of monetary control. The British system, at least up to the introduction of Competition and Credit Control in 1971, had been based upon the administrative control of credit, that is, of bank lending (the assets side of the banks' balance sheet) rather than upon the control of the banks' liabilities, which form the greater part of the money supply. Competition and Credit Control, as the name implies, also sought to control credit, but by different means. One unintended result of the system, stemming in part from the Government's reluctance to use interest rates effectively, was to inflate bank liabilities and hence the money supply. Thus in the second half of the 1970s when attention switched to the monetary aggregates, the system was not well placed actually to control them and the debate on methods of control ensued.

In the words of the Governor of the Bank of England, the question was 'where should the operation of a target system lie on a scale running from the strictly mechanical to the totally discretionary;'[17] In the search for new methods of control the debate was between those who favoured modifications to the existing system and those who believed that the only solution lay in something far more radical, namely, 'monetary base control' or MBC, a system which itself had several variants.

Monetary Base Control was supposed, by a control of varying possible degrees of rigidity, statutory or not, of the monetary base of the inverted pyramid of bank lending, to exert close control over the supply of money. The demand for money, independently determined, would then set the price, i.e. the rate of interest. In short, the authorities would lose all control over the rate of interest which, opponents of MBC argued, would then become extremely volatile, to the disadvantage of the economy generally. Moreover, since the exchange rate is sensitive to relative rates of interest, it too would fluctuate widely. It was also feared that lenders and borrowers would attempt to circumvent control of the banks' monetary base by operating outside the banking system ('disintermediation'). While this might eliminate some of the fluctuation in interest rates and the exchange rate, it would mean that the money supply that *was* being measured and controlled would have lost much of its significance. Proponents of MBC conceded that while all this might be so in the short run the system would eventually settle down, with smaller fluctuations.

The Bank of England, while fully accepting the importance of monetary targets, adopts an approach that is sceptical and pragmatic. Monetary targetting rests upon the belief that there is a reasonably stable and predictable relationship between the monetary aggregates and nominal incomes, but 'The hopes of those who looked for a simple, close and reliable relationship, that would hold even in the short term, have not been fulfilled ... I am totally persuaded that it is a mistake to expect too much precision in such relationships, especially in the short-term.'[17]

Because all the aggregates, including the liquidity measures, are subject to 'unforeseen distortion', 'monetary targets have to be operated pragmatically. The course of the monetary target aggregates of itself thus provides only a first approximation to the overall assessment of monetary conditions ... we need to adopt a somewhat pragmatic approach to intermediate monetary objectives recognising that such objectives are, as their name indicates, no more than a means to an end.'

There is a need for the authorities to justify themselves in the face of the healthy scepticism of financial markets but that need cannot 'be met by the adoption of mechanistic rules which are themselves likely to turn out to have been ill-designed and inappropriate'.

Given this general philosophy of the Bank of England (who, it should be remembered, had done a great deal of research into the matter), it was hardly surprising that the arguments in favour of MBC did not prevail and that the new arrangements introduced in August 1981 were designed only to improve existing methods of control while, it was said, leaving the way open for a move to MBC later should that be desired.

The new arrangements

The new arrangements were, in brief, as follows:

1. The 'Corset' was abolished. (This had already been done.)
2. The practice of continuously 'posting' a Minimum Lending Rate (MLR) was discontinued (with provision for it to be reintroduced at need).
3. The Bank would in future aim to keep interest rates at the very short end of the market within an undisclosed band. This it would do by open-market operations rather than by direct lending through 'the discount window'.
4. The requirement on the banks to maintain a minimum reserve asset ratio was abolished.

These arrangements were in essence a half-way house between full control of the money supply and full control over rates of interest. By abandoning MLR, the official discount rate, and relying more an open-market operations in an expanded bill market, the Bank would influence the *supply* of bank liquidity (and hence the banks' ability to lend and the quantity of money), leaving the markets to set the *price* of money, the rate of interest – but only within the limits of an 'undisclosed range'.

Although the new arrangements were said to (and did) represent 'a significant change' in the way the Bank of England operated in the money markets, and although they were a step along the road to control of the supply of money rather than its price, they were a defeat for the more extreme monetarists. The argument of the latter was logically impeccable: *if* the supply of money was absolutely crucial to everything else then it must be controlled, no matter what. The difficulty lay with that 'if'; the British macro-economic establishment was not convinced that pure monetary numbers were all that crucial: what had to be controlled were 'monetary conditions'. It was all very British and pragmatic; or muddling through, as some might prefer.

However, to take the defeat of the logical monetarists either too tragically or too gleefully would be to misunderstand the nature of the debate, which takes place at two levels. There is the debate within the monetarist camp about the degree of strictness in monetary control that is required and the methods for achieving this; and there is the wider debate between the monetarists and what may be loosely called 'the Keynesians'. The fear on the monetarist side is that a Keynesian approach would look for growth in the economy by an expansion of public borrowing and the money supply which would, so it is believed, generate more inflation than growth. On the evidence of history that is still fresh in our minds, that is not an unreasonable fear. What is absolutely clear from all evidence so far is that the Conservative Government will countenance no such approach; in the face of the deepest recession for more than fifty years it stuck to the MTFS and refused to adopt the Keynesian prescription. *That* is more important for policy than the behaviour and control over the short term of any monetary number or clutch of numbers. If, that is, the overriding policy objective is the elimination of inflation rather than the full use of resources and the reduction of unemployment.

Some problems

By the spring of 1985 monetary policy had, as the *Financial Times* put it, 'got into one of its characteristic tangles' and the Bank of England had 'retired hurt'.[19]

The immediate problem had been the authorities' uncertain response to the exchange rate crisis at the beginning of the year when, after initially taking a relaxed attitude to the fall in sterling and to the rate of interest, they resurrected MLR for one day, hoisting the rate 1½ points to 12 per cent, validated a further rise to 14 per cent and then, with obvious reluctance, endorsed a fall to 12.5–12.75 per cent. The rise in rates had clearly been a response to the exchange rate crisis; the authorities then at first resisted a fall in rates because of a concern not for the exchange rate but for the monetary aggregates and the future rate of inflation; and later justified a further fall on the basis of the recovery in sterling. It was not clear whether it was the money supply or the exchange rate which was to be paramount in the determination of interest rates. The authorities' answer was that it was not so much the money supply as *monetary conditions* that they were out to influence and in doing this they would look at the money supply, the exchange rate and bank lending. And, for good measure they would – or at least the Governor would – have regard to the trend in wage costs when considering the future rate of inflation.

This was all sensible stuff, but it bore a closer resemblance to old-fashioned seat-of-the-pants economic management than to monetarism, even British monetarism.

The uncertainties brought to the fore by the exchange rate crisis revived interest in more fundamental questions: if the exchange rate was now so much more important as an indicator of monetary conditions, if unit costs were a better indicator of future inflation than the monetary aggregates, and if some of the monetary aggregates gave misleading signals, was there any longer any justification for focusing policy on these aggregates and, on the basis of them, imposing extremely high real rates of interest? And were interest rates effective, anyway, in controlling bank lending to the private sector? There was evidence that private demand for bank credit was not particularly sensitive to changes in the rate of interest.

There was, too, the familiar problem associated with the broader monetary aggregate, sterling M3, the Government's first-chosen aggregate. When that aggregate approaches its target limit the institutions may pile up interest-bearing deposits in sterling M3 (which includes certificates of deposit) waiting for interest rates to rise. When the institutions hold off in that fashion the growth of sterling M3 is distorted and it tells us nothing about the future rate of inflation – of which the growth in the money supply is supposed to be an indicator – because the pension funds who hold the money have no intention of spending it on goods, services or real assets.

When the institutions hold off buying gilt-edged it is known as a 'funding crisis'. When too many gilts are sold there may occur an 'overfunding crisis', generating its own distortions in the monetary numbers.

Overfunding

It is one of the primary financial objectives of the authorities to sell as much medium- and long-term Government debt as possible to the non-bank public in order to minimize the effect of the PSBR on the money supply. This is known as funding the debt. 'Overfunding' occurs when the net purchases of public sector debt by the UK non-bank private sector exceeds the PSBR. The purpose of overfunding is to mitigate the effect on the monetary aggregates of bank lending in sterling to the private sector, often the largest element in the growth of the money supply. Table 12.2 shows that a significant amount of overfunding occurred in 1981–82 and again in 1983–84.

Table 12.2   Overfunding, and the purchase of commercial bills by the Issue Department of the Bank of England
(£m)

| | PSBR | Net acquis- ition of public sector debt by the UK non-bank private sector | Under- funding (–) Over- funding (+) (Col 2– Col 1) | Issue Department | |
| | | | | Commer- cial bills purchased | 'Other securities' held at end of the first calendar year* |
	1	2	3	4	5
1979–80	10,018	9,193	–825	765	1,465
1980–81	12,682	10,823	–1,859	2,015	2,195
1981–82	8,629	11,332	+2,703	4,240	4,696
1982–83	8,864	8,439	–425	–787	8,058
1983–84	9,731	12,483	+2,752	3,586	7,461

Source: Financial Statistics, No. 275, Mar. 1985, Tables 6.3 and 11.5
          * Mostly commercial bills. Year ending banking December.

The 'bill mountain'

Traditionally any excess of funds arising from overfunding has been applied to the redemption of Government short-term debt, i.e. the Bank of England buys Treasury Bills. The problem in recent years has been that there have not been enough Treasury Bills and the Bank has had to buy commercial bills (for its money market operations, whether or not overfunding was taking place), creating what has become known as 'the bill mountain'. Purchases and holdings of commercial bills by the Issue Department of the Bank of England are shown in Table 12.2. In 1978 a note issue of £9 bn was backed by £8 bn of Government securities and £1 bn of other securities. At the end of 1984 a note issue of £12.6 bn was backed by £1.9 bn of Government securities and £10.7 bn of other securities, mostly commercial bills. Such bills have also become increasingly important in the Bank's money market operations to relieve cash shortages. In the year beginning 1 March 1975 it bought (gross) £9,364 m. of Treasury Bills and £200 m. of commercial bills; in the year beginning 1 March 1981 the figures were, respectively, £3,810 m. and £39,771 m. (illustrating not only the change in the relative importance of the two types of bill but the much larger scale of intervention to relieve cash shortages).

Commercial bills and the money supply

When the Issue Department buys commercial bills it is in effect temporarily taking over some lending to the UK private sector which would otherwise be provided by the banking system, and this is reflected in the statistical treatment of Issue Department purchases which in the table showing the counterparts to changes in the money stock[20] are shown as 'sterling lending to the UK private sector' and hence as part of the domestic counterpart to changes in the money stock, sterling M3.

On the face of it this implies that purchases of bills contribute to the increase in the stock of money. And indeed the Bank explains that the object of such purchases ' ... is solely to relieve the cash shortage which has arisen in the money market as a result of the raising of government finance in another market for the purpose of influencing the rate of growth of the money supply'.[21] It appears, in short, that the Bank of England is with one hand selling gilt-edged stock to the non-bank public to reduce the growth of the money supply below what it would otherwise be, and with the other hand offsetting this by lending to the private sector on bills. Nevertheless, the Bank maintains that bill purchase

> ... do not have any direct statistical impact on the stock of money, as measured by notes and coin with the public and bank deposits (because) when the Bank buys eligible bills from the market, there is a switch from bills to cash in the assets of the banking system, but no change in

deposit liabilities; there is thus only a shift in the statistical
counterparts to the money stock, with the Bank taking
over, from the rest of the banking system, bill claims on
other sectors. Nevertheless, the operations may be
designed to influence the stock of money indirectly,
through their effects on interest rates.[22]

So, now you see it, now you don't: all that has happened is 'a
shift in the statistical counterpart to the stock of money'. But the
statistical counterparts are not unimportant: they tell us
something. And the effect of the bill purchases has been to leave
the assets of the banking system (and hence its deposit liabilities)
higher than they would otherwise have been.

Bill arbitrage and the money supply

While the purchase by the Bank of commercial bills may not
directly affect the monetary aggregates, it is agreed that the weight
of purchases may create opportunities for bill arbitrage that *do*
affect (i.e. increase) these aggregates, thus offsetting to some,
possibly small, extent, the effect of selling gilts to the non-banks.
The argument runs as follows: to secure what it needs of a limited
supply of commercial bills, the Bank of England has to bid up the
price, driving down the rate of interest to an extent where some
borrowers find it profitable to borrow on bills and redeposit the
proceeds in the inter-bank market, adding to the money supply.
The Bank of England believes that this form of arbitrage is not
quantitatively important at present.[23] It is ironic that overfunding,
which requires the purchase of additional commercial bills, should
contribute to this effect when its very purpose, as we have noted
above, is to mitigate the effects on the monetary aggregates of
bank lending to the private sector. It suggests that it may not be
an effective technique for that purpose.

So, for one reason and another, there was, by 1985, a good deal
of scepticism about the usefulness of the monetary numbers and
the ability of the authorities to control them. They had been
downgraded as an indicator of monetary conditions; they were
inferior as an indicator of future inflation; and they were likely to
be distorted by the very methods used to try to control them.
Despite their shortcomings, and despite the fact that they were,
after all, no more than *intermediate* objectives of economic
policy, they were still a prime focus of policy, and watched with
anxiety. Might it not be more sensible to forget about them? As
the *Financial Times* observed (leading article 1 Apr. 1985), ' ... life
would be much simpler if less attention were paid by everyone

concerned to these intermediate and distorted numbers'. Life became simpler sooner perhaps than the *Financial Times* had hoped: in the autumn of 1985 the sterling M3 target was officially abandoned. A new target, however, was promised in the 1986 Budget. So whilst it may be too early to write the obituary for £M3 it may be appropriate at this juncture to look briefly at the life of this unfortunate aggregate and the manner of its withdrawal from active service.

When the Government introduced its Medium-Term Financial Strategy in March 1980[24] sterling M3 was cast to play a central role. To reduce inflation the Government would 'progressively reduce the growth of the money stock and will pursue the policies necessary to achieve this aim'. The Government had a ' . . . firm commitment to a progressive reduction in money supply growth'. To avoid confusion the money supply was to be measured by one aggregate only and that aggregate was sterling M3. Its annual rate of growth was to decline from a range of 7–11 per cent in 1980–81 to 4–8 per cent in 1983–84. When the MTFS was revised in 1981 sterling M3 was again the only measure of the money supply.

£M3 grew at an annual rate of 19.1 per cent in 1980–81 and 12.9 per cent in 1981–82. In 1982 the 1982–83 target range was raised from the 5–9 per cent in that year in the original plan to 8–12 per cent, higher than the 1980–81 range in the 1980 plan and on a base into which all previous growth had been built. Sterling M3 stayed within its target range in 1982–83 and in 1983–84. In 1984–85 the range was 6–10 per cent and growth was 11.9 per cent. Undeterred the Treasury set the 1985–86 target range at 5–9 per cent.

By September 1985 sterling M3 had grown at 14.5 per cent over 12 months, and since April had grown at an annual rate of 18.5 per cent. The authorities conceded defeat. In its *Quarterly Bulletin* of September 1985[25] the Bank of England noted the conflicting signals being given by the money supply figures and by the exchange rate and said

> . . . the Bank continued to take the view expressed in the June *Bulletin* that . . . the rate of broad money growth was understating the degree of monetary tightness. It was decided, therefore, that for the time being above-target growth of sterling M3 should be accommodated, provided that the other indicators of monetary conditions remained consistent with the achievement of the ultimate policy objectives of declining inflation and sustainable activity

> growth. And ... the authorities did not seek to restrain
> sterling M3 to within its target range by further
> overfunding of the PSBR ...

There are a number of interesting aspects to this passage. First,
it says *the Bank* continued to take a view that it had expressed
earlier. No suggestion here that it was a view jointly held by 'the
authorities' i.e. the Bank and the Treasury. And then there is the
neutral statement that 'it was decided' where one might have
expected 'the authorities decided'. It may be objected that to read
into the suggestion that the Bank was very much in the lead in this
matter is to put excessive weight on a verbal construction. Maybe
so; but the Bank, like the Treasury, is meticulous in its choice of
words. Then there is the Bank's formulation of the conditions in
which excessive growth of sterling M3 might be safely
accommodated. it did *not* say 'provided other indicators suggest
that monetary conditions are tight' (the intermediate objective) but
expressed itself in terms of the 'ultimate policy objectives'. This
formulation confers much greater freedom upon the executors of
policy: a competent polemicist can argue that almost anything is
consistent with the ultimate policy objectives.

The Bank's pronouncement was given the approval of the
Chancellor of the Exchequer at the Mansion House on 17
October. In a lengthy exposition of monetary policy he said that
over the past five financial years sterling M3 had grown by 82 per
cent while GDP had grown by only 54 per cent:

> It has become increasingly evident that both individuals
> and companies wish to hold an increased proportion of
> savings in liquid form. In retrospect it is now clear that we
> have persistently underestimated the strength of this
> demand. We can maintain, and are maintaining, progress
> towards our inflation objectives while sterling M3 is
> growing at a rate well above the top of the range set in
> this year's Budget Statement. To try to bring it back
> within the range – which, with the benefit of hindsight,
> was clearly set too low – would imply a tightening of
> policy which the evidence of other indicators of financial
> conditions tells us is not warranted.

The abandonment of the sterling M3 target had implications for
funding policy, and the Chancellor confirmed the end of the
practice of overfunding: '... short-term considerations came to
make overfundiung almost a way of life. And that cannot make
sense ... Accordingly, we are no longer seeking to control the

recorded growth of sterling M3 by systematic overfunding ... The objective of funding policy is to fund the PSBR over the year as a whole: no more, no less.' Any tightening of monetary conditions would be achieved by a rise in short-term interest rates.

It is often good generalship to abandon an offensive that cannot be won; and even better generalship to argue that this was necessary not because of any fault in the battle plan but because the enemy was too strong. But in the matter of sterling M3 we should not lose sight of the original battle plan and of the absolutely central role to be played by the control of the money supply as measured by sterling M3. The first presentation of the Medium-Term Financial Strategy conceded that *some* policy changes might be necessary but concluded with these words: 'But there would be no question of departing from the money supply policy, which is essential to the success of any anti-inflationary policy.'

'Monetarism is dead – official', said the *Financial Times* in the heading to its leading article on the day after the Chancellor's Mansion House speech. That may be an overstatement; but what remains is far from the early vision. What seemed to remain by the autumn of 1985 was a system of looking at the exchange rate and a large number of monetary aggregates and then setting interest rates to be consistent with ultimate policy objectives. There are numbers of non-monetarists who would find little to quarrel with there; although a lot does depend on who is doing the looking and what the ultimate objectives are.

Summary

To summarize, we may identify the following phases in the development of monetary policy. First, a period up to the end of the 1960s when 'monetary policy' meant 'interest rate policy' and when nobody paid much attention to the monetary aggregates. Attention shifted to a new concept, Domestic Credit Expansion, but this became of diminishing interest as the balance of payments moved into surplus. Control of credit by traditional means became increasingly difficult.

In the first half of the 1970s a new system of monetary management, Competition and Credit Control, led to a huge expansion of both credit and the money supply. The balance of payments moved into deficit, and the rate of inflation accelerated. Policy was still being conducted within a Keynesian framework with wage and price controls as the primary instrument for controlling inflation.

From the mid-1970s, however, the authorities pursued internal objectives for the monetary aggregates. The markets, moving ahead of the authorities, became increasingly concerned with the money supply figures so that the Government was obliged to apply to itself the constraint of a published money supply target. This might be categorized as a period of 'monetary-constrained Keynesianism'.

At the opening of the 1980s the broader monetary aggregate, sterling M3, became the major focus of policy, with its path plotted for several years ahead. New methods of control were introduced, but these fell short of attempting to control the monetary base of the banking system. The authorities allowed the market more influence on interest rates but retained ultimate control.

By the mid-1980s the number of monetary aggregates targetted had been increased and, while target ranges for these continued to be published, the authorities' (intermediate) objective had come to be to influence 'monetary conditions', in judging which the exchange rate assumed greater importance and the monetary aggregates, especially those for broad money, correspondingly less. Criticism focused upon the relevance of the monetary numbers to the real world, partly because some of the authorities' methods of control were capable of distorting the aggregates they were designed to control. Towards the close of 1985 the attempt to control one of the major aggregates was abandoned together with the technique of overfunding. The focus of control appeared to be lengthening from intermediate to ultimate objectives.

The evolution of monetary policy

Pre-1970

1957 May Radcliffe Committee appointed.

1958 Jul. All direct controls on bank lending lifted for first time since the Second World War. Authorities reserve the right to raise liquidity requirements by a new 'Special Deposits' scheme.

1959 Aug. *Radcliffe Report.*

1960 Apr. First use of Special Deposits.

1960 Dec. Bank of England begins publication of *Quarterly Bulletin.*

1962 May First issue of *Financial Statistics* by CSO.

1963   Bank of England publish first statistics of money stock.

Oct.   Liquidity ratio lowered from 30 to 28 per cent.

1964 Dec. Banks asked to curb the growth of credit and given guidance on the direction of lending.

1965 Apr. One per cent Special Deposits called for.

May   Advances limited to 105 per cent of their March level.

1968 Oct. Treasury/IMF Monetary Seminar.

Dec.   First issue of sterling certificates of deposit.

     Bank modifies gilt-edged tactics to allow weakness to be reflected in prices; interest rates rise.

1969 May 'Money supply and domestic credit' published in *Economic Trends*, No. 187.

Jun.   Mr Jenkins releases Letter of Intent to IMF (dated 22 May) containing reference to Domestic Credit Expansion.

Oct.   Conference to commemorate the tenth anniversary of the *Radcliffe Report*.

1970

Apr.   Resumption, in Washington, of Treasury/IMF Monetary Seminar.
Bank guidance – lending not to exceed 5 per cent to March 1971.

Jun.   Article 'The importance of money' by C.A.E. Goodhart in the *BEQB*.

Jul.   Bank repeats lending guidance to banks (see Apr.).

Aug.   In *Economic Trends* No. 202, an article 'A note on definitions of the money supply' introduces M1 and M2. A similar article 'The stock of money' appeared in *BEQB*, Sept.

Oct.   Call for Special Deposits raised from 2.5 to 3.5 per cent for London clearing banks. Banks urged to restrain their lending further.

Dec.   Sir Leslie O'Brien's Jane Hodge Memorial lecture 'Monetary management in the United Kingdom' (*BEQB*, Mar. 1971).

1971

30 Mar. Budget. Chancellor announces intention to explore new techniques of monetary control.

14 May Bank published consultative document *Competition and Credit Control* (CCC); and changes its tactics in the gilt-edged market.

28   Governor's speech in Munich on 'Key issues in monetary and credit policy' (*BEQB*, Jun.).

21 Jul.	Bank publishes *Competition and Credit Control; the discount market*
10 Sept.	Bank announces that CCC to come into effect on 16 Sept. All earlier lending notices lapse after 15 Sept.
16	CCC arrangements come into effect. Bank gives details in *Reserve Ratios and Special Deposits*.
10 Nov.	Chief Cashier of the Bank gives Sykes Memorial Lecturer on CCC. (Extract in *BEQB* Dec.)
Dec.	Bank publishes *Reserve Ratios: further definitions, BEQB*, Dec.

1972

Jan.	Governor's speech in CCC to Finance Houses Association (*BEQB*, Mar.).
Mar.	'The demand for money in the United Kingdom: a further investigation', *BEQB* Mar.
23 Jun.	Pound floated.
7 Aug.	Governor's letter asks banks to make credit less readily available to property companies and for financial transactions.
9 Oct.	Bank Rate to become Minimum Lending Rate from 13 Oct.

1973

Mar.	'Competition and Credit Control: further developments', *BEQB*, Mar.
11 Apr.	'Does the money supply really matter?' Speech by Mr Hollom, Deputy Governor of the Bank of England. (*BEQB*, Jun.).
1 Jul.	Mr Gordon Richardson replaces Sir Leslie O'Brien as Governor of the Bank of England.
19	Bank of England releases Discount Market from agreement, under CCC, to hold 50 per cent of borrowed funds in public sector debt.
11 Sept.	Governor's letter to banks requesting restriction of credit to persons and for property and financial transactions.
Nov.	Collapse of London and County Securities.
17 Dec.	Introduction of Supplementary Special Deposit Scheme (the 'Corset').
19	Beginning of secondary banking crisis.
21	The 'Lifeboat' launched. First meeting on 28 Dec.

1974

Aug.	Secondary banking crisis: criteria for 'Lifeboat' help tightened and limit set to total.

1975

28 Feb.	'Corset' suspended.
Dec.	Qualitatative guidance to banks on lending priorities renewed.

1976

6 Apr.	Budget. Growth of money supply to continue to be contained and consistent with growth of demand.
22 Jul.	First money supply figure: 'expected to grow 12 per cent in 1976-77'. Not a target.
Sept.	Governor discusses monetary targets. *BEQB*, Sept.
10	MLR raised by 1½ points to 13 per cent.
7 Oct.	MLR formula suspended for one day only. MLR up 2 points to 15 per cent.
20	Seventh report from the Select Committee on Nationalized Industries Session 1975-76, No. 672, 'The Bank of England'.
15 Dec.	Revised definitions of DCE. Sterling M3 introduced. Letter of Intent sets target limits for DCE and an expected rate of growth (not a target) for the money supply.

1977

Mar.	'DCE and money supply', *BEQB*, Mar.
11 Mar.	MLR arrangements modified to allow Banks to override formula where this would bring about a reduction in the rate. (See *BEQB*, Jun. 1977, Additional notes to Table 9.)
12 May	'Corset' extended for six months.
Jun.	'Financial forecasts in the United Kingdom', *BEQB* Jun.
27 Jul.	Change of intervention policy.
11 Aug.	'Corset' suspended.
31 Oct.	Sterling uncapped.

1978

Feb.	Mais lecture by Governor 'Reflections on the conduct of monetary policy'. (*BEQB*, Mar.).
11 Apr.	Rolling targets for money supply introduced.
25 May	MLR to be set by administrative action, instead of by formula.
8 Jun.	'Corset' reactivated.
17 Aug.	'Corset' to be continued for a further eight months.
9 Nov.	8-12 per cent monetary target for year from mid-October.

Dec.   'External and foreign currency flows and the money
            supply', *BEQB*, Dec.

1979
6 Apr.   Change of intervention tactics to stem currency inflow.
Jun.   'The gilt-edged market'; 'Monetary base control',
            BEQB, Jun.
23 Oct.   Remaining exchange controls lifted.
15 Nov.   MLR up 3 points to 17 per cent. 'Corset' extended.
            Target for sterling M3 7–11 per cent.

1980
21 Mar.   Green Paper on *Monetary Control* (Cmnd 7858).
26   Budget. MTFS launched.
18 Jun.   'Corset' abolished.
Aug.   Bank changes methods of intervention to allow market
            more influence on interest rates.
9 Sept.   Treasury 'Statement on Monetary Developments.'
24 Nov.   Changes in monetary management.
            Bank background note 'Methods of Monetary Control'
            (*BEQB*, Dec.).

1981
5 Mar.   Third Report of Treasury and Civil Service Committes,
            Monetary Policy, House of Commons Paper, 163-1.
            (Highly critical.)
10   Budget. MTFS updated.
12   Bank publishes *Monetary Control: next steps*, *BEQB*,
            Mar.
12 May   Sir G. Howe, Mais Lecture, on inflation.
5 Aug.   Bank paper *Monetary Control: provisions* (*BEQB*,
            Sept.).
20   New arrangements for monetary control into force.
            MLR no longer to be continuously posted.
18 Nov.   'Monetary sector' to replace the more narrowly defined
            'banking sector'.

1982
9 Mar.   Budget. MTFS updated.
25 Jun.   New arrangements governing borrowing by the
            corporate and public sectors (*BEQB*, Sept.).
            Bank introduces new monetary aggregate, M2.
Dec.   'Composition of monetary and liquidity aggregates and
            associated statistics', *BEQB*, Dec.

1983

15 Mar.	Budget. MTFS updated.
Jun.	End of DCE (no longer calculated).
9	Mr Lawson becomes Chancellor of the Exchequer.
Jun.	'Setting monetary objectives', *BEQB*, Jun. (paper given in May 1982).
1 Jul.	Mr Robin Leigh-Pemberton becomes Governor of the Bank of England.
19	Bank modifies monetary control arrangements with affect from 18 Aug.

1984

10 Feb.	Changes announced to definition of PSBR and sterling M3.
13 Mar.	Budget. MTFS updated. Targets for M0 and sterling M3.
Jun.–Jul.	Bank of England cannot resist market-determined rise in banks' base rate.
26 Oct.	'Some aspects of UK monetary policy', lecture by Governor at University of Kent. (*BEQB*, Dec.).
7 Nov.	Bank discussion paper *The Future Structure of the Gilt-Edged Market*.

1985

11 Jan.	Base rates raised 1 point to 10.5 per cent.
14	MLR re-introduced for one day, at 12 per cent.
28	Base rates raised 2 points to 14 per cent.
19 Mar.	Budget.
20	Base rates lowered ½ point to 13.5 per cent; Bank validates but indicates it wants no further fall.
28	National Westminster and Lloyds Banks cut base lending rate by ½ point; Barclays and Midland fail to follow, but Bank reluctantly endorses the fall.
29	Bank of England concludes £150 m. indemnity agreement for Johnson Matthey Bankers.
12 Apr.	Barclays and Midland Banks cut base lending rate from 13.25 to 12.75 per cent. Bank of England does not endorse and forces discount houses to borrow from it at a penal 13.25 per cent.
	Bank of England publishes *The Future Structure of the Gilt-Edged Market*.
19	National Westminster and Lloyds Banks cut base rates by ½ point to 12. 5 per cent. Bank endorses but indicates it wants no further fall.

12 Jun.	Barclays and Midland Banks cut base rates by 0.25 per cent to 12.5 per cent, bringing them into line with National Westminster and Lloyds.
20	Statement by Chancellor of the Exchequer on Banking Supervision and Johnson Matthey Bankers, presenting the recommendations of the Review Committee. White Paper to be published and Banking Bill to be introduced. Bank of England's Annual Report includes the Bank's account of the rescue of JMB.
9 Jul.	Sterling M3 rises by 2 per cent in 5 weeks to mid-June, 12 per cent up on June 1984.
11	Bank of England cuts its dealing rates by 0.25 per cent and then by a further 0.25 per cent.
12	Clearing banks fail to lower base rates in response to Bank's signal of yesterday.
15	Clearing banks cut base rates ½ point to 12 per cent.
17	Bank of England discourages expectations of a further fall in interest rates.
26	Bank of England cuts dealing rates by ½ point but again acts to discourage expectations of further falls.
29	Clearing banks cut base rates by ½ point to 11.5 per cent.
15 Aug.	Building Societies reduce mortgage rate 1¼ points to 12.75 per cent. Bank of England continues to resist pressure for lower interest rates.
10 Sept.	Sterling M3 rises 2 per cent in banking August to give annualized increase of 16.75 per cent over 6 months.
25	Announced that Mr George Blunden to be new deputy governor of the Bank of England. Also announced, new high level Committee on supervisory policy.
8 Oct.	In banking September sterling M3 again rises excessively to give growth of 14.5 per cent over 12 months and an annual rate of 18.5 per cent since April. M0 rises 4.25 per cent over 12 months, within target range.
17	In his Mansion House speech Chancellor of the Exchequer makes major statement on monetary policy. Sterling M3 no longer to be controlled by overfunding.

Notes and references

1. *Committee on the Working of the Monetary System, Report*, Cmnd 827. Known as the *Radcliffe Report*, after its chairman. Published August 1959.

2. *BEQB*, Vol. 9, No. 3, Sept. 1969.
3. Published in *Economica*, May 1966.
4. 'Monetary analysis of income formation and payments problems', *Staff Papers*, VI, 1, 1957–58.
5. Statistically, any deficit on the current account of the balance of payments represents credit from abroad in one form or another.
6. For details see *Treasury Press Notice* 161/76, 15 Dec. 1976.
7. *BEQB*, Dec. 1981, Jun. 1983, p. 172.
8. *BEQB*, June 1971, Vol. 2, No. 2, p. 192.
9. *Treasury Press Notice*, 9 Oct. 1972.
10. *Treasury Press Notice* 89/78, 25 May 1978.
11. *Official Report*, Vol. 833, No. 84, Col. 1347.
12. *BEQB*, Jun. 1973, Vol. 13, No. 2.
13. *BEQB*, Mar. 1974, Vol. 14, No. I, pp. 37–8.
14. Speech at the Lord Mayor's Dinner 21 October 1976.
15. Speech to the Society for Long Range Planning, 12 November 1979.
16. 'Some aspects of UK monetary policy', *BEQB*, Dec. 1984. That Governor was, of course, appointed well after the introduction of the MTFS. The Governor in post at that time had not, it appears, been enthusiastic about the MTFS. According to the *Financial Times*, 6 May 1982, 'The Bank opposed the Treasury's decision in 1980, under its Medium-Term Financial Strategy, to set fixed monetary targets for more than one year ahead. There was considerable rejoicing in Threadneedle Street when this part of the strategy was made more "pragmatic" ... The Bank informed the public of its distaste for the Medium-Term Financial Strategy through the masterly device of never mentioning the words in its Bulletins.' The article adds that in 1981 the Bank ' ... fought off the attempt of Mrs Thatcher's economic adviser, Professor Alan Walters, to move to a full-scale monetary base system for controlling the money supply'.
17. op. cit., *BEQB*, Dec. 1984.
18. The monetarists' fear of government borrowing may be briefly expressed as follows: If people have money they will spend it. An increase in the money supply, from whatever cause, creates potential spending power. Government borrowing creates money without creating a corresponding supply of purchasable goods. It therefore leads to inflation or to increased imports or both. (Alternatively, if government borrowing is met by private savings, it takes those savings

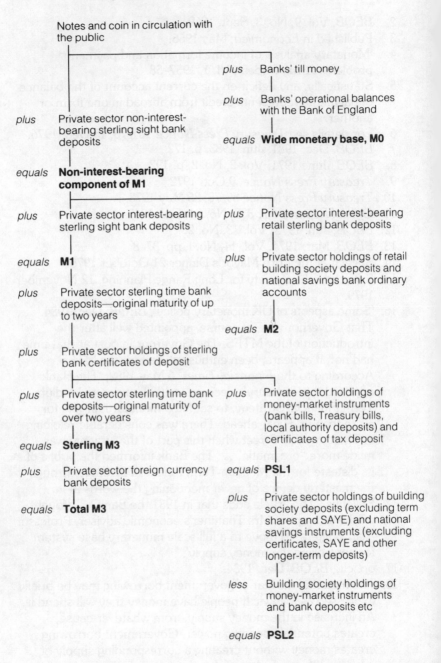

Fig. 12.1   Relationships among the monetary and liquidity aggregates and their components

away form productive use in the private sector, i.e. from where they would be used to produce tradeable goods.) The only legitimate (non-inflationary) increase in the money supply is that which stems from the creation of marketable goods, for then there are the goods to match the money.

19. Leading article 18 Apr. 1985.
20. For example, *Financial Statistics*, No. 275, Mar. 1985, Table 11.5. A different treatment, however, is used in some other tables.
21. *BEQB*, Vol. 22, No. 2, Jun. 1982, p. 201.
22. *BEQB*, Vol. 22, No. 1, Mar. 1982, p. 94.
23. See 'A note on money market arbitrage' in *BEQB*, Vol. 22, No. 2, Jun. 1982.
24. In the Budget Statement and *Financial Statement and Budget Report*.
25. *BEQB*, Vol. 25, No. 3, p. 362.

Figure 12.1 shows the relationships among the monetary and liquidity aggregates.

13

The secondary banking crisis

When you're weary, feeling small,
When tears are in your eyes, I will dry them all;
I'm on your side. When times get rough
And friends just can't be found,
Like a bridge over troubled water
I will lay me down.

Paul Simon

Background

The secondary banking crisis of 1973–75 had its origins in many
things, one of them being, possibly, the Moneylenders Act of 1900.

The period from the late 1950s to the early 1970s was one in
which the London money market and the banking system
developed in a number of ways. London became the centre for
trading in the new Eurodollar (later Eurocurrency) market; partly
because of this, many foreign banks sought to set up shop in
London and were welcomed by a Bank of England anxious to re-
establish London as a major financial centre and sterling as a
major trading currency. It was in large measure the Bank of
England's desire to preserve the reputation of London as a
financial centre and home for the surpluses of the oil producers
that inspired it to act as it did when the crisis came.

More important, perhaps, for subsequent domestic
developments was the growth of what were first known as
'parallel' money markets and later as the 'wholesale' money
market. This was a market which, as the name implies, brought

together lenders and borrowers of large sums of money. On the lending side might be company treasurers with surplus cash for which they needed to find a profitable resting place; and on the borrowing side local authority and company treasurers requiring short-term money. Borrowing and lending in this market were conducted, at least at first, without the intermediation of the traditional high-street banks (the 'clearers') who dealt mainly in 'retail' money – small deposits from many, relatively small advances to a few. Until the introduction of Competition and Credit Control (CCC) in 1971 the clearing banks were not well placed to compete in the wholesale money market, partly, perhaps, because they were more conservative than the newcomers, but mainly because they were constrained by their own interest-rate cartel and by long-established conventions which governed their 'liquidity ratio' (28 per cent of assets had to be held in cash, call money, Treasury Bills and other liquid assets). They were more closely controlled by the central bank, the Bank of England; and by the same token were 'safer' because the Bank of England stood behind them as lender of last resort. In theory no such long stop stood behind the secondary banks, who began to acquire an increasing share of total deposits. When lending restrictions on the clearing banks were lifted in 1971 these banks became 'increasingly prepared to on-lend surplus resources through the medium of the money markets.'[1]

The new banking entrepreneurs by no means confined their activities to the market in wholesale money. There were other opportunities. People were earning good money, were able to save and were looking for something more exciting than National Savings Certificates in which to invest. Investment and unit trusts offered an alternative, provided good returns to the managers of such trusts and generated considerable cash flow for disposal. At the other end of the spectrum from the savers were those who wanted to live now and pay later and who made good business for the hire-purchase finance companies and the second-mortgage dealers. Closer to the Stock Exchange there was money to be made in takeovers and share dealing.

Above all as a money-maker, as time went on, was property. It seemed that God or some Providence had ordained that property values would go on rising for ever. As Galbraith has noted ' ... at some point in the growth of a boom all aspects of property ownership become irrelevant except the prospect for an early rise in price. Income from the property, or enjoyment of its use, or even its long-run worth are now academic.'[2] Certainly values were never expected to fall. Property was the perfect hedge against inflation, especially if you could borrow money at negative real rates of interest (and charge the nominal interest against tax).

The Companies Act 1967

The fringe banking system was growing fast, far outstripping the supervisory capability of the Bank of England and the Board of Trade. Nevertheless, the Bank of England contended that it had the situation under control until 1967 when it was still able to supervise those institutions that were, under existing legislation, classified as banks of one sort or another. All might have been well 'had the statutory position then existing remained unchanged. But', the Bank says, rather plaintively, 'the statutory position did not remain unchanged.' (Bank paper) The Moneylenders Act 1900 exempted from its provisions 'any person bona fide carrying on the business of banking'. Every time the issue was challenged the courts had to decide anew whether a company was carrying on a bona fide banking business. To settle the matter it was decided that the Board of Trade should be given powers to separate the banking sheep from the non-banking goats. Powers conferred by Section 123 of the Companies Act 1967 enabled the Board of Trade to issue 'certificates to companies satisfying them that they could properly be treated for the purposes of the Moneylenders Acts 1900 to 1927 as bona fide carrying on the business of banking'.

Following this 'A large number of companies which were not of sufficient size or quality to warrant the more advanced banking recognitions' (to use the Bank's phrase) obtained certificates. 'The possession of the certificate', said the Bank, 'was proof that the company concerned was not subject to the Moneylenders Act, but in more general and unanticipated ways it allowed the impression to be created that the companies concerned were recognised by the responsible government department as carrying on a banking business, without drawing attention to the fact that they were only so recognised for one narrow purpose.' (Bank paper) With hindsight, at least, it is fair to say that it was perhaps naive of the bureaucracy to suppose that an entrepreneur given a certificate that he was carrying on a banking business would not thereupon feel free to call his business a bank.

Supervision

The Companies Act of 1967 allowed the Board of Trade to call for certain accounts, but it did not provide for any comprehensive system of supervision of Section 123 (or Section 127) companies either by the Department, the Bank of England or anyone else. It is evident that inadequate supervision of a rapidly expanding banking system was a major factor in the banking crisis. A discussion of the Bank of England's supervisiory system and powers at that time would take us beyond our immediate purpose, but those who are interested will find a lengthy description in the Bank's *Quarterly Bulletin* of June 1975.[3]

The officer responsible for banking supervision was the Principal of the Discount Office. Mr Blunden – the author of the article referred to – says, 'The Principal's room has always seen a constant flow of visitors anxious to talk as freely and frankly as they would in the confession box or to a marriage guidance counsellor.' Perhaps, in a way, that sums the matter up: the Bank was still operating in a milieu in which banking was a business for gentlemen. Alas, the London banking scene at that time, and since, included players as well as gentlemen, professionals who played by the rules. And the rules were few and obscure, largely because the Bank did not believe in rules.

The Bank of England looked back wistfully to the time when banking was conducted by gentlemen: 'The Bank and the banking community had naturally always required individual members to adhere to certain well-understood standards of conduct; and new entrants to that community had only been accepted where these standards were met . . . .' Supervision relied not only on an analysis of the accounts and the character and quality of the business, but ' . . . on the Bank continuing to inform themselves about the reputation and quality of the management'. (Bank paper) The Bank, it seems, looked upon the nouveau bankers rather as Lord Reith might have regarded Independent Television and cable television; or, possibly, even BBC Television. Since the banking crisis there has been further evidence that the City is not populated exclusively by gentlemen, to the surprise of no one but the supervising authorities.

The fringe banks had, as we have noted, taken credit business away from the traditional banks. One consequence of this was that the system of credit control operated by the Bank of England (as agent for the Government) through its leverage on the banks it supervised, was eroded. One way to rectify this situation might have been to bring the fringe under Bank supervision. An objection to this was that to bring the fringe outfits under banking supervision would *ipso facto* confer upon them the status of banks recognized by the Bank of England, an outcome that the Bank did not welcome: ' ... for their part the Bank believed that it would be improper and misleading to accord such institutions the status of banks.' (Bank paper) An alternative solution, and the one eventually adopted, was to ' ... remove the constraints whose prolonged application to the banks and the deposit-taking members of the Finance Houses Association (FHA) had enabled the fringe to develop as it had. The expectation was that, perhaps not immediately but in a short while, the fringe would contract to a level of comparative unimportance.' (Bank paper)

Competition and Credit Control

It was these concepts, and this motivation which, in part, moved the Bank, with the Government's approval, to bring forward the ideas embodied in *Competition and Credit Control* (CCC). It is easy to see why, in the climate of the times (the early days of the Heath Administration) the authorities preferred the path of freer and wider competition over that of extended regulation. But in so far as this was expected to lead to the withering away of the fringe banks, the logic of the matter appears suspect, at least with hindsight. If the charge against the fringe banks was that they were indulging in unsound business, business of 'low quality' and high risk, were we supposed to believe that the 'proper' banks would now take over this business? It is true that high risks can be more comfortably borne when there are adequate resources to cover them and that, therefore, the clearing banks, with their much bigger resources, were better placed than the fringe to carry some high-risk business. But it is reasonable to suppose that there would be a significant amount of risky, low-quality business which the clearers would not care to undertake. If that was the case, the fringe would not only not wither away but would, if anything, become more vulnerable, being left with much of the low-quality business.

The new monetary arrangements of CCC which came into effect in September 1971 encouraged banks, hitherto constrained in their borrowing by tradition and in their lending by the Bank of England, to be more aggressive; to match their borrowing to their desired lending rather than the other way round. To get them off to a good start, the lower liquidity ratio of CCC effectively conferred upon them some £700 m. of new lending capacity. In the two and a quarter years following the introduction of CCC, banks' deposits doubled and their advances to customers increased by nearly 150 per cent. It had been hoped that the easier lending regime of CCC would stimulate industrial investment. But although the water was there, the industrial horse was reluctant to drink, for, as the Bank of England put it 'The rates of return foreseen in a still rather stagnant economy did not seem very attractive. This provided a marked contrast with another sector of economic activity, namely properly development.' (Bank paper) Within three years advances of all banks to property companies had grown sixfold and those of 'other banks' alone eightfold. At one point loans to 'finance and property' exceeded advances to the whole of manufacturing industry. Since industrial demand for funds was slow to pick up, the banks had to find another home for their surplus funds. 'They were therefore increasingly prepared to on-lend surplus resources through the medium of the money markets.' And, 'The bulk of the fringe's deposit requirements was met from the money markets, which by the early 1970s included as lenders not only banks, but also industrial and commercial companies and major institutional investors.' (Bank paper)

What part did CCC play in the secondary banking crisis? On one view it had only an incidental role, having about the same effect on fringe banking as feeding cream cakes might have on a case of terminal gluttony – not helpful, but not the cause of death. On another view CCC played a much more important role. For one thing, if the CCC solution had not been applied to 'the fringe problem', then some other solution would have had to be – and it might have been more effective. What really frightened the Bank of England was the involvement of major banks with secondary banks and with the property market; and the fear that any collapse would in the end involve one or more of the big names. And the clearing banks would not have become so involved but for CCC. According to this argument CCC had two effects: on the one hand it enlarged the scale of the crisis by, as it were, paying out long lengths of credit for the fringe operators to hang themselves with; and on the other hand it created a situation in which the collapse, when it threatened, could not, in the eyes of the Bank, be allowed to happen. In short, without CCC there would still have been a secondary banking crisis, but as a purely secondary banking collapse it could conceivably have been allowed to proceed, to muted murmurs of 'good riddance' from the more cautious, and gentlemanly, bankers. The fringe banks, as the Bank of England had envisaged, would indeed have contracted, albeit rather suddenly and messily, 'to a level of comparative unimportance'. Competition and Credit Control may have been ill-thought-through but it was neither a necessary nor a sufficient cause of the secondary banking crisis; what it did was to accelerate the pace, widen the involvement and turn a secondary banking crisis into a banking crisis proper.

To summarize, we may identify the causes of the banking crisis as follows:

1. The rapid expansion of the banking and financial institutions of the City of London.
2. In particular, the provisions of the Companies Act 1967.
3. The failure of the authorities, and specifically the Bank of England, to adapt their supervisory functions to the new conditions.
4. The introduction of Competition and Credit Control.

We now turn to the crisis itself.

The crisis

Speaking to the Institute of Bankers in Scotland in January 1973, the Governor of the Bank of England said, 'I see little to complain of in the more competitive banking world which we have succeeded in fostering. The situation is in some ways less tidy than it was, but that is to be expected when competition is freer. I am sure the banking system is healthier and doing its job better than it did under the old conditions.'[4]

As we have seen, the first part of 1973 was characterized by a succession of international currency crises. At home, a package of public expenditure cuts was introduced in May. The money supply was growing fast and the exchange rate began to weaken. In June, Minimum Lending Rate (MLR) stood at 7.5 per cent, 2 points below the rate of inflation (giving, on rule-of-thumb calculation, a negative interest rate of 2 per cent). It was raised to 9 per cent on 22 June and to 11.5 per cent on 27 July. This rise of over 50 per cent in a little over a month came as a shock to the financial and property markets, whose business relied largely on the beliefs that property values could not fall and interest rates would not rise.

As late as October the Governor of the Bank of England saw no danger. Speaking at the Lord Mayor's dinner, he said, 'Yet I do not suppose that anyone would deny that our banking system – and I speak especially of the big clearing banks – today shows an altogether new vigour and enterprise.'[5]

On 13 November MLR went to 13 per cent. At the end of that month London and Country Securities, a Section 123 bank, ran into liquidity difficulties; and on 17 December the Government introduced a package of economic measures that included a new scheme of Supplementary Special Deposits, designed to restrict the growth of banks' deposits. The secondary banking crisis broke two days later with the threatened collapse of Cedar Holdings, another Section 123 company.

The Governor of the Bank of England called a meeting of the parties involved, some 40 banks and institutions, and kept them in the Bank until a rescue plan was agreed in the early hours of 20 December. The institutions involved provided £50 m., Barclays Bank £22 m. and the Bank of England threw in £2 m. towards any ultimate losses incurred. Later that day Cedar's share quotation was suspended and the rescue package made known.

The 'Lifeboat'

> Throw out the life-line,
> Throw out the life-line,
> Someone is sinking today.
>
> Revivalist hymn

The Governor's prompt and firm action stopped the first domino from falling; but the revelation that such a big finance house was in difficulties shocked the City. Many knew that Cedar was not the only vulnerable bank. The Governor and the Bank took the view that *ad hoc* rescues were unlikely to be enough and that some more permanent arrangements were needed. On the afternoon of Friday 21 December the Governor called a secret meeting of the chairmen of the Big Four clearing banks, and a continuing joint support fund was set in place, the Bank taking a 10 per cent share. Later that day the Bank announced the new support arrangements, without giving details or any indication of the extent of support envisaged. The body that became known as the 'Lifeboat' was launched. Officially it became the 'Control Committee of the Bank of England and the English and Scottish Clearing Banks'. It comprised senior representatives of each under the chairmanship of the Deputy Governor of the Bank.

The market was calmed but the troubles of the secondary banks continued. The Bank of England identified three stages of development of the crisis. In the first phase, up to March 1974, the problem was seen primarily as one of recycling deposits. Twenty-one companies were helped, of which sixteen were Section 123 companies, and some £400 m. was advanced.

Stage two ran from March to December 1974: ' ... it became increasingly clear that the problem had become more complicated than a simple recycling of deposits. Confidence in fringe deposit-taking institutions showed little sign of returning and the collapse of property values was now fully apparent ... in some cases ... what had begun as a liquidity problem had become a solvency problem, making liquidation inevitable.' (Bank paper) The Bank felt that it had to rescue some of the depositors and *this cost was borne wholly by the Bank*, not shared with the clearing banks.

In August 1974 following continued drawings on the Lifeboat's resources, the criteria for assistance were toughened and the clearers' liability limited to £1200 m. Lifeboat support peaked at £1285 m. in March 1975 with the Bank then carrying more than its share of 10 per cent. In all, twenty-six secondary banks and finance houses called on the Lifeboat for help.

At the end of 1974 the Bank rescued Burmah oil, but that was not a Lifeboat operation.

In the Bank's view international confidence was still fragile, a view that led it on to phase three, ' ... support operations on their own account outside the Lifeboat, of which two were of particular significance.' (Bank paper) The two were Slater Walker and Edward Bates and Sons.

The cost

What has been the cost of the rescues? The cost to those private banks and institutions who took part is a matter for their shareholders and members; the cost to the Bank of England, a nationalized industry, is of more general concern. The sources of the Bank's losses may be listed as follows:

1. The early, pre-Lifeboat rescues.
2. Its 10 per cent share of the Lifeboat proper.
3. The cost of support above the £1200 m. limit set by the other participants and agreed by the Bank.
4. The cost of taking assignments of debt in cases of liquidation. These costs fell wholly on the Bank.
5. The cost of 'support operations on their own account' from 1975 onwards. (Slater Walker, Edward Bates and others.)

These costs have never been revealed. Margaret Reid[6] estimates them at around £100 m. (although it is not clear whether she includes all the above items). Whatever the true cost, part of it will have fallen upon taxpayers because the Bank's profits will have been reduced and hence the dividend paid to the Treasury out of those profits. Thus while the major cost was met by the shareholders and customers of the clearing banks, some undisclosed sum came indirectly from public funds.

The Treasury, in its dual role of sponsoring department for the Bank of England and controller of the public purse, the natural guardian of the taxpayers' interests, seems to have been largely passive. With a sterling crisis, a major economic package, a fourfold rise in oil prices, an incomes policy and a state of emergency on its hands, it had enough to keep it occupied. Even if it had had the time and the will to intervene, it would have been incapable of doing so effectively because it lacked banking expertise. It was obliged to leave the matter in the hands of the Bank of England, an arrangement with which, we may be sure, the Bank was well content.

Was the Lifeboat really necessary? There were those at the inaugural meeting who remained unconvinced that it was. It is understandable that the central bank should have been more worried; the history of banking is spattered with crises of confidence that might have been averted had the responsible people taken the right action in time. Banking is, after all, a gigantic conjuring trick that depends for its success upon keeping most of the balls in the air; if they all fall to hand at once disaster and embarrassment ensue.

There can be no doubt that in acting the way it did the Bank of England prevented the collapse of a number of 'banks' and finance houses. Equally it is not to be doubted that had such collapse occurred there would have been misfortune for those immediately involved. What may be doubted is whether the collapse of some twenty-six *secondary* banks (to take the maximum figure) would have brought down the whole structure of British banking. If it would, then that structure would appear to be a good deal more fragile than we commonly suppose it to be.

Even if it is granted that some sort of support operation was indicated we have to ask, as Margaret Reid (1982) does, was what was actually done:

> ... too comprehensive, expensive – and quiet? Could it have been effectively conducted at less potential cost on a more restricted basis? Some senior bankers privately expressed the view at the time that, while personal depositors with troubled fringe and secondary banks should be safeguarded, companies and other institutions which had lent to these banks should have known better and ought to be left to bear the consequences ...
> Another critical opinion was that it was not necessary

in the interests of confidence to rescue all affected banks.
This approach envisaged, as one clearing banker summed
it up privately, that 'if we had from the outset allowed two
or three of the less respected names to collapse in a flurry
of publicity with losses to their depositors, it would have
served them right and would have acted like a quick piece
of surgery on the City, cutting out the canker and
enabling the rest of us to continue the more easily with
our normal business'.

We may, she says, have to accept

... the uncomfortable conclusion ... that the
comprehensive nature of the support operation was
perhaps rather tender to certain banks which had taken
high risks for high rewards in good times and now enjoyed
ready protection in bad times ...

Heads I win, tails I don't lose. But *someone* had to lose; as we
have seen, the rescue was far from costless.

One comes away from the secondary banking crisis with the
impression that of those who contributed to the collapse and who
benefited, directly or indirectly, from the generous rescue, rather
more were likely to be afterwards found enduring the hardships of
Bermuda and the Caribbean than drawing supplementary benefit.
With Margaret Reid, one is left wondering 'whether it was right
that compassion should have been so marked a feature of the
conduct of the rescue. Personal bankruptcies have been relatively
few.'[7]

One outcome of the crisis was the Banking Act 1979 (although
legislation to regulate deposit-taking institutions was anyway
required by the European Community). The Act gave the Bank
supervisory powers overs deposit-taking institutions; and power to
determine which such institutions were banks – the so-called two-
tier system of regulation. Nevertheless, the Act left the Bank with
'flexibility in interpretation' for which the Governor was grateful:
' ... flexibility is preferable to a system of supervision in which
detailed rules and regulations are rigidly codified ... We have
always believed that the broad, strategic interests of supervisors
and supervised in banking business are as one ... '[8]

The secondary banking crisis occurred at a time when the
supervisory powers of the authorities were weak and diffused and
when there seemed little that the Government of the day was not
prepared to subsidize or protect. All would be different, one might
have supposed, in the more bracing climate of 1984 with less

compassion about and the Banking Act in place. A Government prepared to sit out a year-long strike over loss-making coal mines would scarcely be more tender towards a loss-making bullion dealer or minor bank, supposing that the Bank's supervision proved sufficiently flexible to allow such loss to occur. But in October 1984 the Bank re-entered the rescue business.

The Lifeboat re-launched

In October 1984 the Bank of England, under a different Governor, was given another opportunity to display its tenderness towards City institutions.

On 1 October the Bank took control of Johnson Matthey Bankers (JMB) and organized a large stand-by credit from banks and members of the London Gold Market. The action came under widespread criticism, from politicians, notably Dr David Owen, the Press, parts of the City itself and, in muted but unmistakable form, from the Treasury.

Johnson Matthey Bankers, a subsidiary of Johnson Matthey plc, were bullion dealers who had diversified into banking; and it was their loan book, not their activities in the gold market, that was the cause of their difficulties.

Criticism focused on four issues. First, the reason for the takeover as stated by the Bank and the Treasury was to prevent damage that might otherwise have occurred to members of the London Gold Market, of which JMB was an important member. Critics felt that it was one thing for the Bank to rescue a bank to protect the banking system of which it was the guardian, but quite another for it to extend this protection to the bullion market, not part of the banking system.

Secondly, even if it were granted that some action to protect the gold market was justified, this could and should have been done by setting up guarantees for JMB's bullion commitments while leaving the banking side of the business to suffer whatever fate it deserved. It was felt that to nationalize JMB in order to save its loan book was perhaps the least appropriate solution. The Governor's response to criticism of this nature was that the Bank was under great pressure, speedy action was needed and 'one cannot always deliberate over the design of the house when the kitchen is on fire'.[9]

Thirdly, there was the view, held particularly by other banks who were asked to subscribe to the rescue, that JMB, a mediocre, medium-sized bank whose demise would have been unlikely to damage the fabric of the City, should not have been rescued anyway. This was especially so in a climate of

Government opinion which placed great emphasis on the benefits of market discipline and when other, non-City, businesses were being allowed to fail in the name of that discipline.[10]

Finally, there was the matter of the adequacy of the Bank's supervisory arrangements. The Bank had known for some time that JMB was in difficulties and it was felt that the Bank might have acted earlier than it did, before the kitchen caught fire.

The reluctance of some banks to pay for JMB's losses was evidenced by the delay in finalizing an indemnity agreement. By early November the Bank said that 'An indemnity agreement, of which the Bank's share is 50 per cent, has now been agreed to cover up to £150 m. of possible losses over and above those of £167 m. matched by the bank's [JMB's] capital and provisions.'[11] Yet it was not until nearly 5 months later, on 29 March 1985, that the signing of the agreement was announced. The Press reported considerable resentment among participating banks, who did not see why they should pay for somebody else's mistakes. Sir Timothy Bevan of Barclays Bank said in Barclays' *Annual Report* that while it was right to rescue the bank, support should have been given through JMB's parent, Johnson Matthey plc, so that that company's shareholders bore more of the burden.

The Treasury was displeased with the form of the rescue and some friction was apparent between it and the Bank. Evidence of this was in the Chancellor's letter of 31 October to Dr David Owen where, distancing himself from the Bank's action, he said ' ... the Governor neither required nor sought my approval for the operation he undertook ... '; and concluded, 'For my part, I have little doubt that there will be important lessons to be drawn from the JMB failure, and the Bank is reviewing the events surrounding the failure with this very much in mind.'

The Chancellor, however, was not content to leave the matter entirely in the hands of the Bank. On 17 December 1984 he announced the setting up of an Inquiry into the matter with a strong Treasury participation.[12]

In late April and early May 1985 the JMB affair developed in a manner that caused the Treasury much embarrassment. On 25 April, in response to pressure in the House for the publication of the Bank of England's Report on the affair, the Economic Secretary to the Treasury said it was clear that JMB had indulged in some 'extremely unwise and imprudent lending'. On 2 May the Treasury, in a Written Answer to a question, confirmed that the Bank's enquiries had revealed departures from normal prudent banking practice. The answer was laid in the Press Gallery, where it was seen and reported upon, and placed in the letter rack of the Member who had asked the question. The Treasury then withdrew the answer from the Gallery and repossessed it from the MP's letter rack and from *Hansard* on the grounds that it was only a draft and had not been seen by ministers. 'The answer', said the Treasury, 'had no status' because it had been withdrawn and no MP had seen it.

The MP who had placed the question protested that the withdrawal of the reply raised issues of Parliamentary Privilege because his mail had been interfered with and *Hansard* 'forced' to omit the original answer and substitute a revised version. The Speaker upheld the complaint and on 7 May strongly rebuked the Treasury (who had made a full apology) and directed *Hansard* to print the original reply.

On 20 June 1985 the Chancellor of the Exchequer made a Statement in the House on Banking Supervision and Johnson Matthey Bankers. The Review Committee that he had set up on 17 December 1984 had reported, making 34 recommendations of which the two most important were that the two-tier system of banking supervision should be abolished and that there should in future be regular dialogue between the Bank of England supervisors and banks' auditors. A White Paper would be published followed by a Banking Bill to revise the Banking Act of 1979. (That Act drew a distinction between recognised banks and licensed deposit takers with only the latter subject to a rigorous regime of supervision. JMB, despite its small size, ranked and still ranks, as a full bank enjoying, so far as supervision was concerned, a status similar to that of the major clearers). The Bank of England's supervisory arrangements, which could not escape criticism, would be strengthened and reorganised.

The Bank of England's Report and accounts 1985 published on the day of the Chancellor's Statement contained in a lengthy Annex the Bank's account of the rescue.

JMB's losses were estimated at £248 million of which £34 million would fall to be met by the Bank of England. This will not come directly from public funds but it is deducted from the Bank's operating profit and must reduce the payments made to the Treasury out of profits.

The measures set in train by the Chancellor of the Exchequer will no doubt go far to preventing another Johnson Matthey debacle. But the affair itself rumbles on amid accusations by Mr Brian Sedgemore MP of fraud and conspiracy, and official denials of such.

Notes and references

1. 'The secondary banking crisis and the Bank of England's support operations'. A paper presented by the Bank to the research panel of the Wilson Committee and reprinted in the *BEQB*, Vol. 18, No. 2, Jun. 1978. Other quotations labelled 'Bank paper' are from the same source.
2. Galbraith (1961) p. 46.
3. George Blunden, 'The supervision of the UK banking system', *BEQB*, Vol. 15, No. 2, Jun. 1975, pp. 188–94.
4. *BEQB*, Vol. 13, No. 1, Mar. 1973.
5. *BEQB*, Vol. 13, No. 4, Dec. 1973.
6. Reid (1982), an excellent account, to which I am indebted.
7. Reid (1978).
8. Speech, 20 May 1980. *BEQB*, Vol. 20, No. 2, Jun. 1980.
9. *BEQB*, Vol. 24, No. 4, Dec. 1984, p. 473. See also p. 502 for the Governor's further defence of the action taken.
10. The Government's view was expressed succinctly by the then Chief Secretary to the Treasury, the Rt Hon. Peter Rees QC MP, in a speech on 17 April 1985 on Financial Management and the Search for Efficiency: 'In the private sector it is of course for the individual enterprise to concern itself with its own efficiency. Market forces should signal relatively promptly whether or not it is offering value for money. The Government's role, as we conceive it, is to ensure that the market is working smoothly and to provide the right framework for a healthy enterprise to flourish.

    But there is a large area of the economy where the pressures of the market cannot be relied upon to bring about greater efficiency. I refer of course to government itself.' Perhaps Mr Rees was one of those who doubted whether the best way to deal with JMB was to nationalize it.
11. The Governor's letter to Dr David Owen, 9 Nov. 1984.
12. There was to be a Committee under the Governor, to include the Permanent Secretary to the Treasury and other Treasury officials; and a separate official group chaired by the Treasury to examine possible legislative changes.

14

The critics

If, come the revolution, the first tumbril is occupied by the
Cabinet, the second may well carry the official Cabinet, the
Permanent Secretaries of Whitehall departments; a prospect that
numbers of other civil servants might contemplate with a certain
equanimity. But they should beware: they might themselves be
redeployed from the carpeted comforts of Whitehall to cultivate
the paddy fields of Potters Bar, or worse, to administer social
security in Liverpool. All of which is to say that, at the present
time, civil servants, and especially very senior civil servants, are
low in public esteem, suspected of being idle, incompetent,
secretive, devious, collusive, cloistered, sheltered from both
inflation and the disciplines of competition, fireproof, overpaid,
and altogether too powerful.

The Treasury, as part of the civil service, is not only not
excluded but enjoys a privileged place in the demonology. If, short
of the tumbrils, it were decided to shoot just one Permanent
Secretary *pour encourager les autres*, there can be little doubt
that the choice would fall on the Permanent Secretary to the
Treasury; although the enthusiasm for this selection might depend
as much upon whom the Permanent Secretary happened to be at
the time as upon the general principle of the thing.

Criticism of the Treasury and the civil service comes, literally,
from Left, Right and Centre of the political spectrum, although for
different reasons and in different volume. Let us look first at the
fire from the Left. Four people on the political Left, each of whom
has served in government at the policy level, have published
books of their experiences.[1] Each, I suspect would be a willing
volunteer for the firing squad; although whether, in the event, they
would fire at the designated target or at each other is less certain.
It would be imprudent, one feels, to allow Mr Haines to come too

close to Lady Falkender while in possession of a loaded firearm.

Common to the critics from the Left is the suspicion that the civil service is Conservative (capital 'C') or, at least, anti-Labour. This belief seems to rest on the fact that civil servants did not support or implement the political views and policies of the writers. But then neither, it appears, did their Government.

The critics have many interesting tales to tell of struggles with the civil service and of the civil service attempts, as they see it, to obstruct a Labour Government. To get the full flavour of these one must read the books themselves, easily the most entertaining of which is Mr Haines's. We must limit ourselves to their criticisms of the Treasury, which may be listed as follows: The Treasury:

1. is obsessed with monetary and financial matters (the external and internal value of the pound sterling) at the expense of the real economy;
2. (following from (1)) is always eager to recommend deflationary policies (which inhibit longer-term growth);
3. believes that wage increases cause inflation;
4. (following from (3)) is eager to attack wage increases, specifically (Haines) by a statutory incomes policy, and on one occasion tried to bounce the Cabinet into such a policy (Haines);
5. is incompetent.

Charges (1) and (2) are made at greater length by another critic, Professor Pollard, to whom we shall come in due course. Item (3), that the Treasury believes that wage increases cause inflation, was certainly true up until May 1979 if we insert after 'increases' the words 'not justified by increased productivity'. There may still be corners of the official Treasury where this heresy survives; but the only approved doctrine now is that it is only excessive increases in the money supply that cause inflation; excessive wage increases cause only unemployment. One may wonder whether the critics are any happier with this version.

In support of his thesis (at (4)) that the Treasury, in 1975, was determined to impose, against the declared policy of the Government, a statutory incomes policy, Mr Haines gives, in some detail, an account of an occasion in July 1975 when, in his view, the Treasury tried to bounce the Cabinet into a statutory incomes policy in the wake of a sterling crisis – a crisis which, he suggests, was created, or not aborted, by the Treasury and the Bank of England for just that purpose. The full story is in Mr Haines's book. In brief it is that, in a crisis atmosphere, the Treasury produced at ten minutes past midnight a draft statement to be made by the Chancellor of the Exchequer that afternoon, for consideration by the Cabinet at 9.30 that morning. In defiance of both declared Government policy and of a specific instruction from the Prime Minister to the Chancellor, the statement imposed a statutory incomes policy. Under pressure from Mr Haines and Mr Bernard Donoughue (Head of the PM's Policy Unit) the PM had the draft statement withdrawn.

I am not in a position to dispute the facts of Mr Haines's detailed account. But an examination of them exposes the weakness of the idea that 'the Treasury' has a policy of its own. The Treasury cannot submit proposals to Cabinet except over the Chancellor of the Exchequer's initials. And it would be manifestly absurd for the Chancellor of Exchequer to submit to Cabinet proposals, to be presented by him to the House of Commons, with which he was not in full agreement. The implication of Mr Haines's construction is either that the Chancellor was, in defiance of Government policy and the PM's instruction, himself in favour of a statutory incomes policy; or that he was quite out of control of his civil servants. Since the Chancellor was Denis Healey this seems unlikely. Moreover, it implies that the Chancellor had connived in creating or failing to abort a sterling crisis – not something that a Chancellor would lightly do.

The charge that the Treasury is ever eager to impose a statutory incomes policy has suffered from the passage of time. Whatever the Treasury believed in 1977 when Mr Haines was writing, it clearly cannot have believed after May 1979. The vision of Treasury mandarins trying desperately to impose a statutory incomes policy on Sir Geoffrey Howe, Mr Nigel Lawson and Mrs Thatcher lacks conviction. Nevertheless, it is worth examining the idea that the Treasury, or any other department, can bounce, or railroad, the Cabinet into a policy. For this proposition there is evidence from some fairly authoritative sources.

The Treasury and the Cabinet

We should draw a distinction between 'bouncing' the Cabinet, which implies some degree of malice aforethought allied to a deliberate tactic; and 'steering' the Cabinet, something which, it is alleged, goes on fairly continuously.

For an example of bouncing we may take Joel Barnett's account of an episode during the IMF crisis of 1976. In his story of the crisis, Joel Barnett writes:

Some Treasury officials were panicking at the thought that unless Cabinet agreed quickly on such a package, we would not get the loan and all hell would be let loose in the money markets. But the figures changed constantly. Denis Healey was now talking of £1.5 billion in 1977/78, and £2 billion in 1978/79, with the Cabinet paper enshrining this proposal held back until such time as to be late for the meeting. Tony Benn jocularly expressed the view that the 48-hour rule ... had been cut to 15 minutes.[2]

Treasury influence

We should bear in mind that the Prime Minister is also First Lord of the Treasury (even if 'he' is a 'she') and that all recent Prime Ministers have worked very closely with their Chancellors of the Exchequer. Some Chancellors would not move on any major issue without consulting the Prime Minister. Since so much of modern policy is concerned with the economy it is not surprising that the Treasury should have a major input to Cabinet papers. Nor is it surprising that senior Treasury officials should be called upon to brief the Prime Minister on complicated issues, such as those concerned with the European Community. It is also the case, again, no doubt, because of the pervading influence of matters economic, that there is often a middle-ranking Treasury official on secondment in the Prime Minister's Private Office, and others in the Cabinet Office.

Joel Barnett bears witness to the usefulness of this Treasury presence. In Cabinet in March 1977 'there was the usual criticism from Harold Lever and others of "the Treasury", and what was described as nonsensical PSBR definitions, and ritualistic conventions. I may say that Treasury officials knew of these criticisms even before I got back to the Treasury.' 'Sometimes', he observes, ' ... the Prime Minister (in Cabinet) would do my job for me with the appropriate tough question. This was usually no accident, as the Cabinet Office brief for the Prime Minister would be well drafted – often with a useful guidance from my Treasury official. It was even more helpful if the Cabinet Office official was a former Treasury official ... '[3]

Apart from any 'direct line' that the Treasury may have to the Prime Minister and to the Cabinet Office, it is alleged that the Treasury influences policy in a pervasive way. The Cabinet is serviced by Cabinet Committees of Ministers. These Committees are serviced by 'shadow' committees of officials. Crossman argues that policy is 'pre-cooked' in these Cabinet Committees by the civil servants; and that the civil servants strive for a 'coherent Whitehall view' which is 'nearly always a view dominated by Treasury thinking'.[4] A policy agreed by a Cabinet Sub-Committee needs only formal approval by the full Cabinet.

Crossman was writing of conditions some 20 years ago. Joel Barnett, more recently, would not disagree with him. Senior officials of the Treasury and of other Departments have their contacts among themselves and with the Cabinet Office and are able to influence

> the crucial brief that would be put before the Prime Minister or the Chairman of the appropriate Cabinet Committee ... when united these (senior officials) can be devastating, particularly when arguing *against* a proposition.

Having come to their own conclusion, officials would

> then seek by every means at their disposal to carry their Minister with them ... Ministers would come (to Cabinet Committees) with long briefs prepared by officials who had been members of the appropriate Official Committee which 'shadowed' the Ministerial Committee. In fact 'shadowed' is an inappropriate term, for the Official Committee ... usually left their Ministers in no doubt whatever as to which was the best option – the one they recommended.[5]

But manipulating the 'shadow' sub-committees is not the limit of civil service influence on policies: there is also a full Shadow Cabinet of officials. Barnett again:

> There were many instances during our period in office when Ministers suspected the motives of senior civil servants, ... a 'them and us' attitude exists between civil servants and Ministers. No little blame for this must rest with the civil servants themselves and the system they operate. I am thinking of the 'Shadow' Cabinet Committee meetings of officials from all Departments. But most of all I have in mind the officials' 'Cabinet', or weekly meeting of Permanent Secretaries. Plotting is too strong a word, but there is no doubt that officials at those meetings plan how to 'steer' a Cabinet and Cabinet Committees along paths Ministers may not have originally intended.[6]

Mr Tony Benn records a similar view: ' ... when Permanent

Secretaries sit down together [in the 'Official Cabinet'] they do think that they are the ultimate government of the country and that ministers may come and go, but in them resides the ultimate responsibility ... '[7]

Thus, it is argued, the Cabinet is, if not at the mercy of officials, at least at some disadvantage simply because the officials have more information. In his 1983 Reith Lectures, Sir Douglas Wass discussed the problem of providing the Cabinet with adequate information for decision-making. An issue brought to Cabinet is presented by the interested, and therefore partisan, Minister. It is not in his interests to present the Cabinet with arguments against his case, and his case may not be challenged unless another Minister is sufficiently affected to have prepared a counter-case. There is no mechanism to enable the Cabinet as a whole to challenge a departmental view. 'The Cabinet', said Sir Douglas, 'can too easily be railroaded.' Decisions may be taken on inadequate information. It should be noted that the argument here is not that civil servants are railroading the Cabinet, but that a Departmental Minister is able to. It becomes civil service railroading only if the civil servants have already impressed their own view upon the Departmental Minister (and also, it is suggested, upon their colleagues).

Sir Douglas relates the general problem specifically to the Treasury:

> In no area of policy-making does this problem arise more acutely than in the management of the economy, and, in particular, the Budget. The Minister who brings these issues to Cabinet is, of course, the Chancellor of the Exchequer. No other Minister has at his command the back-up of analytical support that the Chancellor receives from his Treasury and Revenue Department officials and from the Bank of England. How can his colleagues be assured that they're getting the whole story and not just the one which the Chancellor wishes them to hear? They have no independent staff. They have indeed no direct access to the official advice which the Treasury provides. Yet they are obliged to come to a view on the basis of what one of their colleagues, a committed party, is telling them. [Until a few years ago the Budget] ... was settled as a personal matter by the Chancellor of the day, and presented to his colleagues as a *fait accompli*. It was a matter of astonishment to me that successive Cabinets should have acquiesced in this procedure ... Today

things are somewhat better, but the Cabinet as a whole remains at a disadvantage *vis-à-vis* the Chancellor, who keeps his powerful control of the sources of official information and advice.[8]

These are brave words from a former Permanent Secretary to the Treasury. What, before he became 'former', would Sir Douglas's response have been to a request from Mr Benn to see official information and advice?

The Treasury as Mafia

The argument so far has been about the power of senior civil servants acting in collusion; about the power of a Departmental Minister (and especially the Chancellor of the Exchequer) within Cabinet; and about the special links that the Treasury has with the Prime Minister's office and the Cabinet. There is another charge brought against the Treasury, namely that it has its agents everywhere within Whitehall. Evidence of this comes from the experience of two Ministers who, as members of Labour Cabinets, scarcely qualify as Left Wing: the late Richard Crossman (a senior Minister in the 1964–70 Government, but never in the Treasury); and Joel Barnett (Chief Secretary to the Treasury in the 1974–79 Government).

It is held that the power of the Treasury extends far beyond the power that flows naturally from its position as holder of the purse because Whitehall is permeated and run by civil servants whose second, if not first, loyalty is to the Treasury. This loyalty (which is, by the same token, disloyalty to the official's own department) stems from two things. The first is that a significant number of Permanent Secretaries of Departments come on promotion from the Treasury; ex-Treasury men are to be found at the highest level all around Whitehall. One reason for this is the Treasury's unique grading structure at the top. Immediately beneath the Permanent Secretary are four Second Permanent Secretaries. These posts carry a Knighthood, with the rations. Given the age structure and usual length of tenure of the Permanent Secretary, only one of these Knights can become Permanent Secretary to the Treasury. So two or three Treasury Knights have to be found Permanent Secretaryships elsewhere to end their civil service days. On two occasions in recent years none of the sitting Second Permanent Secretaries got the top Treasury job, which went instead to a Deputy Secretary who leapfrogged his seniors. When that happens there is a desire to sweeten the pill for those passed over by the award of a Permanent Secretaryship elsewhere.[9]

Permanent Secretaryships apart, there are other top jobs around
Whitehall to which Treasury men can and have been moved.
(Comptroller and Auditor General; Head of the Inland Revenue,
for example); and other Treasury officials go to other departments
on secondment.

The second reason for loyalty to the Treasury is that civil
servants, and perhaps especially the young fliers who populate
Ministers' private offices, see the Treasury as the natural source of
promotion. Whitehall, it is alleged, is infiltrated by a sort of
Treasury Mafia. Crossman, for example, has this to say:

> All the civil servants I worked with were imbued with a
> prior loyalty to the Treasury and felt it necessary to spy
> on me and report all my doings to the Treasury whether I
> wanted them kept private or not. There was nothing I
> could do, no order I could give, which wasn't at once
> known to the Treasury, because my staff were all trained
> to check with the Treasury and let it know in advance
> exactly what each of them was doing ... No doubt this is
> explained in the case of ambitious young men and women
> by the fact that the Treasury is the prime source of
> promotion ... But there are other senior people ... who
> just feel the Treasury is their natural boss; and whereas
> the Treasury and the head of the Civil Service are
> permanent, the Minister changes once every three years
> on average. Why should they worry about giving any
> particular loyalty to me?[10]

In the entry for 4 October 1965 Crossman records an instance
where the Chancellor knew of a private consultation conducted by
one of Crossman's ministers before he (Crossman) did. He told
his Permanent Secretary 'how deeply I resented people in my
Department leaking in this way to the Treasury ... I keenly resent
the behaviour of officials who obviously feel that their first
obligation is to the Treasury ... ' Many higher civil servants were
' ... willing to spy for the Treasury and to align themselves with
the Treasury view even against their own Minister'.[11]

Joel Barnett shows how the system works from the Treasury
end.

> Although I might not be aware ... of the views of one of
> my Ministerial colleagues with whom I was having an
> argument, my officials, through their contacts with their
> opposite numbers in the Department concerned, would
> be able to report to me on the line the Minister would be
> likely to take - assuming, that is, that he would be

following their advice. This frequently turned out to be useful and accurate information.[12]

Civil servants and departmental policy

If it is true, as alleged, that a caucus of senior civil servants can manipulate a whole Cabinet-full of Ministers, how much more likely is it that the ranks of civil servants within a department (including the Permanent Secretary, who sits on the official 'shadow' cabinet) can steer their own minister or ministers? The official side of the department will have been there for a long time and will have a knowledge of the department's business which an incoming minister cannot hope to match. He will learn, but he will be gone again after, on average, two or three years.

Joel Barnett was a strong minister, much respected, and he spent five years in the same job in the Treasury. Was he manipulated?

> Life was not made easier for me by officials putting up long briefs which required, or so it was said, a decision 'immediately'. It did not take long to learn that decisions required 'today' could usually wait a week or more. I had not been long in the job when I turned down a recommendation, and the next thing I knew was that Sir Douglas Henley, the Second Permanent Secretary (Public Expenditure) asked to come and see me. He came in, and began to refer to the case I had rejected. I interrupted him to say I was not prepared to have my life made yet more difficult by officials asking to see me each time I rejected their 'advice'.[13]

'Another tactic deployed by officials is delay.' They 'played it long' in the hope that either the issue or the Minister would 'die'. In one case Barnett found that officials had not put papers (containing recommendations with which they disagreed) before the Home Secretary for three months.[14]

Mr Prior is another Minister 'well aware of what (civil servants) could do to manoeuvre against a policy they did not like'.[15] They could slow it down by endless objections and discussions; they could stir up other Departments to raise objections; they could brief interested organizations; and they could leak to the Press.

Sir Patrick Nairne, a former Permanent Secretary to the Department of Health and Social Security, points to other powers that civil servants have: they can manipulate information and they have discretion over the use of resources within a Department.[16]

As we have seen (Ch. 5), there was a belief that at the time of

334   The critics

the 1976 IMF crisis Treasury officials tried to impose their own policies. Again, early in 1979, says Mr Barnett,

> ... Treasury officials were producing more and more pessimistic forecasts of the PSBR. I was becoming daily more suspicious of their motives, and I know this applied even more in the case of Denis Healey and Jim Callaghan, the latter being in one of his, by now fairly regular, anti-Treasury moods. Substantial public expenditure cuts were 'what officials thought to be necessary'. ... to some extent, I was sure officials were presenting the financial picture as gloomily as they could in order to persuade me, and in turn Cabinet, of the need for what was essentially a major public expenditure cuts package.[17]

In February 1979 the borrowing requirement figures being produced by officials ' ... were much higher than those of outside forecasters, and Denis just did not believe them. I must say, neither did I, and we both assumed that officials were in effect conspiring together to compel us to do more than we would otherwise have wanted to.'[18]

Mr Barnett does not subscribe to the 'political conspiracy' theory of the civil service. He found his civil servants 'intensely loyal, both to me personally and to the Government'. There was just 'a combination of "Natural conservatism" and a genuine belief in the need for public expenditure cuts'.[19]

The Treasury's incompetence

We have dwelt at some length upon the power and influence of the Treasury. If in fact the Treasury has possessed and does possess that power and influence it would be an entirely beneficial state of affairs were the Treasury always right, or mostly right, or, at least reasonably competent. But that, it is alleged, is not so. The charge that the Treasury is in fact incompetent comes most trenchantly from Mr Haines:

> The belief in their own infallibility is one of the Treasury's greatest mistakes ... If only the Treasury more readily admitted its mistakes – which on occasions would be a full-time job – a more balanced understanding of its limitations might prevail ... Not for nothing are the Knights of Great George Street referred to as mandarins: like an Oriental tong, they have their agents everywhere. With a certainty which successive Chancellors have invariably mistaken for wisdom, these financial Fu

Manchus have presided over, nurtured, cossetted and brought to flower almost every kind of economic crisis which can afflict a declining economy ... From 1973 onwards they managed to achieve the worst unemployment since the war, deflation and inflation, recession, rising prices and falling living standards, and all at once, and yet their supremacy is rarely challenged. Give them a problem and they will turn it into a crisis.[20]

If the Treasury is incompetent, then there is something wrong with civil service selection methods, for the Treasury gets the cream.

The Treasury view

A favourite belief of the critics is that the Treasury has a continuing institutional view which does not change, or does not change very much, whatever the Government. Adrian Ham, for example, sees a continuity of thought and policy running from the infamous 'Treasury view' of the inter-war years to the monetarism of the 1980s. It is difficult to see how this view can survive the very sharp policy changes that followed the change of Government in 1979. It is impossible to accuse the official Treasury of embracing both a statutory incomes policy and monetarism, for the two are mutually exclusive. But that may not silence the critics, who seem likely to regard it as mere hair splitting. What the Treasury really does, one can hear them say, shifting their ground, is to use any fashionable stick to beat the unions.

At least one Chancellor of the Exchequer did not subscribe to the monolithic view of the official Treasury:
Mr Healey:

> I would say that of all the departments the one which has the least coherent view of its role is the Treasury. It may have been true in the ten years after the war that all Treasury officials knew exactly how the country should be run, but in my experience none of them knows now. They're deeply divided on many of the central issues. You'll find monetarist officials, people who are neo-Keynesians, people who are pragmatists of one sort or another. I would say that the only constant thing in the Treasury is a desire to see that the figures add up, and that is not always a first priority for ministers.[21]

While the Treasury's forecasts may always have added up arithmetically, they did not always bear a close relationship to what in the event happened.

The Treasury responsible for poor economic performance

Mr Haines's complaint, aside from the suggestion that the Treasury shows an irritating confidence in its own incompetence, is that the Treasury is responsible for all the economic ills that have afflicted the economy in recent years. The argument runs as follows: the British economy has performed poorly, absolutely and relatively. The Treasury is responsible for managing the economy. Therefore the poor performance results from the Treasury's management. It is a plausible syllogism and one that lies at the heart of Professor Pollard's criticisms, to which we now turn.

Professor Pollard levels at the Civil Service, and at the Treasury in particular, some of the charges made by other critics, notably that the permanent officials are too powerful and collusive and that Treasury influence permeates the whole of Whitehall.

But Professor Pollard's target is not quite the same as that of other critics. His polemic is not directed primarily against civil servants as manipulative and frustrators of ministers but, like Mr Haines's criticism, against the Treasury as the single most important begetter of Britain's relative economic decline over the last thirty years. The Treasury is responsible for nothing less than 'the wasting of the British economy' (the title of his book).[22] There are, he concedes, other explanations (which he discusses);[23] but the attitudes and policies of the Treasury are a sufficient cause of our decline and present state.

Pollard will have none of the argument that the Treasury is relatively powerless to influence the real economy: ' . . . we have to conclude regretfully that the Treasury cannot be exonerated on the grounds that its actions have no significant effect: Britain is littered with the very real derelict victims of its policies . . . the actions taken by the Treasury . . . included precisely those measures which made it impossible for the vehicle to move at all.'[24]

Professor Pollard describes Britain's 'staggering relative decline', a decline 'such as would have been considered utterly unbelievable only a little over thirty years ago'. Starting from a relatively advantageous position, Britain has (in GNP per head) been successively overtaken by Norway, Iceland, Finland, Denmark, Holland, Belgium, West Germany, France, Luxembourg, Austria, Australia, New Zealand and Japan. Of the major European countries only Italy is still below us in the per capita GNP league and that only because of the backward condition of Calabria. 'There is no record of any other economic power falling behind at such startling speed.' What needed explaining was not the 'miracle' of growth elsewhere but how we had avoided it. 'Surely it must have required a powerful and sustained effort, or most unusual circumstances, to prevent the world boom from spilling over into Britain as well.'[25] There were unusual circumstances, in the shape of the Imperial heritage, including the sterling balances, and illusions of grandeur; but it was the Treasury, argues Professor Pollard, who provided the sustained effort.

Having documented Britain's slide to near the foot of all the virtuous tables measuring economic performance, Professor Pollard looks for reasons. These he identifies as 'a low level of investment and a contempt for production'. Why was investment so inadequate for so long? The 'one single overwhelmingly important' reason was that 'the whole panoply of government power, as exercised above all by the Treasury, was designed to keep it so'. And 'The contempt for production thus stood at the centre of British policy ... It informs fundamentally all the actions of the Treasury and other central policy-making bodies.'[26]

This seems a little hard on Harold Wilson and generations of Labour and trade union leaders who have been criticized for being obsessed with industry and the production of things, scarcely able to raise their eyes to horizons beyond tons of steel and truckloads of coal; forever complaining that capital was being invested abroad instead of here; and demanding that the funds of 'the institutions' should be directed into 'productive investment'. Nor does it seem consistent with the generous – many would say over-generous – relief given in grants and tax relief. (Until, that is, the Budget of 1984, when Mr Lawson announced the staged removal of capital allowances. Applauding this, the *Financial Times* in its leading article on the day after the Budget said 'The encouragement of investment has been a cornerstone of Treasury doctrine, encouraged by the industrial lobby and enthusiastically backed by governments of both parties, for so long that it seemed a fixture.')

Professor Pollard does give the Labour Government marks for establishing the Department of Economic Affairs but 'The Treasury ... had no difficulty in strangling the DEA at birth ... there was never a real chance of shaking the "balance-of-payments-firsters" in the Treasury.'[27]

He should also have given Mr Healey and the Treasury credit for the determined efforts made from 1973 onwards to promote 'the industrial strategy' and take account of the needs of manufacturing industry. A National Economy Group was established in 1973 under Sir Douglas Wass and became the Domestic Economy Group in 1974 under Alan Lord, brought in from the Department of Trade and Industry. The needs of industrial policy were taken very seriously. An 'industrial dimension' was grafted on to the thrice-yearly National Income Forecasts (NIF) and high level inter-departmental meetings were held to discuss the industrial implications of the macro-economic forecasts both overall and for specific industries.

The central charge that the Professor brings against the Treasury runs as follows: For thirty years the economy has repeatedly gone through the same crisis. Because of a failure to invest and build up an adequate production base, the economy quickly runs into its capacity ceiling when run at a high level of demand, and a balance of payments or currency crisis ensues. The Treasury's routine response to this recurring crisis is to impose restrictions which fall heavily on investment and which undermine confidence; a response that not only does nothing to improve the fundamental deficiency on the supply side, but makes it progressively worse. The Treasury learns nothing from this repeated experience which 'seemed to come each time as a complete surprise to the Treasury and those who accepted its advice'.

But if the Treasury did not learn from experience, entrepreneurs in the private sector did: they expected every 'go' phase to be short-lived and made their investment plans accordingly. ' ... the failure of the Treasury to anticipate this obvious result and ... to fail to learn from the experience of up to ten similar crises, and go on charging again and again like a bull in the *corrida* in spite of the painful and fruitless consequences each time, must be among the most powerful indictments of our policy makers in modern times.'[28]

What then, is the principle that drives policy makers to continue with policies which

> ... have led over a period of three decades, as a matter of experience, to the most devastating economic failure recorded in modern history and do not make sense even in their own terms? ... it is the principle of concentrating first and foremost on symbolic figures and quantities, like prices, exchange rates and balances of payments, to the neglect of real quantities, like goods and services produced and traded ... Whenever there is a clash of interests, the real must be sacrificed to the

symbolic ... No one who has lived through the period and has read or listened to the media will require proof of the single-minded obsession of the Treasury with such issues as balance of payments or inflation: it is the single most consistent thread running through official propaganda and discussion.[29]

That, in summary, is the charge and the evidence. The Treasury has been caught with a symbolic and smoking gun in its hand, kneeling beside the mortally wounded body of the real British economy. But did the Treasury do it? Friends might suggest that to suppose that it did claims too much for the Treasury's aim, that it would have been more likely to have shot its own foot. Misadventure rather than murder. And, anyway, what was the motive? The DPP would no doubt extend his protection. If charged, however, and found guilty, the Treasury might ask for several other offences in the 1920s and 1930s to be taken into consideration.

One cannot but be impressed by Professor Pollard's documentation of Britain's dismal performance. As an economic historian he is able to take a longer and more detached view than the Treasury, up there at the sharp end of economic management ('staggering from crisis to crisis' as critics would put it). One questions whether it is fair to lay quite so much of the blame at the Treasury's door. But then the old, nagging, question obtrudes: who is responsible for setting the agenda and steering the economy in the short and long term if not the Treasury? Lord Soames for one would not exonerate the official Treasury from all blame:

> The trouble is, very often [bad advice] isn't found out for a long time afterwards ... if you take the role of the Treasury, for instance, in the economic and financial decisions that have been made over the last twenty or thirty years, you can ask, 'Why is it that our productivity is so much lower in this country and our production has increased so much less than it has in many of our competitor countries in recent years?' You can't blame that just on the governments ... you can't say that the civil service, in the advice they've given, have had nothing to do with it at all.[30]

Hugo Young and Anne Sloman in their book about the Treasury[31] put the view that 'if the government machine has an impact on the economy the Treasury must surely be its powerhouse ... a fair test for the Treasury might be thought to relate, in the ultimate reckoning, to Britain's economic performance.' They put the proposition to Michael Posner, Economic Adviser to the Treasury 1967–69, Economic Consultant 1969–71, Deputy Chief Economic Adviser to the Treasury 1975–76. He replied:

> It is true that the Treasury is out of touch. During the seventies there was a very considerable effort by successive ministers to bring the Treasury more fully into touch with things. When Mr Alan Lord was a very senior Treasury official, he had responsibility for industrial policy in a way which would have been unheard-of in the Treasury of a decade earlier. Now, I believe that the Treasury's interest in the grass-roots or in the dirty fingernail side of the economy has diminished since then.[32]

Thus, the Treasury must be given credit for trying, at least some of the time. I recall one occasion when the formidable Alan Lord stopped the Government from introducing a particular piece of taxation because he believed it would have had a ruinous effect on a particular section of British industry.

Sir Frank Cooper, Permanent Under-Secretary of Defence 1976–82, also thought the Treasury to be out of touch:

> There's no substitute for real experience, and there are very few people in the Treasury who've had real experience ... The people who work there are very clever. Intellectually they are extremely able, outstandingly so, there's no doubt about that. But they live in an isolated world and a different world from the rest of humanity. And until you change this, you're never really going to get an effective Treasury.[33]

Perhaps this view of the Treasury was put most succinctly by Lord Wilson of Rievaulx: 'The Treasury could not, with any marked success, run a fish and chip shop.'[34]

One of the charges brought against the Treasury is of arrogance and an inability to admit mistakes. How does the Treasury maintain this arrogance, or at least its self-confidence, in the face of evidence of persistent failure? David Hancock's view was that by the time, some years later, that it was generally recognized that a mistake had been made, policy would have moved on and people would be busy with current problems, not re-running history. There was no time for guilt or remorse. He thought that this was ' ... a perfectly healthy mental attitude. It would not be a good thing to have a government department staffed by people who were constantly feeling guilty about things, not all of which they could have influenced.'[35]

There is no doubt much common sense in what Mr Hancock says: like doctors, the Treasury buries its mistakes but does not allow this to impair its omniscient bedside manner. But one corollary is that because 'some years' will have passed before a mistake is generally acknowledged, no one is ever held accountable. You can go on making mistakes until the end and by the time they are seen to have been mistakes you will have retired.

Andrew Britton, a senior economist in the Treasury, later at the NIESR, had a slightly different explanation: officials felt not failure but frustration that their advice had not been taken. ' ... if you ask how they maintain their self-confidence in the face of the appalling mess of the British economy, I think it's because, never having actually taken decisions, they are always able to satisfy themselves that, if they had taken the decisions, they would have taken the right ones.'[36]

Peter Middleton, the present Permanent Secretary to the Treasury, said he did not feel like a defeatist or a pessimist, and did not see why he should: 'I think one has to keep on pursuing policies which increase efficiency ... with a macro-economic background which best promotes that, given the policies of the government of the day. If you succeed in taking steps along that road, by and large you can't be doing anything which harms the British economy, and the chances are that you'll be doing things which do it a great deal of good.'[37]

Well, yes, precisely: if you do beneficial things, beneficial results will follow. But what Permanent Secretary, even of the Treasury, ever knowingly did unbeneficial things – given, of course, 'the policies of the government of the day'?

When people criticize 'the Treasury' it is clear that in most cases what they mean is the official Treasury, the permanent civil servants, the Treasury as an ongoing institution. It is true that civil servants give policy advice – that, in large part, is what they are paid for. But they do not, or should not, *decide* policy; that, constitutionally, is for ministers and the Cabinet, supported by Parliament. If that is so, the verdict of Young and Sloman on the Treasury is the fair and correct one: 'The failures may have been large (and sometimes the successes), but they have been attributable more to governments and political leaders, and above all to uncontrollable events, than to the Treasury as an institution.'[38]

Notes and references

1. Falkender (1975). Marcia Williams (Lady Falkender) was
   Political Secretary to the Prime Minister, Harold Wilson.
   Haines (1977). Mr Haines was Mr Wilson's Press Secretary.
   Ham (1981). Mr Ham was Special Assistant (i.e. political
   adviser) to Denis Healey.
   Sedgemore (1980). Mr Sedgemore was a civil servant who
   became a Member of Parliament and Parliamentary Private
   Secretary to Tony Benn.
2. Barnett (1982), pp. 103–4.
3. Ibid., pp. 123, 141.
4. Crossman (1979), pp. 85–6. *The Crossman Diaries* is a
   selection from *The Diaries of a Cabinet Minister*, a book
   which the then Secretary to the Cabinet, Sir John Hunt, went
   to great lengths to suppress. In *Good Times, Bad Times*
   (Weidenfeld and Nicolson 1983) Harold Evans gives a
   fascinating account of the battle over publication of extracts.
   For example, when asked whether it would be in order to
   print that Mr Crossman had sat in Cabinet, looking out over
   Horse Guards parade, Hunt considered a moment and said
   'Yes. But you may not say who sat on either side of him.' One
   hopes that this was an irritated response to an exasperated
   question. But one has an uneasy feeling that Secretaries to
   the Cabinet do not joke about such matters; that Sir John
   Hunt felt that he was sticking his thumb in the dyke to
   preserve the Establishment from a flood of memoirs from
   Cabinet ministers other than Prime Ministers. Joel Barnett
   was one who walked through the huge breach made by
   Crossman.
5. Barnett (1982), pp, 18, 19, 41.
6. Ibid., p. 188.
7. Young and Sloman (1982), p. 95.
8. *The Listener*, 24 Nov. 1983.
9. When Peter Middleton became Permanent Secretary to the
   Treasury in 1983 he jumped over the sitting Second
   Permanent Secretaries. Anticipating or following this move,
   Sir William Ryrie went to become Permanent Secretary at the
   Overseas Development Administration (Apr. 1982 – and his
   post at the Treasury was abolished); Sir Kenneth Couzens
   became Permanent Secretary at the Department of Energy
   (Jan. 1983); Sir Anthony Rawlinson became Permanent

Secretary at the Department of Trade (Apr. 1983); and David Hancock, widely believed to have been the losing contender for the top Treasury post, became Permanent Secretary to the Department of Education and Science. (Hancock was a Treasury official but at the time of his promotion was a Deputy Secretary in the Cabinet Office.)

10. Crossman (1975), Vol. 1 pp. 615–6. Young and Sloman (1982) write: ' ... it's no use pretending that a private secretary is working solely for his minister ... it's the service which employs him and has his future in its hands. And he is not left long unaware of the state of mind of his Permanent Secretary ... ' (p.92).

11. Crossman (1979), pp. 134–5

12. Barnett (1982), p. 18.

13. Ibid., pp. 19–20.

14. Ibid., p. 21.

15. Young and Sloman (1982), p. 28. Mr Prior was at different times Minister of Agriculture, Fisheries and Food; Leader of the House of Commons; Secretary of State for Employment; Secretary of State for Northern Ireland.

16. Young and Sloman (1982), p. 27.

17. Barnett (1982), p. 180. Elsewhere (pp. 21–2) he writes: ' ... officials were quite brilliant in the different ways they had of "fudging" figures, particularly on expenditure decisions ... In the preparation of a public expenditure White Paper, a whole variety of "assumptions" have to be made (economic jargon for "guessing") about such matters as earnings, prices, shortfall, along with a host of other "estimates". Any one of these variables could ensure that the picture painted was such as to require action of the kind which officials believed to be right. Change this or that "assumption", and abracadabra – the PSBR is about the figure you first thought of!' Mr Barnett makes it clear that he does not accuse officials of cooking the books. 'They would not put their names to figures which, as they saw it, impugned their integrity.'

18. Ibid., p. 182.

19. Ibid., p. 179.

20. Haines (1977), pp. 40–41. The Treasury's address used to be Great George Street before the Great George Street entrance was closed and a new entrance opened in Parliament Street round the corner.

21. Young and Sloman (1982), p. 25.

344   The critics

22. Pollard (1982).
23. Including the behaviour of British trade unions. Our unions
    'have had to be counted among the most irresponsible and
    destructive in Europe ... '. (p. 106). They are anarchic,
    irrational, selfish, ruthless and have the mentally of the
    highwayman. They have barbarized the labour process (p.
    113). But even here the Treasury cannot escape: 'It is not the
    least indictment of Treasury policy that it has converted the
    potentially positive force of British trade unionism into an
    agency that inhibits growth, embitters social relations and
    brings long-established working class ideals into disrepute.' (p.
    118)
24. Ibid., p. 98.
25. Ibid., pp. 2, 3, 6.
26. Ibid., pp. 71, 73.
27. Ibid., pp. 43, 74.
28. Ibid., pp. 54–5.
29. Ibid., p. 72.
30. Young and Sloman (1982), p. 70. Lord Soames, Lord
    President of the Council 1979–81.
31. Young and Sloman (1984).
32. Ibid., p. 104.
33. Ibid., p. 108.
34. Quoted in *The Observer*, 18 Mar. 1984.
35. Young and Sloman (1984), p. 118.
36. Ibid., p. 121.
37. Ibid., p. 125.
38. Ibid., p. 130.

15

The road to 1985

For British economic policy, and particularly for people who worked in the Treasury, the period from 1964 to 1967 was a bitter one, full of tension and anxiety and an atmosphere of crisis that remained for a while even after the devaluation of 1967. Yet in retrospect it appears as the end of an almost golden age of certitude in the management of the economy, an age in which we understood how the economy worked and knew what we were doing. True, there was a problem with the balance of payments, but that was nothing new and we thought we knew that all we had to do to put the matter right was to move a relatively small proportion of the GDP into the balance of payments: politically difficult but economically a solution.

Little else was wrong with the economy: the rate of inflation in recent years had only twice exceeded 4 per cent and in 1967 was 2.4 per cent; the percentage unemployed was below 2.5 per cent; gross domestic product was growing at an average of something approaching 3 per cent a year. Thus, three of the major objectives of economic policy – full employment, growth and relatively stable prices – were being simultaneously achieved. Yet the Chancellor of the Exchequer felt honour-bound to resign for the failure of his policies.

This book has been about the changes and reversals in economic policies between then and now. Domestic economic policy does not take place in a vacuum but in what we may call, clumsily, the economic environment. This environment itself comprises two elements: the objective world and the theoretical world. I use the term 'objective world' rather than 'real world' because the term 'real' as applied to 'economy' is used in contradistinction to 'financial' or 'monetary'; and we are concerned with both worlds. There is a sense in which the theoretical world is part of the objective world, for if theories, or beliefs, are widely held and acted upon they assume some of the properties of an objective fact. But that is a semantic point.

So, before reviewing policy changes we should first consider the changes in the environment.

Changes

We may identify eight major changes.

1. *The exchange rate.* At Bretton Woods a system of fixed exchange rates had been built. Within the constraint of the exchange rate a country could follow whatever domestic policies it pleased. But the constraint was a powerful one: economies had, in a Procrustean way, to be made to fit the exchange rate. A country could, after the courtesy of informing the IMF, devalue its currency, but since exchange rates were regarded as something of a national virility symbol this came to be regarded as a somewhat extreme step. (Nor, as it turned out, were governments any more eager to raise their exchange rate.) If a country ran into continuing deficit on its balance of payments, the only way that competitiveness on trading account could be preserved or increased was through a reduction in domestic costs. There was thus considerable incentive to keep costs down; and the major component of domestic costs was wages and salaries. Trade unions were exhorted to bargain for wage increases no higher than the increase in output; much emphasis was placed upon productivity. With any change in the exchange rate ruled out, the exhortations carried some weight. And with a low rate of inflation trade unionists in this period thought in terms of increases in money wages.

With the exchange rate not available as an instrument of policy (and the money supply of no interest), the main tools of economic management were the rate of interest (set by the authorities, not by the market) and the fiscal balance.

With the demise of the Bretton Woods system the exchange rate became available as a policy instrument; one of the major constraints upon domestic policies was removed and, in the UK at least, nothing put in its place.

2. *Entry to the European Community.* This was not so much a change in the objective world as an additional economic burden –

on taxpayers, on the rate of inflation and on the balance of payments – voluntarily assumed.

3.   *The price of oil.* Between the autumn of 1973 and the beginning of 1974 oil prices increased fivefold. This was both inflationary and deflationary; inflationary because it raised domestic prices, and deflationary (or, more correctly, contractionary) to the extent that the rise in domestic prices was not offset in some way or if oil-importing countries sought to correct an ensuing balance of payments deficit by deflating domestic economies. The rise in oil prices represented a once-for-all shift of real income to the producers. Therefore consumers should lower their own real consumption standards and transfer real resources to the producers. Apart from the political impossibility of doing the first, there was no way that the real income could be transferred to the producers, because their absorptive capacity was too small. Deflation by oil consumers could not correct the balance with oil producers and could result only in a fall in the trade and output of the oil-consuming countries.

oil-consuming economies and to finance the ensuing balance of payments deficits by borrowing back from the oil producers the extra money they had from the higher oil prices and which they were incapable of spending on current output. Larger budget deficits than we had hitherto been accustomed to became necessary to offset the loss of purchasing power of consumers brought about by the rise in oil prices. Thus, the fall in real national income and living standards was postponed at the cost of budgetary and balance of payments deficits and increased foreign borrowing.

4.   *Trade union attitudes.* In the early post-war years unions had bargained for money wages. But as the rate of inflation accelerated the 'money illusion' was dispelled and unions began, quite rationally, to bargain for increases in *real* wages. Less rationally, they sometimes sought to make allowance for both past and prospective inflation. The next stage in their thinking was to bargain not only for real wages but for real take-home pay, after tax increases. The belief became entrenched that everyone was entitled to an annual increase in real income whether or not there had been any commensurate increase in output. Not only did the unions begin increasingly to think in these terms, they were powerful enough to achieve at least some of their aims. This was less an increase in actual power than a recognition of power that was already there and a willingness to use it. The trade unions

may not always have acted wisely or taken a long-term view, but they acted rationally within their terms of reference: their leaders' job was to protect and advance a sectional interest, not to act in the public good. That was the responsibility of government.

5.   *Inflation.* As with entry to the European Community, it is not entirely legitimate to include inflation as a change in the objective world, since it was not so much something imposed upon governments from outside – although the rise in oil prices played an important part – as allowed to happen. Nevertheless, the big rise in the rate of inflation had important consequences, for trade union behaviour, for the transformation of monetarism from an economic theory into a political doctrine, for the control of public expenditure and (because it made the past an unreliable guide to the future) for economic forecasting.

6.   *The power of markets.* The overwhelming weight of the international market in money had become apparent in the early 1970s. As communications technology developed there was added to this weight the ability to move huge sums of money from currency to currency within minutes. Governments and central bankers were obliged to recognize that even acting in concert their control over exchange rates was minimal. Once again the rate of exchange was not available as a policy instrument although it could be used as an indicator of monetary conditions. It was possible to have an exchange rate policy, other than one of benign neglect, but not possible to enforce it with any certitude or outside limits imposed by the market.

The power of the domestic markets in money also grew, from the mid-1970s. In framing their economic measures governments found it increasingly necessary to take account of what the market reaction would be. With the introduction of monetary targets and a commitment to adhere to them, the institutions discovered that by holding off the gilt-edged market they could force a rise in interest rates.

7.   *Monetarism.* The power and influence of the domestic markets stemmed in part from their belief and governments' belief in the theory of monetarism in one form or another, a belief which stockbrokers' circulars in the mid-1970s had played a not insignificant part in fostering. A belief in the importance of controlling the money supply and setting monetary targets was a policy constraint from the mid-1970s and became a dominant influence after 1979.

8.   *North Sea Oil.* The United Kingdom became a major oil producer. This had consequences for the balance of payments, for

the exchange rate, for non-oil exports and manufactures and for taxation.

These were the major changes in the environment in which economic policy was made.

Policies

The extent of the changes in economic policy that took place within our period would have been unbelievable at the outset.

1. *Employment policy.* The period began with the by then traditional commitment to full employment as a major (usually the primary) economic objective, to be achieved by broadly Keynesian methods of demand management founded, naturally, on a Keynesian analysis of how the economy worked. By the end of the period the objective and the analysis had been abandoned (by the government of the day).

2. *Monetary theory and policy.* We moved from a situation in which no one paid the slightest regard to the monetary aggregates to one in which they became a major focus of policy.

3. *Fiscal policy.* At the commencement of the period fiscal policy was the main instrument for demand management; and the Public Sector Borrowing Requirement was unknown. By the end of the period the PSBR had become, along with the money supply, a focus of policy; and it was believed that fiscal expansion created not jobs but inflation.

4. *Prices and incomes policy.* The period began with pay norms, standstills, freezes, and moved to various other versions of statutory, semi-statutory and voluntary policy, some of them novel and most of them successful for a while. The period ended with a complete rejection of all forms of incomes policy. Excessive pay rises, it was believed, caused not inflation but unemployment. The instrument for controlling inflation was the money supply.

5. *Public expenditure.* We began with a new model system (the Plowden system) that rejected the old form of cash control in favour of a sophisticated system of control of real resources related to the expected growth of GDP. The system proved incapable of coping with high rates of inflation (for which it may itself have been partly responsible) and the Treasury was slow to recognize this. We moved, via cash limits, back to the old system of cash control, albeit with some Plowden elements retained.

6.   *Growth*. For the first half of the period not only was there an objective for a reasonable rate of economic growth, there was almost an obsession with accelerating that rate. By the end there was no growth objective; growth was something that must come, or not come, from the private sector: there was nothing the government could do about it, except create 'the right conditions'.

It is a quite extraordinary catalogue of change and policy reversal within the space of twenty years.

Errors and omissions

What may be seen as the major policy failures over this period?

1.   First in time but not in importance was the failure, between 1964 and 1967, to reconcile an overambitious growth plan with the realities of the balance of payments. The conventional wisdom now has it that it was also a mistake not to have devalued sooner, but there is room for two views on that: our subsequent experience with (involuntary) devaluations has not been entirely happy.

2.   Allied to the persistent difficulty with the current account of the balance of payments, was the failure to deal earlier with the incubus of the sterling balances which, because our short-term liabilities exceeded our short-term assets, turned a current account problem into a run on the reserves and a sterling crisis.

3.   We must count as a major mistake, probably *the* major mistake, the 'dash for growth' between 1971 and 1973 in the pursuit of which all fiscal, monetary and exchange rate constraints were discarded. The results were disastrous, and would have been so even without the rise in oil prices which occurred at the end of that episode.

Underlying the errors of 1964 to 1967 and 1971 to 1973 were the beliefs that the economy should and could be run tight up against its capacity limits, and that stoking up domestic demand would generate domestic supply. It could not and did not: it generated inflation and imports.

4.   The failure throughout most of the period to control public expenditure. There are four elements to this: firstly, the setting of public expenditure plans on the basis of estimates of the growth of output which were always too optimistic, and were seen at the time to be so; secondly, the commitment to provide any amount

of cash to pay for plans drawn up in mythical money; thirdly, the failure of the Treasury to control even the mythical money plans; and, fourthly, the failure of the Treasury to realize, much earlier than it did, that the system it was working – the Plowden system – was manifestly unsuited to a period of rapid inflation. Even after the Plowden system had been superseded by cash planning, expenditure continued to exceed plans.

5.   The inability to forecast the Public Sector Borrowing Requirement. The PSBR is a central part of the Medium-Term Financial Strategy, is closely linked to monetary policy – the other major component of the MTFS – and is the determinant of fiscal policy. Yet the Treasury, which is supposed to control the PSBR, has proved unable to forecast it with any acceptable degree of accuracy even over short periods. It is unsatisfactory that the number upon which so much of financial policy hinges should be subject to a margin of error so large that it not infrequently exceeds any fiscal adjustment it is used to justify.

6.   Credit policy and monetary policy. In the attempt to control credit and money we had Bank Rate; Minimum Lending Rate by formula, without formula, abandoned altogether, re-instated; Special Deposits and Supplementary Special Deposits; the authorities tried to control bank lending, directly and indirectly, reserve assets, domestic credit expansion, liabilities, and the money supply in an ever expanding number of definitions.

In 1979 the control of the money supply became the central objective of economic policy. Targets were set for several years ahead but were exceeded, sometimes by a large margin. Control became less effective than formerly. New methods were introduced but control of the monetary base was rejected and the new arrangements still left the authorities with considerable discretion in influencing interest rates and the liquidity of the banking system. The methods used sometimes distorted the numbers they were intended to control. The focus of policy widened from the monetary aggregates to monetary conditions, in judging which the exchange rate became relatively more important and the monetary aggregates less so. Although the money supply was controlled neither convincingly nor in the manner at first envisaged, the *objective* of control, namely the reduction in the rate of inflation, was achieved. When an objective is achieved despite the weakness of the instrument, the relevance of the instrument is called into question.

7.   The failure to handle with any assurance recurrent sterling crises, most conspicuously in 1976 and early 1985. Repeatedly the

authorities gave the impression of being in something of a muddle, not to say panic, with no clear or consistent idea of what they ought to be doing, vacillating between intervention and non-intervention. They never seemed to learn that it is the nature of markets to overreact and that a rate that goes too high will, by definition, come down again; and vice versa.

Economic policy in the last twenty years has had to be made against an international environment that has undergone changes that have on the whole made life difficult. So far as one of those changes was concerned – the rise in oil prices – we in the United Kingdom were better placed than most once our own oil came on stream. Yet we have coped less well than almost any other country, with higher inflation, higher unemployment, lower growth of output and income, a more fragile exchange rate. We have continued our progress towards the foot of every table of virtuous economic indicators.

No one could claim that, except for some modest increase in GDP, our last position is better than our first or that the passage from the one to the other has been marked by success. The rate of inflation, although reduced from its peaks, is still higher than it was in the beginning; unemployment seems immovable at an historically high level; none of the plans for growth has been achieved except for a brief period; public expenditure, taxation and public borrowing have consistently been higher than planned; our trade balance in manufactures, historically in surplus, has fallen into deficit; the exchange rate is weak and unstable. Of the traditional objectives of growth, full employment and relatively stable prices, none has been achieved for more than a transitory period and never all of them at the same time.

The role of the Treasury

The Treasury's self-proclaimed 'main task' is to manage the economy. Yet it would be manifestly unfair to blame the Treasury for every economic disaster since 1964. It has no control, and little influence, over events outside these shores; it cannot be held accountable for the pricing policies of OPEC, the economics of President Reagan or the behaviour of the international money markets.

Less obviously, it has much less control over the domestic

environment than is sometimes supposed. The Treasury has to operate in the social, political and industrial environment of the time. The Treasury cannot be held responsible if British industry failed to innovate, if trade unions acted perversely, if lobbies and special interest groups blocked reforms. As Chancellors of the Exchequer have frequently pointed out, the Treasury has little control over what actually happens in the factories, farms and offices where wealth is created. But we cannot go to the other extreme and suppose that Treasury policy has no effect whatsoever on the efficiency of the economy and upon such matters as the internal and external value of the currency. If we suppose *that*, then the Treasury might as well shut up shop as manager of the economy. There may be those who would say 'hear, hear' to that, taking the view that the management of the economy is too serious a thing to be left to the Treasury (the view that inspired the creation of the Department of Economic Affairs).

The Treasury has two, overlapping, faces: there is the 'official' Treasury, the Treasury as an ongoing institution (the Treasury that most critics have in their sights); and the Treasury as a Department of State headed by ministers taking political decisions. While it is right to distinguish between officials who advise on policy, and ministers who decide policy, the collegiate nature of much policy-making at the higher levels should not be overlooked: officials do play an important part in making policy.

We should render unto the Treasury no more than that which is the Treasury's; which would include responsibility for controlling expenditure and forecasting the PSBR, for regulating the money supply and for the tactical management of the exchange rate. In all these matters one is left with a lingering impression of muddle, a feeling that everything might have been done better. It is a puzzle to know why this should be so when the Treasury is undoubtedly full of very clever people.

Appendix: Statistics

As noted in the Preface, the statistics given here are the latest available at the time of writing and, because of revisions, may not always agree with those in the text which are from publications of the time.

Note: Billion (bn) = 1,000 million, — means Nil, .. means not available

Table A1   GDP, public expenditure, consumers' expenditure
and personal disposal income – Year-on-year
change at constant prices

Year	GDP at 1980 factor cost*	Public expenditure†	Consumers' expenditure at 1980 market prices	Personal disposable income per capita
1964	5.1	4.4	3.1	3.5
1965	2.7	6.4	1.5	1.3
1966	1.9	6.2	1.8	1.7
1967	2.8	13.4	2.4	0.9
1968	4.5	–0.9	2.8	1.3
1969	1.6	0.3	0.6	0.5
1970	2.0	3.4	2.7	3.6
1971	2.5	2.9	3.1	0.7
1972	1.4	7.1	6.1	8.2
1973	7.9	7.3	5.1	6.6
1974	–0.7	12.6	–1.4	–0.9
1975	–0.7	–1.0	–0.7	0.4
1976	3.8	–1.8	0.3	–0.5
1977	1.1	–8.2	–0.5	–1.1
1978	2.9	4.8	5.6	7.0
1979	2.2	0.2	4.5	5.4
1980	–2.1	1.5	–0.4	1.2
1981	–1.3	2.7	–0.3	–2.6
1982	1.6	1.6	0.7	0.3
1983	3.4	1.6	4.0	2.3
1984	1.4	1.7‡	1.7	2.1

Sources: GDP, consumers' expenditure and personal disposable
income are from the *United Kingdom National Accounts*
1985 Edition (*The CSO Blue Book*) Tables 1.5, 3.9, 3.11 and
3.17.
Public expenditure. No consistent series from 1964 onwards
is published and the Treasury is unable to provide one.
The series here is taken from *Economic Trends* No 301
November 1983 Table 1a p. 145 up to 1979; and from Cmnd
9428 of January 1985 for the remaining years. Up to and
including 1973 Public Corporations Market and Overseas
Borrowing (PCMOB) is excluded and from 1974 included.

*   Based on expenditure data

†   Financial Years beginning in the year shown

‡   Estimate

Comment: The table shows
The excess growth of public expenditure, compared with the growth of GDP, in 1965–1967; and the reversal in 1968 and 1969.
The sharp acceleration in the growth of GDP in 1973, the excess growth of public expenditure in 1972 and 1974 and the contraction in the next three years, especially in 1977.
The negative growth in personal disposable income and/or consumers' expenditure in 1974–1977, largely the consequences of counter-inflationary policy, followed by substantial recovery in 1978 and 1979.
The recession of 1980, 1981; and the recovery in 1983 associated with consumers' expenditure.

Table A.2 Unemployment, wages and salaries, and output

Year	Unemployment excluding school-leavers		Wages and salaries per unit of output 1980=100	Output per person employed 1980=100
	Number* 000	per cent		
1964	394	1.4	21.4	75.4
1965	338	1.4	22.2	76.7
1966	353	1.3	23.4	77.8
1967	547	2.3	23.8	80.2
1968	574	2.5	24.3	84.0
1969	566	2.4	25.2	85.7
1970	602	2.5	27.6	87.5
1971	776			
	709	3.1	30.1	89.9
1972	787	3.4	32.8	92.3
1973	555	2.4	34.9	95.7
1974	559	2.4	42.5	94.0
1975	871	3.7	55.4	92.6
1976	1,091	4.6	60.9	95.2
1977	1,271	5.3	65.0	97.9
1978	1,253	5.2	72.4	100.5
1979	1,173	4.8	82.7	102.3
1980	1,487	6.1	100.0	100.0
1981	2,307	9.5	108.6	101.8
1982	2,669	11.0	113.0	105.6
1983	2,912	12.1	118.1	109.8
1984	3,047	12.6	122.2	111.5
1985	3,181	13.2	..	..

Sources: *Economic Trends Annual Supplement* 1985 Edition; and Department of Employment.

* Annual average. From 1971 revised series based on claimants instead of, as formerly, registrations. From 1983 some men aged 60 and over no longer had to sign on.

Table A3   Rate of inflation and purchasing power of the pound

Year	Index of retail prices (Jan. 1974 = 100)	Rate of inflation measured by RPI (per cent)	Consumers' Expenditure Deflator* (1980=100)	Tax and Price Index† (Jan. 1978 = 100)	Purchasing power of the pound (pence)
1964	55.8	3.3	21.9	..	100
1965	58.4	4.7	23.0	..	96
1966	60.7	3.9	24.0	..	92
1967	62.3	2.6	24.6	..	90
1968	65.2	4.7	25.7	..	86
1969	68.7	5.4	27.2	..	81
1970	73.1	6.4	28.8	..	76
1971	80.0	9.4	31.2	..	70
1972	85.7	7.1	33.3	..	65
1973	93.5	9.1	36.0	..	60
1974	108.5	16.0	42.2	50.2	51
1975	134.8	24.2	52.2	63.0	41
1976	157.1	16.5	60.4	80.4	36
1977	182.0	15.9	69.4	95.3	31
1978	197.1	8.3	75.7	100.0	28
1979	223.5	13.4	85.9	106.1	25
1980	263.7	18.0	100.0	123.2	21
1981	295.0	11.9	111.5	140.4	19
1982	320.4	8.6	121.1	162.3	17
1983	335.1	4.6	127.4	170.7	17
1984	351.7	4.9	133.8	177.9	16

Sources: Central Statistical Office

*   An alternative method of calculating the purchasing power of the pound derived from national accounts estimates of consumers' expenditure.

†   Introduced in August 1979, and calculated back to 1974. It incorporates the effects of changes in direct and indirect taxes as well as prices. It measures the increase in *gross* taxable income needed to compensate taxpayers for any increase in retail prices.

Comment: The lowest annual rate of inflation recorded in the period was 1.1 per cent in February 1964. In November 1967, when the pound was devalued, the annual rate was 1.9 per cent. The highest annual rate was 26.9 per cent in August 1975. The rate first went into double figures, 10.3 per cent, in June 1971.

In 20 years the pound has lost five-sixths of its value: a pound in 1984 would buy what 16p would in 1964; or, it would require £6.30 in 1984 to buy what £1 would in 1964.

Since it was introduced in 1979 the Tax and Price Index (TPI) has risen by 67. per cent, against 57.4 per cent for the RPI, implying an increase in the tax burden. The lowest year-on-year change in the TPI was 1.5 per cent in June 1978, when the change in the RPI was 7.4 per cent, indicating that at this time only a very small increase in gross pay was required to maintain the standard of living.

Table A4   Money supply and the exchange rate

Year	Change in £M3* (per cent)	Exchange rate†	
		Against US$	Sterling exchange rate index‡ 1975 = 100
1964	5.3	2.80	..
1965	8.4	2.80	..
1966	3.5	2.80	..
1967	9.8	2.75	..
1968	7.5	2.39	..
1969	2.0	2.39	129.4
1970	8.8	2.40	128.1
1971	15.4	2.44	127.9
1972	25.6	2.50	123.3
1973	27.4	2.45	111.8
1974	10.9	2.34	108.3
1975	6.1	2.22	100.0
1976	9.8	1.80½	85.7
1977	9.5	1.75	81.2
1978	15.5	1.92	81.5
1979	13.4	2.12	87.3
1980	18.8	2.33	96.1
1981	13.4	2.02½	95.3
1982	9.3	1.75	90.7
1983	10.4	1.52	83.3
1984	9.7	1.34	78.8

Sources: Bank of England, *Economic Trends Annual Supplement* 1985 Edition.

* Change (+) during the year. From 1979 excluding public sector deposits.
† Annual average.
‡ Formerly known as the Effective Rate.

Table A5   Monetary targets – Annual percentage rates of growth

Date target set	Period of target	Target aggregate	Target range	Out-turn
Dec. 1976	12 mths to Apr. 77	£M3	9–13	7.2
Mar. 1977	12 mths to Apr. 78	£M3	9–13	16.4
Apr. 1978	12 mths to Apr. 79	£M3	8–12	11.3
Nov. 1978	12 mths to Oct. 79	£M3	8–12	13.4
Jun. 1979	10 mths to Apr. 80	£M3	7–11	10.0
Nov. 1979	16 mths to Oct. 80	£M3	7–11	17.5
Mar. 1980	14 mths to Apr. 81	£M3	7–11	19.1
Mar. 1981	14 mths to Apr. 82	£M3	6–10	12.9
Mar. 1982	14 mths to Apr. 83	£M3	8–12	11.1
		PSL2	8–12	10.8
		M1	8–12	12.1
Mar. 1983	14 mths to Apr. 84	£M3	7–11	9.5
		PSL2	7–11	12.2
		M1	7–11	13.5
Mar. 1984	14 mths to Apr. 85	£M3*	6–10	11.9
		MO	4–8	5.6
Mar. 1985	14 mths to Apr. 86	£M3	5–9	..
		MO	3–7	..

Sources: Financial Statement and Budget Reports; Bank of England

* New definition, excluding public sector deposits. Out-turn for earlier years excluding public sector deposits: 1982–83, 10.7%; 1983–84, 9.6%.

In May 1985 the Treasury announced changes in the method of targetting (see Economic Progress Report, No. 177, May 1985). Instead of being measured at an annualised rate from the February base, progress of the aggregates would be measured at 'the 12-month growth rate'. This rate is not defined but it appears to mean growth over the corresponding month a year earlier. The Treasury says ' ... it has been decided that the target ranges will in future apply continuously to that 12-month growth rate, rather than to growth between the beginning and end of the target period. It will therefore no longer be necessary to specify either a 14-month target period or a particular base month.'

The new method of measuring the growth of the money supply, which seems to have been adopted for cosmetic reasons, is the same as that used for several other indicators including the rate of inflation as measured by the

Retail Price Index. The growth rate will now be affected not only by what happens in the current year but by what happened a year earlier; the figures will look better when a particularly bad month in the previous year drops out, and vice versa.

Comment: The target range decreases in one-point steps from 1976 to 1981 and then again from 1982 to 1985. But the target base is moved up each year, so that the growth in the previous period, including any overshoot, is built in to the new base ('base drift'). The annualized growth rate of sterling M3 over the period from June 1979 to April 1985 was 13.0 per cent.

Table A6   Public Sector Borrowing Requirement – Forecasts and out-turn (£bn)

Year	Forecasts				Error†		
	Budget*	Autumn Statement	Budget. Year just ending	Outturn	Budget	Autumn Statement	Year just ending
1967–68	1.5	..	2.0	2.0	–0.5	..	0
1968–69	1.0	..	0.3	0.5	+0.5	..	–0.2
1969–70	–0.3	..	–0.6	–0.5	+0.2	..	–0.1
1970–71	–0.2	..	0.6	0.8	–1.0	..	–0.2
1971–72	1.2	..	1.3	1.0	+0.2	..	+0.3
1972–73	3.4	..	2.9	2.5	+0.9	..	+0.4
1973–74	4.4	..	4.3	4.5	–0.1	..	–0.2
1974–75	2.7	6.3‡	7.6	7.9	–5.2	–1.6	–0.3
1975–76	9.1	..	10.8	10.6	–1.5	..	+0.2
1976–77	12.0	11.0	8.8	8.5	+3.5	+2.5	+0.3
1977–78	8.5	7.5	5.7	5.6	+2.9	+1.9	+0.1
1978–79	8.5	8.0	9.2	9.2	–0.7	–1.2	0
1979–80	8.3	8.3	9.1	10.0	–1.7	–1.7	–0.9
1980–81	8.5	11.5	13.5	12.7	–4.2	–1.2	+0.8
1981–82	10.6	10.5	10.6	8.6	+2.0	+1.9	+2.0
1982–83	9.5	9.0	7.5	8.9	+0.6	+0.1	–1.4
1983–84	8.2	10.0	10.0	9.7	–1.5	+0.3	+0.3
1984–85	7.2	8.5	10.5	10.1‡	–2.9	–1.6	+0.4

Sources: *Financial Statements; Financial Statement and Budget Reports; Financial Statistics; Economic Progress Report*, No. 160, Sept. 1983.

* Budget forecasts do not take account of any subsequent policy changes affecting the PSBR.

† The error is the out-turn minus the forecast, with sign reversed, indicating the direction of the error (+ shows forecast too high, – too low). The Treasury calculates the average errors from 1972–73 to 1982–83 at 1982–83 prices at, respectively, £4.4 bn, £2.5 bn and £0.9 bn. The biggest errors occurred in the period 1974–75 to 1977–78. The issue of *Economic Progress Report* referred to above carries an interesting article on forecasting the PSBR and the causes of errors.

Table A7 The balance of payments of the UK (£ m.)

Year	Current account	Investment and other capital transactions	Allocation of SDRs etc.	Balancing item*	Balance for official financing†	Trade in oil
1964	−371	−311	—	−13	695	..
1965	−79	−316	—	42	353	..
1966	129	−579	−44‡	−97	591	..
1967	−284	−504	−105ᵉ	222	671	..
1968	−264	−755	−251ᵉ	−140	1,410	..
1969	485	−169	—	371	−687	..
1970	795	549	133‖	−57	−1,420	..
1971	1,089	1,792	125	265	−3,271	..
1972	191	−673	124	−783	1,141	..
1973	−1,018	119§	—	128	771	−941
1974	−3,317	1,527§	—	144	1,646	−3,357
1975	−1,582	154	—	−37	1,465	−3,057
1976	−913	−2,977	—	261	3,629	−3,947
1977	−128	4,169	—	3,320	−7,361	−2,771
1978	972	−4,137	—	2,039	1,126	−1,984
1979	−736	1,865	195	581	−1,905	−731
1980	3,100	−1,503	180	−405	−1,372	315
1981	6,528	−6,972	158	−401	687	3,112
1982	4,033	−3,317	—	−2,000	1,284	4,643
1983	3,127	−4,847	—	900	820	6,976
1984	1,121	−5,658	—	3,221	1,316	7,136
1985Ψ	1,596	−3,084	—	1,620	−132	6,161

Source: United Kingdom Balance of Payments 1984 and 1985 Edns (The CSO Pink Book) and CSO Press Notice No. 114 5 Dec 1985.

* The net total of errors and omissions.

† The sum of the preceding columns, with sign reversed. A positive balance represents a need to borrow and/or run down the reserves; a negative figure indicates the repayment of debt and/or an addition to the reserves.

§ Including capital transfers of −£59 m. (1973) and −£75 m. (1974).

(Continued)

‡ Gold subscription to IMF.

ø Exchange Equalisation Account loss on forward commitments.

‖ Including gold subscription to IMF –£38 m.

Ψ First 9 months.

Comment: Statistics published in March 1968 (*Economic Trends*, No. 173) showed a current account *deficit* in 1966; and a deficit of £514 m. in 1967.

The table shows the strong recovery in the current account in 1969, 1970 and 1971 and the rapid deterioration in 1972 and 1973.

The first oil price shock came at the end of 1973 and in the next five years (1974–1978) the deficit on oil trade was £15 bn; despite this the current account improved by £4.3 bn. After 1979 the current account moved into comfortable surplus aided by the growing surplus in the trade in oil. By 1982 the oil surplus was providing almost the whole of the current account surplus. The non-oil balance fell into increasing deficit so that in 1983 and 1984 together there would, but for oil, have been a current account deficit of nearly £10 bn (all other things being equal). The balance of trade in finished manufactured goods (not shown in the table) deteriorated from a surplus of £4.0 bn in 1980 to deficits of £2.5 bn in 1983 and £3.6 bn in 1984.

Table A8   The sterling balances and the reserves

End of period	Sterling balances* £bn	Reserves†	
		£bn	$bn
1964	2.4	0.8	2.3
1965	2.3	1.1	3.0
1966	2.3	1.1	3.1
1967	2.1	1.1	2.7
1968	1.9	1.0	2.4
1969	2.3	1.1	2.5
1970	2.5	1.2	2.8
1971	3.2	2.5	6.6
1972	3.6	2.4	5.6
1973	3.7	2.8	6.5
1974	4.6	2.9	6.8
1975	4.1	2.7	5.4
1976	2.6	2.4	4.1
1977	2.9	10.7	20.6
1978	2.6	7.7	15.7
1979	3.3	10.1	22.5
1980	4.7	11.5	27.5
1981	4.8	12.2	23.3
1982	5.6	10.5	17.0
1983	6.6	12.3	17.8
1984	7.9	13.6	15.7

Sources: Bank of England Quarterly Bulletin, various issues; The United Kingdom Balance of Payments (The CSO Pink Book), various editions; Financial Statistics, No. 276, Apr. 1985.

* Exchange reserves held in sterling by central monetary institutions and international organizations (other than the IMF).

† Comprises gold, convertible currencies, Special Drawing Rights (from 1970) and the reserve position in the IMF (from 1972).

Valuation. From the end of March 1979 the reserves have been revalued annually. Until end-1978 gold is valued at the official price of SDR35 per fine ounce and SDRs and convertible currencies are valued in dollars at historic middle or central rates. Thereafter they are valued at market-related rates. Total reserves expressed in dollars are converted to sterling at end-year middle market closing rates.

Comment: The sterling balances exceeded the reserves,
sometimes by a considerable margin, up to and including
1976.
   Over the years the value of the reserves has been
enhanced both by coverage and valuation changes
(although the annual revaluation can lower the value).

Bibliography

Barnett, J. (1982) *Inside the Treasury*. Deutsch

Brittan, S. (1971) *Steering the Economy*. Penguin Books

Brown, G. (1972) *In My Way*. Penguin Books

Browning, P. (1983) *Economic Images*. Longman

Cockerell, M., Hennessy, P. and Walker, D. (1984) *Sources Close to the Prime Minister*. Macmillan

Crossman, R. (1975, 1976, 1977) *The Diaries of a Cabinet Minister* (3 vols). Hamilton and Cape

Crossman, R. (1979) *The Crossman Diaries*, ed. Anthony Howard. Hamilton and Cape

Evans, H. (1983) *Good Times, Bad Times*. Weidenfeld and Nicolson

Falkender, Lady (1975) *Inside No 10*. Weidenfeld and Nicolson 1972; new edition New English Library

Friedman, M. (1977) 'From Galbraith to economic freedom', *Institute of Economic Affairs Occasional Paper 49*

Galbraith, J. K. (1961) *The Great Crash*. Penguin Books

Galbraith, J. K. (1962) *The Affluenct Society*. Penguin Books

Gilmour, I. (1983) *Britain Can Work*. Martin Robertson

Haines, J. (1977) *The Politics of Power*. Cape

Ham, A. (1981) *Treasury Rules*. Quartet Books

Hennessy, P., see Cockerell

Howard, A., see Crossman

Keegan, W. (1984) *Mrs Thatcher's Economic Experiment*. Lane

Keegan, W. and Pennant-Rea, R. (1979) *Who Runs the Economy?* Maurice Temple Smith

Keynes, J. M. (1936) *The General Theory of Employment, Interest and Money*. Macmillan

National Institute of Economic and Social Research. *Reviews*

Pennant-Rea, R., see Keegan

Pliatzky, L. (1982) *Getting and Spending*. Blackwell

Pollard, S. (1982) *The Wasting of the British Economy*. Croom Helm

Radcliffe, Lord (1959) *Committee on the Working of the Monetary System*, Cmnd 827. HMSO

Reid, M. (1978) 'The secondary banking crisis – five years on', *The Banker*, December

Reid, M. (1982) *The Secondary Banking Crisis 1973–75*. Macmillan

Riddell, P. (1983) *The Thatcher Government*. Martin Robertson

Sedgemore, B. (1980) *The Secret Constitution*. Hodder and Stoughton

Sewill, B. (1975) 'In place of strikes', in *British Economic Policy 1970–1974*. Hobart paperback No. 7. The Institute of Economic Affairs

Sloman, A., *see* Young

Stewart, M. (1977) *The Jekyll and Hyde Years*. Dent

Walker, D., *see* Cockerell

Wass, Sir Douglas, *The 1983 Reith Lectures*. BBC

Williams, Marcia, *see* Falkender

Young, H. and Sloman, A. (1982) *No, Minister*. BBC

Young, H. and Sloman, A. (1984) *But, Chancellor*. BBC

Index